Manhood
and the
American
Renaissance

Manhood
and the
American
Renaissance

David Leverenz

Cornell University Press

Ithaca and London

First published 1989 by Cornell University Press.

International Standard Book Number 0-8014-2281-7
Library of Congress Catalog Card Number 88-47914

Printed in the United States of America

Librarians: Library of Congress cataloging information appears on the last page of the book.

The paper in this book is acid-free and meets the guidelines for permanence and durability of the Committee on Production Guidelines for Book Longevity of the Council on Library Resources.

*To Anne Rutledge, again,
and to Allison, Elizabeth,
Trevor, and Nell*

Contents

very least, they have helped me to discover what I wanted to be stubborn about.

For help going well beyond this book I thank Melvyn New, who lured me to the University of Florida and then shepherded me through some difficulties I didn't even see. For awesome competence on the word processor I thank Dee Nesbitt, who expeditiously transcribed a staggering number of drafts. Thanks go also to the Division of Sponsored Research at the University of Florida, which funded two summers of writing.

As my dedication implies, my deepest acknowledgments go to my family, especially to Anne Rutledge, for whom manliness and womanliness mean even less than ambition. Living with these five strong and loving people has brought me into my own strength of loving. The experience has also brought me far enough beyond manhood to be able to see it operating in myself daily, and that's no small journey.

My more formal acknowledgments go to *Nineteenth-Century Fiction*, now *Nineteenth-Century Literature*, which printed an earlier version of Chapter 9 in the March 1983 issue, vol. 37, 552–575, © 1983 by the Regents of the University of California (used with permission); to *PMLA*, which published a slightly different version of Chapter 2 in the January 1986 issue, vol. 101, 38–56; and to *Criticism*, which published a slightly different version of Chapter 4 in the Summer 1987 issue, vol. 29, 341–370. I thank T. Walter Herbert, Jr., Lee Clark Mitchell, and Allon White, for inviting me to give talks (with vigorous discussions) at Southwestern University, Princeton University, and the University of Sussex, respectively; and Norman N. Holland, Andrew Gordon, Bernard J. Paris, and my other colleagues at GAP (Group for Applied Psychoanalysis), for their lively and heteroglossic responses to my excerpts on Whitman.

DAVID   LEVERENZ

Gainesville, Florida

Acknowledgments

A great many people have helped me with this book. I've tried to be quite scrupulous about acknowledging specific aid in my notes. More comprehensively, I thank Zelda Bronstein, T. Walter Herbert, Jr., Mary Kelley, and Lee Clark Mitchell for incisive comments on various vexed chapters, especially Chapter 3. At midpoint the two readers for Cornell University Press were encouraging and usefully blunt. After the manuscript had been submitted, Lawrence Buell's lengthy commentary for Cornell pointed me toward a great many final tinkerings, as did that of my colleague John Seelye. Both of them took me to task for my coercively kinky reading of *Moby Dick*; I've tried to scale down the tone, though I'm afraid I've kept the argument. Faith Berry and Terry H. Pickett generously provided information about Frederick Douglass, as Herbert Levine did about Whitman. Samuel Kimball, Peter Middleton, and Neal Tolchin gave me hours of good talk about Melville and much else, as well as alert responses to Chapter 10. Judith Bailey gave the manuscript an expert editing. Thanks also to Bernhard Kendler for his attentiveness throughout and for his gentle nudges to get on with it. Finally, Frederick Crews has given me enthusiastic support and canny advice at several crucial junctures. In various aspects of my life I tend to be accommodating in little conflicts, stubborn as a mule on issues that really matter to me; so with the suggestions of all these readers. At the

Manhood
and the
American
Renaissance

AHAB (*advancing*)

(*During the ensuing scene, the carpenter continues sneezing at times.*)

Well, manmaker! . . .
Sir?
Hold; while Prometheus is about it, I'll order a complete man after a
desirable pattern. Imprimis, fifty feet high in his socks; then chest mo-
delled after the Thames Tunnel; then, legs with roots to 'em, to stay in
one place; then, arms three feet through the wrist; no heart at all,
brass forehead, and about a quarter of an acre of fine brains; and let
me see—shall I order eyes to see outwards? No, but put a sky-light on
top of his head to illuminate inwards. There, take the order, and
away.
Now, what's he speaking about, and who's he speaking to, I should
like to know?

Herman Melville, Moby Dick

Men who make themselves felt in the world avail themselves of a
certain fate in their constitution which they know how to use. But they
never deeply interest us unless they lift a corner of the curtain, or betray, never so slightly, their penetration of what is behind it. 'Tis the
charm of practical men that outside of their practicality are a certain
poetry and play, as if they led the good horse Power by the bridle, and
preferred to walk, though they can ride so fiercely. Bonaparte is intellectual, as well as Caesar; and the best solders, sea-captains and railway
men have a gentleness when off duty, a good-natured admission that
there are illusions, and who shall say that he is not their sport? We
stigmatize the cast-iron fellows who cannot so detach themselves, as
"dragon-ridden," "thunder-stricken," and fools of fate, with whatever
powers endowed.

Ralph Waldo Emerson, "Illusions"

Introduction

In 1980, when my book on the Puritans had just come out, one of my
more well-known colleagues sat down in my office to read the jacket
flap. "Oh," he said, with a touch of disdain. "You're actually saying
something."

This book, too, is actually saying something—more readably, I hope.
My colleague's spontaneous reaction expressed the prevailing postro-
mantic values of the profession, which most admires the dazzle of
critical sensibility playing over texts. I should have been saying something *about* saying something—about representation and language. Assertions about "reality" and history seem flat by comparison. Assertions
about the reality and history of feelings, such as those I hazard in both
books, tend to look like horse-drawn carriages on a superhighway.

"History is a nightmare from which I must awake," Stephen Daedalus
truculently notes in *Ulysses*.[1] As the heirs of Joyce and modernism,
various recent literary theorists have claimed for literature a special
power of intellectual language play, liberating the reader's mind from
the oppressiveness of historical circumstances. Literary language, they
say, subverts and explodes social conventions of meaning. Great works
of literature now loom like Martian protoplasms beyond the white
picket fences of normal social discourse.

Well, yes and no. The deconstructionist movement has been enor-
mously useful in highlighting the clashes of meaning rather than the

unity and coherence in what we take for literature. Equally important, deconstructionism has helped to shift critical attention from issues of moral sensibility to issues of power and ideology. My book could not have been written without the impact of that reorientation.

Nevertheless, while the profession of English criticism has moved from New Critical unities and ambiguities toward deconstructive gun-fights at Meaning Gap, the effect has been to bind many readers all the more tightly to texts for their own sake, with history at arm's length. As Frank Lentricchia's subtle and empathetic account of some contemporary theorists concludes, literary theory has headed into a linguistic cul-de-sac. Theory needs to confront history, he says. Geoffrey Hartman more plaintively finishes one of his recent books on theory by wondering why history departments and English departments don't talk to each other any more.[2]

The problem has a great deal to do with how institutions reward specialization. But it also reflects a presumption of alienated intellectuality. Classic male writers in mid-nineteenth-century America help to inaugurate the modernist tradition of alienated mind play. Unlike many critics, I try not to collude with the tradition. I have been far more influenced by feminism and psychoanalysis than I have been by deconstructionists, in part because feminism and psychoanalysis are feelingful modes of interpretation. Their ways of seeing have helped me to articulate the complex yet evasive connections among creativity, gender socialization, and class and family backgrounds.

As the length of each chapter attests, I have also tried to demonstrate that close readings don't have to preclude "saying something." They can open out from textual issues to social history. Finally, while much of this study invites a "new historicist" label, especially my intermittent use of self-fashioning as a locus for gender ideologies and class conflicts, my approach also resists the new historicist tendency to focus exclusively on power, economics, and ideology. I think that their focus ironically reinforces what I take to be the reigning American ideology of manhood, which orients the self toward power, not feelings.

"It takes a great deal of history to make a little literature," Henry James remarks in his 1879 study of Hawthorne, the first notable book about an American writer.[3] Unfortunately, joining social history with the American Renaissance has become one of the most intractable problems in American literary criticism. Beyond or within the general post-romantic predisposition of literary theory, American criticism tends to present its classic texts as if they were break dancers surrounded by policemen. "Melodramas of Beset Manhood," Nina Baym has called the tradition.[4] Moreover, there is the undeniable fact that the best literary criticism has a suppleness and complexity lacking in the best social criticism, which frequently seems tangential or reductively allegorical.[5]

The vital relation between classic American writers and history, I argue, can be located in the broad pressures of class and gender ideology, not in the specific links between texts and political or cultural contexts. Emerson, Hawthorne, Melville, Thoreau, and Whitman find their most original voices in responding to the pressures and conflicts of American manhood. All five writers felt self-consciously deviant from prevailing norms of manly behavior. Their anxiety of influence had more to do with gender ideologies in the American marketplace than with strong precursors in English literature.

My first four chapters develop my sense of what it means to read American Renaissance writers in that social frame. The first chapter, on manhood and self-refashioning in the American Renaissance, examines the rhetorical strategies of conversion and unsettlement used by Hawthorne, Melville, Stowe, Thoreau, Whitman, and more briefly Emerson. All use the possessive individualist as a straight man for their diverse transformations. Chapter 2 moves to a more explicitly political discussion of class and gender issues in considering how Emerson used "man-making words" to rouse himself from depressive feelings of inferiority. Chapter 4 focuses on Frederick Douglass's rewriting of the fight that made him a man, to show the startling change in his 1855 view of manhood and class.

Chapter 3 sketches three ideologies of manhood in the antebellum Northeast: patrician, artisan, and entrepreneurial. The older ideologies of genteel patriarchy and artisan independence were being challenged by a new middle-class ideology of competitive individualism. The artisan tradition of manhood has stimulated and constrained the best of American radicalism, as a great many recent social historians have demonstrated.[6] At least in my judgment, however, the artisan tradition became tangential to the fundamental class conflict in the Northeast from the 1820s through the 1850s: the battle for dominance between the old mercantile and landowning elite and the new middle class of entrepreneurial businessmen. The new middle class won, and its ideology of manhood as competitive individualism still pervades American life. Emerson was right to see Napoleon as its "representative man" and a brutal struggle for dominance, not freedom, at its core. Meanwhile, the new working class of wage laborers brought into being by industrialism found its class consciousness continuously co-opted by artisan norms of manhood and middle-class expectations of upward mobility.

Thus the real social conflict involved the two upper classes. As Catherine Gallagher concludes, a similar class conflict in England ended just the other way, with the gentry reestablishing control by 1870.[7] In the American Northeast, the writer's social position seemed marginal, precariously poised between fading gentry status and professionalization for a feminized middle class reading public. Male writers in particular found themselves situated on the edge between contending classes. Patrician, almost without exception, in their backgrounds and self-expectations, they were ambivalently fascinated and horrified by the aggressive materialism they witnessed in their fellow men and perhaps by the rivalries they felt in themselves as well. Their best writing has a weirdness quite absent from that of their English counterparts. Their voices seem more deliberately deviant, at once urgent and detached, moral and grotesque.[8] The writing we now canonize buzzes like Socratic gadflies about the chrysalis of what has become the most middle-class country in the world.

In the second half of Chapter 3, I use four texts to explore my most basic thesis, that any intensified ideology of manhood is a compensatory response to fears of humiliation. I've come to question the psychoanalytic view, now adopted by many feminist critics, that manhood compensates for various fears of women and mothering. I think male rivalry is a more basic source of anxiety, though the language of manhood makes ample use of maternal scapegoating. Nor has my discussion of manhood been much influenced by recent works in men's studies, primarily because those histories tend to accept feminist views of manhood as patriarchy.[9] Such views are probably accurate in describing women's experience of men in the home, but they don't reflect men's experience of each other at work, where most American men measure themselves. If women writers portray manhood as patriarchy, male writers from Melville to Sam Shepard, David Mamet, and David Rabe portray manhood as a rivalry for dominance.

Women writers illuminate class and gender conflicts in American life with exceptional clarity, even starkness, as Chapters 5 and 6 explore. To paraphrase Alfred Habegger's argument, their domestic realism anticipates the later age of realism in the nineteenth century, notably the works of the two great "sissies," Howells and James.[10] The male texts canonized as the American Renaissance, on the other hand, tend to blur class issues, articulating an alienated and intellectualized self-consciousness of deviance. The genteel rhetorical strategies of Caroline Kirkland and Sarah Hale reflect patrician models of how to manipulate your man, in sharp contrast to the evangelical, middle-class thrust of Susan Warner's *Wide, Wide World* and Harriet Beecher Stowe's *Uncle Tom's Cabin*, which present patriarchal power as the source of impassioned resentment.

Four more chapters then consider some works of Hawthorne and Melville in detail, with Dana and Parkman as launching pads. There, I discuss the narcissism and deviousness embedded in various texts, notably *The Scarlet Letter* and *Moby Dick*. Readers may feel skeptical or uncomfortable when I emphasize Hawthorne's fears of homosexual rape or argue that Ishmael and Ahab are twinned in their desire to be beaten. Beating fantasies, I assert earlier, are at the heart of other major texts as well, especially *Uncle Tom's Cabin*. Though I too balked at first, I've come to see such fears and fantasies as the deep structure of manhood. Their presence in classic American texts constitutes profound sensitivity as well as ideological complicity.

Throughout, I argue that such a social perspective can help us to see these writers freshly, beyond conventions of the victimized artist in a philistine land. Their texts act within nineteenth century traditions of social rhetoric as well as premodernist traditions of intellectual alienation. In very different ways, American Renaissance writers try to disorient and convert their readers, especially male readers, from one style of manhood to another. In an age when possessive individualism was running wild, surrounded on every side by men striving to beat down other men, these writers fashion styles of self-dispossession. They make it impossible for anyone to pin them down.

What frustrated contemporary readers, who wanted moral simplicities to steer their lives by, may delight academics like myself, who need literary complexities to write books about. Nonetheless, I experience as much frustration as delight in responding to these classic texts. I try not to collude with the intellectual strategies they use to transcend social and personal conflicts. I feel impatient with Emerson's idealism, Melville's metaphysics, Hawthorne's ambiguities, Thoreau's sardonic pugnacity, and Whitman's incorporative detachment, not to mention the defensive strategies of more conventional male writers. I see them as men struggling with what it means to be a man. More specifically, I argue that their best work takes fire from complex feelings about male rivalry for dominance. The pervasive ascendancy of the work ethic for men and domesticity for women transformed class conflicts into gender pressures. Far from being simply victimizing, this frame helped to goad the best male writers from feelings of depression, shame, and deviance to creative power. Yet the inescapable mystifications of manhood remain in their voices.

Like the writing I think about here, this book has its own social frame. More transparently than with most literary criticism, my rereadings emerge from several experiences in my own life, especially my involvement in child care. I suspect that some degree of gender role reversal has been quite common to upper-middle-class American men in the last fifteen years. If the two decades before 1850 brought competitive individualism to middle-class American men, the age just before Reagan and Rambo brought feminism and the two-career family, at least to men like me. As one result, I now read classic American texts quite differently.

My partial role reversal didn't consciously affect the way I read books until midway through a class on *The Scarlet Letter*, when I suddenly erupted in fury at Dimmesdale for getting away scot free from his child care responsibilities. At that point I felt immersed in attending to our two-year-old while my wife finished law school and launched her new career. As deconstructionists stormed the ramparts of the profession, teaching professors to question how texts unravel themselves, whether texts exist, and how language had constituted our bourgeois selves, I was unraveling toward a different sort of question: why don't millions of mothers throw their babies out the window? My outrage at Dimmesdale had more than a touch of envy in it. The man could work at his writing all day long. Yet my experience with child care—more than a conventional man's, much less than a traditional woman's—led me to read *The Scarlet Letter* with new eyes.

Before, I would never have noticed when Dimmesdale responds to his daughter's acting up by saying to Hester, "Pacify her, if thou lovest me!" Now, I was irresistibly reminded of a family wedding at which one of my relatives looked down at his bawling child, then stared at his wife. "Your child is crying," he said. Appalling yet enticing, those sex-role divisions. I grew up in a home where they were rigorously felt, and the definition of manliness as competitive success in one's work still lodges in me like lava, miles deep.

The Emerson chapter, too, comes from reading with new eyes—the eyes of a parent, not a trans-parent. I had been struggling with Emerson for well over a year when I picked up Gay Wilson Allen's biography. There, I read that Emerson's father had been extremely disappointed in the boy for not being able to read by the age of three. That detail leaped out at me, since our four-year-old wasn't even close to reading, nor could I imagine forcing him to try. Up to then I had accepted Quentin Anderson's sense of William Emerson as something of a wimp, whose sickness and death supply a psychological context for Emerson's willed optimism.[11] To reconceive Emerson's father in the eyes of a sensitive, scared little boy, who saw a severe and exacting parent rather than the "absent father" depicted by current criticism, illuminated Emerson's depressions for me. It gave me a way to explicate his transformative prose in psychological terms. It also helped me to appreciate Emerson's effort to free himself from his father's class-bound idea of social success. For all that, as Ishmael says of the white whale, manhood becomes the symbol.

My involvement with all four of our children—a boy and a girl, born in 1978 and 1981, and two stepdaughters now in their twenties—led to another experience outside the bounds of career ambition: a three-year immersion in school politics. In 1982 I ran with two other candidates against three incumbents for our local school board, in Highland Park, New Jersey. We were enraged by the board's attempt to establish an elitist "Gifted and Talented Program," which segregated the academically advanced children in the fourth and fifth grades for most of the school day. During the course of that extraordinarily heated campaign, we realized that we had launched a class war, in a town populated mostly by liberal Democrats. Why I was going against my class would take me well beyond the scope of these pages; suffice it to say that we won the battle and lost the war. Readers interested in my various experiences with politics and manhood, gaucheries and all, can look up my stories in the Autumn 1986 *Southwest Review*.[12] Here my point is simply that as a privileged, upper-middle-class white male, brought up in Princeton and educated at a fine college and graduate school, I had never "seen" the centrality of class before, even though it stared me in the face every day across the river, where I taught at Rutgers, New Jersey's state university. From that experience comes one of my most basic arguments, that gender pressures help to bury class conflicts.

In the scale by which most men I know measure themselves, being a citizen doesn't matter much. That might have been important in the old gentry days, when to be a citizen meant to exercise power among one's peers. Emerson himself served on the Concord school board in the mid–1830s. Now, to be on a school board took me away from the only kind of power that my thoroughly professionalized colleagues take seriously: the power of one's writing to make an impact on other professors. Several friends seemed mildly baffled that I was wasting so much time on community issues. Sometimes I was too.

Happily, it all fed this book. To be sure, as Emerson so grudgingly acknowledged, temperament has its say. I shy away from a full-court Marxist press in part because I'm ambivalently drawn to middle-class individualism and in part because sustained anger makes me uncomfortable. As Walt Whitman once said to Horace Traubel, *"Be radical— be radical—be not too damned radical."*[3] Perhaps my emphasis on "self" does tend to exaggerate individual experience and minimize social groupings. Nevertheless, my pleasure in close readings makes me a retrograde new historicist, one who believes that "self" and "experience" matter. Moreover, if my experiences with child care and town politics have inched me beyond my role socialization, they have also encouraged an Emersonian spirit of self-trust. Despite my many quarrels with Emerson, I've written this book with something of his relish for intellectual nonconformity, and with an Emersonian faith that what has been vital for me will prove useful for other readers as well.

1

"I" and "You" in the American Renaissance

One of the most curious facts about the American Renaissance is that all five currently canonized men changed their names. As he emerged from his teens, Ralph Emerson switched to his middle name of Waldo, partly because he disliked his first name and partly to honor his Waldensian ancestors, who had fled from social persecution. In the first edition of *Leaves of Grass*, Walter Whitman, Junior, shortened his printed name to the more informal Walt, his nickname since childhood. David Henry Thoreau reversed his name to Henry David soon after he quit his first job as a teacher. As a Concord farmer contemptuously remarked, "Henry D. Thoreau—Henry D. Thoreau. . . . His name ain't no more Henry D. Thoreau than my name is Henry D. Thoreau. And everybody knows it, and he knows it. His name's Da-a-vid Henry and it ain't never been nothing but Da-a-vid Henry. And he knows that!"[1]

Along with the rest of his family, Herman Melvill added an *e* to his last name when he was twelve, after his father had shamed, enraged, and impoverished his mother by going bankrupt twice and dying delirious. Hawthorne added a *w* to the name Hathorne shortly after he graduated from college, ostensibly to have it read the way it sounded. He also may have wanted to emphasize his patriarchal "hawthorn tree" roots in his father's family history, unmanning himself from his mother's Manning side, especially from her brother Robert, the dominant adult in his childhood. Yet he was dedicating himself to writing stories that would expose the cruelty of his Hathorne ancestors. As he says in "The Custom-House," he became "an idler" on the "topmost bough" of his "family tree," as "sufficient retribution" for his forefathers' "sins."[2]

Except for Melville, who always stands outside any pattern, the changes imply a self-conscious mixture of alienation, self-assertion, and dependence. To play a variation on Stephen Greenblatt's model of "Renaissance Self-Fashioning," their literary voices begin with a self-fashioning beyond yet within the identities given to them by their parents and their culture.[3] The pattern probably works better as metaphor than as reality. Nonetheless, it does intimate a certain quiet prickliness at the outset of their literary experiments in self-reliance. Their arm's-length relationship to social expectations proved to be amply repaid by the often more than arm's-length distance accorded to their works by American readers.

I

Like manhood, "The American Renaissance" is a collective fiction, transforming insecurity into strength. F. O. Matthiessen's nationalistic label appropriates the European Renaissance as a model for the extraordinary six-year burst of literary creativity in the Northeast from 1850 to 1855. Out of those years came five current classics: *The Scarlet Letter* (1850), *Moby Dick* (1851), *Uncle Tom's Cabin* (1852), *Walden* (1854), and *Leaves of Grass* (1855). There was also a host of other memorable books, from such strange, self-defeating satires as *Pierre* and *The Blithedale Romance* to more conventional works like Emerson's *Representative Men* and Longfellow's *Hiawatha*, along with best sellers such as Susan Warner's *Wide, Wide World*, Maria Cummins's *Lamplighter*, and Fanny Fern's *Ruth Hall*. Hawthorne's career, which had sputtered along on short stories for two decades, suddenly took on massive international magnitude when he produced no fewer than five books in three years, including a book of children's stories and a campaign biography of a college friend who was to become one of our most forgettable presidents, Franklin Pierce.

Matthiessen's label seems odd. How could this burst of creativity be a *re*birth, analogous to the Renaissance rediscovery of Greek and Roman classics? Nonetheless it has stuck, losing its touch of defensive bravado as the texts it proclaims have become unquestionably "major."[4]

In proportion as classic American literature has gained near parity with English literature, at least in American universities, so the term *American Renaissance* has come to look innocuously descriptive.

A more intractable oddness is the relative unpopularity of these texts, then and now. Of the books we now think of as classics, only *Uncle Tom's Cabin* seized the public by the button. It sold 305,000 copies in its first year of publication. By 1948 it was out of print, disparaged by critics and ignored by Matthiessen, who mentions it only once, while sympathizing with Emerson's uneasy detachment from popularity. In contrast, *The Scarlet Letter*, easily the most popular of the books now considered to be great literature, sold only 10,000 copies in its first five years. As one explanation, male writers emphasized their deviance. "I observe that all the bookish men have a tendency to believe that they are unpopular," Emerson notes in his 1848 journal.[5]

The entry has a touch of complacent irony, since Emerson was one of the few such men to have become well known, in part because of his indefatigable labors on the lyceum circuit. Beyond the irony, his entry indicates a basic fact about the intense self-consciousness of "bookish men" in a country without an institutionalized, educated elite to check the headlong rush of men toward commerce. One after another, foreign observers recounted their astonishment at the obsession of American men with business, business, and only business. As Fanny Wright lamented, what she had taken "for the energy of enlightened liberty... was, perhaps, rather the restlessness of commercial enterprise" (1828). "All men who live in democratic times more or less contract the ways of thinking of the manufacturing and trading classes," Alexis de Tocqueville concluded in *Democracy in America* (1840). "Their minds take a serious, deliberate, and positive turn"; they pursue "some visible and proximate object"; they lower the flight of the imagination "to the level of the earth." Such preoccupations constrain both great art and great feeling. "No men are less addicted to reverie than the citizens of a democracy," he continues, "and few of them are ever known to give way to those idle and solitary meditations which commonly precede and produce the great emotions of the heart."[6]

Writer after writer, too, railed against the indifference of practical men to literature. Longfellow, for instance, speaking at his and Hawthorne's Bowdoin graduation in 1825, traced his country's lack of a "polite literature" to the pervasive distrust of pleasure and luxury. "We are a plain people, that have had nothing to do with the mere pleasures and luxuries of life: and hence there has sprung up within us a quicksightedness to the failings of literary men, and an aversion to everything that is not practical, operative and thorough-going." Melville's letters to Hawthorne and Hawthorne's four prefaces to his romances show a combative, defensive self-consciousness about not conforming to their audience's expectations, either as allegorical romancers or as men who had chosen the social role of writer. When Emerson visited Wordsworth in 1833, Wordsworth soon launched into an attack on American culture, with Emerson's tacit approval. Americans "are too much given to making of money & secondly to politics," Wordsworth said. "And I fear they lack a class of men of leisure—in short of gentlemen to give a tone of honor to the community."[7]

"The best feat of Genius is to make an audience of the mediocre & the dull," Emerson wrote in his journal for April 5, 1847. That had been the impetus behind *The Dial*, to which Emerson and Margaret Fuller had given so much time a few years earlier. Even after *The Dial*'s failure, Fuller's candid and incisive review of American literary achievements and prospects concludes that "the most important part of our literature, while the work of diffusion is still going on, lies in the journals" (1846). They "form at present the only efficient instrument for the general education of the people." The problem, as she puts it, is very simple: "a new country where so large a portion of manly ability must be bent on making laws, making speeches, making railroads and canals."[8]

Fuller's public optimism about re-forming the manly multitude does not carry over to some of her private letters and conversations. American literature is "boyish," she once said to William Henry Channing, who recalled her "contrasting its boyish crudity, half boastful, half timid, with the tempered, manly equipoise of thorough-bred European writers." Writing from Chicago to her friend Channing (August 16, 1843), Fuller speaks with despair of how beautiful the landscape is, yet how empty all the men are of spirit. "Its beauty has filled me with rapture, but among *men* oh, how lonely! . . . they seem to me to tend so exclusively to bring the riches out of the earth." She finds little to sustain Channing's dream of disseminating his new journal out West:

> It has been a cause of true grief to me, dear William, that I could do nothing in aid of your purposes, simply for this reason, that I have had no intercourse with any one, with whom I should naturally introduce a mention of objects such as your periodical is intended to pursue. Always it has been that I should hear from them accounts of the state of the country, in politics or agriculture, or their domestic affairs, or

hunting stories. Of me, none asked a question.... My friend, I am deeply homesick, yet where is that home?[9]

A decade later, Sarah Hale's revised edition of *Northwood* comprehensively indicts the manly American spirit of enterprise: "It is the love of money, the craving desire to accumulate property, the entire devotion of the heart and soul, mind, might and strength, to the one object of increasing or preserving an estate, that bows down the lofty intellect of men, and makes their sordid souls as grovelling as the appetites of the brutes that perish. This inordinate thirst for riches is the besetting sin of Americans; situation, institutions, education, all combine to foster it." As if to confirm such laments, a contemporary governor of Michigan complacently observed, "Like most new States, ours has been settled by an active, energetic and enterprising class of men, who are desirous of accumulating property rapidly."[10]

To writers of both sexes, conventional American manhood seemed blithely inhospitable to any kind of literary spirit. Recurrently Emerson contrasts himself with the ruthless practical men he finds all around him. "I feel, meantime, that those who succeed in life, in civilized society, are beasts of prey," he writes in his journal for March-April 1847. "It has always been so." Staying in hotels always mortifies his well-being, Emerson muses three years later. "The people who fill them oppress me with their excessive virility, and would soon become intolerable, if it were not for a few friends, who, like women, tempered the acrid mass." A late Emerson essay, "Worship," begins with several tart paragraphs on the necessity to acknowledge the brutalizing impact of worldly men. The presence "of fate, of practical power, or of trade... tyrannizes at the centre of Nature." At one point, in considering the attacks on him, he responds with redoubled detachment, at once smug, childish, and impersonal. "I am never beaten until I know that I am beaten," he has a "remarkable person" say. "I meet powerful brutal people to whom I have no skill to reply. They think they have defeated me. It is so published in society, in the journals; ... and yet I know all the time that I have never been beaten; have never yet fought, shall certainly fight when my hour comes, and shall beat."[11]

There is a strong class dynamic at work in writings like these. Emerson's sniffy transcendence of "powerful brutal people" resembles the pervasive tendency of patrician men of affairs to invoke the fall of the Roman Empire in response to Jacksonian democracy. As Robert Ferguson concludes, conventional men of culture, most of them lawyers, were unable to cope with "the dynamism of the expanding nation" and the democratization of politics. William Charvat's still indispensable book on American authorship in the nineteenth century argues that classic male American writers tend to come from a patrician class on the ropes at the hands of Jacksonian entrepreneurs. Except for Whitman, much of the now celebrated "quarrel with the reader" in the midcentury male canon has the vaguely oxymoronic hope of creating readers both manly and patrician. The broad social context for such rhetorical quarrels is the writers' self-conscious resistance to the growing middle-class and female market for fiction and to authorship as a feminized profession.[12] Only Thoreau and Whitman, Whitman less ambiguously, come from artisan and farmer backgrounds.

As a practical matter, Longfellow, Fuller, and Emerson were right to say that writers lacked social supports. So too did artists and scholars. The channels of success all seemed to flow one way. "This country possesses neither the population nor the endowments to maintain a large class of learned idlers," wrote James Fenimore Cooper in *Notions of the Americans*. To make a social impact, he declares, a man must speak directly, naturally, vigorously, forcefully, without many learned allusions. Real learning—and, implicitly, real manhood—comes through "the jostlings of the world," where a man who may be "existing in a state of dreaming retrospection, lost in a maze of theories," comes up against antagonists at every turn. The emphasis on practical persuasion makes for "bold and sturdy discussions," mostly about law and politics, but also for a striking homogeneity of sensibility. "I have never seen a nation so much alike in my life, as the people of the United States, and what is more, they are not only like each other, but they are remarkably like that which common sense tells them they ought to resemble," Cooper concludes. As Hawthorne mused, to choose a vocation requiring idleness "was fatal in New England. There is a grossness in the conceptions of my countrymen; . . . they can anticipate nothing but evil of a young man who neither studies physic, law, nor gospel, nor opens a store, nor takes to farming." Tocqueville would put it most pithily. Americans think themselves the freest men on earth, he said in *Democracy in America*, but actually they are the most unfree, because they have the most limited range of opinion.[13]

Male writers—at least the ones now collected as "the American Renaissance"—sought alternative states of manly creativity, whose powers flow from that same "state of dreaming retrospection" that Cooper dismissed. Melville expressed the impasse most starkly, if with a certain self-pity. "The calm, the coolness, the silent grass-growing mood in which a man *ought* always to compose,—that, I fear, can seldom be mine," he writes to Hawthorne in a well-known passage. "Dollars damn me;... What I feel most moved to write, that is banned,—it will not pay. Yet, altogether, write the *other* way I cannot. So the product is a final hash, and all my books are botches." Elsewhere, in accepting his English publisher's offer for *Moby Dick*, Melville notes the two overwhelming problems of being a writer in America: the lack of an international copyright law, without which American publishers stole the work of established English writers at the expense of developing a national literature, and worse, the indifference of men to literature. "This country & nearly all its affairs are governed by sturdy backwoodsmen—noble fellows enough, but not at all literary, & who care not a fig for any authors except those who write those most saleable of all books nowadays—i e—the newspapers, & magazines."[4]

The quotations could be multiplied a hundredfold. My point is not to accept at face value these accounts of literary victimization but to highlight the self-consciousness of being deviant from prevailing norms of manhood. Michael Davitt Bell has rightly emphasized the pervasive self-doubt, guilt, and strategic evasiveness underlying the ostensible choice of "romance" as a literary genre at this time. As his remarks on the sociology of literary vocation suggest, the label of romancer "could validate, or at least give substance to, their sense of alienation."[5] One of my central arguments is that American Renaissance writers did not liberate their voices from their class background and "polite" English models until they began to struggle with, rather than dismiss, the middle-class ideology of manhood taking hold in American public life. They made a potentially hostile or indifferent audience, men preoccupied with competing for money and property, part of their rhetorical strategies. Gender expectations are as crucial a context for antebellum male writers as they are for female writers in the Northeast before the Civil War.

Another inducement to alienation and nonconformity for male writers was their awareness that the audience for serious literature was shifting from patrician men of public affairs to middle class women, from men in power to women at the leisured margin of power. In 1798 Charles Brockden Brown had sent a copy of *Wieland* to Vice President Thomas Jefferson. Brown presumably hoped his tale of the mind's factions, passions, and interests would bring Jefferson back from incipient republican anarchy to a Federalist vision of paternal self-discipline and elite controls. By the 1840s, when Poe wanted to publish his sketches of the New York literati, he chose the magazine outselling every other American magazine of its day by three to one, *Godey's Lady's Book.*

While Susan Warner, Harriet Beecher Stowe, and other women writers captured the new mass market of bourgeois women readers in the Northeast, various male writers brooded about what Hawthorne in a notorious 1855 letter called "a d——d mob of scribbling women." Actually most writers were still men, and few women dared deviate from the pervasive expectation that as professional writers their duty was to inculcate domestic virtues. Men could aspire to literary genius, Nina Baym and Mary Kelley point out, while women had to replicate stereotypical maternal values. Nonetheless, writers such as Melville and Thoreau, who directly challenged their readers, had to await the transformation of American higher education before their works received widespread applause. Eventually their secure place in the hearts and close readings of professors would gain them the respect if not the affection of the American middle-class reading public.[16]

In short, the problematic popularity of books we now acclaim as canonical texts reflects the problematic status of bookish men in the nineteenth century, especially those men who tried to be writers rather than clergymen, lawyers, or professors. They were the first generation of American writers to reject the eighteenth-century "gentleman amateur" model of literature as a neoclassical adjunct to genteel citizenship. They were at odds with at least two basic aspects of the marketplace: middle-class male norms of practicality and competitiveness and a suddenly visible female audience.

At the simplest level, the "scribbling men" of the American Renaissance open a modernist sparring match between avant-garde writers and bourgeois readers. Their writing, as Walter Benn Michaels has said of *Walden*, has false bottoms.[17] Whether in the guise of fiction or essays, their devious voices deliberately undermine the stabilizing interpretive expectations of their readers: consistent characters, gripping plots, coherent genres, uplifting moral themes. What Melville gleefully says of Hawthorne's titles has frequently been applied to Hawthorne's short stories as well: "It is certain, that some of them are directly calculated to deceive—egregiously deceive—the superficial skimmer of pages."[18] Melville's own voices are flagrantly inconsistent, especially in his masterpiece, *Moby Dick*. Whitman and Emerson, of course, openly cherish inconsistency. It helps them gain access to the mind's spontaneous powers.

Insistently Hawthorne and Melville veer toward what Ishmael self-mockingly calls "a hideous and intolerable allegory," the one genre contemporary readers disliked. From Scott and Cooper they appropriated the label of romance, a much more acceptable genre of improbable historical adventures, as a veil for their real interests. Hawthorne and Melville used "romance" as a deceptive strategy, not as a coherent literary genre, to legitimate their explorations of the unloving heart's wicked truths (Hawthorne) and the unloving universe's wicked metaphysics (Melville).[19] Sensitive reviewers such as E. P. Whipple felt very uneasy with Hawthorne's hypnotic prying, so disturbingly at odds with his sweet, moral, and genteel narrative voice, which so many readers praised as "natural" and "feminine." Almost everyone backed off from Melville's extravagant oscillations from rhapsody to malice in *Mardi*, *Moby Dick*, and especially *Pierre*.[20]

As covert acts of fight, and flight, American Renaissance texts have received a very good press from twentieth-century academic critics. Classic American literature has generated an unusual profusion of critical paradigms. Each paradigm presumes victimization by bourgeois society as the starting point for the writer's alienated imagination. We have the American Adam, a World Elsewhere of style, the Imperial Self, the prophetic and redemptive American Self, the Romance as a sacrifice of relation, the chaste marriage of wilderness males. Nina Baym has perceptively labeled these paradigms, all established by male critics, as "Melodramas of Beset Manhood."[21] They highlight textual elements converting feelings of social and sexual alienation into an aggrandized verbal status for autonomous, brotherly, or disembodied male consciousness, while demeaning powerful men and passionate women.

In the last fifteen years a complementary set of paradigms has emerged from feminists studying women's fiction before the Civil War: the Cult of True American Womanhood, the feminization of American culture, the ideology of sentimental domesticity and moral mothering, the female world of love and ritual, the intrepid heroine transforming her powerless condition. There has been much disagreement among feminist critics about whether popular women's fiction conforms to the bourgeois myths of an early capitalist social structure or whether women's fiction finds ways of expressing women's feelings, openly or duplicitously.[22]

Within a rhetorical context of separate gender spheres, male writers developed premodernist styles to explore and exalt their sense of being deviant from male norms, while women writers developed evangelical or more broadly moral narrations of domesticity to articulate the needs of a largely female reading public. Later writers such as William Dean Howells and Henry James might accept with relative equanimity the "sissy" role given to male writers in an industrializing society. But from 1830 to the 1850s, the writer's role and the writer's audience were more uncertain, especially for men.[23] American Renaissance self-refashioning—of reader as well as writer—develops as a common rhetorical response to these social conditions.

II

Faced with the pervasive ascription of deviance, male and female writers tended to manage feelings of alienation, anger, and self-doubt in opposite ways. Men adopted intellectual strategies of self-splitting and reader disorientation—the false bottoms that academic critics love to expose. Women wrote impassioned and often duplicitous moral dramas, mirroring the values and conflicts of genteel and evangelical women readers. Nevertheless, both men and women writers make the refashioning of self and reader a central process in their texts. From *The Wide, Wide World* to *Uncle Tom's Cabin*, from *Walden* to "Song of Myself," American Renaissance writers build much of their rhetorical energy by dramatizing a process of conversion, and by directly addressing readers whose values have to be transformed.

Unlike the women writers, classic male writers dramatize their own self-refashioning by destabilizing their narrations. They evoke uncanny feelings of being drawn into the continuously changing self as if it were quicksand in a lightning storm. A self-possessed "you" often becomes a point of departure for the flight of the self-dispossessing "I," whose delight in multiple perspectives and linguistic play invites readers to jump free of their slavery to a striving, anxious, manly ego based on ownership, work, competition, and social position. Ironically, the "I-you" relationship also intimates rivalry. A lurking competitiveness reappears in the flights of self-refashioning, reinscribing the tensions of manhood.

Sometimes rhetorical refashioning of the reader takes the form of direct assault, as in the first paragraph of *Typee*, which Melville had to censor for the American edition. In the uncensored version his narrator mocks "ye state-room sailors" who drink champagne punch and rail

against "those good-for-nothing tars, shouting and tramping over-
head." In *Pierre*, Melville extravagantly satirizes a genteel, feminized
audience in the person of one Miss Angelica Amabilia of Ambleside,
who asks the young poet-hero to grace her album with "some nice little
song." As other perfumed albums pile up on Pierre's shelves to await
his responsive verses, Melville sardonically muses about his hero's situation: "The true charm of agreeable parlour society is, that there you
lose your own sharp individuality and become delightfully merged in
that soft social Pantheism, as it were, that rosy melting of all into one,
ever prevailing in those drawing-rooms." Melville's brief satire clearly
implies that for him a "drawing-room" should be a place where a writer
"draws the sword of his own individuality" as an "ugly weapon" to
expose false prettiness. To borrow a helpful distinction from recent
theories about readers in texts, Melville's assault on his hapless *characterized* reader (female) prepares the way for a truculent appeal to his
implied reader (male).[24] As Emerson counsels himself in one of his 1844–
1845 journal poems,

> I will not read a pretty tale
> To pretty people in a nice saloon
> Borrowed from their expectation
> But I will sing aloud & free
> From the heart of the world[25]

Surprisingly, in *Uncle Tom's Cabin*, Harriet Beecher Stowe also attacks
"nice" parlour readers. In chapter 12, for instance, after Tom has
witnessed the suicide of a young black mother whose child has just
been sold, Stowe suddenly addresses readers who think as the slave
trader thinks and can't feel as Tom feels. Haley's "heart was exactly
where yours, sir, and mine could be brought, with proper effort and
cultivation," she writes, and she repeatedly excoriates northern politicians who cultivate such heartless attitudes in the name of national
union. But Stowe has more than Daniel Webster in mind. By the end
of the chapter, her implicit appeal for reader refashioning has shifted
to direct accusation. Building reader response right into her text, she
asserts with extraordinary vehemence that their refined Christian comfort has produced the system of slavery.

Haley, discovering the woman's absence after she has jumped into
the river at midnight, simply sits down "discontentedly" with his account
book, and marks down "the missing body and soul" in the "losses"
column. Immediately Stowe voices the responses of her readers.

"He's a shocking creature, isn't he,—this trader? so unfeeling! It's dreadful, really!"

"O, but nobody thinks anything of these traders! They are universally despised,—never received into any decent society."

Then she lowers the boom. "But who, sir, makes the trader? Who is most to blame?" she asks.

The enlightened, cultivated, intelligent man, who supports the system of which the trader is the inevitable result, or the poor trader himself? You make the public sentiment that calls for his trade, that debauches and depraves him, till he feels no shame in it; and in what are you better than he?

Are you educated and he ignorant, you high and he low, you refined and he coarse, you talented and he simple?

In the day of a future Judgment, these very considerations may make it more tolerable for him than for you.

This is a Jeremiad, as Jane Tompkins has argued for the whole novel.[26] The last shall be first and the first shall be last. Yet the first have the capacity for refashioning the social system if they can refashion themselves. Men, in particular, have to admit Tom's soft, gentle, domestic sensibility to their hard, dominant, calculating, Anglo-Saxon habits of thought. If Stowe's characterized readers here look like a snooty high-society couple, the implied reader is motherly, including the maternal sensibility buried in male readers. Stowe encourages a relatively comfortable reader refashioning—at least for those who don't own slaves—by frequently acknowledging the reader's upper-class status at the same time as she urges moral improvement.

Stowe's advocacy of maternal sympathy could not be more opposed to Melville's scorn for feminization. She seeks to bring out feminine sensibilities in men of power; Melville seeks to restore manliness to writing, even at the price of self-castration, as the "Enceladus" episode near the end of *Pierre* makes clear. Yet both writers use reader refashioning as a common rhetorical tool. They construct a characterized genteel reader to be accused and transformed, either directly or through indirect satire, for the common end not of comic mockery but of conversion from class and gender stereotypes to imaginative life and fellow feeling.

Where Stowe presumes great intimacy between writer and reader, male writers presume a wary distance. *Uncle Tom's Cabin* speaks with and for her feelingful readers, often voicing their thoughts. The last installment of her serialized version says good-bye to her readers as "children" embraced by her maternal values and voice: "Farewell, dear children, till we meet again." While Stowe confidently presumes an intimate readerly engagement, the four traditionally canonized male texts—*The Scarlet Letter, Moby Dick, Walden,* and "Song of Myself"—all begin with a shared rhetorical device reflecting the writer's sense of alienation from readers.[27] Each writer self-consciously constructs a "you," with varying degrees of appeal and accusation. The "you" becomes a foil for the writer's rejection of conventional manliness. He ostentatiously adopts a posture of meditative laziness, not hard-working ambition.

In "The Custom-House," the first paragraph ambiguously describes Hawthorne's readers as capable both of completing "the divided segment of the writer's own nature" and of "violating" his "inmost Me." Then Hawthorne presents himself in ambiguous relation to manhood. He is both an "idler" on the topmost bough of his sternly disapproving patriarchal family tree and a man half-possessed by his workplace, needing to be converted from its masculine norms to an implicitly feminine sensibility. Thoreau begins *Walden* with a simpler opposition to work and conventional manhood. Mocking his village neighbors and readers for working too hard, he laughs at the young men possessed by their possessions, who push before them "a barn seventy-five feet by forty, its Augean stables never cleansed, and one hundred acres of land, tillage, mowing, pasture, and wood-lot!" As he concludes, "men labor under a mistake."

Melville, too, introduces Ishmael as a surrogate and a goad for his readers, landsmen "nailed to benches, clinched to desks." He gives a jaunty list of reasons for preferring to gaze at the water from the easygoing fraternity of the foredeck rather than the higher slavery of command. Whitman, of course, celebrates himself as the most ostentatiously lazy man of all. He leans and loafs, observing a spear of summer grass. Moreover, his first line's claim to "celebrate myself" turns out to be both an invitation and a coercive prediction to the self-alienated reader: "And what I assume you shall assume."

In each case the fun not only liberates the writer from reader expectations but fictionalizes the forceful, practical, ambitious, hard-working American male as a limited reader. The conventional man has no real consciousness. He has been driven into social bondage by his work. Such a reader stares out from manly drudgery with resentful yet yearning eyes, like one of Ishmael's water gazers, half aware that living might somehow be more natural and that his sense of self might be enlarged.

Walden, for instance, immediately establishes an antagonistic stance toward its readers, whom Thoreau characterizes as townspeople. After Thoreau announces that he is speaking of himself only because other people have asked him to, he turns their seemingly natural questions about his life at Walden Pond into mirrors for their own resentful or anxious self-preoccupations. At the extreme, "some, who have large families," ask him "how many poor children I maintained." Opposing the nonsensical self-sacrificing in the name of work that he sees all around him, Thoreau proclaims his own self-reliant egotism and addresses his pages "to poor students," not yet fully cast in the molds of adult life. His real subject, at least for the first few chapters, is the contrast between himself and his readers. He presents himself as a rather cavalier and patronizing anthropologist, bent on studying "you who read these pages, who are said to live in New England."

These readers, "serfs of the soil," are really serfs of conventional manhood. "They have got to live a man's life, pushing all these things before them." Such conventions of "a man's life," Thoreau argues, have nothing to do with true manhood. They make men into machines. "Actually, the laboring man has not leisure for a true integrity day by day; he cannot afford to sustain the manliest relations to men; his labor would be depreciated in the market. He has no time to be any thing but a machine." The market has made men alive only to things and property, not to true manhood.

Thoreau's attack intensifies. "It is very evident what mean and sneaking lives many of you live, . . . lying, flattering, voting, contracting yourselves into a nutshell of civility, or dilating into an atmosphere of thin and vaporous generosity." His satiric thrusts use metaphors from nature to subvert social relations: men live as skulking animals, contract themselves into nutshells, or close and dilate like clams. The pun on "dilating," also implying a verbal expansiveness or holding forth, simultaneously has his neighbors evaporating like a "thin and vaporous" atmosphere even as they talk empty words into that atmosphere. In either case, their chameleon self-transformations expose an absence of self.

Thoreau's uses of nature to describe village unnaturalness launch a full-scale rhetorical attack. Aiming to make his audience as nervous as possible about their lack of autonomous moral authority, he contracts himself into a nutshell of incivility to dilate upon their lack of manhood. He is the real man; they are the slaves. "It is hard to have a southern overseer," he says; "it is worse to have a northern one; but worst of all when you are the slave-driver of yourself." His readers have a "stereotyped but unconscious despair" because "there is no play in them." They live for the market, not for their potential divinity. They measure their worth only by how their profits stand in relation to their neighbors', not by taking up the only question worth asking: what is "the chief end of man"?[28]

Thoreau refashions himself beyond the oppressed manhood of his neighbors in at least three ways. First, he turns feelings of depression and alienation into aggressive satire. Second, he links himself to natural processes of seasonal change and rebirth. Third, he links natural processes to verbal processes of linguistic transformation, especially through puns and paradoxes. Throughout, he oscillates between a prickly opposition to social conformity and a self-effacing attentiveness to nature. In practicing what his mentor preaches, he plays porcupine to Emerson's amoeba. Under his transformational uses of language and his manly braggadocio lie his unacknowledged fears of humiliation and his partially acknowledged rivalry. A contradictory rhetoric of self-refashioning as purification and rebirth, whether through pure nature or purified words, keeps circling back to attack the social conditions that make him feel contaminated and unmanly.

Most simply, Thoreau tries to transform depression into aggressiveness. As Sacvan Bercovitch discovered, the first version of Thoreau's celebrated epigraph is the ode to dejection that he claims to disown. The epigraph, repeated in the second chapter, declares: "I do not propose to write an ode to dejection, but to brag as lustily as chanticleer in the morning, standing on his roost, if only to wake my neighbors up." The first, censored version: "I could tell a pitiful story respecting myself . . . with a sufficient list of failures, and flow as humbly as the very gutters."[29]

In the past twenty years or so, a good many critics have begun to talk about Thoreau's predilection for excremental language. To put it bluntly, in saying that "I could . . . flow as humbly as the very gutters," Thoreau implies that he feels like shit. That feeling, displaced and transformed, underlies a great deal of the language play in *Walden*, from the knotty puns and paradoxes to the delight in linguistic transformation and verbal aggression.[30] At the very beginning he mocks his neighbors for endlessly pushing before them their Augean stables, so hopelessly filled with animal dung, not realizing that they themselves will be "soon ploughed into the soil for compost." Why do they do it? Only to store up a little profit "in the brick bank."

By the end Thoreau has found his profit in a different kind of bank: the metamorphosis of the forty-foot bank of clay in the spring thaw, where rebirth and etymology become indistinguishable pleasures in his description. Yet he wants his manliness both ways; he wants both to flaunt his natural brag to his dung-driven neighbors and to show himself flowing as humbly as nature's gutters. Even in his extravagantly uneconomical first chapter, "Economy," he simultaneously scorns the villagers' criteria for profit while showing how by their own standards he got a better return for his labor. Here, more blatantly than elsewhere in *Walden*, rivalry lurks under his seeming detachment. If he has been made to feel like shit, he learns to flow while throwing it back at his neighbors.

In *American Romanticism and the Marketplace*, Michael T. Gilmore astutely describes *Walden* as "a defeated text," an "ahistorical maneuver" against the marketplace, which for Thoreau is "a site of humiliation." For Gilmore, Thoreau's attempt to transform his autobiography into seasonal myth and universal metaphor abstracts his text from history. Paradoxically, the abstracting process brings back the reification and commodification he wants to flee.[31] I would add that the market for Thoreau includes not just products and profits but male rivalry, the competitive arena in which he and especially his father so conspicuously failed to measure up. What Thoreau fears is more than being made to feel like a thing or a machine; it's being made to feel ugly, despised, physically loathsome and emotionally helpless.

Perhaps he also invited humiliation sometimes. "I once set fire to the woods," he noted in his 1850 journal. In 1844, whether with a strange, self-punishing malice or with gross ineptness, this expert woodsman let his fire get out of control while cooking fish with a friend. It destroyed three hundred acres. Worse, Thoreau simply sat on a high rock to "enjoy" the "glorious spectacle." It may well have been the townspeople's vehement rage that drove him to Walden in the first place. More broadly, humiliation, not reification, is the real terror of the entrepreneurial marketplace, as I argue in Chapter 3.[32] Thoreau's last transformational metaphor, the bug emerging from the table, reinscribes the buglike, walled-in, excremental feeling of self even as he takes such pleasure in its spontaneous self-refashioning.

In reviewing *Walden*, George Eliot remarked that it seemed to her "a bit of pure American life (not the 'go a-head' species, but its opposite pole)." By the "opposite pole" she meant to suggest how *Walden* shares the American spirit of "innovation" and "independence," however "unpractical and dreamy" the book seems to be.[33] One can take her insight further. Thoreau does indeed stand as the undialectical opposite of "the 'go-ahead' species": acerbically critiquing American men, yet inversely mirroring the preoccupations of American manhood. In the midst of his detached observations, a continuing sense of rivalry and confrontation belies his attempt to refashion himself as a natural flow of words about nature. Emerson makes a similar remark when he speaks of Thoreau's no-saying. "There was somewhat military in his nature, not to be subdued, always manly and able, but rarely tender, as if he did not feel himself except in opposition."[34]

Thoreau's language of self-refashioning is most vital, I think, when it is implicitly saying no. Yet his combative, evasive voice continually claims to detach his eye from his I, his affirmations of nature from his satirical thrusts. As D. H. Lawrence said of Crèvecoeur, "Absolutely the safest thing to get your emotional reactions over is NATURE."[35] Thoreau found in his observations of natural and linguistic processes an alternative to feeling himself in opposition: not feeling himself at all.

III

Melville's Ishmael shares many of Thoreau's traits. He too relishes quarreling with his readers, and he too seeks ways of transforming his feelings of depression and humiliation. Like Thoreau's, his self-refashioning takes him toward a fascination with etymology and a blending of his voice with oceanic nature. Unlike Thoreau, Ishmael mocks his own intellectualizing as well as his slavish readers. He tries to draw us into a spontaneous fraternity of intellectual chums. Moreover, he finds a way of dramatizing intense feelings of humiliation, by telling Ahab's story.

Ishmael's first act of self-presentation tweaks readers who expect something else: his name and his history. In saying "Call me Ishmael," he imperiously thwarts the reader's curiosity about who he really is. His next opening brings me up short again: "Some years ago—never mind how long precisely." Ishmael implicitly characterizes his readers as people who want precise labels and time frames for self and story. Rather than tell me who he is and when it happened, he makes me self-conscious about my need to know. His opening has become so memorable in part because of its peremptory, playful surprises. He teases the reader, anticipating responses and denying expectations.

Simultaneously, he characterizes himself as a storyteller. If he badgers his audience, it's as if to say, Settle down, relax, I'm in charge here and I'm about to tell you a fascinating tale. From the first, his mask of truculence betrays a minute attentiveness to the reader's potential hostility. By the end of the first paragraph he even claims to be our representative.

Why is that first paragraph so appealing? If I pause and do a close reading, it gets more and more annoying. After initially challenging and undermining my expectations for conventional storytelling, or at least exposing the conventionality of those expectations, Ishmael launches a series of explanations for why he went to sea. He was poor; he was bored. No, he needed to be "driving off the spleen, and regulating the circulation." Here the phrasing intimates that his calm, assured voice is a pose. His self-controlled tone detaches him from the self that needs controlling. It's not *his* spleen and *his* circulation, themselves ambiguous metaphors for uneasy emotions, especially anger, but "*the* spleen" and "*the* circulation," disowned and depersonalized. He seems at a vast distance, in space and time, from his feelings and his body. Somehow, going to sea comfortably unites detachment with the "driving off" of rage and the "regulating" of inward disorder.

Or does it? The next, tumultuous sentence almost loses control altogether, barely held in check by its string of "Whenevers." Whenever (which implies frequently) he gets depressed, again depersonalized as "grim about the mouth"; whenever he gets *really* depressed, with "a damp, drizzly November in my soul"; whenever he becomes "involuntarily" obsessed with death, "pausing before coffin warehouses, and bringing up the rear of every funeral I meet; and especially whenever my hypos get such an upper hand of me" that he feels like "deliberately" and "methodically" knocking people's hats off—then he goes to sea. His recurrent depressions surge toward violence yet oddly disown bad feelings.

Knocking off a row of top hats seems rather funny, in fact. The image suddenly deflates the ominous buildup. Perhaps Ishmael is just being self-mocking. In any case, going to sea brings back self-control, or rather, brings back the mask of control and drives off the devil of self. Yet only four sentences into his narrative, Ishmael's voice seems impossibly contradictory: at once contentious and mocking, yet comfortably detached, regulated in its cadences, yet chaotic in what he says. Is there a self here at all?

The contradictions, which all swirl about the issue of anger, become more intense. "This is my substitute for pistol and ball," he calmly affirms. A good close reader extrapolates from the measured yet desperate hostility of his previous sentence: going to sea must be his substitute for killing someone. Now he has escalated knocking off hats to murder, while preserving his self-control by doing his usual trick, objectifying and disowning his feelings as the depersonalized objects "pistol and ball."

Then, suddenly, aggression once more becomes depression, escalated to suicide. "With a philosophical flourish Cato throws himself upon his sword; I quietly take to the ship." He goes to sea to save himself; he goes to sea to kill himself. Which? The more slowly I read this passage, the more aggravating its calmly balanced cadences become. But Ishmael does not allow me to read it slowly. What seems to be a psychological morass turns out to be a mirror for the reader. As his last surprise, he says there is no surprise, because any male reader can see all these feelings in himself.

"There is nothing surprising in this," he concludes. "If they but knew it, almost all men in their degree, some time or other, cherish very nearly the same feelings towards the ocean with me." His five artful qualifiers ("If they but knew it, almost . . . in their degree, some time or other, . . . very nearly") allow an illusory measure of safety. I'm brought to the brink of joining him, yet I'm not forced to come all the way. Ishmael's final sleight-of-hand trick is to say these are "feelings towards the ocean," when all along the ocean has been the place of escape from feelings.

Ishmael's philosophical flourishes both hide and expose an abusive, violent depressive, unable to own his anger. At the same time as I pry open that reading of his heart, I'm aware that he's toying with my own heartstrings. From start to finish he has assembled in his voice a contradictory set of readerly conventions, intended to mirror my own unacknowledged alienations and to unsettle my complacency just as I settle down to read this sea story. In every sense, I'm being taken— taken out to sea, yet taken into myself.

So why is his voice so appealing? Partly because it seems more like rhetorical play than personal anxiety. And partly—a contradiction— because he seems so brash and playful, yet vulnerable and confiding, all at once. Also, his unintegrated, obsessive, depressive, self-avoiding self turns out to be the reader's as much as his own. In particular he mirrors male readers like myself, those of an intellectual turn who, for whatever reason, may be uncomfortable with anger. Both his imperious confidence and his startling openness, if not looked at too closely, make me trust him or, perhaps I should say, seduce me through the quiet anger he half controls in himself and half awakens in me.

After the introductory paragraph Ishmael speaks directly to his landsmen or townsmen readers, as *Walden* does, but with sympathy rather than detached contempt. Surveying all the varieties of "you" who stand surreally "fixed in ocean reveries," he sweeps through city and country with a grand accumulation of rhetorical questions, all in the second person, culminating in his emphatic assertion that the story of Narcissus is "the key to it all." Then Ishmael throws away the key with another exposition, this one rather more comic and defensive, to explain why he goes to sea as a sailor rather than a proud commander. Not Narcissus but Fate rules the second half of the chapter. "Who aint a slave? Tell me that." He pugnaciously defends his choice of being pushed around, as if we were all in the same kennel.

The initial contradictions make wider and wider circles through his narrative. For instance, I can easily dissociate myself from the "you" addressed in "The Mast-head," "ye ship-owners of Nantucket!" But I feel uneasily affiliated with the "thee" he more sympathetically addresses, the patrician Platonist or "Childe Harold" who forgets his identity in an implicitly masturbatory reverie. While Ishmael's rhetorical dislocations begin the refashioning of himself and his reader, making "you [who] live under the blessed light of the evangelical land" receptive to the unfixed, oceanic fluidity of spontaneous thought, he strangely distances himself from the dangers of his own masthead fluidities. At the same time he fixes himself ever more tightly to the fated yet narcissistic quest of his commander, whose obsessive search for manhood makes him the slave of rage.[36] Ishmael's final vortex is his beginning: the *Pequod* becomes a coffin warehouse, and he brings up the rear of Ahab's funeral, an orphan in the wake of his disowned double.

After Ishmael establishes his gruff and jaunty, yet attentively needy chumship with his readers, we tend to fall away from landsmen's rigidities of self toward his oceanic improvisations. We quickly reject the nonsensical land-bound responses of the lounging aristocrats who listen to Ishmael's "Town-Ho Story." These characterized readers care only about social labels and categories: What is a Lakeman? Where is Buffalo? Who or what are Canallers? Do whales have christenings to give them Christian names? Yet the pleasures of Ishmael's self-decentering follow in the wake of Ahab's self-rigidifying quest for manhood. By the end, as Ishmael fades into a passive invisibility, the drive to be Ahab and the fear of being Pip, or the craving for dominance and the fear of being a coward, turn out to be the same thing: a pair of boy-men bonded by their cosmic humiliations.

Whitman, too, structures "Song of Myself" not just as a quasi-mystical journey, an inner dialogue to integrate himself, or a grand rhetorical integration of his country's divisions, three influential interpretations, but as an intermittently badgering address to his characterized reader, whom he frequently invokes as "you." His great mother bear of a voice seeks to refashion his readers from possessive individualism to a natural wholeness coextensive with his own egotism. He needles and cajoles us to give up our obsession with property and our own ego, even the egotism of mastering the meanings of his poem, so that we can find ourselves blessed with the universal properties of his flowering, flourishing soul.

If Thoreau learns to flow as humbly as the thawing gutters of a spring bank, Whitman claims to flow as grandly as the cosmos itself or as intimately as fingers caressing a body. His self-refashioning therefore seems much more continuously grandiose, at once embracing and mirroring all his separate readers. A flagrant mixed signal, the poem says (1) he can "incorporate" us beyond private ownership and competitive self-reckoning and (2) my Self is bigger than your self. Yet the drama of his self-refashioning lies in the failure of his operatic "I" to consummate union with his silent "you." Under his serene confidence about representing and transforming his audience lies a recurrent feeling that if we don't join and complete him, he will be left standing there, small, separate, and alone. D. H. Lawrence's "greasy little Esquimo" who chuckles outside the egg of Whitman's Allness is really Whitman's double.[37]

In section 2, Whitman addresses the reader with a hectoring hopefulness. "Have you reckoned a thousand acres much? Have you reckoned the earth much?" His second question mocks the reader's concern with the first. Those who "reckon" themselves by reckoning their accumulations will never experience themselves as blades of grass, part of nature's processes. Then Whitman forces his questions still further, to jolt readers who remain proud of their self-alienating possessiveness, including their acquisition of poetic meanings. "Have you practised so long to learn to read? / Have you felt so proud to get at the meaning of poems?" Stop, he says. "Stop this day and night with me and you shall possess the origin of all poems."

An intimate stay with him, just a day and a night, will introduce readers to the act of reading as a spiritual intercourse. Such an intercourse can reorient us from acquisitive skills to a genuine self-possession, felt as both intimacy and self-discovery. It will lead, as intercourse does, to "origin," both birth and procreation. The reader will experience himself as a continuous original, through continuous rebirth. At the same time, the reader merges with the writer, to experience the writer's caressing creativity as his own.

All this is a sympathetic summary of what I take Whitman to be doing. To take him seriously, however, both scares and annoys me. Not only is he attacking me for trying to make sense of him, but he is also playing the grand seducer. Stripped of its prophetic grandiosity, his speech promises me the moon for a one-night stand. First he tries to make me uncomfortable with my analytic distance by equating analysis with pride and possessiveness. Then he inflates my potential pride and possessiveness by saying that a casual dalliance with him can give me the origin of all poetic creativity. I could merge with Shakespeare, Dante, Milton, Homer, even Whitman himself, at the moment of their greatest inspirations. Where he invokes intimacy, he means possessive fusion, veiled by the comfortable womblike bath of his abstractions.

To promise me such creative reading effectively denies the basis of real intimacy in separate selves. As with Ishmael's first paragraph, to slow down and think about it brings on a rather surly distance, at least in me. Perhaps that's why Whitman's confident prophecies implicitly urge readers not to think at all. To be blunt, both his grandiose promises and his implicit homoeroticism make me, as a heterosexual male, recoil. At the same time I'm forced to acknowledge how conventionally manly and "up tight" my response appears, compared to his relaxed and luxuriously inviting voice. It makes me feel rather too close to Emerson, who once said that there were parts of *Leaves of Grass* "where I hold my nose as I read."[38]

Whitman partially restores my ease with him by acknowledging his incorporative coerciveness. "I know perfectly well my own egotism," he declares in section 42 of "Song of Myself," "And would fetch you whoever you are flush with myself." "My words itch at your ears till you understand them," he nags in section 47. "It is you talking just as much

as myself . . . . I act as the tongue of you, / It was tied in your mouth . . . .
in mine it begins to be loosened." Curiously, despite my anxious annoyance at what sometimes looks like a homosexual rush, I like his
bold brag about my hidden strength of self, even when he claims to be
my tongue. I welcome his call to "fetch" me "flush with myself," so long
as "myself" includes me as well as him, and so long as his "I" evokes
a vaguely arrogant spirit rather than a specifically desiring body.

My resistance leaps into consciousness when he gets too physical with
me. "You there, impotent, loose in the knees, open your scarfed chops
till I blow grit within you," he shouts in section 40. Here Whitman's
confidence building sounds perilously close to fellatio. "I dilate you
with tremendous breath . . . . I buoy you up." Why do I tighten and
fend him off at such moments, when I unabashedly revere the won-
drously mystical homosexual intercourse of section 5? Because there
he makes love with a "you" who is "my soul," part of himself, not me.
In the abstract I can flow with the serenely biblical majesty of his self-
integration, while physically I can watch, fascinated, as an uncoerced
bystander.

A great deal has recently been made of Whitman's androgyny. Alienated from the masculine conventions of his time, he integrates maleness
and femaleness (Albert Gelpi), or finds his creative vitality in writing
"not-poetry" out of his fragmented sexual ambiguity (Sandra Gilbert).[39]
Despite his ostentatiously conventional, if antiliterary artisan's pose facing the title page of the first edition, Whitman uses his voice for a self-
administered gender-bypass surgery. He speaks as a fatherly midwife,
urging impotent readers to push, push, push our own strong selves
into the open air. That voice I like. It mixes birthing with a grandi-
loquent potency. He also speaks as if he were one long kiss, much
longer than the kisses he loved to give wounded soldiers, breathing his
inspiration into my lungs. Though that voice makes me uncomfortable,
I do yearn for the fatherly power and the unstinting mother love he
promises.

On the other hand, despite his quasi-parental androgyny, Whitman's
voice also proclaims a very phallic self-extension, which seems inseparable from his will to inseminate, embrace and dominate. He will be the
new father of his country, "jetting the stuff of far more arrogant re-
publics." David Reynolds links Whitman's "I" to the swaggering of a
Bowery "b'hoy," and Jeffrey Steele nicely exposes how Whitman's seemingly androgynous claims to "act as the tongue of you" mask what he
calls "the poet's power over the feminized reader."[40] If I resist his

specifically homosexual desires, I resist them not simply out of erotic anxiety but also because Whitman makes me feel feminized or non-existent, rather than either masculine or androgynous.

Eventually I come to think that my ambivalent resistance to his invitation has been part of his rhetorical strategy all along. His claims for reader refashioning, whether playfully punning or grandly fusing, require the continuing separateness of the heterosexual male reader's conventionality from his own homoerotic vision of self-integration. His joyous self-empowering depends on imagining readers who continue to hover between no and yes.

His first three lines typify the whole. They simultaneously acknowledge the reader's resistance, in the reader's own language, and presume to transform conventional meanings of *self*, *assume*, and *belong*.

> I celebrate myself,
> And what I assume you shall assume,
> For every atom belonging to me as good belongs to you.[41]

Here, for the reader, *assume* means "hypothesize," and *belongs to* means "own" or "possess." Before saying anything about the "I" being celebrated, Whitman imagines his readers as those who care about analyzing and owning. Yet he immediately transforms the meaning of *assume* into biological absorption. And he redefines *belongs to* as atomic interchangeability. In just these first three lines the atoms of the reader's body, like conventional assumptions about *assume* and *belongs to*, have been separated from the reader's ego, for a mutual conversion.

These three lines brilliantly condense the process of the poem, which strives to make the reader feel how "good" it would be to forsake an alienated, thinking, calculating ego for an organic flow of universal particulars. Yet the lines also acknowledge the reader's distance from that vision. The "I" who celebrates his inclusive self has little in common yet, except atoms, with the "you" whose separate ego may or may not assent to the poet's "assumption." In fact, the poet's sense of celebration presumes a distance from his balky reader. "You" becomes the platform for the poet's progress toward metamorphosis.

In sections 2–4, Whitman expands his critique of his readers by associating them with "Houses and rooms," those who "talk of the beginning and the end," and "Trippers and askers" who surround him. Positioning his voice "Both in and out of the game, and watching and wondering at it," he detaches himself from "mockings and arguments" to establish his visionary, watchful readiness. His voice caressingly names all these aspects of the world as part of the self he celebrates, yet "they are not the Me myself." At once affectionate, amused, and detached, he offers his model of calm self-doubling and self-witnessing as a way for the reader, too, to stand "Apart from the pulling and hauling," where he once sweated in the fog "with linguists and contenders." Whitman's rhetorical strategy is exactly what he says he himself is: double, at once a mocking argument and a detached expectancy. It depends on characterizing the reader as contentious, confined, perhaps befogged by his own argumentative sweat, for its calming, punning "air" of natural breathing and receptive "inspiration."

Then, in section 5, the extraordinary homoerotic coupling of "I" with "you," or self and soul, dramatizes the ecstasy of self-conversion. Thereafter the reader can choose whether to be in the self or out of it, watching and wondering at its metamorphoses. Throughout, whether Whitman addresses the reader as a potential convert to his absorptive intimacy or reduces the reader to a bystander's role of witness to the poet's self-refashioning, he gives his "you" perpetual powers of refusal. The rhetorical relation he establishes implies an abyss of distance as much as a promise of fusion. His last line—"I stop some where waiting for you"—acknowledges that the reader hasn't yet come along.[42]

Beneath Whitman's peremptory yet confiding voice, so Ishmael-like in its promise of chummy fraternity yet much more serenely caressing and continuous in its cosmic narcissism, lurk doubleness and rivalry. Several psychoanalytic critics, most recently David Cavitch, have seen in Whitman's voice an identification with his mother, warding off not only his fear of his father's brutality but the deeper fear of being like his father, isolated, surly, and baffled by failure. Both Cavitch and Paul Zweig detect a great deal of rivalry with his father in the genesis of "Song of Myself." Whitman's language of reader absorption and self-refashioning paradoxically allows him to express his rivalry with his father's manliness while celebrating his triumphant transformation beyond male rivalry. In Vivian Pollak's fine phrase, he gains an "empathetic self-control."[43] The self he celebrates is a fiction of perpetual incorporation and continuous birth, both manly and motherly, or egotistical and oceanic. He presents himself as begetter and midwife for the reader. Yet the triumph of Whitman's self-celebration requires a resisting reader, implicitly male, and surly too, if my responses are any guide, to be cajoled, bullied, and caressed for his own good. Even Whitman's homoerotic desire requires heterosexual posing to trane and incorporate traditional manhood in his omnisen-

, the center of "Song of Myself" betrays a self very much
h his celebration of self. Section 28, in playfully, yet fearfully
g what it feels like to masturbate, evokes Whitman's terror
at b g abandoned to the touch of his body, utterly alone, without
"fellow-senses" or any other kind of fellowship. Later, in section 37,
he suddenly feels overmastered by the beggarly identities that flow
through him. These are the only two places in the poem where his
grand celebration of Self with a big *S* seems to break down. Momentarily
we see a little self, isolated and shamed, whether he is being watched
by his own senses as his traitor-self masturbates, or he watches himself
"sit shamefaced and beg." For just an instant the greasy little Esquimo
emerges from the egg of Whitman's Allness. Then, like Ben Jonson's
brave infant of Saugantum, he pops back in, while the surge of the
Papa-Mama lover voice rolls on and on, over the resisting reader who
is Whitman's rival, double, father, and stranger-friend.

IV

So far I've tried to show the presence of a common rhetorical pattern
in the diverse masterpieces of Thoreau, Melville, and Whitman. A
conventionally manly "you" is accused and appealed to, as double,
potential convert, and comrade for the self-refashioning "I." Male rivalry looms under the fraternity, I've argued, and the rivalry returns
in the self-refashioning. Homoerotic desires also gain partial voice,
especially with Whitman, though critics have detected latent homosexual leanings in the other two writers as well. My argument is really the
underside of Leslie Fiedler's well-known claim that classic American
literature expresses a mythic male bonding in the wilderness.[44] Fiedler
is certainly right to emphasize the myth, which he explains as a fantasized flight from heterosexual anxiety into a chastely homoerotic chumship. I see the myth as an attempt to make desires that are felt as
unmanly and deviant look both natural and universal. At the same
time, the myth of chumship and the rhetoric of metamorphosis bury
fears about male rivalry.

An implied "I-you" relationship also helps to structure Hawthorne's
introduction to *The Scarlet Letter.* The opening sentences of "The
Custom-House" invite Hawthorne's "indulgent reader" to complete his

"intrusive" self. Or rather, he flirts with a possibility he then denies: that as "I again seize the public by the button," he may find "the one heart and mind of perfect sympathy," who could "find out the divided segment of the writer's own nature, and complete his circle of existence by bringing him into communion with it." This intrusive, aggressive, yet self-mocking and faintly guilty author seems to be seeking a combination of wife and double in his readers. But he quickly withdraws from the possibility of being so nakedly seen and received: the effort would be "scarcely decorous." Nonetheless, his mind will remain "frozen" and his speech "benumbed" unless he stands "in some true relation" to his readers. Therefore he picks a halfway point. He imagines his reader as "a friend . . . though not the closest friend," ambiguously "apprehensive"—suggesting both sympathy and fear—as the writer ventures upon an autobiographical reminiscence.

In backing off from the hope of perfect sympathy to a skittish distance, Hawthorne implicitly characterizes his readers as the indulgent doubles of his intrusive self. Real intimacy of any kind, he concludes, brings the danger of "violating" what he calls "the inmost Me." Having defined the reader as both a sympathetic, apprehensive friend and someone capable of intrusive violation, he rests content with his divided self and his divided narration, which will oscillate between ambiguous sympathy for Hester's inmost Me and fascination with Chillingworth's intrusive violation of Dimmesdale's hidden heart.

The extraordinarily complex and devious maneuvers of this opening paragraph, describing the right relation between writer and reader, typify Hawthorne's approach to narrating any kind of intimacy. Intimacy, for him, brings the threat of violation, which he experiences with a "divided" sensibility. One "segment" of him is a sympathetic woman's heart, capable of being both passionate and violated; the other segment is a man's mind, capable of ruthless intrusion. His self-presentation turns out to be a representation of how unnatural men can become when imprisoned too long in an all-male "Custom-House." Such men use heart-sympathy as a veil for their covert purposes of malice and revenge.

The narrator of this prefatory sketch certainly does not seem to be a malicious man. But the outraged resentment of the first Whig reviewers has some truth in it. While Hawthorne takes care to distance himself from the malice and revenge he attributes to his Whig successors, his ostensibly nostalgic, affectionate portraits of the superannuated Custom-House men clearly carry a good deal of satirical bite. More profoundly, his account of his own self-refashioning from a patriarchal man of business to a man of painful female sensibility is a way of accusing conventional manhood by dramatizing it in himself. Hawthorne's "I" implies "you" without taking the risk of saying so. Both in his portraits of the Custom-House officers and in his self-presentation, Hawthorne exposes manliness as unnatural and potentially persecuting, epitomized in his heartless Puritan ancestors.

Hawthorne most obviously mocks conventional manly values through his portrait of the Custom-House officers' bent for system and measurement. The narrator's first act, on discovering the scarlet letter, is to measure it: "each limb proved to be precisely three inches and a quarter in length." Throughout "The Custom-House" Hawthorne frames similarly precise measurements—such as the three and a half hours during which the flag flies vertically from the rooftop—with a more powerful and untidy nature. Hawthorne's satire of how nature has reduced the permanent inspector to his dinners and his instincts yields to his more genial portrait of the old general, now the collector. This man had been a killer. Yet now "there was never in his heart so much cruelty as would have brushed the down off a butterfly's wing." The general seems more like "a young girl" in his appreciation of flowers than like an old soldier prizing his laurels. The imagery here clearly foreshadows the wild red rose growing beside the Puritan prison, and intimates the ultimate power of female nature to help kind feelings break through the most patriarchal facade.

The narrator's loving, lingering portrait of the old general sharply contrasts with his crisp sketch of "a man of business." This man, he declares, is custom itself. "Bred up from boyhood in the Custom-House," the man finds in his work "the regularity of a perfectly comprehended system." He is "the Custom-House in himself; or, at all events, the main-spring that kept its variously revolving wheels in motion." Patently inverting the values of the narrative soon to follow, the man of business thinks stupidity is "little short of crime," while a "stain on his conscience" seems reducible to "an error in the balance of an account, or an ink-blot on the fair page of a book of record." In short, the narrator concludes, he is "thoroughly adapted to the situation which he held."[45] The man has become no more than his work, and his social role expresses society as mechanical order, with no awareness of feelings.

The man of business is the modern version of the pitiless Puritan judges, so unfit, as the narrator says, to "meddle" in questions of the heart. Dimmesdale's self-falsifying accommodation to his social role will expose the inward consequences of stifling feeling to abet a conventionally manly self-definition through work and ambition. Hester's ringing question to Dimmesdale in the forest is really meant for all of Hawthorne's male readers: "And what hast thou to do with all these iron men, and their opinions?" (142).

More immediately, the narrator dramatizes his own conversion from habits of measurement and analysis to fearful sympathy with a woman's suffering. He first experiences his self-transformation as he puts the letter on his chest and feels it "communicating itself to my sensibilities, but evading the analysis of my mind." His movement from analysis to sensibility prepares the reader to acknowledge values alien to the all-male marketplace: those rooted in intuition, nature, and the potentially erring heart, and ultimately expressed through writing romances.

The narrator's conversion is less a self-castration, as John Irwin has argued, than a rhetorical pose artfully constructed to nudge his readers from conventional manly values.[46] But "The Custom-House" has a Chillingworth-like underside. Overtly Hawthorne disowns any complicity in conventional male politics. He presents himself in grotesque and lugubrious detail as a "beheaded" victim of the revengeful Whigs when they returned to power (35–36). He prides himself, he says, on not having acted in that spirit when he took office. His lengthy account of his public humiliation points an accusing finger while detaching his own behavior from such pedestrian political rivalries.

Yet what did he actually do when he took office? For one thing, as Stephen Nissenbaum has discovered, he authorized political kickbacks.[47] Moreover, he immediately fired several old men, who then died. His ponderously airy euphemisms make the old men's beheadings easy to miss. Nonetheless, Hawthorne clearly implies that he killed them, without remorse.

"I must plead guilty to the charge of abbreviating the official breath of more than one of these venerable servants of the republic," he declares. "They were allowed, on my representation, to rest from their arduous labors, and soon afterwards—as if their sole principle of life had been zeal for their country's service; as I verily believe it was—withdrew to a better world." Mockingly he pleads guilty; complacently he says he offered them "a sufficient space . . . for repentance" of their "evil and corrupt practices, into which, as a matter of course, every Custom-House officer must be supposed to fall." Then he washes his hands of the whole affair with a mordant epigram: "Neither the front nor the back entrance of the Custom-House opens on the road to Paradise" (14).

Reading this passage, as a student once said in class, is like walking on a sponge.[48] When the sponge compresses, what looks like a confession of guilt comes to look much more like malice. For just an instant the narrator allows a dangerous self-exposure, one that explains his seemingly strange declaration of emotional affinity with his persecuting Puritan ancestors. "And yet, let them scorn me as they will, strong traits of their nature have intertwined themselves with mine," he affirms, offering no further explanation (12). Here is the closest he comes to practicing what he preaches at the very end of his narrative: "Be true! Be true! Be true! Show freely to the world, if not your worst, yet some trait whereby the worst may be inferred!" (183). His "worst" is not guilt but ruthless malice, projected for the most part onto his rivals and veiled by a genial yet guarded sympathy for suffering.

Once again, self-doubling and male rivalry loom under the rhetoric of self-refashioning. Hawthorne's fears seem exceptionally intense and unintegrated. He fears being invaded and possessed by readers, as Dimmesdale fears Chillingworth's penetrating scrutiny. He also fears the Chillingworth in himself. To anticipate my argument in Chapter 9, the narrator's preoccupation with these fears leads him toward a narcissistic resolution of the Dimmesdale-Chillingworth tensions, at the expense of his sympathy for Hester's story. As he does with the old men he fires, without ever quite saying so, he ultimately sends her down the road away from paradise to a sinner's dust, and perhaps to hell.

Emerson does not use the "I-you" mode in his essays. Rather, his strategy for self- and reader-refashioning frequently begins by establishing a "we" pregnant with self-reliance yet bound to social conformity. To liberate the "eye" in the "we" is Emerson's variant on the rhetorical strategy I've been describing. Paradoxically, his prose is as man-making as Melville's or Thoreau's, while his self-refashioning dramatizes a Hawthorne-like transformation from the unthinking customs of manhood to a woman's spiritual receptivity.

The first paragraph of "Nature" asserts a "we" that has to be undone. "Our age is retrospective," he begins. "It builds the sepulchres of the fathers." We are aging children, groping "among the dry bones of the past," without "an original relation to the universe." Instead of honoring our fathers, we should be assuming manly powers of our own. His tone is imperious, challenging, even covertly angry, as Joel Porte has demonstrated, in its ironic use of biblical allusions.[49] Yet the "we" he invokes is slavish as well as potentially manly. Bound to deferential social conventions of the fathers, we don't realize we are also "embosomed" in mother nature and her streaming "floods of life."

Emerson's rhetorical self-refashioning climaxes with his startling account of becoming a "transparent eyeball," probably the best-known image in all of his prose. His transformation requires the paring away of a "mean egotism" as well as social relations. As Emerson describes his mystical moment, his identity happily vanishes along with his ego. "Standing on the bare ground,—my head bathed by the blithe air, and uplifted into infinite space,—all mean egotism vanishes." The dangling participle signals an emptying I. When head becomes eye, he can forget friends and family alike. They disappear over the horizon of the world's master-servant relationships. "The name of the nearest friend sounds then foreign and accidental. To be brothers, to be acquaintances,— master or servant, is then a trifle and a disturbance."

The passage remains so memorable, I think, because its grotesque central image brings back the body and the feelings he wants to leave behind. "I become a transparent eyeball. I am nothing. I see all." The force of Emerson's parallel syntax moves him toward the "Universal Being" that rolls round with the next period. But the force of his "eyeball" image keeps him starkly physical. If we visualize the eyeball, and we have to just a bit despite its transparency, we see Emerson reduced to something small, jellylike, naked, and rather silly, with every part of his body cut off except a central blob. The universe shimmers inside him. Yet from the outside he looks alien, exposed, and vulnerable, vaguely like a deformed baby. His voice alone carries him through to invulnerable strength. The cadences reverberate with the abstracted momentum of power as if nothing else could be real.

My own response here hovers between awe and ridicule. It wasn't just malice that made Christopher Cranch, a contemporary cartoonist, draw Emerson as a quasi-Martian eyeball in the woods. Cranch seized on the opening with exactly the conventional man's earthbound spirit of attack that Emerson both feared and disdained. Here Emerson's vulnerability peeps out, inviting aggressive mockery, despite his own imperious distancing and his exemplary invitation to join him in experiencing power as receptive fluidity rather than aggressive domination.[50]

Emerson's body continually betrayed him, with eye diseases, diarrhea, pain, and simple awkwardness. When he went ice skating with Thoreau and Hawthorne, he seemed to topple, skating as if he were "pitching headforemost, half lying on the air." When Longfellow was debating whether to join an Adirondack hunting party, he found out that Emerson was going too, with a gun. "Then somebody will be shot!" he said, and refused to talk about it further.[51] Emerson lumped his body together with everything else that wasn't his mind. It was his "NOT ME." His body took him sprawling into the world, and the world continuously made him feel inadequate, foolish, vulnerable, and open to attack.

A candid entry in Emerson's journal for October 1837 shows his conscious struggle to disengage from his battered ego and join what he calls "the All":

> The victory is won as soon as any soul has learned always to take sides with Reason against himself; to transfer his *Me* from his person, his name, his interests, back upon Truth & Justice, so that when he is disgraced & defeated & fretted & disheartened and wasted by nothings, he bears it well, never one instant relaxing his watchfulness, & as soon as he can get a respite from the insults or the sadness, records all these phenomena, pierces their beauty as phenomena, and like a god oversees himself. Thus he harvests his losses & turns the dust of his shoes to gems.
>
> Keep the habit of the observer & as fast as you can, break off your association with your personality & identify yourself with the Universe. Be a football to time & chance the more kicks the better so that you inspect the whole game & know its uttermost law.[52]

The soul can choose to be either an observer or a personality. On the one side, Emerson sets the benign abstractions of reason, truth, justice, and the universe. On the other, he sets himself down as a football. The "victory" comes when he can affirm the reality of the abstractions over the reality of the kicks. Then he can rise above the rivalry and brutality that makes his feelings and his body seem so helpless and crippled.

Emerson's baffling, bloblike idealism emerges from an often explicit animus against the kicks and humiliations of ordinary male competitiveness. This particular journal entry has a touch of cosmic thumbsucking as he first formulates what soon becomes his mature philosophy. "The more kicks the better" sounds more petulant than brave. Later Emerson will return with greater confidence to his discovery that through attentive observation of one's own mind a man can "transfer his *Me* from his person" and oversee himself "like a god." A serene self-doubling animates Emerson's paradoxical uses of "we" to announce his social challenge to the fathers, yet to detach himself from any social identity that could be kicked.

As with Thoreau, who shares Emerson's penchant for self-doubling as well as for aggressive puns, the language of "Nature" intimates marketplace rivalry even as the voice rises above the marketplace. Directly before the "transparent eyeball" passage, Emerson punningly contrasts the poetic eye's vision of the landscape with that of ordinary men who divide it up into farms. "Miller owns this field, Locke that, and Manning the woodland beyond. But none of them owns the landscape. There is a property in the horizon which no man has but he whose eye can integrate all the parts, . . . [and] to this their warranty-deeds give no title." Michael T. Gilmore and Walter Benn Michaels have emphasized similar marketplace ironies of property and title in Thoreau's sense of economy and Hawthorne's sense of romance.[53] The ironies depend on laying airy "title" to a detached quality of observation, implicitly triumphing over possessive men with language's potential for dispossessing and transforming any man's manhood.

All five canonized male writers, therefore, empower their voices partly by turning to rhetorical strategies of self-refashioning and reader-refashioning. Their strategies transform various feelings associated with deviance and male rivalry. The discovery of the inadequate reader as an implicit or explicit rhetorical device helped to liberate male American writers from upper-class British conventions of taste, wit, and polish to address an American audience without feeling fettered to American readers. Exuberant, yet alienated idiosyncracies of self-refashioning build from tensions between "I" and "you." A complex rhetorical relationship, not fantasies of an imperial, representative, or victimized self, sustains male creativity in the American Renaissance.

To focus on this literature as social rhetoric, as I've tried to do here, brings out issues of manhood, especially male rivalry and fears of humiliation. I now want to explore the social frame of American manhood in more political terms. First in a chapter on Emerson, then in a more general chapter on class and gender contexts, I argue that contemporary American ideologies of manhood express and mystify class conflicts, while blocking feelings about heterosexual intimacy.

2

The Politics of Emerson's
Man-Making Words

Several years ago I heard of a scholar who got tenure at one of our best universities primarily because of a brilliant manuscript he'd written about Emerson. The book had been accepted by Oxford University Press, with glowing reader reports and suggestions for only a few minor revisions. But in the course of doing these revisions, the writer changed his mind. So he withdrew his book and completely rewrote it. Again he submitted the manuscript, again it was accepted with great enthusiasm, and again he changed his mind. The years have been passing, and there is still no sign of that Emerson book.

Anyone who has tried to write about Emerson hears that story with a mixture of delight and terror. Apocryphal or not, it shows the ferocious difficulties inherent in trying to make sense of his prose. One of his subtlest readers, Jonathan Bishop, announces at the outset of his study that "there is something at the heart of Emerson's message profoundly recalcitrant to the formulations of the discursive intelligence." James Russell Lowell called him "a chaos full of shooting-stars." Emerson himself read his words with bemusement. "Here I sit & read & write with very little system," he wrote to Carlyle in 1838, "& as far as regards composition with the most fragmentary result: paragraphs incompressible each sentence an infinitely repellent particle."[1] That doesn't seem to bother him at all; he seems quite nonchalant about it. He goes on to talk about his garden.

Emerson is intrinsically baffling. Yet Emerson's critical stock has never been higher. He has become the avatar of the strong mind heroically overcoming personal and social limitations to liberate its genius. That's especially odd because Emerson has never had an interpretive community. Eric Cheyfitz is among the most candid about the problem: "Putting Emerson aside, we cannot remember what we have read or if we have read anything."[2] From the beginning of his lecturing career Emerson's eloquence has been received by most of his audience with floundering incomprehension. His western listeners wanted something "burlier and more definite." Artemus Ward drew belly laughs across the country, and taught Mark Twain how to give a comic lecture, by doing a grave burlesque of Emerson's abstracted hesitations and disjointed juxtapositions.[3]

From the 1840s to the 1980s, however, Emerson's cultural centrality has been assured not by general assent but by the advocacy of two very different pressure groups: intellectuals and businessmen. In political terms, we could call them his interpretive constituencies. Emerson's prose begins to make sense not in and of itself or in relation to intellectual and literary traditions but as an implicitly political response to contemporary American expectations about becoming a man.[4] His contradictions speak to his contradictory constituencies.

In recent years two prominent national figures have traveled the country to preach Emerson's greatness: Harold Bloom and Woody Hayes. These two infinitely repellent particles have more than a little in common. Both men are strenuously embattled champions of combat. Like the late Ohio State football coach, the Yale professor is self-confessedly preoccupied with being "strong." Both men graphically evoke the anxieties of competition with other strong men, and both delight in the will that perseveres beyond recurrent defeat. Bloom and Hayes have very different Emersons, of course. Hayes affirmed the country's dominant gospel of competitive success, while Bloom delights in the mind's revelatory gnostic leaps beyond social convention. One spoke to postindustrial businessmen and the athletes who entertain them, while the other speaks to an alienated elite who seek to repair what Bloom in *The Anxiety of Influence* calls "the disease of self-consciousness."[5] But the bottom line of the Bloom-Hayes connection is that both speakers revere Emerson because Emerson inspires feelings of access to manly power.

Emerson's voice gains its own access to power as he becomes what he calls for, a man speaking to men in a country where "the young men were born with knives in their brain."[6] Transforming the desperate competitiveness that he saw around him and within him, Emerson developed a style of imperious nonchalance, a manliness beyond any competition. "I never argue," he once said to a questioner. For him power means an inward experience of spontaneous metamorphosis, not a public rivalry for dominance. Paradoxically, his calls for self-reliance rest on his faith in self-decentering. To be incessantly reborn from a disembodied, cosmic womb-mind becomes his alternative to the conventional arts of manly disputation and animates his hopes for a new kind of manly language. As Emerson confidently demands of the universe in his 1841 journal, "Give me initiative, spermatic, prophesying man-making words."[7]

Emerson's language of man making launches some wonderfully destabilizing flights. He unsettles the vocabularies of businessmen, merchants, and landed gentry who are imprisoned in their rivalries for money, dominance, property, and status. He senses the vacuum of self-confidence filled up by those social codes. In particular, Emerson calls for men like himself and his brothers to abandon his father's patrician conformity and create a new elite. But while his most forceful rhetoric unmans the manly types, his contradictory affirmations of individual will and intellectual infinitude blur the conflicts that give vitality to his prose. His "man-making words" hold his own rivalries and resentments in suspension, while his presentation of power absorbs without acknowledging the class conflicts that intensified the ideology of manhood from 1825 to 1850.

As one crucial consequence, the women's world of relations and feelings becomes irrelevant. Though Emerson challenges the social definitions of manhood and power, he doesn't question the more fundamental code that binds manhood and power together at the expense of intimacy. Emerson's ideal of manly self-empowering reduces womanhood to spiritual nurturance while erasing female subjectivity. "Self-Reliance" takes for granted the presence of faceless mothering in the mind, an ideal state of mental health that he sums up in a memorable image: "The nonchalance of boys who are sure of a dinner."

Emerson's various paradoxes reflect contradictions in the emerging ideology of individualism, which erected an ideal of free, forceful, and resourceful white men on the presumption of depersonalized servitude from several subordinated groups. Such solitary male freedom, as Emerson slowly discovers, depersonalizes himself as well. To empower his voice, Emerson's rhetoric requires as its speaker a free-floating self whose nonchalance deliberately rides above emotional commitment and social groupings. In taking his female support system for granted and in reducing intimacy to faceless nurturing, Emerson cuts himself off from experiencing feelings except through rivalry and detachment. While he may have triumphed over his father, he has ceased to recognize himself.

In "Experience" he can't even mourn for himself, projected through the death of his son—only for the loss of access to power. The essay's seemingly brutal candor about being unable to feel masks an uglier and more evasive note of depressive accusation, directed at the women who take care of him. If "Experience" shows his intellectual tenacity, it also reveals the self-cauterization exacted by the American ideology of manhood, an ideology that Emerson ambivalently resists and intensifies.

I

Emerson's early essays proclaim an explicit rhetoric of man making. "The American Scholar," "The Divinity School Address," and "Self-Reliance" in particular insist on manly power as the essence of mental energy and rail against what society does to manhood. Men have lost the "fountain of power," he says in "The American Scholar." "Yes, we are the cowed,—we the trustless." "The state of society is one in which the members have suffered amputation from the trunk, and strut about so many walking monsters,—a good finger, a neck, a stomach, an elbow, but never a man." "The main enterprise of the world for splendor, for extent, is the upbuilding of a man." "Society everywhere is in conspiracy against the manhood of every one of its members," he declares in "Self-Reliance." "We are parlor soldiers," "city dolls," "a mob." A true man should be a "firm column" who, as soon as he realizes his inborn power, "throws himself unhesitatingly on his thought, instantly rights himself, stands in the erect position," and "works miracles." "The Divinity School Address" makes similar claims. "Once man was all; now he is an appendage, a nuisance." "Now man is ashamed of himself; he skulks and sneaks through the world." The quotations could be tripled. Emerson seeks "man-making words"; he wants "the institution of preaching" to become once again "the speech of man to men."[8]

John Jay Chapman was the first to call attention to Emerson's obsession with being a man. Emerson has nothing essential to do with philosophy, Chapman says in his still compelling 1898 essay. "We must regard him and deal with him simply as a man." Emerson's manhood comes into being through an agonized struggle with the "atmospheric pressure" of his country's intellectual timidity. "He felt he was a cabined, cribbed, confined creature, although every man about him was celebrating Liberty and Democracy, and every day was Fourth of July. He taxes language to its limits in order to express his revolt. . . . If a soul be taken and crushed by democracy till it utter a cry, that cry will be Emerson."[9] Harold Bloom translates Chapman's manly Emerson into a modernist mode that emphasizes the subversive play of Emerson's voice as well as the desperate cry. Eric Cheyfitz, challenging and re-translating Bloom, says that Emerson's manly eloquence really transforms his sense of his own female defects, especially his sense of powerlessness and his inability to make up his mind.[10]

That fantasy of transformation may seem bizarre and sexist, as in fact it is. Yet other male readers have sensed something similar in the relation of Emerson's manhood to femaleness. The elder Henry James, whose letters to Emerson have the needy and exuberant tone of Melville's letters to Hawthorne, finally decided "that Emerson himself was an unsexed woman, a veritable fruit of almighty power in our *nature*." He came to that conclusion, he says, after repeatedly locking himself up with Emerson in his bedroom.[11]

The elder James often complained to his friend about his intense love and his intense frustration. Both feelings came from the same source: Emerson's serene refusal to meet James's need for manly leadership. Where James wanted forceful arguments that he could follow and contend with, Emerson seemed already elsewhere, attending another inspiration. His "difficult staccato," as John Morley called it, fascinated and infuriated James, who expostulated in an 1843 letter, "Oh you man without a handle! . . . shall one never be able to help himself out of you, according to his needs, and be dependent only upon your fitful tippings-up?" Jonathan Bishop sympathizes with James's frustrated response, and he also casts it in masculine-feminine terms. "It is possible to feel that Emerson does not step forward enough, does not play a proper 'masculine' role," he says. Elsewhere Bishop comes close to calling Emerson a flirt.[12]

I suspect that the temptation to call Emerson a woman, one that Bishop and James momentarily indulge and that Cheyfitz ambiguously expands into a book, is finally a conventional male response to frustrated possessiveness. Feeling vaguely uneasy with the kind of manliness

Emerson is interested in, and given so little to advocate or argue with, these three male readers try to account for their bafflement by affixing the label of "female" to his power. Emerson himself would do that trick in a more demeaning way when he got back at his dead father's awesome severity by recurrently accusing the genteel clergy, his father's profession, of effeminacy. The label of "woman" indirectly acknowledges how insinuating and comprehensive Emerson feels to these readers and how dangerous William Emerson seemed to his son. But it also suggests that Emerson's power proves more frustrating than liberating to the manliness of some of his most candid devotees.

As Cheyfitz says, Emerson implicitly or explicitly rejected not just one but three vocations that could have channeled his powers of eloquence into conventional manly roles: the pulpit, the press, and politics. All three would have required more organized modes of persuasion.[13] For the young minister, intellectual instability began as a self-confessed defect, then grew to be the signal of his receptivity to spontaneous power. To be a real man, for Emerson, meant exactly what the elder James attributed to him: being free of handles. In a society that defined manhood competitively by possessiveness and possessions, Emerson would define manhood paradoxically by abandonment and self-dispossession. His nonchalance often makes grasping men look foolish.

Barbara Packer finds the right note when she speaks of Emerson's insouciance, his air of unselfconsciousness, the "curiously evasive action" of his mind in effacing himself from his own prose powers. That provokes a characteristic critical response, she says, of asserting that Emerson was unconscious of something absolutely essential to his text.[14] He seeks the shock of unconscious or transconscious power through his voice without mediation or control. "Man-making words" knock down the social walls by which we protect ourselves from being perceivers instead of possessors. Perceivers of what? "Gleams," he says, intuitions, spontaneities, fluidity, infinitude—he's not sure what. But he's utterly confident that it's the only real power, that it flows through the mind, and that he can best express it when he abandons argumentation for an imperious nonchalance.

"I wish to be a true & free man, & therefore would not be a woman, or a king, or a clergyman, each of which classes in the present order of things is a slave." Becoming a man, Emerson came to feel, meant escaping conformity either to the rivalries of the marketplace, where men became things, or to the suffocations of domestic gentility, where men became women.[15]

To be a real man, as every foreign observer remarked of Americans at this time, was to have strong opinions on a narrow range of subjects while bending one's life and liberty to the pursuit of money and property. But American men weren't nearly as practical as they claimed to be. Their fanciful speculations reminded Harriet Martineau of the Irish. Barbara Packer picks up on that insight to emphasize that American money making had much less to do with greed than with proving one's worth. As she says, Americans "did not really want money, but the sense of self-esteem its possession would confer." She and Joel Porte connect Emerson's reliance on spiritual capital and mental mobility to the boom-and-bust cycles of American capitalism at takeoff point.[16]

This was an America, as the younger Henry James would later say, with only three kinds of people (and by people he meant men): the busy, the tipsy, and Daniel Webster. Emerson chose to be a Webster of the spirit. He reconceived eloquence as the free flight of the mind through the mind, "dispossessed" from what he calls in an 1845 journal entry, "the adhesive self." The entry builds its eloquence by self-consciously naming and revising the conventions of manly social action.

> It is the largest part of a man that is not inventoried. He has many enumerable parts: he is social, professional, political, sectarian, literary, & of this or that set & corporation. But after the most exhausting census has been made, there remains as much more which no tongue can tell. And this remainder is that which interests. This is that which the preacher & the poet & the musician speak to. This is that which the strong genius works upon; the region of destiny, of aspiration, of the unknown. Ah they have a secret persuasion that as little as they pass for in the world, they are immensely rich in expectancy & power. Nobody has ever yet dispossessed this adhesive self to arrive at any glimpse or guess of the awful Life that lurks under it.
>
> For the best part, I repeat, of every mind is not that which he knows, but that which hovers in gleams, suggestions, tantalizing unpossessed before him. His firm recorded knowledge soon loses all interest for him. But this dancing chorus of thoughts & hopes is the quarry of his future, is his possibility, & teaches him that his man's life is of a ridiculous brevity & meanness, but that it is his first age & trial only of his young wings, but that vast revolutions, migrations, & gyres on gyres in the celestial societies invite him.[17]

The power of the passage depends not simply on an opposition between mind and society but on the ability of Emerson's voice to transform the usual manly preoccupations: "interest," "rich," "expectancy & power," "interest" again, "quarry," possession and dispossession. Like a good businessman he takes inventory; like a good citizen he takes a census; he adds up every item of "firm recorded knowledge" but finds his interest and profit in the "remainder," "which no tongue can tell," *tell* meaning "reckon" as well as "say." We should be hunters or miners of a different kind of quarry, the quarry of the mind, where a "dancing chorus of thoughts and hopes" unpossesses our possessiveness.

The nonchalance here comes largely through the puns, which mine and undermine the common meanings of manly words to illuminate their spiritual possibilities. Emerson's manliness is a state of transformation, in which he springs loose the play of meanings from the "properties" of words which have become fixed by their social uses. "The one thing which we seek with insatiable desire, is to forget ourselves, to be surprised out of our propriety," he says at the end of "Circles." "The way of life is wonderful: it is by abandonment" (*CW* 2:190).

Emerson frequently invokes a Neoplatonic sense of ultimate form and generative harmony which joins birth, passivity, and power in a cosmic vagueness. But his more pungent descriptions of power often connect thinking to abandonment in every sense. His epigrams pop up like loons from a vast fluidity. While the great lines make him the patron saint of overachievers, the explicit self-decentering liberates a jaunty aggressiveness against strong social men.

"God offers to every mind its choice between truth and repose," he writes in "Intellect." "Between these, as a pendulum, man oscillates." The man who chooses repose "will accept the first creed, the first philosophy, the first political party he meets,—most likely, his father's." But the man of truth "will keep himself aloof from all moorings and afloat. He will abstain from dogmatism, and recognize all the opposite negations between which, as walls, his being is swung" (*CW* 2:202; *JMN* 5:112). The mind's passive pendulum oscillates between, not beyond, the strong walls of the fathers. Thinking exposes their dogmatic negations by abandoning their fixity.

Take, for instance, one of his most astonishing destabilizations of manhood, a passage near the start of "The Transcendentalist." Emerson's flight of scientific fancy transforms solidity into motion, earth into space, nouns into verbs and then into even less determinate participles. As mass converts to pure energy, sturdy self-reliance becomes a dazzling imaginative openness, as soft as air and as pliable as language itself. Yet throughout, as we finally discover, the passage's power floats on a startling emptiness.

> The materialist, secure in the certainty of sensation, mocks at fine-spun theories, at star-gazers and dreamers, and believes that his life is solid,

that he at least takes nothing for granted, but knows where he stands, and what he does. Yet how easy it is to show him, that he also is a phantom walking and working amid phantoms, and that he need only ask a question or two beyond his daily questions, to find his solid universe growing dim and impalpable before his sense. The sturdy capitalist, no matter how deep and square on blocks of Quincy granite he lays the foundations of his banking-house or Exchange, must set it, at last, not on a cube corresponding to the angles of his structure, but on a mass of unknown materials and solidity, red-hot or white-hot, perhaps at the core, which rounds off to an almost perfect sphericity, and lies floating in soft air, and goes spinning away, dragging bank and banker with it at a rate of thousands of miles the hour, he knows not whither,— a bit of bullet, now glimmering, now darkling through a small cubic space on the edge of an unimaginable pit of emptiness. And this wild balloon, in which his whole venture is embarked, is a just symbol of his whole state and faculty. (*CW* 1:202)

This wonderful send-up of old Boston bankers and new "venture" capitalists launches them on a "wild balloon" of intellectual speculation, as panic inducing as the wild economic speculations that had launched the Panic of 1837 five years before.[18] First Emerson presents the materialist in language that mimics the man's voice as well as his world view. Pithy phrases and reductive verbs evoke a rather truculent fellow who aggressively sports his certainties, almost to excess. His hard-sounding words and choppy phrases mock the stargazers and dreamers. For him knowledge means simply opinions and work, in the good old American way: "where he stands, and what he does." This is a man who holds tight to the minimum: "he at least takes nothing for granted."

The passage then introduces him to the "nothing" that he *should* take for granted. As soon as he "ventures" into questions beyond his knowledge, he discovers uncertainties whose powers he can ride but never own. While the pleasures of discovery are "easy to show" with simple astronomy, it's the easy showmanship of Emerson's voice that conveys his real argument: to relish dislocation. He turns the materialist's hard-edged language into a receptive softness, lightening the *s*'s and loosening the rhythms to a more extended flow. If the assertions seem bizarre at first, the voice seems oddly assured and inviting, much more expansive than the skeptical materialist seems to be. Casual and informal ("he need only ask a question or two"), welcoming and even chummy ("he also is a phantom . . . amid phantoms"), the speaker can leap from fact to imagination in a phrase. Emerson intimates that real security rests not in "the uncertainty of sensation" but in the uncertainty of what lies "before his sense."

Then the long, magnificent transformational sentence flings the materialist toward everything he has mocked. Finespun theories take him "spinning away" from foundations; dreamers find him part of their "wild balloon." His deep, square, cubic blocks turn out to be "no matter" at all, at best "a small cubic space" on the edge of a boundless space. Motion becomes everything that matters. The materialist discovers himself first self-possessed, as a sturdy capitalist, then unpossessed, as a whirl of mind. Since he's also a characterized reader, we too experience a giddy displacement from a sturdy world to "a bit of bullet" hurtling through a universe that offers no place to take a stand. At the apex of receptive perception, the "whole" darts along the edge of an immeasurable hole. We gain power only by acknowledging our perpetual motion through "an unimaginable pit of emptiness."

The passage is self-consciously dazzling. It's a bravura showpiece of finespun rhetorical effects. Yet it's also self-consciously scary, especially in its precipitous ascent or plunge, we can't tell which, from womblike security to abandonment. We stand on a world "which rounds off to an almost perfect sphericity, and lies floating in soft air." Yet that transforms to "a bit of bullet, now glimmering, now darkling" in a void. Are we lying in the lap of immense intelligence, as he says in "Self-Reliance," or are we riding a gunshot to nowhere?

In the next paragraph Emerson explicitly demands that we relocate power in the mind, not in society, government, property, and "sensible masses." Yet like the materialist, we have to accept dislocation as the price of our access to the mind. And if we perceive ourselves rightly, we see that "mental fabric is built up on just as strange and quaking foundations as his proud edifice of stone."

II

Why is Emerson so at ease with this kind of eloquence? How can he announce his imperatives in such a nonchalant tone, while manly power draws on female fullness and emptiness in his themes? Close readings would take us further and further toward deconstruction for its own sake. Instead of deconstructing his prose I want to reconstruct his politics. We have to shift our focus from his contradictory language of mental process to the social manhood his rhetoric addresses. What does he want his power of eloquence to do?

The usual thing to say about Emerson's politics is that while he sometimes seems elitist, he actually has a radically egalitarian vision of what people can be. I propose the reverse. Emerson calls for a new cultural elite, whose ideal of manly conversion to intellectual activity both dramatizes and transcends class conflicts. Emerson's claims for the potential convertibility of every man to intellectual power veil a politics that divides people into a new elite and the mob. He dreams of an intelligentsia that could preserve the patrician valuing of culture over business and politics, while he also dreams of revaluing culture by investing the capital of American manhood. For Emerson the mind is the richest liquid asset.

The ideal of a manly intellectual elite allows Emerson to reject alliance with the new middle class of businessmen and professionals, whose aggressive competitiveness disturbed and offended him. Emerson also rejects alliance with his own "cultivated classes," which, as he says in "Self-Reliance," seem "timid," with at best a "feminine rage" (*CW* 2:33). Disengaging from those two groups, and from the ministry and the Whig party straddling the line, he incorporates their contrary modes of social power in the self-abandoning mind, which he equates with the flow of the cosmos.

From that extraterrestrial base Emerson addresses his politics of man making to all the potential constituencies that might enable his cultural elite to thrive. But Emerson's business and intellectual constituencies have used him from the start to fortify their separate turfs. This rivalry reflects the nascent condition of capitalist dominance and elite alienation Emerson strives to transcend and transform.

As "The American Scholar" proclaims, "Man Thinking" has to be rescued from a fading gentility, for whom manly power means patriarchy, property, and social status, and from the rising class of businessmen, for whom manly power means entrepreneurial competition and money making. Emerson especially reaches out to his real cultural constituency, the feminized clergy in the middle. "The so-called 'practical men' sneer at speculative men," he says, "as if, because they speculate or *see*, they could do nothing. I have heard it said that the clergy,—who are always more universally than any other class, the scholars of their day,—are addressed as women: that the rough, spontaneous conversation of men they do not hear, but only a mincing and diluted speech" (*CW* 1:59).

Emerson's attempt to rescue the clergy from the contemptible status of women both confronts and evades his lifelong resentment of his minister father, who died when he was almost eight. Until Gay Wilson

Allen's recent biography of Emerson, various psychological and social critics followed Quentin Anderson's lead in locating Emerson's sense of selfhood within the broader American context of the search for the absent or failed father. But Allen's biography, and Joel Porte's *Representative Man*, make Emerson's resentment clear and abundant.[19] Allen begins his biography with an account of the writer's profound and enduring hostility to William Emerson, who not only plunged him into the ocean for curative baths when he was six but expected him to be reading before the age of three. Young Ralph Waldo grew up among incessantly competitive brothers, presided over in the early years by a father who makes Joseph Kennedy look like Mr. Rogers.

From the beginning Ralph was a relative failure, unable or unwilling to measure up. "Ralph does not read very well yet," his father complained to a friend, a week before his son's third birthday. The boy continued to disappoint his father, who supervised all the boys' education with a stern and demanding hand. Three of Ralph's brothers—a fourth was retarded, and a fifth died very young—seemed to thrive in this atmosphere of high expectations. William, Charles, and Edward always excelled, while Ralph always lagged behind. The family felt that all the Emerson boys were "born to greatness," and Ralph became keenly conscious of being the "ugly duckling," as Allen calls him. While the other three boys graduated from Harvard at or near the top of their classes, Ralph graduated thirtieth in a class of fifty-nine. He became class poet only because the first six choices turned it down.[20]

All three brothers then went out into the wide world and fell apart. William, the eldest, had great difficulty establishing himself as a lawyer, frequently became sick, and starved himself for a time. Edward went violently crazy in 1828, thrashing about in a manic-depressive frenzy that lasted at least a week. He needed two men with him every minute, to hold him down. Ralph, now Waldo, wrote to William with a graphic description of their brother's derangement and concluded, "But what's the need of relating this—there he lay—Edward the admired learned eloquent thriving boy—a maniac." This was the brother to whom Waldo felt closest. Seven years later, in 1835, Edward died. As Allen says, "Edward's devouring ambition to excel would destroy his health; and Charles, no less ambitious than Edward, was torn by self-destructive anxiety." Charles died a year after Edward, in 1836. Only then, looking over Charles's journals, did Waldo discover the depth of his brother's self-doubts, "melancholy, penitential, self-accusing" (*EJ* 148).[21]

How did Emerson escape? The early years of his journal teem with similar self-flagellations for not being great. He too suffered periodic illness, especially eye diseases and diarrhea, often when facing tasks about which he felt anxious or ambivalent.[22] From this man-breaking family, how did he find his man-making words?

At least three strategies helped Emerson to resist and transform his family's expectations. First, he developed what Allen calls his "self-protecting frivolous streak."[23] Second, he slowly became able to see his father as a member of a class losing power. Third, he discovered that he could disengage from his anxious, competitive self by splitting mind from feelings. All three strategies led him to reconceive power as thinking.

In his July 1828 journal Emerson ruminates about "the constitutional calamity of my family," especially the "towering hopes" that had been "buried" with brother Edward's fall. He concludes by thanking Providence for his defects. "I have so much mixture of *silliness* in my intellectual frame," he says. Where Edward "lived & acted & spoke with preternatural energy...my actions (if I may say so) are of a passive kind. Edward had always great power of face. I have none." Yet "all this imperfection...is a ballast—as things go—is a defence" (*EJ* 67). When William wrote home from his garret in New York to say he had been ill, Waldo wrote back to remind his brother "that all the Emersons overdo themselves." He urged William to try out the laziness he had been enjoying.

But his brothers, as Allen says, were "career-haunted."[24] In mulling over Charles' death, Emerson is baffled at first by the shocking disparity between his brother's strong character and the self-hatred revealed in Charles's journal. Finally, six months later, he concludes that "like my brother Edward, Charles had a certain severity of Character which did not permit him to be silly—no not for moments, but always self possessed & elegant whether morose or playful; no funning for him or for Edward" (*EJ* 147–148, 153 [May, November 1836]). This "self possessed & elegant" character mirrored their father's "power of face." Father had always dismissed playfulness as "levity." Subverting that dictum, a quiet inward playfulness gave Emerson a habit of mind that Allen calls "intellectual strolling." Silliness also encouraged a more benign self-inspection. "It was a kind of gift for humor, an ability to look at himself from the point of view of a detached bystander, to see his shortcomings not with the tragic regret of his Aunt Mary but as the comic failures of a limited person."[25]

His Aunt Mary, William's sister, had become the dominant force in the Emerson family after his father's death, and Emerson was always much more devoted to her than to his self-effacing mother. He liked to call her "Father Mum." His aunt's quasi-Calvinist intensity of faith made her sharply critical of her brother's worldly gentility, even while he lived. Aunt Mary's critiques gave the young boy some measure of freedom to think of his father's power as worldly rather than spiritual. But she too expected young Ralph to be a minister, preaching her own faith. Emerson's gift for detachment protected him from the accommodation and guilt that both his strong-minded instructors tried to induce. He was able to fend off his father's demands that he push himself harder academically and his aunt's demands that he share her evangelical self-denial.[26]

Emerson's lifelong gratitude to his aunt, despite his disengagement from nearly everything she wanted him to do, suggests that her real effect was to help him start to get free of his father, whose death must have complicated and arrested his ambivalent feelings. Mary helped the boy begin to see William Emerson not as the originator of awesome power but as the product of a Boston gentility that was already starting to lose social dominance. Emerson's father had dined with the governor on the day Ralph was born. He had the governor over for a party in his home the day after, presumably while his wife was upstairs with the baby. He was personable, relatively tall, immaculately dressed, and always the consummately polished gentleman. Urbane to the core, he became "the confidant and companion of the social and political elite of the city, who in religion might be Unitarian, Congregationalist, or Episcopalian, but in politics were rigid Federalists." As the pastor of the First Church of Boston, he "was at ease in this mercantile society," for which he performed every Sunday, reading his unmemorable sermons in "a charming baritone voice" with "perfect enunciation."[27] He was at the center of social power, and he knew it. He would make sure that his sons got there too.

But social power was changing. Emerson's conscious politics remained relatively aligned with the Whigs, the party that inherited the Federalist mantle of wealth while straining for a broader evangelical appeal. His deeper politics developed from a love-hate relationship with his class. "All conservatives . . . have been effeminated by position or nature," he declares in "Fate," "born halt and blind, through luxury of their parents, and can only, like invalids, act on the defensive."[28] His insistent taunting of the elite "fathers" was as much a rescue fantasy as a wish for generational parricide. This class should be the source of magnificent souls. For "ordinary persons" to be materialistic "does not shock us," he writes in his September 1832 journal. "But we cannot forgive it in the Everetts & Cannings [*sic*] that they who have souls to comprehend [truth] should utterly neglect it & seek only huzzas & champagne" (*EJ* 85–86). Throughout the 1840s he peppers his journals with scornful remarks about various new parties of the rabble. As he says in early 1845, "A despair has crept over the Whig party in this country. They the active, enterprizing, intelligent, well meaning, & wealthy part of the people, the real bone & strength of the American people, find themselves paralysed & defeated everywhere by the hordes of ignorant & deceivable natives & the armies of foreign voters...and by those unscrupulous editors & orators who have assumed to lead these masses. The creators of wealth and conscientious, rational, & responsible persons...find themselves degraded into observers, & violently turned out of all share in the action & counsels of the nation" (*EJ* 333).

If Emerson's class made him a Whig, his dream of power brought him partially beyond his class to search for a more forceful elite. From the beginning of his adulthood he had hoped for fame as a writer or orator. Gradually, throughout the 1820s and early 1830s, his recurrent journal entries on that theme reflect not only a greater self-confidence but a growing willingness to quarrel with his class. Disengaging from his accommodation to the conventional ministry, he sought a more confrontational social preaching in which words might roll back "the cloud of ceremony & decency" over "smooth plausible people" and convert them to spiritual force. Like Luther's, he wrote in 1832, such words should be "half battles" (*EJ* 87). "The whole secret of the teacher's force lies in the conviction that men are convertible," he writes in 1834. "Get the soul out of bed...and your vulgar man, your prosy selfish sensualist awakes a God & is conscious of force to shake the world" (*EJ* 123).

An evangelical political fantasy spurs Emerson's hopes. It emerges as early as 1823, when a lengthy journal entry discusses the dangerous marginality of respectable men on the frontier. There "the offscouring of civilized society" threatens to engulf the nation. In considering the problem, Emerson couples the country's need for moral oracles with his own need for greatness. There is great danger, he says, "that the Oracles of Moral law and Intellectual wisdom in the midst of an ignorant & licentious people will speak faintly & indistinctly." If that were to happen, "human foresight can set no bounds to the ill consequences of such a calamity." But if the oracles of the elite could regain social power, "if the senates that shall meet hereafter in those wilds shall be made to speak a voice of wisdom & virtue, the reformation of the world would be to be expected from America. How to effect the check proposed is an object of momentous importance. And in view of an object of such magnitude, I know not who he is that can complain that motive is lacking in this latter age, whereby men should become great" (*EJ* 29). Here is the "egg, embryo, and seminal principle" (*EJ* 69) of Emerson's political vision. His personal greatness will come as he emboldens other respectable speakers. His calling will be to increase their impact in the senates of his frontier country. If they "shall be made to speak a voice of wisdom & virtue," Americans can bring about "the reformation of the world." Emerson dreams of re-forming their voices. He will bring a marginal elite from timidity to power.

This is a conventional úpper-class fantasy of the time, shared by Whig leaders and John Calhoun alike. For Emerson to empower his own voice requires one further quarrel with his class, a quarrel that gives public legitimacy to his conflicts with his father. He reconceives the lower orders of people as a source of energy as well as a frightening barbarism to be "checked" by respectable speech. He discovers how to tap Jacksonian energies by developing a rhetoric that simultaneously accuses dead patriarchs while imagining the cowed self's potential to convert the mob. Here Emerson finds his most forceful language of power by shifting from a narrow ideology of class to a broader ideology of manhood. Presenting the manly self as a seemingly dialectical process that synthesizes contemporary class tensions, Emerson incorporates Jacksonian rebelliousness and entrepreneurial resourcefulness into his vision of an intellectual elite in the making.[29]

In 1833 Wordsworth told Emerson that America had no culture because it lacked a leisure class (*EJ* 113–114). A year later Emerson writes in his journal that perhaps Jacksonian democracy may be a symptom of the cure as well as the disease. "I suppose the evil may be cured by this rank rabble party, the Jacksonism of the country, heedless of English & of all literature—a stone cut out of the ground without hands—they may root out the hollow dilettantism of our cultivation in the coarsest way & the new-born may begin again to frame their own world" (*EJ* 125, also 128). Here, he takes up not only Jacksonian energy but also the language of birthing. He comes close to the theme of "Nature," though not to the imperious, irreverent voice opening that essay by saying that our age "builds the sepulchres of the fathers" only to rob their graves. "Why should we grope among the dry bones of the past?" Emerson wants birth, not cemetery grubbing for his father's bones. We should be "embosomed" in nature, "whose floods of life stream around and through us" and invite us to natural energies of our own (*CW* 1:7).

Rarely, however, does Emerson find manhood in the dignity of labor. He seeks a natural nobility of genius. As early as 1827 he muses that "those writings which indicate valuable genius treat of common things. Those minds which God has formed for any powerful influence over men, have never effeminately shrunk from intercourse with unnurtured minds. . . . They have taken hold with manly hand on its vulgar wants" (*EJ* 62). But the manliness is in the hand of "genius," not the minds of the vulgar. For him Daniel Webster personified the political possibilities of manly genius. Emerson's growing disillusionment with Webster reflects the decline of his hopes for reempowering an elite through "intercourse with unnurtured minds." As he wrote in the early 1840s, "Any form of government would content me in which the rulers were gentlemen, but it is in vain that I have tried to persuade myself that Mr Calhoun or Mr Clay or Mr Webster were such; they are underlings, & take the law from the dirtiest fellows. . . . they are not now to be admitted to the society of scholars."[30]

Emerson's attitude toward workers has something of Thoreau's contempt for the Irish, though without *Walden*'s puckish mockery. He takes them more seriously, with a more profound contempt. They are the herd, the mob, the mass, "bugs and spawn," at best a kind of larvae. In the two broad groupings into which Emerson usually divides society, the workers will forever be inert, unless a few self-reliant men bring them to intellectual vitality. "The life of labor does not make men, but drudges," he writes in May of 1843. "The German and Irish millions, like the Negro," he says in "Fate," "have a great deal of guano in their destiny."[31] Toward the end of "Nature" Emerson goes so far as to say, "you cannot freely admire a noble landscape, if laborers are digging in the field hard by" (*CW* 1:39).

Emerson's language of man making takes him temporarily beyond his class to challenge his father's demands for genteel success. He struggles out of recurrent and often fierce depressions in which he caustically takes inventory of his inability to meet his own perfectionist standards, really his father's expectations. He wins that struggle by reconceiving his father's demands in broader social terms, as crippled conformity to patrician norms that were thwarting a great variety of entrepreneurial sons. "The land stinks with suicide," he wrote to himself in 1837 (*EJ* 164). His most pugnacious essays, especially "The American Scholar" and "The Divinity School Address," have young versions of his father, his brothers, and himself as his actual and characterized audience. Emerson wants to save their souls. He prophesies a new mode of manhood which will shatter genteel controls to incarnate a truly revolutionary elite.

In "History," with which Emerson begins his first volume of selected essays, he all but directly attacks his father, ostensibly by describing the evils of "priestcraft." The passage condenses and universalizes Emerson's own childhood struggle.

> The priestcraft of the East and West . . . is expounded in the individual's private life. The cramping influence of a hard formalist on a young child in repressing his spirits and courage, paralyzing the understanding, and that without producing indignation, but only fear and obedience, and even much sympathy with the tyranny,—is a familiar fact explained to the child when he becomes a man, only by seeing that the oppressor of his youth is himself a child tyrannized over by those names and words and forms, of whose influence he was merely the organ to the youth. (*CW* 2:16)

In one long, highly charged sentence Emerson sums up his liberation. First comes the hard tyranny of his formalist father, so "paralyzing" as to produce only "fear and obedience, and even much sympathy with the tyranny." Then, after the deep breath of the dash, comes a sudden ease of perception: the tyrant is himself a child, merely an "organ" for society's forms. When the child "becomes a man," his mind can see, accuse, and transform his social bonds.

"The American Scholar" is his finest public drama of accusation and transformation. Emerson begins and ends that address by speaking of the "indestructible instinct" that has miraculously survived "amongst a people too busy to give to letters any more." His peroration makes the opposition more pungent. Poignantly, if indirectly invoking the fates of his two brothers, he declares that the world of business is killing the young. "There is no work for any but the decorous and the complaisant. Young men of the fairest promise . . . are hindered from action by the disgust which the principles on which business is managed inspire, and turn drudges, or die of disgust,—some of them suicides."

The "remedy" begins "if the single man plant himself indomitably on his instincts." Then comes a swift sequence of brilliant transformational turns. The single man's "planting" will be the axis on which "the huge world will come round to him." That turning will bring about "the conversion of the world" (*CW* 1:69). As it does so often, his voice builds its prophetic confidence from converting accusation into a demand for metamorphosis of selves, words, and social meanings. Change itself will bring the experience of power. The 1848 revolutions, he later says disparagingly, will probably lead to the same old thing, "a scramble for money.... When I see changed men, I shall look for a changed world."[32]

Emerson's man-making words proved personally liberating and socially galvanic. But his contempt for laborers and his tendency to see society as divided into a few real men and the masses ultimately crippled his rhetoric as well as his hopes. It wasn't simply his refusal to get organized—a prerequisite for any kind of political success—that left his dream stranded in himself. It was also a failure of social vision. Emerson's attentiveness to the play of his mind liberates his tussle with contemporary definitions of power and manhood, but his faith in the infinitude of the private man evades his own ambivalence about rivalry. Moreover, his call for the conversion of individual men to self-reliant thinking blocks awareness of how his rhetoric builds on several kinds of power struggles in the Northeast: between fathers and sons, between ministers and gentry, and between the gentry, the new middle class, and the new working class being created by industrialization.

Various recent social histories by Paul Johnson, Anthony Wallace, Mary P. Ryan, Joseph Kett, Nancy Cott, and Daniel Walker Howe broadly agree that a drastic change in social conditions came about from 1825 to 1850, especially for men. The dominance of small patriarchal shops and a patrician class yielded to the rise of entrepreneurial managers and professionals in conflict with wage laborers. There's much disagreement about whether the complementary rise of evangelical fervor functioned primarily to teach workers self-discipline or to give mothers an intensified domestic role and some measure of influence in their communities.[33] But it's clear that expectations for young men were in a confused transition from patriarchal and agrarian or mercantile norms. After 1840, Joseph Kett says, the isolated, ambitious male self was expected to rise beyond his father in a world where everyone felt "marginal and insecure." Emerson's emphasis on mental fluidity, while serenely transposing what Mary Ryan has called "the open and anxious question" of male identity at this time, finally denies the conflicts to which his rhetoric implicitly responds.[34]

In his later essays, less able to find power surging through his voice, Emerson more explicitly refuses to take sides. "Politics," for instance, says of Democrats and Whigs what had become conventional, that "one has the best cause, and the other contains the best men." Yet Emerson adopts a plague-on-both-your-houses tone. "The spirit of our American radicalism is destructive and aimless," he asserts; it grows from "hatred and selfishness." "On the other side, the conservative party, composed of the most moderate, able, and cultivated part of the population, is timid, and merely defensive of property" (*CW* 3:122–123). His solution retreats to detachment and conventional character building, a tepid reduction of his earlier self-abandoning metamorphoses.

The rather sniffy and querulous tone of "Politics" shows his disillusionment with any prospects for social man making by 1843. But his cause had been lost from the start, because his rhetoric of man making aimed to bring an elite to cultural dominance at just the moment that the elite class was being displaced from social leadership. In fact, his cause was really the old Federalist cause for the leadership of reasonable patricians, with the difference that Emerson emphasized spontaneity rather than reasoning as the road to intellectual power. Yet that too could be seen as an old Federalist dodge: to appropriate the language of one's opponents for a politics that maximized the presence of "representative men" while minimizing the differing social interests of different groups.

That was how the Federalists had preserved the power of the propertied gentry against the "new men" in passing the Constitution, Gordon Wood concludes. "The result was the beginning of a hiatus in American politics between ideology and motives that was never again closed. By using the most popular and democratic rhetoric available to explain and justify their aristocratic system, the Federalists helped to foreclose the development of an American intellectual tradition in which differing ideas of politics would be intimately and genuinely related to differing social interests." An "encompassing liberal tradition . . . often obscured the real social antagonisms of American politics."[35] Emerson's politics of man making, by any measure, helped that tradition to thrive, long after the Whigs went the way of the Federalists. He was more his father's son than he knew.

III

Emerson's championing of a manly cultural elite reinforced his most personal form of self-protective transformation: a disengagement from anxious rivalry by separating his mind from his feelings. He depoliticizes power by imagining a self that watches the mind's powers flow into his voice. If his father is the covert target for his most polemical public addresses, the man who is accused for his own good, Emerson himself becomes the ideal implied reader: the spectator and midwife of our common amniotic self-in-the-making. To be that kind of reader conceals the inescapable connection between power and social conflict and deliberately disconnects power from personal feeling.

"One cannot think at all, Emerson is prepared to say, as long as one is the victim of feeling." That summation by Jonathan Bishop is the other side of Bishop's praise for Emerson's "quasi-physical agility of the free mind."[36] Feeling for Emerson meant pain, powerlessness, resentment, and the perils of the body—all of which he dumped on the laboring masses. His grand disdain for those whose sense of self comes from their daily tasks, needs, and relations reflects his discomfort with his own body and his fear of intimacy. As he says in "The Poet," "The centrifugal tendency of a man" seeks "passage out into free space... to escape the custody of that body in which he is pent up, and of that jail-yard of individual relations in which he is enclosed" (*CW* 3:16). Relations bring on a sense of being trapped; the passage into intellectual space brings nonchalance. There, he can yield to aggressiveness with tranquillity, voicing its thunder charges as a natural flow of self-discoveries.[37]

The numbed, truculent return of depressiveness in Emerson's later essays, especially in "Experience," shows that without power he feels abandoned and empty. The only relationship he has allowed himself to value is the bond between power and manhood. When that self-abstracting greatness breaks down, Emerson experiences himself as faceless. He blames that facelessness on the women who care for him at the margins of power, while he relegates them to the margins of his text.

Toward the beginning of "Self-Reliance," Emerson speaks of "the nonchalance of boys who are sure of a dinner" as "the healthy attitude of human nature." An adult man, on the other hand, "is, as it were, clapped into jail by his consciousness.... Ah, that he could pass again into his neutrality!" Then his opinions "would sink like darts into the ear of men, and put them in fear." A true nonchalance will bring fear to other men, because it strips them of their social conciliations. "A boy is in the parlour what the pit is in the playhouse; independent, irresponsible.... he tries and sentences them on their merits, in the swift summary way of boys," with no troubling over interests or consequences (*CW* 2:29). Here is one of Emerson's most direct amalgamations of "parlour" and "pit," as he asserts the power of the free mind to make men like his father cringe.

Once again we have a passage that seeks to unfix parlor men and plunge them into panic, or awe. At the center of aspiration stands that fine introductory phrase, "the nonchalance of boys who are sure of a dinner." The line itself has a nonchalant and boyish lift. It lopes along with an iambic swing and strong, steady, wide-open vowels, then springs into a dactylic sprint with the word "boys." Yet the boys' breezy freedom, like the line's jaunty stride, depends on being "sure of a dinner," not sure of themselves. And what about the girls? One can picture them in the kitchen with the angels of the house, getting more faceless and sexless by the minute while they put out the meals for their lounging brothers. To achieve a bold male self-reliance presumes a depersonalized female support system. What dinnertime is to a boy, the cosmos will be to the mature soul. This source sustains the private infinitude that buoys self-confidence and restores the wondering little boy to the dispirited man.

Emerson's presumption raises questions about his mother, about whom we know almost nothing. Quiet, patient, dutiful, not very pretty, but with "kindly dark eyes," she bore eight children, lost three, and "never complained, regarding affliction and hardship as the will of Providence." Much more devout than her husband, Ruth Haskins Emerson took as her one personal prerogative an hour of privacy every morning for religious meditation. Always reserved, she never raised her voice. Gay Wilson Allen concludes that "her reserve and habitual restraint of emotion in speech" not only "created an intangible atmosphere of remoteness" but more specifically gave young Ralph "an inhibited emotional life."[38]

Allen, Jonathan Bishop, and John Jay Chapman all finally blame Emerson's inhibited mother for the restricted range of feeling in Emerson's prose.[39] I think his ambivalence about his father and male rivalry was more basic. These three knowledgeable and loving readers unwittingly mimic Emerson's own depressive strategy of displacing resentment. Blaming mother is the other side of taking mother's nourishment for granted. It's comparatively safe. Both responses evade the primary arena for Emerson's resentment: the struggle for a feeling of power. Symptomatically, his responses to mothering recast intimacy as a power relation, in which dependence or isolation are the only options. The reduction of woman's subjectivity to a mothering role legitimates male uses of rage, disdain, and dependency to restore feelings of power.[40]

One could argue that since Emerson's family provided so many reasons for emotional withdrawal, his mother became his first model for disengaging from competition. But the main point is that, like everyone else, Emerson seems to have taken Ruth for granted, though she lived in his house for over twenty years, from 1830 until her death. Did she share the resentments that Aunt Mary voiced, that Lidian, his wife, would sometimes release in her many years of "black moods," and that evangelical piety explicitly submerged in women, as Susan Warner's 1850 best seller, *The Wide, Wide World,* makes abundantly clear? We will probably never know. She was just there, like the dinners. She coped, she endlessly dealt with the family's money problems after her husband's death, she probably disagreed with Aunt Mary about how to raise baby Caroline, and she kept her feelings to herself and her God. Allen's massive biography doesn't even bother to mention her death, in November of 1853, except in the chronology.

Emerson felt ambivalence about his unacknowledged dependence, to be sure. A startling poem written shortly after his mother's death momentarily voices some of his need for her, with a weird fusion of blaming and self-blaming. After six lines ruminating about how thinking cripples feeling, his poem ends:

> His mother died,—the only friend he had,—
> Some tears escaped, but his philosophy
> Couched like a cat sat watching close behind
> And throttled all his passion. Is't not like
> That devil-spider that devours her mate
> Scarce freed from her embraces?

Erik Ingvar Thurin rightly describes this poem as a self-accusation, in which Emerson blames himself for having "treated his mother as roughly as Hamlet treats his." Underneath, however, lies submerged ambivalence. With a maudlin self-pity Emerson names his mother as his "only friend" and accuses his mind of being a "devil-spider" which throttles his passion for her. Yet an opposite reading lurks here: Emerson has just been "freed from her embraces" by her death, making mother the implicit devil-spider. In either case, the female devours her mate.[41] Retreating from exploring his emotional vulnerability with his mother, or with any other woman for that matter, Emerson elsewhere tends to reduce women to the stereotype Thurin examines: a support and undeveloped complement for manly greatness.

The death that really mattered to Emerson was the death in 1842 of his five-year-old son, named for himself. He felt, as he wrote to Thomas Carlyle, as if an eye had been plucked out. On his deathbed, his last coherent words were, "That beautiful boy."[42] Yet his poem "Threnody" makes it clear that his feelings about his son's death are really thoughts about his own inability to be born. Waldo seemed to him the divine mind, now blocked from fruition in the world. The boy's nonchalance, which so delighted Emerson, would never again embody the father's man-making dreams.

"Experience" ruthlessly explores Emerson's sudden, permanent aging. He no longer experiences himself as universal or representative. Instead, he finds his life defined mostly by its surfaces. If, as Clark Kerr once said, a college president's fate is to be nibbled to death by ducks, Emerson discovers that he has been nibbled to near death by a fate more boring than ducks: marriage, family, conversations, social routine, and his own temperament. The essay amounts to a private prospective wake for himself. He sits by the bier of his hopes, alternately crabby, depressed, hopeful, baffled, dyspeptic, philosophical, wistful, resolute, resigned, remembering the good times, and puzzled, too, by his inability to mourn.

Beneath the prevailing mood of depressive acquiescence, Emerson harbors what Joel Porte has called "an undercurrent of bitterness at life's forcing him to sing *vive la bagatelle* so bravely." Almost every critic finds "Experience" deeply moving, in part because of Emerson's candor about himself. For Stephen Whicher, the essay shows Emerson openly struggling with his skepticism about transcendent dreams. For Barbara Packer, the essay exposes the mature self's "secret cruelty." Yet how candid is he? Where Packer hears Emerson admitting that he can't find his feelings, Porte detects an oblique anger at the Being that has robbed him of his son. "Anger, however, is not Emerson's strong suit." Instead, he retaliates by robbing Being of reality.[43]

For me the essay has an uglier evasiveness. While Emerson disowns his feelings by denying reality to anyone else's, he partially vents his unacknowledged resentment as a glancing snideness about the dull lives of the women who care for him: his wife and his mother. The essay is not just "disturbing" and "shocking," as various critics have rightly said, but also deliberately insulting to those readers to whom grief and intimacy have meant something. For Emerson such feelings are only the bitter unrealities of Mother Nature. Oscillating between a puzzled calm and a crusty petulance, he accepts and indicts the female surfaces that have blocked his access to creative energy.

The opening poem sets the scene: "Little man, least of all," walks aimlessly among the legs of his masked guardians, the Lords of Life. Mother Nature, seeing his "puzzled look," takes little man by the hand and whispers, "Darling, never mind!... The founder thou! these are thy race!" (*CW* 3:25). The poem evokes its own puzzle, which the essay expands upon. Do the Lords of Life emanate from man's littleness of mind, blocking his access to divinity and power with idle dreams, faces, and games? Or do the surfaces emanate from Mother Nature, who indulgently comforts and praises man for fathering her fraudulent creations? "Darling, never mind!" becomes her ominous message as well as her comfort. Mother has nothing to do with mind. In fact mother rather likes it when man feels so belittled. Then her powers can come into view.

This judgment might be an unfair extrapolation from a gnomic epigraph, except that the essay recurrently returns to a mood of passive blaming. The urgency about manhood that suffuses the earlier essays has vanished. The word *man* itself rarely appears. Instead, in circling about the surfaces of ordinary life, Emerson keeps rediscovering the omnipresence of mother and the frustrations of a child. "The child asks, 'Mamma, why don't I like the story as well as when you told it me yesterday?' " The response: because stories, like any lasting relationships, become monotonous. We were "born to a whole"; now we endure particulars. The "plaint of tragedy" here has a touch of accusation. Our most intimate relations, whether to art or to people, have an "absence of elasticity" and give "no power of expansion." Power may go to the muscles, but culture "ends in headache." Those who think about it can feel "quite powerless and melancholy.... Unspeakably sad and barren" (*CW* 3:33–34). Better not to think about it, mother implies.

For a time at least, Emerson seems to speak in Mother Nature's realistic voice. "The whole frame of things preaches indifference," he concludes a few lines later. "Life is not intellectual or critical, but sturdy." If things are in the saddle and ride the mind, nonetheless life's sturdy frame rewards "well-mixed people" who enjoy without questioning. Why? Because the world belongs to Nature, and like a good mother, "Nature hates peeping." Now Emerson attributes a little more oppressiveness to mother's alliance with Nature: "our mothers speak her very sense when they say, 'Children, eat your victuals, and say no more of it' " (*CW* 3:35). Good mothering tells little man to shut up, in effect, and adjust himself to littleness.

Emerson has learned to be both accommodating and hidden. "A man is like a bit of Labrador spar" at best, deep and beautiful in just one place, while "the Power which abides in no man and in no woman" hops like a bird from spar to spar, and "for a moment speaks from this one, and for another moment from that one" (*CW* 3:33–34). Better to "awake, and find the old world, wife, babes, and mother," with "the dear old devil not far off." Better to seek the "mid-world," where Nature "comes eating and drinking and sinning," and where "her darlings" have no interest in divinity. "If we will be strong with her strength," we have to live in the present and present ourselves as Nature's creatures (*CW* 3:36–37).[44]

That voice of resigned acceptance is a mask. By the end of his paragraph on the "darlings" of the mid-world Emerson is pleading with himself to dismiss the illusory surfaces of life. "But thou, God's darling! heed thy private dream: thou wilt not be missed in the scorning and skepticism: there are enough of them: stay there in thy closet, and toil, until the rest are agreed what to do about it." These are not man-making words. Let Nature's people treat you like a stubborn child, he says; let them prescribe remedies for "thy puny habit." While big people pound on the closet door to force recalcitrant little dreamers into the world, the child-man knows that life itself is a dream. If energy flows into the midworld, at least "dig away in your garden, and spend your earnings as a waif or godsend to all serene and beautiful purposes" (*CW* 3:38).

The puzzle of the opening poem has taken a larger turn. Does the midworld emanate from a dream, or does Nature create the hapless dreamer? The answer depends on Emerson's shifts of mood, from detached hope to dependent blame and back again. Yet blame keeps returning. Why, he asks, have scholars been such traitors to the mind? Because "nature causes each man's peculiarity to superabound. . . . Irresistible nature made men such" (*CW* 3:38). "Fate" makes the accusation more directly. "Men are what their mothers made them."[45] Ultimately the failure of power to be intellectual rather than worldly comes from how mothers bear and raise us. The passages that critics put forward to celebrate the mature vitality of "Experience" show Emerson conjuring up his old ecstasies of rebirth and metamorphic surprise. But the discovery of power has yielded to "infantine joy and amazement" (*CW* 3:41) for its own sake, as man-making words have yielded to mother-made temperaments.

No longer "man talking to men," Emerson ends up talking to himself, explicitly about failure and implicitly about women. "A man is a golden impossibility," he now concludes, no matter how plain it is "in the street and in the newspapers . . . that manly resolution and adherence to the multiplication-table through all weathers, will insure success" (*CW* 3:38–39). Besieged by frivolous conversations, the man of thought has to take refuge in a "preoccupied attention" and a higher aim, an aim whose "other politics," he knows, is irreconcilable with worldly impact. Once, he had imagined otherwise. "But I have not found that much was gained by manipular attempts to realize the world of thought." The "eager persons" who try to experiment with visionary dreams on earth "acquire democratic manners, they foam at the mouth, they hate and deny." So Emerson disowns both his anger and his hopes. The best we can do, he says, is "dress our garden, eat our dinners, discuss the household with our wives," and then forget those trivial surfaces "in the solitude to which every man is always returning" (*CW* 3:47–49).

Emerson's numbed and prickly mood does have a larger social dimension, though in a mode quite opposite from the prophetic rhetoric of the earlier essays. His brief experience editing *The Dial* had already shown him that oracular intellectuality had little potential for man-making impact. Baffled by the possibility that the American future might be demanding a self-narrowing specialization and a divergence between intellectuals and businessmen, not a protean self-expansion, Emerson was thrown back on the isolation of his own temperament. He had lost confidence in equating himself with the embryonic possibilities of a new social elite.

"We are like millers on the lower levels of a stream, when the factories above them have exhausted the water," he ends the first paragraph of "Experience." "We too fancy that the upper people must have raised their dams." As striking as his sad, passive, powerless tone is the uncertainty of self-location. Emerson shifts the source of blame for his state of confused deprivation from "factories" to "the upper people," as if stranded midway between a genteel disdain for the emergence of heavy industry and an older peasant consciousness of arbitrary, self-serving lords. All he can be sure of is that he feels shut off from water and clear vision. His confusion slips into metaphors that indirectly expose mother's control of our birth. The "Genius" who stood by the door poisoned our drink with lethargy as we entered, and now we've lost our way on the stairs of life and consciousness. Or was it that she withheld something? "Did our birth fall in some fit of indigence and frugality in nature, that she was so sparing of her fire and so liberal of her earth, that . . . we have no superfluity of spirit for new creation?"

"Ah that our Genius were a little more of a genius!" (*CW* 3:27). In either case, mindless mother has shut off little man's creativity.

A language reducing both power and love to property gives Emerson some momentary if ironic solace. The death of little Waldo now seems no more than the loss of "a beautiful estate," a "great inconvenience," like "the bankruptcy of my principal debtors" (*CW* 3:29).[46] But from beginning to end he still yearns for creative power, what he at last invokes as the "great and crescive self, rooted in absolute nature," which "supplants all relative existence, and ruins the kingdom of mortal friendship and love." If this "magazine of substance" were to rise again to its full phallic, yet receptive explosiveness—the closest he gets to rage—it would expose the impossibility of every relationship, even marriage, the "gulf between every me and thee" (*CW* 3:44).

This widening gulf is what Emerson thinks experience teaches. Throughout, however, a vindictive, patronizing subtext drives the voice that claims to have no emotions. "Two human beings are like globes, which can touch only in a point," he concludes; "the longer a particular union lasts, the more energy of appetency the parts not in union acquire" (*CW* 3:44). Emerson's impersonal geometry disconnects desire from intimacy as well as from marriage. His brutal self-abstraction balances his wife's thirty years of depressions. Whenever I read that passage, I want to write in the margin, "Poor Lidian."

Poor Lidian indeed. Ellen Tucker Emerson speaks of the "dungeon" of her mother's resentful thoughts, "in which she suffered for so many years." Despite her "hot & fiery" temperament, Lidian seems to have been a near invalid from the early 1840s until the 1870s, with recurrently disabling depressions that may have been augmented by Emerson's detached self-preoccupation. Ostensibly her depressions came on as she realized how far her husband had diverged from religious orthodoxy.[47] But surely Emerson's half-conscious contempt showed through.

"We are not very much to blame for our bad marriages," he writes in a later essay, "Illusions," striking the same note with a more complacent truculence. "We live amid hallucinations; and this especial trap is laid to trip up our feet with, and all are tripped up first or last." As he universalizes his self-pity and his inability to love Lidian, Emerson once again both blames and thanks "the mighty Mother who had been so sly with us." If that mother has tripped him up with a bad marriage, at least "we find a delight in the beauty and happiness of children that makes the heart too big for the body." Self-pity, however, is the note that endures here, much less deviously than in "Experience." "Like sick men in hospitals, we change only from bed to bed, from one folly to another; and it cannot signify much what becomes of such castaways, wailing, stupid, comatose creatures, lifted from bed to bed, from the nothing of life to the nothing of death."[48]

My deflationary reading of "Experience" opposes almost every recent critical assessment.[49] Though Emerson's business constituency shies away from the essay's depressive complexities, intellectuals have found more and more to praise. At the December 1983 Modern Language Association convention, in welcoming deconstructionist approaches, Lawrence Buell noted that "Experience" is "the hottest text these days." It self-destructs its own meanings; it exposes Emerson's resistance to his own will to power; it presents him as *bricoleur* of his own text, at odds with what the essay calls the "rapaciousness" of a self whose senses have fallen into the world. As an ironic, yet yearning exposure of the will to power, the essay may be a deconstructive masterpiece. In its approach to feeling, the essay seems to me annoying, petulant, and evasive at almost every turn.

"Experience" has almost nothing to do with Emerson's real experience, which springs and recoils from male rivalry. His dream of manly power gains its broader appeal from its implicit rebellions. The wild, fizzing energy of his early prose throws off his father's yoke with a great deal of anger as well as play. His imperious nonchalance liberates him from fear and addresses the fear he sees in the cowed men all around him. Emerson was able to empower his voice in a world he experienced as disempowering. As a student once said, he writes sentences that you want to tack on the wall or send to a depressed friend. Now he has lost touch with those energies. What seems to be a crusty self-encounter is really self-avoidance. Its most inhumane by-product is his displacement of anxiety about manhood into passive indictments of mothering.

Those critics who praise the ethical and social mission of Emerson's allegedly representative self minimize or miss the mystifications that protect him from conflict. The social connections I have proposed encourage a different sense of his major texts. We can see how the earlier essays transform conflicts in himself and his audience by provoking, dramatizing, and prophesying an elite manhood of the mind. We can also see how "Experience" retreats from his hopes for manly transformation to a private depressiveness that fitfully snipes at the women he takes for granted. Emerson's obsession with power reflects the fears of failure, the desperate rivalries for success, and the fluidity of a social frame in which power itself was uncertainly shifting from one group of men and one mode of manhood to another. In disengaging the mind from personal and political struggle, his major essays inaugurate the tradition of alienated liberalism that is still the dominant ideology in American literary criticism.

Reading Emerson at his best is like body-surfing the cosmos, a cosmos inside one's own mind. To float too long there, suspended in close reading, can lead to a more precious alienation, the modernist pleasures of the text detached from social history. Focusing on the politics of Emerson's voice—whom does he address and why, with what fears and hopes?—can reconnect his literary language to the realities of American lives, including his own. As a contemporary journalist said, his voice had shoulders that he himself lacked. His prose anticipates the speeches of Eugene V. Debs as well as the poems of Walt Whitman. He plays some of the first variations on a pervasive American theme: the "Melodramas of Beset Manhood" that shape so much of what is currently canonized in our literature and criticism.[50]

In this chapter I've tried to lower Emerson's critical stock to the level of his assets. I share a baffled fascination with his free-floating flights of language, and I deeply admire his efforts to rescue his mind from depressive turmoil. The anxious competitiveness that pressed on him can still seem more natural than the air we breathe. Nevertheless, Emerson's partial liberation from male rivalry leads to a politics of man making that trivializes women and feelings, while his passion for the mind's abstracted buoyancy strips power of conflict, as if it were a river in air.

At times when I think that I've cut through Emerson's fog of self, it's hard to disengage from his disengagements without wanting to dismiss him entirely. In other moods, the free play of his self-consciousness can seem endlessly absorbing. The way beyond the perpetually circling problem of Emerson's appeal is not to take a stand within that paradoxical either-or but to see how his language resonates with the unresolved tensions of his life and culture. If his limitations then seem inseparable from his achievements, his resisting response to history gains a surprising intimacy. We can see him more clearly as a man, struggling with himself as well as with his time.

3

Three Ideologies of Manhood, Four Narratives of Humiliation

Situating Emerson in his social and family contexts raises at least two immediate questions. First, how legitimate is it to apply a class conflict analysis, especially the relatively simple one I have suggested, to the social changes occurring in the Northeast between 1825 and 1860? Second, how central could Emerson's feelings about his father be to his calls for man-making words and self-reliance, when other contemporary figures who share his individualism have quite different family backgrounds?

I will postpone the latter question until the second half of this chapter. In the first part, I will briefly consider class issues, touching on both contemporary social historians and American Renaissance writers. Despite the ongoing disagreements among social historians and despite the enduring paradox of a middle class that denies it exists as a class, I conclude that to speak of class conflicts as a social frame for the American Renaissance is both plausible and useful. The overriding issue is how class dynamics become subsumed in gender ideologies. More particularly, I argue that as the male workplace became quite separate from the home, competition intensified, and men defined manhood much more exclusively through their work. Beneath a greater preoccupation with manhood and competition, for artisans and entrepreneurs alike, lies a greater fear of humiliation.

I now propose a more general theorem. Anyone preoccupied with manhood, in whatever time or culture, harbors fears of being humiliated, usually by other men. The sources of humiliation may be diverse, in parents or the loss of class position, in marketplace competition or other fears of being dominated. A preoccupation with manhood becomes a compensatory response. To adapt a term from John Von Neumann's game theory, manhood becomes a way not of dominating, though domination may be a by-product, but of minimizing maximum loss. While the loss may be symbolized as castration, its emotional roots lie in a man's fear that other men will see him as weak and therefore vulnerable to attack.[1]

Manhood begins as a battlefield code, to make men think twice before turning and running, as any sensible man would do. Womanhood begins as a domestic code, centered on child rearing. As collective fictions, these codes function ideologically, representing a particular group's prescriptions for behavior as if the norms were both natural and universal. They serve to invigorate yet also to constrain the individual will for the benefit of the group: so men will protect the group from enemies, and so women will raise the children and solace the men. The great paradox of manhood and of womanhood, as perhaps of any ideology, is that what can be socially functional can also be personally dysfunctional. Men get killed; women get stifled.

In the United States, especially after 1820, the primary battlefield has been economic competition. In such a competitive world, where men come to measure their worth primarily through their work, the greatest fear is to be shamed or humiliated by other men. Manhood functions to preserve self-control and, more profoundly, to transform fears of vulnerability or inadequacy into a desire for dominance.

As a short-term defensive strategy in competitive situations, manhood can be undeniably inspiriting. The problem develops when manhood comes to feel like one's whole self. Then an ideology designed to manage and master fear becomes, paradoxically, a way of intensifying and burying fear, so deeply that, as in Ahab, it generates a monstrous need to dominate. *Moby Dick* is a voyage toward suicide, the vortex of a self-hating self unable to step beyond the inward, downward pull of manhood and humiliation. That vortex came to be felt with special intensity in the antebellum Northeast as industrialization separated the home from the workplace, where entrepreneurial values placed far more emphasis on risk and competition.

In what follows, I sketch three ideologies of American manhood. I think of them as paradigms, akin to Max Weber's ideal types, conceptual categories never fully existing in the world yet useful for studying more complicated social stresses. The patrician paradigm, which helped to sustain a relatively small colonial elite composed of merchants, lawyers, and landed gentry, expresses manhood as property ownership, patriarchy, and republican ideals of citizenship. The artisan paradigm, expressing the values of a much larger producing class upon which the elite depended, defines manhood as freedom, pride of craft and, to a lesser degree, citizenship, along with a good deal of ambivalence about patriarchal deference.

Though a good many tensions emerge from the continuing interdependence of artisan and patrician classes, as Marxist historians have emphasized, I argue that the basic class conflict between 1825 and 1850 comes with the rise of a new middle class, for whom manhood is based much more exclusively in work and entrepreneurial competition. Traditional norms of dignity and social status, implying as they do a relatively stable world of small villages, can mitigate the basic connection between manhood and humiliation. In a world of much greater mobility and competition, manhood becomes a more intense anxiety. For middle-class American males at midcentury, before the quick rise of a managerial class and large-scale bureaucratic organizations eased the stress and risk of competition, manhood took on a conscious and unconscious power of self-definition analogous to the more blatant power of class in Europe.

To discriminate among ideologies of American manhood can illuminate the implicit class basis for gender codes, especially male codes that mystify class conflicts by aggrandizing self-isolation, whether through artisan ideals of freedom or entrepreneurial ideals of competition. Such self-isolation, which I believe most American men now take for granted, always carries a heavy interior price.

I

One of the most basic themes in American history has been the widely shared belief that the possibilities for individual upward mobility effectively blur class lines. Benjamin Franklin first gave mythic status to the rags-to-riches dream in his *Autobiography*. Elsewhere he emphasized the "happy mediocrity" of the American situation, so relatively free from class hierarchy and tyrannical aristocratic institutions. In the decades before the Civil War, especially in the Northeast, the idea of being self-reliant or a "self-made man"—a phrase apparently coined by Henry Clay in 1832—amounted to an obsession. Appropriately, Clay associates the phrase with the dominant values of American individualism. As he says during a lengthy speech defending tariffs, "In Kentucky, almost every manufactory known to me, is in the hands of enterprising and self-made men, who have acquired whatever wealth they possess by patient and diligent labor."[2]

In the past few years, various studies have suggested a middle-class frame for the paradoxes of American individualism. Its ethic of hard work, self-control, and material rewards rested on the presumption that everyone could be successful. The very term *middle class* came into use in the 1830s, replacing "the middling orders" or "the middling sort," to emphasize the paradoxical possibility of upward mobility for everyone.[3] Part of the reason class lines have been so blurred in America, I think, is that the triumph of middle-class values and the economic system fostering them has been so overwhelming.

From Crèvecoeur onward, the American emphasis on opportunity for anyone who can reconceive himself as a "new man" has usually been seen as a freedom from class constraints. To Henry James, Hawthorne's obsessive scrutiny of the individual heart took on such urgency and anxious magnitude because of "the absence of a variety of social types and of settled heads" under which the individual "may be easily and conveniently pigeon-holed." The absence of class labels makes for "interrogative and tentative" assessments of character. F. O. Matthiessen repeatedly emphasizes the American tradition of "Protestant inwardness," in contrast to the English tradition of social stratification and manners, as an enabling frame for the American Renaissance. His terms have set the direction for a generation of literary studies.[4] Though a good many recent social historians, especially Mary Ryan and Sean Wilentz, are reintroducing the idea of class consciousness and class tensions in their studies of this period, such perspectives still meet with widespread skepticism. After all, what could it mean to assert that a "new middle class" comes into being between 1825 and 1850, when the middle class has allegedly been rising since the twelfth century?

Edward Pessen has been among the most forceful proponents of the traditional view of America as an agrarian republic, populated largely by farmers and artisans, with urban immigrant masses on the bottom and a relatively stable elite on the top.[5] The newer historiography stresses the complexity and the dynamism of class change during the antebellum period, as well as the contradictions and confusions in social awareness. My emphasis on the triumph of a new middle class over the old Federalist-Republican elite may strike some as too Marxist and others as not Marxist enough—that is, not sufficiently attuned either to the ideological contradictions in each group or to the elite's function as an upper bourgeoisie rather than an aristocracy. Several recent social histories emphasize the plurality of subgroups and the shifting dynamics too simply stabilized as "class." Nevertheless, these histories also emphasize the ideological tensions among mercantile, artisan, and entrepreneurial interests, while disagreeing about the presence of outright class conflicts.

In his 1837 farewell address, Andrew Jackson voiced the resentful class consciousness of the lower orders. "The agricultural, the mechanical, and the laboring classes have little or no share in the direction of the great moneyed corporations," he said.[6] This view, a convention even then, has been preserved in the orthodox Marxist approach to class conflict. For such writers, to focus on the middle class obscures the fundamental conflict between the bourgeoisie and the emerging working class. Strains between a bourgeois elite and more middling managers or between professionals and entrepreneurs and mercantilists are finally family squabbles, of only transitional interest compared to the struggle of the working class toward autonomous self-consciousness and social power.[7]

The great problem with Marxist hopes for proletarian class consciousness in the United States is that the middle class won, and keeps winning. The most sophisticated Marxist study to date, Sean Wilentz's *Chants Democratic: New York City and the Rise of the American Working Class, 1788–1850*, brilliantly details the rise of working-class consciousness in 1830s New York, as wage-labor relations begin to replace patriarchal shops on a large scale, amid enormous confusion and uncertainty. While his analysis is more complex than Paul Johnson's social-control model for Rochester during the same period, Wilentz and Johnson come to much the same conclusions. Nevertheless, Wilentz's book should actually be subtitled "the Rise and Fall of the American Working Class." His analysis of the 1840s shows more and more strain as he tries to explain retrograde nativist and temperance movements as if they expressed the continuing surge of working-class consciousness.

Despite Wilentz's obvious and admirable wish to be the E. P. Thompson of the American left, his book chronicles the tragedy of a working class that clearly existed by 1850—Wilentz's great achievement is to make that unmistakable—yet continually found its self-awareness co-opted and dispersed by artisan ideals of manhood and middle-class ideals of individual upward mobility. As Wilentz himself agrees, the United States "has long been a lower-middle-class nation that lives by spurious middle-class myths and visions."[8] Foremost among those myths is the faith and fantasy that any man can "make it big."

However much one might wish it otherwise, the fundamental class struggle in the Northeast from 1825 to 1850 came not from conflicts between workers and bosses but from the challenge of a capitalist middle class to an entrenched mercantilist and landholder elite. The "new men," as Gordon Wood has called them, the aggressive speculators and undeferential entrepreneurs, set a different tone for the uses of power as well as manners. In Wood's recent reformulation of his conclusions, "the scrambling, individualistic, acquisitive society that suddenly emerged in the early nineteenth century" made work the new measure of a man's value. The zest of ordinary men for the marketplace challenged the traditional disdain of the gentry for market interests, a disdain "at the heart of classical republicanism."[9] In a still-compelling article, "American Romanticism and the Depression of 1837," William Charvat argues that most members of the New England writing elite were not much touched either by the Panic of 1837 or by the problems of the new working class, which they tended to label and dismiss as the traditional poor. Thoreau's relentless mockery of the Irish in *Walden* can be taken as symptomatic. "What really disturbed the writers of the day," Charvat concludes, "was not the poor, whom we have always with us, but the new commercial middle class. . . . They were turning us into a money-mad nation without value, without principles." From the other end of the social scale, on his artisan's promenade in "Song of Myself" (sections 41–42), Whitman lingers over his proud mechanics while pitying the urban capitalists who never feast but walk about "with dimes on the eyes."[10]

In *Disorderly Conduct* Carroll Smith-Rosenberg finds a similar change from what she calls "a golden age for American artisans" (1740–1830) to a great variety of employee-entrepreneur wage relationships thereafter. Unlike Charvat, Smith-Rosenberg stresses the disintegration of the patriarchal family and the rise of a world where young men could not follow in their fathers' footsteps. The newly emerging bourgeoisie "could scarcely be considered a solidified class," she observes. Eventually absorbing the older mercantile elite, it included wholesale merchants, smaller shopkeepers, industrial entrepreneurs, and professionals as well. Moreover, at least in some of the major cities, "downward economic mobility far exceeded upward movement." Unstable in membership, starkly insecure in prospects, this was a class defining itself far more by its fear of falling into the working class than by its hope of rising further. As does Mary Ryan, Smith-Rosenberg implies one of the great paradoxes of American capitalism: a middle class far more conscious of the working class than either class is conscious of itself.[11]

The conflict had not become a class war in conventional European terms. Instead, it became an ideological tension felt in terms more of gender than of class. What did it mean to be manly? Was manliness the independence and self-respect of the craftsman or the ability of an entrepreneur to best his competitors and exploit resources, human as well as material? Did a man's self-respect depend on a sense of being free and equal to any other man or on a struggle to be dominant?

The patrician paradigm defined manhood through property, patriarchy, and citizenship. It was the ideology of a narrow elite: merchants, gentry, large landowners, lawyers—in old English as well as old Marxist perspective, the upper bourgeoisie.[12] Its manly ideal of character, public service, and paternalism had much in common with British aristocratic ideals of honor, though with more emphasis on sturdy independence, except in the South. So long as mercantile capitalism dominated economic production in the Northeast, this ideal of manhood held relatively comfortable sway.[13]

The artisan paradigm defined manhood in Jeffersonian terms, as autonomous self-sufficiency. A man worked his land or his craft with integrity and freedom. Longfellow's "The Village Blacksmith" catches the myth:

> His brow is wet with honest sweat,
>   He earns whate'er he can,
> And looks the whole world in the face,
>   For he owes not any man.

As one can tell from the patrician paternalism of Jefferson and Longfellow, this ideal of manhood worked well with mercantile capitalism, which depended for its raw materials on independent yeomen farmers and whose characteristic mode of production was the small patriarchal village shop.[14]

For instance, in Royall Tyler's popular drawing-room comedy *The Contrast* (1787), Colonel Henry Manly represents just what his last name implies, a forthright, brave, and honorable master, visiting the big city to secure pensions for the soldiers who fought with him in the Revolution. Manly's servant, Jonathan, becomes his exaggerated mirror, a simpleminded bumpkin who continually makes a fool of himself with his brash assertions. Manly, too, looks like a "Bumkin" to the sophisticated, amoral Billy Dimple.[15] The plot's "contrast" plays with the unsophisticated ways of Manly and his servant only to champion their American values of sincerity, generosity, and tender sentiment, as opposed to the quasi-aristocratic urbanity of Dimple and his pretentious servant, Jessamy. At the end, secure in his manliness, Colonel Manly can reject out of hand Dimple's challenge to a duel. The code of aristocratic honor, which survived through the Civil War in the South, yields without a fight to the soldierly simplicity of the new Revolutionary elite. When manhood beats manners, every true American can live happily ever after.

True, Colonel Manly seems much too old-fashioned and sobersided at first, especially to the witty young ladies. Several modern critics have found him priggish.[16] A bit of a Mr. Knightly, or a Samuel Johnson with a broom up to his tonsils, he lectures his sister about coquetry, lectures the audience about dissipation, and refuses to bring his tone down from lofty gravity to the badinage that flutters all about him. Blundering Jonathan presents himself as Manly's still more "unpolished" double, singing "Yankee Doodle" just before Manly invokes a litany of republican virtues to inveigh against luxury and travel. With his first lines, in act 2, Jonathan bristles at Jessamy's label of servant: "Servant! Sir, do you take me for a neger,—I am Colonel Manly's waiter." Yes, he admits, he does black the colonel's boots, "but I am a true blue son of liberty, for all that. Father said I should come as Colonel Manly's waiter, to see the world, and all that; but no man shall master me: my father has as good a farm as the colonel."[17] Jonathan's comic denial, like Manly's ponderous diction, seems both pompous and true to the spirit of Yankee independence.

As Cathy Davidson has pointed out, in genre as well as plot the play affirms what Jonathan rejects, the class structure of master and servant. Davidson tellingly cites an advertisement in the *New York Packet*, requesting the "Ladies and Gentlemen" at the play, "as soon as they are seated, to order their servants out of the boxes." While differentiating Colonel Manly's decency from aristocratic vices, the play also affirms a sophistication glancingly at odds with the exaggerated postures of self-assertion in its heroes. Between the lines, one can detect a fear of being taken for "a neger," a dependent social inferior, in the play's citified framing of country manhood. More obviously, a calculating spirit looms in the final lines of the pater familias, Van Rough, who hands his daughter over to the colonel because Manly looks like "a man of punctuality" who can talk "very prudently" and "mind the main chance." He likes that phrase so much he says it again: "Come, come, no fine speeches; mind the main chance, young man, and you and I shall always agree."[18]

The elite might agree among themselves about the main chance, but they were well aware of potential class conflicts. James Madison's Federalist Paper number 10 sounds pre-Marxist in its candor about the necessity to preserve class "factions" while minimizing their dangers.

> The most common and durable source of factions has been the various and unequal distribution of property. Those who hold and those who are without property have ever formed distinct interests in society. Those who are creditors and those who are debtors fall under a like discrimination. A landed interest, a manufacturing interest, a mercantile interest, a monied interest, with many lesser interests, grow up of necessity in civilized nations, and divide them into different classes, actuated by different sentiments and views.

These social divisions, he affirms a little earlier, occur because all men are created *un*equal. Some men are better at securing property than others, and government's chief function must be to protect their right to do so. To dream of a "uniformity of interests" is "impracticable," he says, because of "the diversity in the faculties of men from which the rights of property originate.... The protection of these faculties is the first object of government." "From the protection of different and unequal faculties of acquiring property, the possession of different degrees and kinds of property immediately results: and from the influence of these on the sentiments and views of the respective proprietors ensues a division of the society into different interests and parties."[19]

Both the patrician and artisan paradigms, despite the artisan's ideal of freedom, imply patriarchal habits of deference. In *The Federalist Papers*, Madison and Alexander Hamilton emphasize the strength of representative government over a democratic model, in part because they believe the lower orders will tend to vote for an elite representative who will think more about the good of the whole. Hamilton, especially, waxes enthusiastic about the likelihood that farmers and tradesmen will put their interests in the hands of their betters.[20] Madison, on the other hand, has a much more pessimistic understanding of the intractability of "the passions and the interests." His concern was to fashion a government based not only on representation but also on checks and balances. In such a government faction could check faction, and power-hungry men would be blocked from tyranny by men leading other constituencies. As he puts it in his equally well known Federalist Paper number 51, "Ambition must be made to counteract ambition."[21] Like Hamilton, however, Madison implied that a representative elite would be more likely to weigh the good of the whole than to succumb to provincial factions.

In practice, many artisans shared the patrician emphasis on citizenship and the good of the whole. The result was what Nick Salvatore has called, in a different context, "deferential democracy."[22] In the world that Eugene V. Debs grew up in, an artisan's sense of manhood was based primarily on his work and to a somewhat lesser extent on his role as father and husband. A man must provide for his family, and he must be "a model of industry and honesty." This code of manhood "also required an active political participation and the fulfillment of one's duty as a citizen." Such an ideal of work could deny existing class interests and stress a common purpose in part because it existed in such a small-town world. Several recent critics see Whitman's "Song of Myself" as an attempt to restore artisan cohesion to an urban world fragmenting into class and national divisions. Ostensibly based on pride of craft, the "skilled worker's vision of manhood" depended on what Salvatore calls "a fundamental cohesion within their society and culture."[23] In a larger, more amorphous marketplace world, where a man felt more and more like a hand, the already romanticized ideal of community could no longer be presumed as a frame for manly freedom and pride of craftsmanship. Skilled labor now seemed more like exploitation and oppression.

Faith in a patriarchal elite had its intimate counterpart in the patriarchy of the home. Though Jay Fliegelman's *Prodigals and Pilgrims* argues for a basic change from stern to benign fathering from 1750 to 1800, the assumption of father's primacy as father remains unquestioned. Considerable psychological conflict roils under the surface of both paradigms, especially in the artisan model, where independence is uneasily yoked to filial deference. "Yankee Doodle," the song Jonathan sings in *The Contrast*, catches the surface: a jaunty fantasy of a land without masters and servants, where

> Father and I went up to camp,
> Along with Captain Goodwin;
> And there we saw the men and boys,
> As thick as hasty-pudding.

Moreover, in this paradise of happy male camaraderie, they fire off a huge "swamping gun," which " made a noise—like father's gun, / Only a nation louder." Washington Irving's "Rip Van Winkle" (1819) patronizes and celebrates another folk version of father-son bonding, as Rip survives both the Revolution and his nagging wife to take his place beside the patriarchal cracker barrel along with his look-alike son. Much more complex works, such as *The Last of the Mohicans* (1826) and Melville's first novel, *Typee* (1846), also move toward ostentatiously patriarchal nostalgia in their depictions of the grandfatherly tribal leader Tamenund and the Typee chief Mehevi.[24]

Many of Whittier's poems—"Democracy" (1841), for example—fuse an impassioned faith in equality with a more formally idealized patriarchal manhood:

> Oh, ideal of my boyhood's time!
> 　The faith in which my father stood...
>
> The generous feeling, pure and warm,
> 　Which owns the right of all divine;
> The pitying heart, the helping arm,
> 　The prompt self-sacrifice, are thine....
>
> By misery unrepelled, unawed
> 　By pomp or power, thou seest a Man
> In prince or peasant, slave or lord,
> 　Pale priest, or swarthy artisan.

The Old World terminology, as well as the abstractedness of the poem, bespeaks the falseness in his idealized fusion of artisan democracy with patriarchy. Elsewhere in this poem, Whittier associates such manhood with Christ, the ultimate artisan democrat and the ultimate in self-sacrificing sons.[25]

Another text that startlingly fuses artisan values with both patriarchal and genteel deference is Walt Whitman's early temperance potboiler, *Franklin Evans; or The Inebriate. A Tale of the Times* (1842). Though Whitman later dismissed it as something he wrote in three days for seventy-five dollars, and though it is certainly no better than the "damned rot" he said it was, the story holds some interest as an artisan fantasy. Despite Sean Wilentz's hopes for finding incipient class consciousness in the artisan temperance movements of the 1840s, Whitman's hero, son of a mechanic and carpenter who died when the boy was three or four, flagrantly aspires to be a gentleman. Like Hawthorne's Robin Molineux or like the Franklin he may have been named for, Franklin Evans heads for the big city to better his station. Unlike Robin, he is slavishly alert to which men are really gentlemen, who "were the really well-bred people of the house," or who has "a perfect pattern of perfection in his dress and manners."

Unfortunately, the young man lacks the requisite self-reliance. His "great failing... —weakness of resolution, and liability to be led by others—" again and again leads him to drink, prohibiting him from "attaining once more a respectable station in society." Only at the very end does Whitman explicitly indict saloons—"these pestilent places, where the mind and the body are both rendered effeminate together"— as enemies of manhood. Throughout, however, the story clearly links upward mobility to manly self-control, and the dream of conventional genteel respectability always glimmers in the distance. "Visions of independence and a home of my own, and the station of a man of property, floated before my eyes." Moreover, Franklin Evans's journey begins with a seemingly unrelated stagecoach tale of father-son conflicts among drunken Indians. A young man's drunkenness, it becomes amply clear, makes potentially helpful and fatherly gentlemen give up on him. As in Horatio Alger's tales for a later generation, patriarchal deference is presented as indispensable for any artisan youth aspiring to genteel status.[26]

The classic text for a young man's upward mobility from artisan to patrician patriarchy is Franklin's *Autobiography*. The first part (1771) is written to his illegitimate son William, then forty years old and the governor of New Jersey, later a Tory. Partly from pride, partly in hopes of bridging their incipient estrangement, and partly to encourage his son's deference to him, Franklin presents his life as a model of how to rise from artisan beginnings to patrician success and influence. Buried in the prescriptions for hard work, good connections, graceful writing, and civic usefulness is his conflict with his own father, who prevented young Benjamin from going to sea and apprenticed him to various artisan trades.

Overtly Franklin's resentments seem directed at his elder brother, from whom he runs away to start a new life in Philadelphia. One can easily read between the lines to see that his father thought Benjamin was dangerously hotheaded and incapable of the deference apprenticeship requires. When Franklin resolves to leave his brother and head south, his father clearly forbids him. "I determin'd on the Point: but my Father now siding with my Brother, I was sensible that if I attempted to go openly, Means would be used to prevent me." So he goes secretly and, as he never quite admits, against his father's will. He begins his rise by breaking a contract and running away.

Later, in describing how he returns to Boston and flaunts his wealth at his brother's print shop, Franklin takes care to dramatize both his triumph over his brother and his obedience to his father. This time father, after weighing at length the letter from the governor whom his youngest son had managed to impress, refused to let his eighteen-year-old boy set up in business but "gave his Consent to my Returning again to Philadelphia, advis'd me to behave respectfully to the People there, endeavour to obtain the general Esteem, and avoid lampooning and libelling to which he thought I had too much Inclination." Recurrently thereafter Franklin refers approvingly to the advice of his father, while he continues the lampooning and near libeling that brought him both business and notice.

As he ambiguously sums up his successful self-refashioning, "(thro' this dangerous Time of Youth and the hazardous Situations I was sometimes in among Strangers, remote from the Eye and Advice of my Father) . . . I had therefore a tolerable Character to begin the World with, I valued it properly, and determin'd to preserve it." He talks about himself as if he were a suitcase. Having learned how to market himself, and how to mask his contentious egotism, he now can wheel his character through the streets as his most valuable piece of property. His success has at least as much to do with his mobility, malicious wit, and ability to impress cosmopolitan men as with any deference to his artisan father's advice. Yet, he feels constrained to cast his achievements within the conventions of patriarchal deference, partly with an eye to his son and partly to submerge his adolescent rebelliousness in mature patrician paternalism.[27]

The basic class tension came from the undeferential, ambitious entrepreneurs and speculators who challenged patrician modes of power. Mary Kelley calls the victory of the new men the greatest social transformation in American history. While that judgment may seem excessive, it catches some of the stress of the time, as men struggled to redefine for themselves what it meant to work. Lemuel Shaw, Melville's father-in-law, played a crucial role as chief justice of the Massachusetts Supreme Court in redefining the gentry's ideal of property rights from an absolute end in itself to an instrumental means. His conception of the corporation as an individual allowed for corporate expansion. While his rulings also connected incorporation to public regulation, the effect was to maximize competition.[28] Traditional artisan ideals of manliness as independence, hard work, and pride in one's labor, the backbone of American rhetoric then and now, were also being challenged in a marketplace emphasizing competition, risk, and calculation, with all the instability attending the economic change to industrial capitalism. Instability itself, the sense of not knowing one's place, was another prime source for obsessive competitiveness.

Franklin himself was a ruthless entrepreneurial competitor, mixing wiles and pugnacity to dominate his rival printers, one of whom he drove to Barbados. He fell back on Deborah Read for a wife only after he failed to gain one with a hundred-pound dowry. Just a year after running away, when Franklin returned to Boston, he relished humiliating his brother by flaunting his fine clothes, watch, and silver in front of James's employees. James did not forgive him until he was dying, many years later. Conversely, in recounting how Franklin himself was humiliated by Governor William Keith's betrayal, he studiously underplays his anger. Seizing the main chance, he uses the letter to do Andrew Hamilton a favor; seizing the *Spectator's* style, he assesses Keith with a measured, impersonal judiciousness.

While Franklin clothes the reality of his entrepreneurial success in the appearance of retrospective patrician mellowness, a newer generation would seek the main chance with less attentiveness either to self-image or civic usefulness. The greatest paradox in the triumph of the capitalist middle class is that its collective success depended on maximizing individual competition, which thrives on the zest for dominance and the fear of failure. What Mary Ryan has called the "ebullience of artisan culture" depended on a relatively stable village world with strong kinship ties. That world was giving way to a much more rivalrous, alienated, and uncertain market, with visions of greater gain and precipitous falls on every hand. As Melville puts it at the beginning of *Pierre*, the greatest of patriarchal families now "rise and burst like bubbles in a vat."[29] Earlier ideologies of manhood stabilized self-esteem by linking it to institutionalized social structures such as class and patriarchy. The ideology of manhood emerging with entrepreneurial capitalism made competition and power dynamics in the workplace the only source for valuing and measuring oneself. Manhood therefore became much more fundamental to a man's unconscious self-image.

In *Cradle of the Middle Class*, foremost among the recent social histories arguing for the growth of a new middle class during this period, Mary Ryan finds a decisive change in the social expectations for adult men. As the role of father became more peripheral or intermittent, the complementary myths of the self-made man and the cult of true American womanhood fostered a narrow intensity of will, work, and self-reliance in the man, while the family became the domestic cradle for nurturing little republicans of the future. Sons became strangers to their mothers at an early age. Joseph Kett's study of American adolescence also finds a striking change in the 1840s toward heightened expectations for boys to be hardworking and self-disciplined.[30]

Ryan also argues for a complementary paradox. If the intensified individualism of the new middle-class male responded to heightened competition, it also reflected the need of middle-class families to protect their children. While "the fragmentation of the patriarchal household economy" led to much greater gender separation, the family remained as the basic survival unit. According to Ryan, parents strove not to be upwardly mobile so much as to maintain their family's middle-class status. Along with the fear of individual failure came the fear I have already mentioned, that children might fall into the emerging working class. Male self-reliance and female domesticity became complementary tactics to preserve the family's class status. The legacy of such families to their children became not property but education, which could give them the skills necessary for commercial or professional careers. The very definition of *career* changed, from a horse at full gallop to lifelong progress in a stable profession.[31]

There is vitality and zest as well as risk and fear in the entrepreneurial spirit, to be sure. This was the age of "Go ahead!"—of try, fail, land on your feet, and try again. A radical such as Fanny Wright found a stabilizing energy in the midst of the unstable marketplace, giving men a fixed purpose while excluding women from healthful work. The "universally marked difference between men and women," she wrote during an American tour in 1825, came from men's "fixed and steady occupation," which gave "habitual exercise" to all their energies. Without that kind of work, American women lacked the "good health and good nerves" she saw in adult American men. More particularly, and here I differ from Ryan, the norm-setting entrepreneurs relished the struggle to gain some measure of dominance in the marketplace. Money was a means and a tangible yardstick of prowess. They thought of themselves much as George Stigler, a Nobel Prize–winning economist, so appreciatively describes their successors, as "men of force": "The competitive industry is not one for lazy or confused or inefficient men: they will watch their customers vanish, their best employees migrate, their assets dissipate. It is a splendid place for men of force: it rewards both hard work and genius, and it rewards on a fine and generous scale." Or as Vince Lombardi put it, in a phrase that has been widely misquoted, these are men for whom "winning isn't everything, but wanting to win is."[32]

Probably the first literary record of the self-made entrepreneur in the New World is Cotton Mather's fulsome praise of Governor William Phips, by all accounts except Mather's an Ahab of the second order. Kenneth Silverman calls him just a "choleric adventurer" who cursed up a storm, regularly knocked people down, and occasionally threw things at governors before he became one himself. Mather relishes stories of how Phips quelled mutinies on his ships and how he dominated people on ship and shore. The bookish clergyman, filled with a good measure of choleric feelings himself, had various reasons for making his celebration of Phips the lengthy coda to *Magnalia Christi Americana* (1702), including political gratitude. Beyond his political and psychological pleasure in depicting Phips's rise from obscure shepherd to great power, Mather presents Phips as the kind of man who can thrive in America: the exploitative, even brawling entrepreneur who seizes his chances and makes the most of them. The will to dominate is as fundamental to Mather's portrait as is the claim, almost a coinage of "self-made man," that Phips was "*A Son to his own Labours!*"[33]

A trickle of such men in the 1690s had become a torrent by the 1830s. True, these men of force, who gathered such great rewards from the economy they spurred, were not the ordinary men Ryan focuses on. As she argues, problematically I think, families socialized their middle-class boys not to become aggressive entrepreneurs but to aim for achievement and respectability. Nevertheless, what mothers wanted and what the business world wanted could be quite different.[34] The bullyboys now set the pace and the model for manhood in the marketplace. The social structure no longer restrained them. The artisan ideal jostled with a new ideal of manhood, one previously accessible only to kings, court politicians, and great military leaders. Faced with a middle-class man of force, anyone on the other side of his dominance must have felt a little more fearful, a little less free. Sean Wilentz quotes an Irish artisan speaking at a New York labor rally in 1850: "Even in this liberal country, the middle class stands above the workingmen, and every one of them is a little tyrant in himself, as Voltaire said."[35]

Emerson explicitly describes the new middle-class man in terms of ruthless power. In *Representative Men* (1850), he personifies the new middle class as Napoleon, the ultimate man of force. Napoleon, he says, represents "the class of business men . . . the class of industry and skill." He has all the virtues and vices of "the middle class of modern society; of the throng who fill the markets, shops, counting-houses, manufactories, ships, of the modern world, aiming to be rich." Utterly lacking in civilized generosity, "never weak and literary," "egotistic and monopolizing," "a boundless liar," Napoleon is always on stage to be seen and to manipulate his audience. He is "a monopolizer and usurper of other minds," to the end of exercising power and making "a great noise."[36] Emerson's patrician disdain is clear. His admiration for Napoleon's force is also abundantly present. Many members of the elite had portrayed Andrew Jackson in much the same way.

It seems at least plausible, then, to see class conflicts shaping the issue of what did it meant to be a man. Not only recent social historians but contemporary writers sometimes dramatize social change with class-linked characterizations of manhood. In *The Blithedale Romance*, for instance, as I argue in chapter 8, Hawthorne personifies the dispossessed elite in Coverdale and Old Moodie, both narcissistic and shallow "men of show." They are ineffectual, if meddling bystanders for the exploitative new Napoleons of power, Hollingsworth and Westervelt, whose name means "western world."

Part of the dark comedy of Melville's "Bartleby, the Scrivener," comes from the inability of the genteel narrator to fit Bartleby into the class niches personified by Turkey, the down-at-the-heels deferential gentleman, and Nippers, the young and ambitious, if mechanical "new man" preoccupied with ward politics. The nameless narrator defines himself quite comfortably as an appendage of the old elite. He thinks of himself as prudent, unaggressive, safe and snug amid his legal briefs and Christian civilities. Yet the story exposes him as a false self. His need for walls makes him unable to deal with anger, moral equality, or strong subjectivity, in himself or others. Struggling to extend his conventionally benevolent sympathies, he blurts out his presumption of dominance and his preoccupation with property rights. The narrator starts to feel "unmanned," he says twice, at being dictated to by an underling. "What earthly right have you to stay here?" he finds himself expostulating.

"Do you pay any rent? Do you pay my taxes? Or is this property yours?" The narrator cures his "state of nervous resentment" by restoring himself to Christian benevolence, at once self-controlled, dominant, and charitable. For a moment, however, he has exposed both his implicit connection to Bartleby's equally unexpressed anger and his reliance on traditional patrician conventions to secure his sense of identity. By the end he unwittingly becomes linked with Monroe Edwards, the "gentleman forger."[37]

As with psychoanalysis, the uses of class analysis in American literary criticism have encouraged a reductive allegorizing. I open myself to the same charge here. I am indebted to the pathbreaking studies by Carolyn Porter, Myra Jehlen, and especially William Charvat, whose *Profession of Authorship in America* (1968) now seems to me as significant as Charles Feidelson's *Symbolism and American Literature* (1953). No analysis of classic American writing, however, has come close to the brilliant Marxist synthesis that Raymond Williams in *Culture and Society* achieves for English literature.[38] The reason, I think, has to do with the relative prominence of gender consciousness over class consciousness in American self-perceptions. Perhaps that in turn has something to do with the relative absence of an empowered and leisured aristocracy. As Michel Chevalier concludes his *Society, Manners, and Politics in the United States*, "The higher classes in the United States, taken as a whole and with only some exceptions, have the air and attitude of the vanquished; they bear the mark of defeat on their front." For Alexis de Tocqueville, the only aristocratic "counterpoise to the democratic element" was the lawyers, not "the rich, who are united by no common tie."[39]

Partly because the middle class has come to be so diffusely triumphant, American men tend to define their self-respect much more stringently through their work than through any other aspect of their lives. Accordingly, the contradictions and intensities of gender ideology refract various class tensions subsumed in the workplace and the work ethic.[40] With the three paradigms I have outlined, we can begin to discriminate among ideologies of American manhood, while also linking manhood with psychological tensions. The ferocity of market competition and entrepreneurial rivalry peaked and subsided between 1840 and 1870, as a new managerial class soon evolved to contain the risks inherent in large-scale capitalism.[41] Nevertheless, the preeminence of men such as Lee Iacocca, George Steinbrenner, and Donald Trump, or the preeminence of football as our national sport, points to the continued power of entrepreneurial manhood as an ideology of dominance subsuming other modes of gender and class consciousness for many if not most American men.

II

The rest of this chapter considers the emotional dynamic that I see as the key to an intensified ideology of manhood. I focus on four texts: Hawthorne's *The House of the Seven Gables*, Melville's "Benito Cereno," Thoreau's essay on John Brown, and Whitman's "There Was a Child Went Forth." These texts differ in innumerable ways. Yet they share at their center a drama of humiliation, from which their voices recoil and diverge.

Only Thoreau resolves the experience with an ideology of manly self-reliance. Hawthorne frames Jaffrey's pursuit of Clifford with a blend of patrician and feminine values, while Melville mordantly deconstructs every kind of class-based social identity as masks for dominance and humiliation, epitomized in the shaving scene. In his hands, language itself becomes exposed as a tool of social power. Whitman responds to his father's brutality in more Emersonian fashion, with an absorptive detachment transcending any and all emotional threats.

The House of the Seven Gables presents a new Napoleon of power in traditionally patrician terms. Old Colonel Pyncheon aimed all his "iron energy of purpose" at augmenting his "patrimonial property," the conventional patrician definition of manly status.[42] In the process, he wrongfully deprived the artisan Maule family of their little homestead. While the Maules stifled their "resentments" and remained "always plebeian and obscure" at the lower end of the artisan scale, one Pyncheon male in each generation has preserved Colonel Pyncheon's rapacious characteristics (25). Now, while the narrator indulges in a ponderously patronizing account of Hepzibah Pyncheon's fall from leisured gentility into the prosaic necessity of running a shop, her brother Jaffrey triumphantly bears the old Pyncheon manhood into the new market society. Bold, hard, and indirect, he exudes an "animal" protrusiveness, from his nose to his cane to his boots (116). His "hard, stern, relentless look" signals his ruthless drive, "trampling on the weak, and, when essential to his ends, doing his utmost to beat down the strong" (119, 123). On the verge of becoming governor, Jaffrey reaches for power and prop-

erty with "a certain hot fellness of purpose, which annihilated everything but itself" (129).

So far this picture of manhood would seem to contradict my sense
of the three paradigms. Jaffrey conflates the new man and the old patrician. For the narrator, too, society consists of aristocrats and plebeians, from his mocking sympathy with Hepzibah's loss of a lady's
status to his description of "aristocratic flowers, and plebeian vegetables"
(87). The narrative's basic structure of patrician guilt and artisan retribution confirms the narrator's sense of unchanging, preindustrial
class conflict. Taking that conflict as a given, the narrator transposes it
into a gender war, exposing the dangers of manhood on both the artisan
and patrician sides.

If Jaffrey reeks of patrician dominance, Holgrave conceals an equally
dangerous lust for power. Just as he hides his identity as a Maule, his
manifest transformation from artisan into artist veils a latent disposition
to dominate. Initially Holgrave looks like one of the new men, a more
dangerous version of Nippers in "Bartleby." Rumor has it that he gives
"wild and disorganizing" political speeches to "his banditti-like associates" (84). More seriously, he has a certain "magnetic" quality, "taking
hold of one's mind" with his half-hidden powers (94, 85). These powers
display themselves as he tells Phoebe the story of how Alice Pyncheon
was mesmerized and inadvertently killed by his ancestor (187–210).[43]

Unlike Jaffrey, Holgrave deliberately forswears the possibility "of
acquiring empire over the human spirit." As he is about to "complete
his mastery over Phoebe's yet free and virgin spirit," his "reverence for
another's individuality" makes him break the spell (212). By the end,
his residual craftsman's integrity and implicitly patrician chivalry rescue
him from his own Jaffrey-like inclinations toward heartless exploitation.
After he exorcises the dangerous manhood welling up inside him, he
gains Phoebe's love by promising "to conform myself" to established
society. "The world owes all its onward impulse to men ill at ease," he
now reflects. He looks to Phoebe's "poise" to stabilize "any oscillating
tendency of mine" (306–307).

From the narrator's patrician point of view, therefore, the three
paradigms don't work, except perhaps as shifting ideological alliances.
One could argue that the entrepreneurial predisposition to vie for
dominance by humiliating rivals infects both Jaffrey's patrician identity
and Holgrave's artisan identity. While the new man in Jaffrey drags
him down to death, Holgrave detaches himself from vengeful rivalry,
reintegrating his values by conflating the two older paradigms. But that

description sounds almost as allegorical as the narrator's own explanatory mechanisms. Besides, the narrator blatantly uses class conflict as a stalking horse for indicting male dominance, with Phoebe as the allegorical center of danger. Before Holgrave nearly mesmerizes her, Jaffrey nearly rapes her with his leering protrusiveness as he tries to kiss her, or at least the narrator thinks so. "The man, the sex, somehow or other, was entirely too prominent" (118). Fortunately, by the end both the possessive and the sexual dangers erupting from manhood have been safely contained.

Unfortunately for the narrator's attempts at interpretive stability, the plot, such as it is, belies his traditionalist class explanations and undercuts his self-feminizing attempt to transform class conflict into a gender war. While the narrator's rhetoric talks of plebeians vs. aristocrats and sets up expectations for Holgrave's revenge against Colonel Pyncheon's descendant, the only real drama of the plot focuses on Jaffrey's pursuit of Clifford. His oppressive, highly sexualized encounter with Phoebe turns out to be just a prelude to his "evident purpose of forcing a passage" to Hepzibah's terrified brother. Not sexual desire but the desire for Clifford's knowledge about a will, and thus for more property, goads the anger and "red fire . . . darkening forth, as it were, out of the whole man" (129). Holgrave is simply a bystander to this drama of male invasiveness. He functions as an implied reader, trying to figure out what Jaffrey wants from such a nonthreatening child-man. He comments to Phoebe, "Judge Pyncheon! Clifford! What a complex riddle" (179). If Jaffrey's ostensible motive is property, his energy manifests a will to prove his power by humiliating or even annihilating Clifford, as the weaker man's agonized recoil makes clear.

From the beginning, Clifford has been associated with Uncle Venner, the ultimately noncompetitive male, as well as with a vaguely decayed patrician class. Uncle Venner's failure to vie for conventionally manly success complements Clifford's "feminine" portrait (60–61). Each man has been labeled as deficient in his wits. To the narrator Clifford also seems deficient in his heart, able to muster only a shallow aestheticism. The manlier Pyncheons had "persecuted" him until his spirit was "thoroughly crushed" (60, 113). Even his soap bubbles are pierced by Jaffrey's nose (171–172). As Hepzibah says, trying to defend Clifford from Jaffrey's pursuit, "Why should you wish to see this wretched, broken man[?]" (233). Their encounter "would be like flinging a porcelain vase, with already a crack in it, against a granite column" (242).

Then suddenly comes liberation. As Jaffrey waits for Clifford to appear at last, the terror of male brutality to which the narrative has been building suddenly transposes into two giddy narratives: Clifford's wild train ride and the narrator's slow, vindictive circling around Jaffrey's ominous, threatening body, sitting motionless in a chair. Both sides of the split narration express release from the incipient drama of male dominance and humiliation. The narrator goes so far as to say that Clifford "had been startled into manhood and intellectual vigor," or at least into a diseased resemblance to manhood (258). Much more memorably, the narrator's voice takes on a startlingly malicious glee as he hectors Jaffrey's dead body. While Clifford has fantasies of merging with all humanity, the narrator reverses the dominance-humiliation paradigm, pulling out every rhetorical stop to taunt and goad Clifford's bullying, penetrating persecutor. Then slowly both sides of the split recede into more decorous order.

The great problem with *The House of the Seven Gables* as a narrative is that it never precipitates its conflicts, except metaphorically in the narrator's explanatory framings. While he orients his readers toward preindustrial class conflict and a profeminine indictment of manhood, his plot builds toward male rivalry. Just as the man who embodies the spirit of the new men is about to destroy a helpless embodiment of the old patricians, the narrative veers away from confrontation. After allegorical manhood strangles itself, the fading patrician finds a new vigor. "That strong and ponderous man had been Clifford's nightmare" (313). Now Clifford can happily live out his days "within five minutes' saunter" of Uncle Venner (317), while Holgrave inherits the Pyncheon property without a fight.

The Blithedale Romance and *The Scarlet Letter* are more compelling narratives, I think, in part because both stories give greater scope to the drama of one man trying to invade and possess another's soul, the drama I see as Hawthorne's secret subject. In *The House of the Seven Gables* the narrator takes such self-conscious control of his story that he guts the plot, imposes a traditional class interpretation on the real conflict, and uses manhood as a universalized foil for his feminized patrician values, which the artisan-artist restores. In his claims for genre as well, Walter Benn Michaels suggests, Hawthorne uses romance to restore the property rights of impoverished aristocrats, in an imaginative realm permanently immune to appropriation by people like Jaffrey.[44]

If Hawthorne retreats from man-to-man conflict by idealizing traditional patrician values in a feminine mode, Melville offers no way out except through a sadistic muteness. In "Benito Cereno" (1855), Melville uses the story of a slave revolt to deconstruct both middle-class and patrician conventions of manhood. His narration is an act of malice against white male American readers, humiliating them at every level of meaning.

On the surface, the narrator presents the story as an allegory of good vs. evil. The Iago-like Babo has destroyed the honor and soul of Don Benito, the hapless Spanish patrician whose dignity and honor have been cannibalized as completely as his friend's body, consumed by the blacks and now carried on the ship's prow. As Carolyn Karcher has pointed out, Don Benito epitomizes a type known as the "Southern Hamlet," a waffling intellectual who vestigially embodies the patriarchal manhood of the old plantation.[45] Captain Delano represents not only naïve innocence but a bluff presumption of dominance. While Delano looks on uncomprehendingly, Babo shaves his master in a terrifying ritual of dominance and humiliation, the most malicious dance of manhood in any text of the American Renaissance.

By the end, Christian order has been restored. The devil is beheaded, and the Old South dies an appropriately emasculated death. After all, from Delano's perspective it has only itself to blame for "the negro." Like Holgrave, the good-hearted bystander takes control without any apparent conflict. Innocence and charity prevail, and the right white man is in charge at last, along with the capitalist order in which the narrator, too, can speak of "carrying negro slaves, amongst other valuable freight."[46]

One problem with this interpretation is that it makes modern readers feel uncomfortably racist. Significantly, until the 1960s almost every American critic adopted the narrator's allegory of white good vs. black evil without a qualm. Yet unlike Hawthorne's narrator, Melville's narrator subverts his own Christian allegorizing with a disorienting mockery of the hero, whom he humiliates at every turn. If Babo is Iago, Delano becomes an unwitting parody of Othello, prevailing through the brute strength he attributes to blacks only after he has been manipulated nearly out of his wits.

What becomes the authority for Delano's reinstated authority? Only a legal document, written to justify his "generosity and piety ... incapable of sounding such wickedness" (86) and penned by a Spanish official representing both king and pope. The legitimacy for Delano's benign command rests on a fusion of two ancient modes of power, now superseded by the new American order. Unmasked, the authority for "objective" language becomes simply power, nothing else. While the winners write history, Babo remains mute: "On the testimony of the sailors alone rested the legal identity of Babo" (91).[47] One needs to go outside the text to a Nigerian dictionary to discover that while his name evokes "baboon" to whites, in Hausa *babu* means "no."

Anyone's sense of "identity," the story implies, is a construct of power relations. Intermittently the narrative subverts all attempts at meaning making by deconstructing language itself as a tool of social dominance, with a mute indeterminacy as the only residue. Simple ironies about Delano and racial stereotyping mask profoundly Derridean ironies about the hierarchizing and silencing inherent in all language.

If by the end Delano looks like a black buffoon while Babo's brain, "that hive of subtlety," becomes everyone's "leader" (91), the inversion demolishes Delano's conventional presumptions. Like the narrator in "Bartleby," his patronizing affection for underlings reflects his unquestioned assumptions about "natural" authority. He can't see what is going on because he can't imagine that a white man isn't in charge of Don Benito's ship. Instead, he comfortably imagines his own role in "lightly arranging" Don Benito's fate (32).

Those ironies are the easy ones. The really disorienting malice of the story exposes the drive for dominance in all human relations, and the presumption of dominance in narration itself. Modern readers wanting to root for the blacks reverse the narrator's categories of good and evil, while trying to minimize the white reader's recoil at the document's account of black atrocities. At the vortex of the story looms neither black nor white but a grey indeterminacy in which all social categories are masks of power. As the key symbol for that indeterminacy, the carving on "the shield-like stern-piece" of Don Benito's ship depicts "a dark satyr in a mask, holding his foot on the prostrate neck of a writhing figure, likewise masked" (6).[48] The masked figure of dominance and prostration appears first as a symbol, then in the drama of the shaving scene, and finally in the narrator's account of the blacks' defeat.

The narrator begins his account of the final battle by blatantly encouraging readers to root for the sailors. They were heroically "fighting as troopers in the saddle, ... plying their cutlasses like carters' whips." At last, "with a huzza, they sprang inboard." Suddenly, at the center of this glorious battle of good men vs. bad, the narrative strangely moves toward metaphoric undecidability. "For a few breaths' space, there was a vague, muffled, inner sound, as of submerged sword-fish rushing hither and thither through shoals of black-fish." The masks of human character momentarily lift, to display the indiscriminate violence on which power depends. Then, as the whites gain the upper hand, the narrator resumes the comfort of his racist metaphors. "Exhausted, the blacks now fought in despair. Their red tongues lolled, wolf-like, from their black mouths" (72). The narrator is an interpretive parasite, letting his own tongue speak for whoever comes out on top.

If, as I argue in Chapter 6, Harriet Beecher Stowe uses blacks in *Uncle Tom's Cabin* to empower white middle-class women, Melville uses blacks in this story to terrorize white middle-class men. While mocking Delano, the New World's representative man, Melville exposes the matrix of dominance and humiliation which frames Delano's rise to innocent mastery. The New Man wins; ergo he is guiltless; ergo his innocence is sanctified as public authority. From Delano's point of view, modern America can relax. There won't be a Civil War, since all the Don Benitos and all the slaves will mutually self-destruct, leaving the men of the Northeast benignly in charge of the ship of state. Besides, the ancient fusion of Catholicism with kingship to legitimate aristocratic manhood has yielded without a struggle to a new fusion of Christianity and capitalism, legitimating the entrepreneurial manhood of the new middle class. Delano doesn't need to struggle for dominance; he presumes it, right from the start. Like Holgrave, he therefore functions as an implied reader or, in his case, an obtuse nonreader of the power dynamics all around him.

At the center of the story is the title figure, not Captain Delano but Don Benito. He is a man being beaten, from his cowering spirit to his empty, artificially stiffened scabbard. Like the "leaden ocean," he is "finished, soul gone, defunct" (42). More than a study in ironic narration, "Benito Cereno" permits no way out of Benito's experience of protracted humiliation except either to relish the narrator's bashing of Captain Delano or to relish the whites' collective resumption of racist domination as the triumph of good over evil. The only other alternative is to give up on language altogether, as Melville quietly seems to be doing.

No longer do his narrations exult in the spontaneous overflow of powerful thinking. After writing *Moby Dick*, perhaps even while writing its final chapters, Melville abandons his half-Emersonian sense of language as self-empowering. Now language seems to him an alien medium, invasive rather than expressive. Repressing originality and creativity in masks and conventions, it functions as a tool for one group's power over another, no more. What looks like a linguistic thrust toward muteness and indeterminacy is really Melville's dead-end fusion of despair with sadism. If he can't get readers to appreciate his mental high jinks, he will deconstruct all the categories by which we define ourselves. To read "Benito Cereno" closely, at least for me, is to feel racist, superior, baffled, humiliated, and nonexistent, all at once.

A man is being beaten: that becomes the central drama of both "Benito Cereno" and *The House of the Seven Gables*. In later chapters I take up that drama in *Moby Dick, The Blithedale Romance, Uncle Tom's Cabin*, and various other American Renaissance texts. Melville's spare ironies look more modern, or modernist, than Hawthorne's equivocal retreats from midcentury manhood to the shelter of civilizing women. Yet each narrative keeps returning to the spectacle of male humiliation, whether latent, as in *House of the Seven Gables*, or stunningly manifest, as in "Benito Cereno."

Reading these texts closely gives us access to feelings that "real men" would immediately disown. Part of the entrepreneurial paradigm's ideological effectiveness is the constant rhetorical call to meet defeat with renewed energy. Don't linger over failures; pick yourself up and get back in the race with zest and gusto. In that respect, male writers of the American Renaissance use their alienation from competitive norms of manhood to voice feelings and fears labeled unmanly by the now-dominant code.

Yet entrepreneurial ideology could not be the only source for fears of humiliation. As a recent study by Richard Ochberg makes clear, obsessively ambitious middle-class men tend to have fathers who humiliated them. In response, such men try to gain self-esteem through self-control and emotional detachment.[49] Writers, being more alert to feelings as well as more alien from manly norms, express the welter of ambivalent emotions suppressed in the rhetoric of individualism. Emerson clearly had such a father, and detachment helped to constitute his literary self-empowering. Hawthorne, too, had such a father figure in Robert Manning.

The case cannot be made so easily, however, for Thoreau, Whitman, and Melville, each of whom had fathers who might be perceived as weak, if intermittently severe. To borrow a concept from Freud, the key issue is overdetermination. The precipitous loss of class status, the presence of a dominating father, the deviance of one's father from manly norms, the oppressiveness of middle-class gender ideology, even the social perception of male writers as unmanly—all could abet a literary focus on the drama of humiliation. At the same time, the diverse narrative strategies adopted by male writers to control this drama show some complicity with the gender ideologies they struggle to critique.

III

The primary stimulus for Emerson's preoccupation with manhood, I have argued, was his latent, enduring feeling of being humiliated by his father. Yet what of Thoreau or Whitman, or Frederick Douglass for that matter, who emerge from quite different family backgrounds to share a similar ideology?

Thoreau's essay on John Brown is peppered with Emersonian calls to manhood. Brown's raid on Harper's Ferry in 1859 galvanized Thoreau into an obsession with the man, whom he had met only twice before without knowing much about Brown's aims. Now Thoreau's mind took fire. For three days he wrote voluminously of nothing else in his journal, and his public defenses of Brown's violence mark a startling swerve in his political thinking. Manhood proved to be more basic to Thoreau than consistency to his previous advocacy of nonviolent civil disobedience.

As several recent critics remark, Brown clearly represents Thoreau's sense of himself. Thoreau praises Brown because he "had the courage to face his country herself when she was in the wrong." Brown's life showed an uncompromising adherence to ideas and principles, his discourse revealed a "directness of speech" with a lurking "volcano" underneath, and he dared to persist to the end despite gross failures and ignominy. "For once we are lifted out of the trivialness and dust of politics into the region of truth and manhood," Thoreau declares. In his "manly directness and force," in his "simple truth . . . He was too fair a specimen of a man to represent the like of us."[50]

By the end of his impassioned plea, Thoreau explicitly compares Brown to Christ. This "hero in the midst of us cowards . . . shows himself superior to nature. He has a spark of divinity in him." He is "such a man as it takes ages to make, and ages to understand." "You who pretend to care for Christ crucified, consider what you are about to do to him who offered himself to be the saviour of four millions of men." Thoreau relentlessly drives home this comparison. "Some eighteen hundred years ago Christ was crucified; this morning, perchance, Captain Brown was hung. These are the two ends of a chain which is not without its links. He is not Old Brown any longer; he is an angel of light" (189–190).

Thoreau acknowledges that he almost fears to "hear of his deliverance," since Brown's death, like Christ's, will do so much more good than his life (190). Richard Lebeaux sees Thoreau's intense involvement with Brown's fate as his way of starting to work through his own approaching death.[51] Yet the last word of Thoreau's essay is "revenge." "When at least the present form of slavery shall be no more here," then, he says, we can weep for Captain Brown. "Then, and not till then, we will take our revenge" (191). Whatever his approach to making peace with death, Thoreau seems more eager to link himself with a scorned hero's martyred rage.

Overtly Thoreau's rage indicts editors who refuse to publish pro-Brown pieces. Covertly, as William Howarth and Richard Bridgman emphasize, Brown gave him a way of focusing his personal as well as writerly rage: against Concord and against the American social structure—the marketplace where his father failed, the forced compromises and self-diminishments of small-town life. Thoreau's sense of Brown's manly heroism briefly purifies him. "How many a man who was lately contemplating suicide has now something to live for!" he says (188), echoing Emerson's transformation of suicide into courageousness at the end of "The American Scholar." Several critics have taken that line as possibly autobiographical.[52]

If Thoreau was transformed from depression to manly anger by Brown's fate, his Emersonian conversion would seem to have quite different psychodynamics. His mother, not his father, was conspicuously dominant. As neighbors saw it, Cynthia Thoreau overindulged her son and overshadowed her cheerful, unobtrusive, rather hapless husband. A recent essay presents her as brilliant and maliciously witty, quite the opposite of Emerson's self-effacing mother.[53]

Thoreau and Emerson do share a similar sense of class humiliation, in that their families gave both of them a sense of high-status expectations in the midst of impoverished circumstances. Yet Thoreau seems to have shown little of the competitive anxiety that Emerson had to struggle with. Emerson himself faulted Thoreau for not having more ambition. Like so many arrogant sons of doting mothers, Thoreau seemed born to self-reliance.

Nonetheless, we can speculate about the little lower layer. Alice Miller's studies of the gifted children of narcissistic mothers offer a great many parallels to Thoreau, especially to what I think of as his Corio-lanus side. As Lawrence Buell emphasizes, Thoreau quested all his life for a heroic military self-image, and he finally found it in John Brown.⁵⁴ His "Plea for Captain John Brown" seems icy with abstract anger com-pared to the witty, playful, changeable surfaces of himself in *Walden*. Far under both surfaces, revised out of *Walden* and almost wholly in-accessible in the later essay, swim Emerson-like depressions, fears of inadequacy, and fears of not being able to measure up to the self-image he and his mother had set for himself.

More rigid in life, more playful in prose than Emerson, Thoreau differs from his mentor in many of his fears, especially his lifelong fear of tuberculosis, which made him take seriously the Grahamite pre-scriptions for chastity as well as various contemporary notions about food.⁵⁵ Their dissimilar false bottoms cover a shared fear of not being adequate to the selves they were expected to assume. From that latent specter of humiliation, whether brought on by father or by mother, springs much of the struggle and transformational energy in their prose.

Thoreau shared Emerson's fall from patrician security to economic difficulties, though from a less exalted social position; Whitman, by contrast, was born to hard times. Yet class looms much larger in Emer-son's sense of self-consciousness, at least when he addresses social issues. Thoreau is more dismissive; Whitman is more incorporative. Each one therefore seems to be a more radical individualist, and each offers greater room for disconnecting his writing from class perspectives.

Thoreau's "Plea for Captain John Brown" discovers manhood in the realm of truth and unswerving principle, manifested as heroic violence against a society that tolerates slavery. Whitman's "There Was a Child Went Forth," probably his most autobiographical poem, takes an op-posite stance, in several ways. For Whitman, manhood is his father's problem. It is a family pressure to be transcended, not a spirit of self-reliance to be emulated. Faced with the pressures of conventional man-hood, at first generally and then specifically in his father, the child blithely makes it no more and no less than anything else he encounters. He takes it into himself and moves on. Here, as elsewhere, Whitman's characteristic defense against emotional threat is mental detachment and sensory incorporation, not Thoreau's defiance. The result is to magnify the child's receptiveness while obliterating his responsiveness. All social experience becomes simultaneously narcissistic, unreal, and rhetorical.

At the center of the poem is his father's brutality. The rest of the poem denies that center.

> The mother at home quietly placing the dishes on the suppertable,
> The mother with mild words.... clean her cap and gown....
> a wholesome odor falling off her person and clothes as she walks by:
> The father, strong, selfsufficient, manly, mean, angered, unjust,
> The blow, the quick loud word, the tight bargain, the crafty lure
>
> [Whitman's ellipses]

While recent biographers point to the idealization in Whitman's portrait of his Quaker mother, they confirm his portrait of his father. As Paul Zweig puts it, there are "no real mothers . . . in Whitman's writing, but only a voluminous mother-legend: beautiful, sacred, sweet-scented." Zweig also emphasizes that Whitman wrote this poem as he was taking over his father's family position and in some respects his father's character. Zweig goes so far as to call Whitman's father his "muse." The poet found a "liberating complicity" with his father in the making of his first true poems, if not in the poems themselves.

Fundamental to his father was the oscillation between anger and isolation. "Walter, Sr., was known to have a terrible temper, which he alternated with equally terrible silent spells."[56] Any child growing up in such a family must have felt deep fear and anger about such a capriciously aloof and brutal man. But not the child Whitman describes. Whitman protects the child against the startling, sudden appearance of the father, in the poem and in life.

First he establishes a calm, controlling, ample voice, with the strong sure cadences of a benign patriarch, announcing the child's birth:

> There was a child went forth every day,
> And the first object he looked upon and received with wonder or pity or love or dread, that object he became,
> And that object became part of him for the day or a certain part of the day.... or for many years or stretching cycles of years.

This opening three-line stanza gives the child a biblical, yet democratic grandeur. The formal beginning, vaguely evoking the Christ child, also establishes a rhetorical paradox: "a child went forth every day." The line implies a double image: a nearly grown child walking out of the house to confront the world, rather confidently, or, as the next lines imply, a child who is being reborn every day.

Whitman also declares a still more paradoxical proposition about all newborn boys. Every man-in-the-making becomes part of the objects he perceives, while those objects become part of him. Feelings come along with the objects: "wonder or pity or love or dread." But such feelings, however intense, are momentary compared to the "stretching cycles" of time and birthing. Objects come and go, while the experience of being born and incorporating whatever you see returns to the receptive consciousness day after day, year after year.

As Whitman's most general defense against feeling surprised and threatened by his father's arbitrary explosions, he makes growth equivalent to perceptual symbiosis. That man can't hurt me, because I can absorb him. A secondary defense minimizes the child's terror of uncontrollable, helpless responses by listing and framing feelings in an abstract, welcoming, propositional voice. A third, related defense makes one's parents a subcategory of "object," a neutralizing word. Finally—Whitman's defenses are as comprehensive as the rest of him—he shelters the wondering child with the voice of a benign rather than threatening father. The tension returns with the paradox. They become me, yet I become them. Who are "they"? Who, for that matter, am "I"?

The next three stanzas lead up to the entry of the father in two ways: by dramatizing the child's curiosity about natural objects and then by introducing some characteristics of manhood. The lovely, quasi-seasonal procession of nature's things, beginning in March, implies the springtime of the soul, with lilacs, grass, flowers, birds and farm animals.[57] The list culminates in a wondering pun on the word *curious*: "and the fish suspending themselves so curiously below there . . and the beautiful curious liquid." The fish and the liquid, like the child, share an inviting strangeness. As he grows through April and May, everything becomes "part of him," while the other half of the paradox—his becoming a part of them—has seemingly been forgotten. The child seems receptive, yet undisturbed by what he receives, much as the pond receives the fish.

At that point come three images of manhood and womanhood, in relatively quick succession.

> And the old drunkard staggering home from the outhouse of the tavern
>   whence he had lately risen,
> And the schoolmistress that passed on her way to the school . . and the

> friendly boys that passed . . and the quarrelsome boys . . and the tidy
>   and freshcheeked girls . . and the barefoot negro boy and girl,
> And all the changes of city and country wherever he went.
>
> His own parents . . he that had propelled the fatherstuff at night, and
>   fathered him . . and she that conceived him in her womb and birthed
>   him . . . . they gave this child more of themselves than that,
> They gave him afterward every day . . . . they and of them became part
>   of him.

The procession of male images begins with the first person the child encounters: the old drunkard, up from the outhouse—not exactly a role model. Then we meet "the friendly boys" and "the quarrelsome boys," going to school. The boys are defined by equal and opposite states of fraternity and fighting, while "the tidy and freshcheeked girls" seem meant to be looked at. To the rear, presumably poor, come the "barefoot" negro boy and girl. All seems comfortably stereotypic, like a Norman Rockwell painting, though the joining of friendly with quarrelsome boys anticipates his father's mercurial temperament, while the schoolmistress and the girls anticipate his mother's tidy calm. The effect of this list is to promote our sense of the child's perceptive, inclusive detachment from any social image of gender.

Only at this point, in a third stanza just two lines long, do we meet the child's parents. They come to us, and to him, as abstract, biological stereotypes: father propels "the fatherstuff"; mother conceives and births him. The tone conveys a retrospective, rather impersonal gratitude. They "gave this child more of themselves" than simply fatherstuff or birthing, the poet says affectionately and impatiently, as if taken aback that anyone could doubt it. Yet the next line begins, rather ambiguously, "They gave him afterward every day." It could mean that afterward they gave to him, every day. Or, the more straightforward reading implies that their gift was simply time, the "afterward" of ongoing days, somehow equivalent to their gift of themselves, as "they and of them became part of him." Again there is no mention of the child's becoming part of them, nor will there be for the rest of the poem. Instead, he already includes his parents in his steady journey beyond them.

At last, after the child has absorbed his parents, we find out who they are. The abrupt contrast between mother and father makes father seem all the more jolting and scary. Whitman's adjectives take the child on a quick downhill slide from artisan conventions of manhood to the reality of blows and shouts: "The father, strong, selfsufficient, manly, mean, angered, unjust, / The blow, the quick loud word." Then comes a sudden swerve, demeaning father's business practices: "the tight bargain, the crafty lure." It all comes as a shock, at least to me, even on rereading. But the poet's voice smoothly carries the boy on, treating the father as just a part of the house, like the furniture:

> The family usages, the language, the company, the furniture . . . .
>   the yearning and swelling heart,
> Affection that will not be gainsayed . . . . The sense of what is real . . . .
>   the thought if after all it should prove unreal

"Affection that will not be gainsayed" seems to imply the boy's love for his father, despite the blows. Yet "the yearning and swelling heart," which comes first, links that affection to adolescent passions, as the heart turns outward from the family, the company, and the furniture.

The veiled ambiguity of feeling here is subtly done and quickly dropped. Instead of probing to find which of these objects or people he has strong feelings for, the child suddenly turns to a more abstracted preoccupation of adolescence: is any of this real? With that question, after flirting with being more loving than his father, he makes first his father and then himself unreal.

A series of musing doubts, by which Whitman transposes all lingering issues of feeling into questions of perception, leads to the suspended conclusion of the poem. The child, at once a wise baby and a "curious" young man, looks at all that family intensity from an immense wondering distance.

> The doubts of daytime and the doubts of nighttime . . . the curious
>   whether and how,
> Whether that which appears so is so . . . . Or is it all flashes and specks?
> Men and women crowding fast in the streets . . if they are not
>   flashes and specks what are they?

These are the last people we meet, as the child tussles with appearance vs. reality in the midst of adults pressing toward adult ends. The rest of the poem drifts off through urban objects to shadows and the ocean, anticipating the child's death as a final merger of his life with the reader: "And these become of him or her that peruses them now."

It is a strangely touching poem, not much commented on.[58] Part of what touches me is the poem's serene, controlled enfolding of the father's threat. The child goes forth from his father, never to return, while he moves more continuously with womb, mother, and ocean. After the child reduces father to an experience no more or less important than anything else he meets, he reduces everything still further, to "flashes and specks." Father recedes to a mote in the mind's eye, which can absorb everything yet make anything unreal.

The mother's tidy quiet and "wholesome odor" have a place in the poem's sense of growing, too, perhaps more than Whitman's claims for abstracted distancing and blurred merger let us see. I imagine the mother as someone who tries to tidy up everything emotional, rather ineffectually on the surface, placating father and protecting her boy. Yet she loves her man's moods, because his irascible out-of-control rages make her feel more in control. Father was one of "the quarrelsome boys," just a type, as mother and son both know. She gives her child a loving watchfulness and a calm disengagement from stress—both in the game and out of it. From her he gains the capacity to be double: serenely looking down at his father, while looking up at him, afraid. As Mitchell Breitwieser nicely puts it in a different context, "What we call 'Whitman' is always both the blessing sun and one of the naked, helpless things it blesses."[59]

Embracing and transcending emotional tensions by its absorptive detachment, the poem also voices Whitman's doubling with complex power. It joins a baby's first sense of the world, whether as flashes and specks or what William James called "a blooming, buzzing confusion," with a mature man's alertness to his own changing mind. More deeply, the poem awakens an Oedipal pleasure: to gain power over a dangerous, unloving father simply by a fluid attentiveness to life as it happens by. Like Bartleby's nonchalance, it effectively "unmans" the conventional man. As an imaginative transformation of fear into serenity it offers both a tidelike comfort and a lurking, quite pleasurable malice. When one is faced with a tightfisted father, a lazy receptivity might well be the best revenge.

Unlike Emerson's similar strategy of detached incorporation, Whitman's has an artisan's muscle as well as an entrepreneur's expansiveness. As important as supplanting his father in the home was working as a newspaperman, then as a housebuilder and contractor in the years just before Whitman found his original poetic voice. He had to rebel not only against his father's threatening presence, or at least the memory of it, but against the more diffuse cultural oppression of the patrician world of letters. Whitman's revolutionary language, Paul Zweig says, was "not only literary but class warfare." As Whitman once said to Horace Traubel, "I resolved at the start to diagnose, recognize, state, the case of the mechanics, laborers, artisans, of America—to get into the stream with them—to give them a voice in literature: not an echoed voice—no: their own voice—that which they had never had before.... to welcome them to their legitimate superior place—to give them entrance and lodgement by all fair means."[60]

Yet it was warfare in the strangest of modes: a fusion of love and death, an elegiac celebration of the artisan in the city. Whitman's "sprawling, entrepreneurial poems of the 1850s" celebrated a world that was fading, as both Zweig and M. Wynn Thomas emphasize. If Walter Whitman, Sr., who failed as an artisan carpenter, symbolized its decline, his son's voice caresses the alienated fragmentation of urban life as if the whole nation were just a traditional village street, full of friendly yet curious passersby.[61] In short, Whitman's genial receptivity fends off social as well as personal conflicts. Emphasizing his personal contexts can highlight the class and psychological tensions latent in his idea of self, though subsumed in his majestically promenading poses of love and self-love.

No obvious psychological pattern links Thoreau and Whitman to Emerson. If one forced it, one could argue that all three men shared a common childhood matrix in which mothers may have supported their sons' self-reliant challenges to men who at first seemed awesome or scary, then who lost their sons' respect. Emerson does not seem to have found such strength in his mother, however, and Thoreau's father resembles William Emerson in neither status nor severity. He seems to have been a quiet and easygoing artisan, rather anxious about money and rather dominated by his wife. Thoreau kept looking for awesome fathers and being disappointed, especially in Emerson. As he read Emerson's letters from England while staying with Lidian and the family in 1847, his disillusionment with his mentor's conventional side may have liberated his self-reliant literary voice.[62] Unless one applies an ahistorical Oedipal model across the board, the childhood differences seem as striking as the similarities. Certainly there is no common pattern of class humiliation.

Instead, Whitman and Thoreau refract Emerson's advocacy of self-reliance through their own manly lenses, with opposite results. Thoreau champions manhood as heroic violence for truth; Whitman absorbs and transcends manhood, the source of father's fearful brutality. While his public voice champions the self by joining an artisan's insouciance with entrepreneurial brag, this poem shows Whitman's readiness for self-diffusion in response to intimate threats. The link, it seems to me, has less to do with the common patterns in childhood backgrounds or class perspectives, which in any case have to be speculatively inferred, sometimes quite arduously. Rather, the three writers share an ability to transform private feelings of humiliation into a shared public rhetoric of self-reliance. The accessibility of that rhetoric reflects the pervasiveness of individualism and middle-class aspirations among all classes.

Adopting the contradictory Emersonian blur of artisan and entrepreneurial ideologies, Thoreau and Whitman shift toward a greater radicalism. They emphasize artisan traditions of independence, not patrician hopes for empowering a new cultural elite. In my next chapter I will examine how a very different kind of Emersonian radical, Frederick Douglass, discovers the reality of class in America and shifts his sense of manhood from artisan freedom to entrepreneurial power.

4

Frederick Douglass's
Self-Refashioning

As the third of Emerson's radical contraries, Frederick Douglass offers the most extreme test case of the class and psychodynamic problems addressed in my last chapter. He was a black man and a slave, not a New England patrician. Far from having a censoriously attentive father, he was never sure who his father was. Yet by his own account he was a self-made man, strongly advocating individualism throughout his public career and insistently emphasizing manhood. When he refashions his autobiography to suit his upward mobility, his redefinition of manhood shows a startling increase in class consciousness.

The 1855 edition of Douglass's autobiography, *My Bondage and My Freedom*, is almost three times as long as his 1845 *Narrative*, not only because he added another ten years of life but because he extensively revised the first version. He took special care with the climactic moment in his *Narrative*, his fight with the slave breaker Covey. In both versions he identifies this as the experience that made him a man. A close reading of the revision shows Douglass's discovery that manhood embraces not only an artisan ideal of independence but an entrepreneurial sense of power.

Douglass's revision also shows his new ability to appropriate the linguistic capital of his genteel audience. He now recognizes that American manhood means not freedom so much as dominance and the fear of humiliation, masked with a persona of dignified self-control. On the

surface he blends patrician gentility with his earlier passion for freedom. Underneath, his shift toward an entrepreneurial ideology of manhood reflects the rise of a new middle class to social dominance in the
antebellum Northeast. Despite his ardent, lifelong public feminism,
Douglass's preoccupation with manhood and power all but erases any
self-representation linking him to women, family, and intimacy or to
lower-class black people.

In the *Narrative*, Douglass does not say much about manhood. There,
at the end of the fight, he emphasizes his equality with Covey and his
triumphant feeling of freedom, despite the four years he would remain
a slave and the six months he would stay on with Covey. His description
of the fight is abrupt, physical, highly dramatic, almost desperate, with
a good deal of anxiety latent in the prose.

The revision emphasizes Douglass's discovery of manhood, which he
now equates with power and moral dignity. Using a striking new voice
filled with genteel self-consciousness, literary allusions, and sophisticated ironies, Douglass plays down his original representation of his
anxiety and desperation. Now he emphasizes his self-control and Covey's humiliation. He refashions himself as a master not only of Covey
but of his white Christian audience's cultured language. He thereby
demonstrates his linguistic as well as physical control. He shows that
he is more Christian, more self-disciplined, and more manly than his
bullying master. Under Douglass's seemingly relaxed gentility lies his
new understanding, which he states explicitly, that manly dignity depends not on freedom but on the ability to use "force" and "power."
"A man, without force, is without the essential dignity of humanity,"
he now concludes. "Human nature is so constituted, that it cannot *honor*
a helpless man, although it can *pity* him; and even this it cannot do
long, if the signs of power do not arise."[1]

I

The rewriting of the fight is worth examining in considerable detail.
The 1845 account of it comes at the end of one paragraph, several
pages long. The fight climaxes the paragraph's description of some
continuous incidents involving Covey, all framed by Douglass's remark
in the previous paragraph: "You have seen how a man was made a
slave; you shall see how a slave was made a man."[2]

Douglass's voice is simple, direct, familiar, yet with a certain balanced formality. He writes as if he were speaking to an audience both sympathetic and more sophisticated than he can claim to be. Part of the drama of the fight, in fact, is his depiction of a self caught between unsophisticated slaves and a tyrannical white master. How can he become free not just physically but mentally? How can be become a man whom white readers can respect?For him these questions are synonymous, as the second edition makes clear. The strength and limitation of the fight description in the *Narrative*, which most readers find more gripping, lies in his restriction of the drama to the struggle between him and Covey, without articulating the implied struggle for respect from his readers.

Douglass leads up to the fight by describing his escapes from Covey, to whom his master had "put me out, as he said, to be broken" (*N* 69). Douglass ran away, returned, and ran away again. On his next return he happened to visit Sandy Jenkins, "a slave with whom I was somewhat acquainted." Sandy Jenkins "told me, with great solemnity, I must go back to Covey," but with "a certain *root*, which, if I would take some of it with me, carrying it *always on my right side*, would render it impossible for Mr. Covey, or any other white man, to whip me." The sixteen-year-old boy first resists the idea. "To please him," however, Douglass agrees (*N* 80–81).

As the runaway returns, Covey surprises him by speaking kindly. Could it be the root? No, Douglass recollects that it is Sunday, and Covey, like so many other brutal masters, claims to be a churchgoing Christian. On Monday, then, "the virtue of the *root* was fully tested" (*N* 81).

So far Douglass has defined his self-consciousness largely in ambivalent relation to Sandy Jenkins. He clearly feels superior to the slave's traditional superstitiousness, yet he is not altogether sure that the root wouldn't work. His behavior also reflects ambivalence about obeying Covey. While Douglass keeps distancing himself from the root by italicizing it, he confesses a tentative receptiveness to Sandy Jenkins's suggestion, as well as a tentative resolve to be more obedient. "Long before daylight" on Monday morning, when he is called to go care for the horses, he "obeyed, and was glad to obey" (*N* 81).

Then Covey seizes him with a rope.

> As soon as I found what he was up to, I gave a sudden spring, and as I did so, he holding to my legs, I was brought sprawling on the stable floor. Mr. Covey seemed now to think he had me, and could do what he

pleased; but at this moment—from whence came the spirit I don't know—I resolved to fight; and, suiting my action to the resolution, I seized Covey hard by the throat, and as I did so, I rose. He held on to me, and I to him. My resistance was so entirely unexpected, that Covey seemed taken all aback. He trembled like a leaf. This gave me assurance, and I held him uneasy, causing the blood to run where I touched him with the ends of my fingers. (N 81–82)

This passage is highly dramatic: simple, short phrases filled with action, interlaced with suppressed emotional uncertainty. Douglass first calls him "Mr. Covey." Then, much less deferentially, "I seized Covey hard by the throat." That resolution comes at the end of a long, suspended sentence whose phrases hold action in abeyance until the end, when "I seized him" and "I rose." Next three short, punchy sentences reverse Covey's initial thrust. The syntax effectively mirrors the fighting.

In the midst of the action, however, a certain self-consciousness and formal distancing persist. Douglass wonders, at least retrospectively, "from whence came the spirit" to fight. Stylistically we can see Douglass's spirit in his verbs: "I resolved ... I seized ... I rose." A six-foot boy is beginning to feel his manhood. Yet Douglass is not at all firm in his resolve. Only when Covey "trembled like a leaf" does he start to feel "assurance. "

That assurance is not very assured. In the last sentence's ambiguous phrasing, "I held him uneasy, causing the blood to run where I touched him with the ends of my fingers." The syntax implies Douglass is as "uneasy" as Covey; the word points both ways. After all, it was a dangerous matter to assault one's master—an act punishable by death, Douglass later declares (N 101–102). Here he backs off from his first rush of assertiveness, "I seized Covey hard by the throat," to the much more equivocal, almost diffident verbs, "held him," "touched him," or even less, touched him only with the "ends" of his fingers, which, seemingly without intention, were "causing the blood to run." The drama and the anxiety of combat exist here in equal measure. Beneath, of course, lies the deeper anxiety of a young black man daring to challenge white authority.

Douglass's revision is quite different. At the onset, called to care for the horses on Monday morning, Douglass no longer presents himself as someone happy to obey. Now he simply "was obeying his order." Covey enters not with dramatic suddenness but as the stock villain, heavily loaded with biblical metaphors: "Covey sneaked into the stable, in his peculiar snake-like way" (*MB* 149). Instead of emphasizing the physical drama of the rope, which he briefly defers, Douglass stresses Covey's moral inferiority. His tone puts him in control, from the start.[3]

The rest of the paragraphs—and there are many paragraphs here— expand Douglass's sense of control. He shifts the drama from physical combat to a class conflict: gentility being affronted by one of the lower sort.

> I now forgot my *roots*, and remembered my pledge to *stand up in my own defense*. The brute was endeavoring skillfully to get a slip-knot on my legs, before I could draw up my feet. As soon as I found what he was up to, I gave a sudden spring, (my two day's rest had been of much service to me,) and by that means, no doubt, he was able to bring me to the floor so heavily. He was defeated in his plan of tying me. While down, he seemed to think he had me very securely in his power. He little thought he was—as the rowdies say—"in" for a "rough and tumble" fight; but such was the fact. Whence came the daring spirit necessary to grapple with a man who, eight-and-forty hours before, could, with his slightest word have made me tremble like a leaf in a storm, I do not know; at any rate, *I was resolved to fight*, and, what was better still, I was actually hard at it. The fighting madness had come upon me, and I found my strong fingers firmly attached to the throat of my cowardly tormentor; as heedless of consequences, at the moment, as though we stood as equals before the law. The very color of the man was forgotten. I felt as supple as a cat, and was ready for the snakish creature at every turn. Every blow of his was parried, though I dealt no blows in turn. I was strictly on the *defensive*, preventing him from injuring me, rather than trying to injure him. I flung him on the ground several times, when he meant to have hurled me there. I held him so firmly by the throat, that his blood followed my nails. He held me, and I held him. (*MB* 149)

In this passage, only part of the equivalent excerpt from the first version, Douglass shows no uncertainty either about the root or about fighting Covey. Covey, whose plans are "defeated" right from the start, is a low-class "brute," a "cowardly tormentor," and a "snakish creature" from first to last. Throughout, too, Douglass seems remarkably at ease, both aggressively controlling the fight and patronizingly above it. A genteel chumminess with the reader pervades his narration, especially in his gratuitous aside, "He little thought he was—as the rowdies say— 'in' for a 'rough and tumble' fight." Such phrasing titillates genteel readers with the spectacle of one of their own able to mix it up on equal terms with a rowdy.

That particular sentence has much the same tone as Harriet Beecher Stowe's self-conscious entry into Aunt Chloe's kitchen, in chapter 4 of

Uncle Tom's Cabin. Stowe makes the narrator's genteel self-consciousness, and her admiring patronage of Chloe's exotic language, quite
explicit:

> Let us enter the dwelling. The evening meal at the house is over, and
> Aunt Chloe, who presided over its preparation as head cook, has left
> to inferior officers in the kitchen the business of clearing away and
> washing dishes, and come out into her own snug territories, to "get her
> ole man's supper"; therefore, doubt not that it is her you see by the
> fire, presiding with anxious interest over certain frizzling items in a
> stew-pan, and anon with grave consideration lifting the cover of a bake-
> kettle, from whence steam forth indubitable intimations of "something
> good."[4]

Here is gentility at its most genial, poised between a patronizing mockery of a black slave's pretensions to be a general and a wholehearted
admiration of Chloe as quintessential woman, in command of her natural turf. The first vernacular quotation, "get her old man's supper,"
precipitates Stowe's extravagantly ornate linguistic recoil: "therefore,
doubt not that it is her you see by the fire, presiding . . . and anon with
grave consideration lifting . . . from whence steam forth indubitable in-
timations . . . " If there is mockery of pretentiousness here, it goes both
ways. The homely nouns of the kitchen—"stew-pan," "bake-kettle"—
deflate the narrator's parlor pomposities.

The result is a curious double message. One affirms a class hierarchy
with the narrator and reader securely perched at the top, watching
Chloe and her still more "inferior officers" bustling at the bottom to
serve her man after they have served the whites. Within this hierarchy,
another message affirms and respects the majesty and glory of women's
experience in the kitchen. What seems to be humble *can* be exalted;
what seems to be high can be brought low. The passage is one of the
subtlest, most concrete renderings of Stowe's "last shall be first" evangelism, her glorification of women's experience, and her narrative uses
of class hierarchy to frame these effects.[5]

Feminists have emphasized such "duplicity," that is, the speaking of
contradictory messages with equal zeal, as a uniquely female strategy
for nineteenth-century Anglo-American writers. Frederick Douglass,
however, also uses genteel language and class consciousness to bring
about a reversal much like Stowe's, with a similar double message. In
one message, he allies himself with the reader to confirm how high he
has risen, how from the last he has joined the first. Covey is the brute;
he is the rightful master, in part because he is the master of himself.

His voice displays a relaxed sophistication. Among other things, *My Bondage and My Freedom* demonstrates that genteel discourse should not necessarily be equated with feminization, though Stowe certainly takes it in that direction. Douglass appropriates it to display his new-found manly dignity.

The other message, much more blatantly than in Stowe's affirmation of women's commanding the kitchen, displays a frank aggressiveness. While he claims to be "strictly on the *defensive*," parrying Covey's blows but never dealing them out, Douglass also declares himself "as supple as a cat," and curtly records, "I flung him on the ground several times." He switches the image of the trembling leaf from Covey, whose quivering in the first version gave young Douglass some much needed assurance, to his own previously cowardly self "eight-and-forty hours before," when Covey could have made him tremble. The shift reinforces his own firmness now. In both these seemingly contradictory messages, his genteel self-control and his aggressiveness, Douglass displays a newfound sense of power, felt as both dignity and dominance.

When I first read Douglass's claim to be "strictly on the defensive" while fighting Covey, I laughed out loud. The assertion seemed so improbable as to look like deliberate posturing, especially since the claim is missing from the first version. Why would he emphasize his defensiveness here and, more flagrantly, later in the revision, when he kicks another white man but remains defensive toward Covey?

In the most obvious explanation, Douglass is anxious about being blamed for fighting a white man. He takes care to allay any hint that a black man's dangerous rebelliousness is going beyond proper bounds. His anxious repetition of his claim to be merely defensive exposes the fragility of his genteel voice and of his bond with the reader. For several years I interpreted the passage along those lines.[6]

But two factors call that interpretation into question. For one thing, both autobiographies conspicuously minimize the danger of being punished for fighting a white man. If, as he says, the penalty for striking a white man is death, the *Narrative* tucks that information away in the midst of a much later fight, and *My Bondage and My Freedom* mentions it only at the end of this incident, as Douglass muses over Covey's unwillingness ever to prosecute the matter.[7] Since Douglass does kick the other white man, the issue seems unimportant both to his self-consciousness at the time and to his later self-presentation. Second, and perhaps more crucial, though harder to judge, his tone seems too much at ease for such anxiety. His expansive, playful fraternity with white genteel readers seems too comprehensive to be so brittle.

I think the more likely interpretation is that Douglass wants to emphasize his mastery of every aspect of the situation, even when his claim for self-control might seem improbable to the point of comedy. He wants to show that he could remember and respect the law—don't hit someone in authority—while actually fighting his boss, who seems not to respect anything except his church-going self-image. Douglass also wants to show that he was forcing Covey to a draw with the equivalent of one hand tied behind his back. In every way, the former slave presents himself as mentally as well as physically Covey's superior, from his agile parrying to his self-restraint to his rather prissy tone.

One can do still more with the long passage I've quoted. In describing how he first seizes Covey, Douglass's revisions accentuate his self-distancing, as if one self were watching another doing the fighting. The first version declares simply, "I resolved to fight; and, suiting my action to the resolution, I seized Covey hard by the throat; and as I did so, I rose." The second: "At any rate, *I was resolved to fight*, and, what was better still, I was actually hard at it. The fighting madness had come upon me, and I found my strong fingers firmly attached to the throat of my cowardly tormentor; as heedless of consequences, at the moment, as though we stood as equals before the law." Disowning the straight-forward thrust of the first version, Douglass shifts the focus toward his self-consciousness. A sophisticated, urbane man seems startled and delighted to discover that his body has a will for fisticuffs. The italics for "I was resolved to fight" emphasize its importance yet also its unusualness, as though he has to talk himself into a shout. His next phrase—"and, what was better still, I was actually hard at it"—also implies some self-distancing. Under the sophisticated veneer one can detect Douglass saying the equivalent of, "Gee, look at that. I'm actually fighting!" He continues the distancing by calling it the "fighting madness," which "had come upon me," and he concludes his narration of bemused self-discovery by noting that "I found my strong fingers" oddly attached to Covey's throat. Immediately comes another self-conscious reflection: "as though we stood as equals before the law."

Here Douglass presents himself as a man of refined culture hurried half unawares into action. He seems at a distance from his body and at a great distance from anger. His self-presentation has as much to do with his ability to appropriate the language and self-image of a genteel reader as with the sixteen-year-old boy who fought the slave breaker. He is having it both ways: defending himself, while remaining above the fray. Disowning anxiety, anger, and aggressiveness has now become a settled rhetorical tactic of self-control, not an ongoing dramatic ambivalence.

At the same time, however, the syntax continues to present Douglass as much more aggressive. When he actually draws blood from Covey, Douglass removes all hint of being "uneasy." He concludes his paragraph with three terse sentences: "I flung him on the ground several times, when he meant to have hurled me there. I held him so firmly by the throat, that his blood followed my nails. He held me, and I held him." In the first sentence, Douglass flings Covey down, returning and reversing Covey's intention. In the second sentence Douglass's body is firmly in charge, right down to his nails: where they led, Covey's blood "followed." The last sentence shows the two antagonists at a standstill, syntactically as well as physically immobilized. Equality has been achieved, on the ground and in the balanced phrasing.

The genteel comedy of mastery continues. "My resistance was entirely unexpected, and Covey was taken all aback by it, for he trembled in every limb." Deleting the inspiriting effect of Covey's trembling on him, Douglass instead adds some dialogue. " '*Are you going to resist*, you scoundrel?' said he. To which, I returned a polite '*Yes sir*;' steadily gazing my interrogator in the eye" (*MB* 149). If the fight has proved Douglass's physical equality, his voice dramatizes his genteel cool. The joke, once again, is the reversal of roles: master is the scoundrel, while slave is the dignified "sir." What might seem to twentieth-century readers like a put-on fits nicely into nineteenth-century readers' expectations for ostensibly deferential self-control. It also fits Douglass's new self-image. He is a writer now, attuned to the conventions of genteel irony.

Unable to defeat this strapping boy by himself, Covey calls for help. Here again the two versions strikingly diverge. In the 1845 *Narrative*, "Mr. Covey soon called out to Hughes for help. Hughes came, and, while Covey held me, attempted to tie my right hand. While he was in the act of doing so, I watched my chance, and gave him a heavy kick close under the ribs. This kick fairly sickened Hughes, so that he left me in the hands of Mr. Covey" (*N* 82). As before, Douglass's emphasis is on physical action, dramatically rendered in short, pithy phrases. The drama is that of a canny underdog getting even. Douglass's continuing ambivalence about authority quietly manifests itself once more in his alternation between "Mr. Covey" and "Covey."

The "Mr.," like the uncertainty and the sense of being an underdog, disappears in the 1855 version:

> He called for his cousin Hughes, to come to his assistance, and now the scene was changed. I was compelled to give blows, as well as to parry them; and, since I was, in any case, to suffer for resistance, I felt (as the musty proverb goes) that "I might as well be hanged for an old sheep as a lamb." I was still *defensive* toward Covey, but *aggressive* toward Hughes; and, at the first approach of the latter, I dealt a blow, in my desperation, which fairly sickened my youthful assailant. He went off, bending over with pain, and manifesting no disposition to come within my reach again. The poor fellow was in the act of trying to catch and tie my right hand, and while flattering himself with success, I gave him the kick which sent him staggering away in pain, at the same time that I held Covey with a firm hand. (*MB* 149–150)

The parenthetical aside to the reader, "as the musty proverb goes," gives the game away. Forswearing the tense immediacy of the first version, Douglass is after bigger game than drama now: not winning a fight with Covey but appropriating the reader's language and status. The passage seems elephantine in its self-congratulation. Douglass pities the "poor fellow" Hughes even as he kicks him, and "he left me in the hands of Mr. Covey" changes to "I held Covey with a firm hand." He shows no hint of fear, or even of suspense. Douglass's voice seems everywhere at ease and confident, almost breezy. The tone belies his assertion, at the moment of kicking Hughes, that he dealt the blow "in my desperation." That was the self of the first version. Here it survives only in a phrase, not in the voice or the action.

The culmination of Douglass's implicit mastery comes in the next paragraph, where his revision turns an uncertain combat into an overwrought barnyard joke. Douglass tells Covey he means to resist; he refuses to be treated like a brute any longer. The first version has Douglass reporting what was said, while the second gives direct dialogue, one of the few changes promoting dramatic immediacy. Then Covey reaches for a stick to knock Douglass down. The first version reads: "But just as he was leaning over to get the stick, I seized him with both hands by his collar, and brought him by a sudden snatch to the ground" (*N* 82). Here is the second version: "But, just as he leaned over to get the stick, I seized him with both hands by the collar, and, with a vigorous and sudden snatch, I brought my assailant harmlessly, his full length, on the *not over* clean ground—for we were now in the cow yard. He had selected the place for the fight, and it was but right that he should have all the advantages of his own selection" (*MB* 150). First Douglass adds "harmlessly," continuing his emphasis on how defensive and respectful he could be toward his "assailant" in the midst of a knock-down brawl. As before, that claim helps to demonstrate Douglass's dominance, this time with the spice of complete humiliation. He has flung the slave breaker into cow shit. Not content with that triumph, he adds a heavy-handed piece of irony, saying the equivalent of "Covey got what he chose" in much more ponderous diction. Ostensibly voicing his sense of justice and fairness, Douglass rubs in his ability to turn the tables. He is the master, and the proof of his dominance is Covey's humiliation.

This is a new sense of power and a striking self-refashioning. As before, Douglass's double message reinforces both his genteel dignity and his physical dominance. His goal is no longer to present the drama of a fight for self-respect but to affirm the self that has risen so far from that fight. Looking benignly down on the crude tussle, Douglass takes a great many stylistic pains to exhibit his ability to control himself as well as his master. An intermittent but unmistakable delight in humiliating Covey coexists with a more pervasive tone of genteel amusement at the raffish doings of his self gone by.

The result of the fight is relatively anticlimactic, though Douglass's revision draws it out at much more length. Covey appeals to several blacks, male and female, who rebuff him. "We were all in open rebellion, that morning." Finally, after two hours, Covey lets the boy go, claiming to have whipped him. As Douglass proudly reminds his readers, "He had not, in all the scuffle, drawn a single drop of blood from me," whereas Douglass had drawn blood from him. Once more Douglass takes care to repeat, rubbing in his power, that he had drawn blood while restraining himself, since "my aim had not been to injure him, but to prevent his injuring me" (*MB* 151).

During the remainder of the six months, Covey never attempted any more physical discipline with Douglass, nor did he raise the matter in any way. Douglass infers that Covey was probably not only ashamed of failing to win but afraid that his reputation as a slave breaker would be irreparably harmed. In the second version Douglass adds that he sometimes tried to goad him into another fight. "It is, perhaps, not altogether creditable to my natural temper, that, after this conflict with Mr. Covey [note the "Mr." now], I did, at times, purposely aim to provoke him to an attack, ... but I could never bully him to another battle" (*MB* 152–153). The happy transition from cowed boy to "bully" shows how completely Douglass has won his new sense of manhood.

The 1845 *Narrative* presents the fight as one long blur, in one long paragraph. A second, short paragraph supplies the interpretive framing, by linking manhood with freedom and resurrection. The 1855 version, after many paragraphs that demonstrate Douglass's interpretive control, significantly alters and intensifies his emphasis on manhood, now linked to force, dignity, and power. Here is Douglass's first conclusion:

> This battle with Mr. Covey was the turning-point in my career as a slave. It rekindled the few expiring embers of freedom, and revived within me a sense of my own manhood. It recalled the departed self-confidence, and inspired me again with a determination to be free.... It was a glorious resurrection, from the tomb of slavery, to the heaven of freedom. My long-crushed spirit rose, cowardice departed, bold defiance took its place; and I now resolved that, however long I might remain a slave in form, the day had passed forever when I could be a slave in fact. (*N* 82–83)

This series of pithy allegorical oppositions does not especially highlight manhood, which stands as the preliminary term for other more specific words: self-confidence, freedom, defiance. The real center is not manhood but his conversion experience. In the midst of his "career as a slave," a nice irony implicitly predicting a second and higher career, a dead self has been resurrected, brought back to life. Despite Douglass's reliance on cliches not felt as cliches, as a student once put it, the passage is effective in part because it simplifies and clarifies his emotional uncertainties. His new firmness of resolve finds an appropriate echo in the firmness of his eloquent antithesis: temporarily "a slave in form" but nevermore "a slave in fact."

The second version may give readers something of a shock. Not only does Douglass's high-minded prissiness move to higher ground, but his claims for manhood nearly eclipse his previous emphasis on freedom and resurrection.

> Well, my dear reader, this battle with Mr. Covey,—undignified as it was, and as I fear my narration of it is— was the turning point in my "*life as a slave.*" It rekindled in my breast the smouldering embers of liberty; it brought up my Baltimore dreams, and revived a sense of my own manhood. I was a changed being after that fight. I was *nothing*

before; I was A MAN NOW. It recalled to life my crushed self-respect and my self-confidence, and inspired me with a renewed determination to be A FREEMAN. A man, without force, is without the essential dignity of humanity. Human nature is so constituted, that it cannot *honor* a helpless man, although it can *pity* him; and even this it cannot do long, if the signs of power do not arise. (*MB* 151).

To his credit, Douglass removes "Well, my dear reader" from his third edition, in 1892. Otherwise, except for deleting the italics for "life as a slave," the passage remains unchanged. It presents Douglass's self-refashioning in exceptionally exaggerated form, as the double message he intends it to be. He is a respectable man who knows how to use genteel instead of "undignified" language. He also knows how crucial the use of force is to the "dignity" of manhood.

On the surface, all Douglass's revisions seem prompted by his explicit wish to dignify his narration of what seems to him now a vulgar experience. Nevertheless, Douglass's emphasis on manhood shows that his sense of dignity has more to do with power than with decorum. To gain "honor" from white genteel readers, the real constituency for power in America, he has to demonstrate that he is a man of force as well as refinement. Without force comes the inevitability of being pitied, then being forgotten. The opposite of dignity for him is not simply vulgarity but humiliation: the spectre of being "a helpless man."

A second paragraph recasts the issues more conventionally, in terms closer to the first version. Twice Douglass declares that Covey was a "tyrant," and he reaffirms that "my long-cowed spirit was roused to an attitude of manly independence" (*MB* 151–152). Here he emphasizes his "resurrection from the dark and pestiferous tomb of slavery, to the heaven of comparative freedom" (*MB* 152), though the new adjectives tend to blunt the impact of the original. Yet Douglass's sense of what manhood means has as much to do with being what he calls, in italics, "*a power on earth*" as with being independent. Replacing "cowardice" with "bold defiance" is not enough. His earlier conversion to an artisan's sense of freedom as equality, self-confidence and defiance of tyranny now uneasily coexists with an entrepreneur's expansive sense of power. Significantly, Douglass ends his chapter with another addition, a quotation from Byron's *Childe Harold*: "Hereditary bondmen, know ye not / Who would be free, themselves must strike the blow?" The quotation recapitulates Douglass's double message. It is at once a genteel literary allusion and an unambiguous call for slaves to use force as the only way up from humiliation.

II

How can we account for such a drastic self-refashioning? Most modern readers like the *Narrative*'s voice much better. Certainly I do. The revision seems arch, smug, pretentious, excessively genteel and self-conscious, even phony. Douglass seems more concerned with presenting a self-image than describing a fight. The taut drama has been lost, for the most part, both at the level of action and at the more subtle level of voice, where the emotional tensions of the first version have given way to claims for self-control, mastery, and dignity. Why would Douglass do it?

The simplest answer would be to please his readers. Douglass wrote the 1845 autobiography partly to prove that he and his stories were real and not a fraud. He was writing for a narrowly defined abolitionist constituency and to bring other white readers into the cause. From his very first paragraph, he presumes white norms for self-presentation. His opening sentence supplies precise details about his place of birth. Then, with a deft implicit irony, he can't meet white expectations for equally precise details about time and parents: he doesn't know the year, he doesn't know his father, he saw his mother only four or five times in his life. Readers would feel shock and sympathy. In the revision, Douglass's sense of his white audience has expanded. For nearly two years he had been lionized in England, and he had broken with William Lloyd Garrison, acrimoniously so. For some years he had been publishing his own abolitionist newspaper—first called the *North Star*, then simply *Frederick Douglass's Paper*—one of the first black men to publish a newspaper in the United States. Douglass, in this interpretation, would now be reaching out to a broader-based reading public.

It therefore seems reasonable to argue that Douglass fashions a self to appeal to this wider audience. He presents himself as righteously affronted but never out of control and rarely un-Christian, even when defending himself against a Christian slaveowner. Emphasizing comedy much more than desperation, he especially enjoys employing what Henry Louis Gates, Jr., has described as a basic trope in black literature: chiasmus, or reversal.[8] The master is presented as snake, the slave as angel. Douglass's voice seems at ease with white American values of Christianity, upward mobility, elegant expression, and self-reliance. Only within that frame does he define freedom and manhood. His rebellion, Douglass implies, has happily made a self worthy of his audience.

Yet the second edition did not sell as well. Whereas the *Narrative* sold thirty thousand copies in the first five years, *My Bondage and My Freedom* sold only eighteen thousand copies in the first two years, after which sales apparently tapered off.[9] Of course one could say that Douglass had misjudged his readers or that people did not want to buy the second edition if they had read the first. Or one could say that readers who prefer the first version, then and now, indulge their racism. The exotic spectacle of an angry, anxious young black boy struggling to rise out of great physical difficulties has more appeal than the mature dignity of a cultivated black man unabashedly at ease among the high bourgeoisie.

There may be some truth in both arguments, but on balance, it seems more likely that Douglass made his revisions primarily to please himself, not his readers. If anything, the 1845 *Narrative* seems written out of an ambivalent need to comply with his abolitionist audience's expectations, and to gain their approval.

William Lloyd Garrison's preface makes the audience expectations very clear. He promises readers that Douglass's story will secure their "sympathy and affection . . . by the many sufferings he has endured, by his virtuous traits of character, by his ever-abiding remembrance of those who are in bonds, as being bound with them!" In short, readers can expect a narrative in the tradition of the heroic fugitive, though Douglass gives no details of his actual flight until the third edition. For Garrison, Douglass stands as the type of the Christ-like, tormented slave, bonded to his fellow sufferers rather than to his readers. His stories will bring the audience to tears with "his pathos" or rouse complacent readers "to virtuous indignation by his stirring eloquence against the enslavers of men!" By his eloquence Douglass will also prove he is "a MAN," not a thing. The fact that his high attainments have come from "but a comparatively small amount of cultivation" gives the lie to a slave code that makes him "a piece of property, a beast of burden, a chattel personal" (*N* v–vi).

The rest of Garrison's rather florid preface speaks as much of Garrison as of Douglass. Garrison all but overtly announces himself as Pygmalion for the untutored youth he has discovered and raised so high. Throughout, he says, Douglass "has borne himself with gentleness and meekness, yet with true manliness of character." Properly docile to his abolitionist betters, in other words, he can be allowed to expose his previous masters. Douglass seems to be living proof both of the brutalizing effects of slavery and of any slave's potential for self-improvement, properly

guided, "considering...how few have been his opportunities to improve his mind since he broke his iron fetters" (*N* viii–ix). To state
Garrison's ostensibly sympathetic innuendo more crudely: Douglass's
simple style shows that the former slave remains more brutalized than
self-improved. In a left-handed way, the remark indicates the depth
of genteel disdain for direct, uncomplicated, dramatic narration. Garrison seems to be apologizing to his readers, much as Douglass would
later apologize for his "undignified" telling after he had taken such
care to remove the first version's marks of unsophistication.

Above all, Douglass represents to Garrison a man's unquenchable
desire for freedom. The *Narrative*'s "most thrilling" passage, Garrison
declares, "is the description DOUGLASS gives of his feelings, as he stood
soliloquizing respecting his fate, and the chances of his one day being
a freeman, on the banks of the Chesapeake Bay—viewing the receding
vessels as they flew with their white wings before the breeze, and apos-
trophizing them as animated by the living spirit of freedom. Who can
read that passage, and be insensible to its pathos and sublimity?" (*N*
xi). To stress the "pathos" of a black boy dreaming of "white wings"
indicates the presumption of white superiority implicit in Garrison's,
and Douglass's, idea of freedom. For both men, those "receding" wings
seem "animated by the living spirit of freedom." Waldo Martin's intellectual biography, *The Mind of Frederick Douglass*, offers many examples of Garrison's arrogant, often racist paternalism.[10]

Garrison's expectations give Douglass little room for complex individuality and almost no room for aggressiveness or imagination. "I am
confident that it is essentially true in all its statements," Garrison affirms,
"that nothing has been set down in malice, nothing exaggerated, nothing drawn from the imagination" (*N* x). Douglass partly conforms to
Garrison's militant pacifism in recounting his representative, docu-
mentable experiences. Yet he also partly resists. While no one has ever
proved Douglass wrong about the incidents he describes, recent scholarship has made it clear that some of his character portraits, especially
of his master Thomas Auld, were indeed maliciously exaggerated.
Douglass himself acknowledged as much in his later years.

At three key points in Douglass's *Narrative*, one can read between
the lines to see Thomas Auld's decisive intervention in his favor: when
he is "the first, last, and only choice" from all the slaves to go to Baltimore, when he is sent back to Master Hugh instead of to vicious Master
Andrew, and especially when he miraculously is returned to Baltimore
instead of being killed or sent down south after his abortive rebellion.

In each case, Douglass perfunctorily thanks "Providence" (*N* 47, 61) or "some cause or other" (*N* 99). Denying any dependence, he lays into Auld with relish and vitriol. He stresses his master's severity instead of his solicitude partly, Dickson J. Preston suggests, to express a certain hot-headed rebelliousness in his own temper. As Preston also says, Douglass's eagerness to please his audience could have shaped the "malice" in his narration. Douglass may have exaggerated his account of Auld's Christian cruelty to conform to the abolitionists's expectations for stories about brutal slaveowners.[11]

One can see here a larger dimension to the *Narrative*'s expression of ambivalence about obeying or rebelling against Covey. Obeying and rebelling against white masters constituted a basic pattern of Douglass's life, until he broke with Garrison and assumed his full public stance of self-reliance. The abolitionists wanted him to keep his plantation speech and stick to the facts of slavery. Instead, resolutely dignified, formal, and savvy from the first, Douglass soon came to assert himself as an independent public man. As he did so, his changing sense of manhood shaped his changing sense of himself. From the first, he chooses to present himself in the manly image of a self-made loner.

Ostensibly his break with Garrison came over two political issues. Wendell Phillips's "Letter" prefacing the *Narrative* makes explicit what Garrison's conclusion implies, that in their view the Constitution was a proslavery document and therefore of no moral validity. Phillips explicitly calls for secession, declaring that he would welcome the day when New England would be "cutting loose from a blood-stained Union" (*N* xviii). More practically, Garrison and his group urged people not to vote.

In the late 1840s Douglass came to think that the Constitution could guarantee black rights. After the *Narrative* was published Douglass went to England for twenty-one months, partly to evade any possible capture. Returning in 1847, a much more worldly man as well as a more accomplished writer and speaker, he almost immediately began to quarrel with Garrison. Waldo Martin notes the father-son dynamics in their controversies, as did Douglass himself.[12] The former slave who had presented himself as a man of sorrows, graphically describing the gashes in his feet big enough to put a pen in, was becoming a man of letters as well as a canny man of power.

The decisive split came not only over the issues of voting and the Constitution but also over Douglass's increasingly vehement argument for other kinds of political action, including the use of force. His 1853 novella, *The Heroic Slave*, celebrates an 1841 revolt on a slave ship.[13] From 1848 on, he had become friends with John Brown, who stayed with Douglass for three weeks in 1858, perhaps while he was planning his 1859 raid on the arsenal at Harper's Ferry. A direct link has never been proved. Nonetheless, Douglass prudently fled to Canada for a time after Brown was captured.

A black boy aching for white wings had become an astute and embattled political manipulator, well aware of the need for a dignified public persona. Douglass had also discovered the realities of class. His ambitions had developed well beyond the "gentleness and meekness" Garrison had prescribed for him. Where Garrison had stressed Douglass's yearning for freedom as the boy looked at those white sails, another kind of yearning appears several times in the *Narrative*: to be a man in the "big house."

Early in the *Narrative*, toward the end of chapter 2, Douglass describes the slaves' reverence for what they called "the *Great House Farm*," Colonel Lloyd's extravagantly august plantation mansion. "Into all of their songs they would manage to weave something of the Great House Farm. Especially would they do this, when leaving home. They would then sing most exultingly the following words:—'I am going away to the Great House Farm! / O, yea! O, yea! O!'" Only when he was outside what he calls "the circle" of slave experience, Douglass says, did he begin to understand the woe in these songs, which "always depressed my spirit, and filled me with ineffable sadness." The songs gave him "my first glimmering conception of the dehumanizing character of slavery" (*N* 30–32).[14] Though Douglass does not say so explicitly, he implies that the slaves' anguish of deprivation and their rapturous hopes for deliverance joined in their vision of the Great House Farm, the symbol of oppression, glory, and repose.

As usual, Douglass puts his own consciousness at a distance from slave traditions. Nonetheless, his own dreams have that song as their unstated refrain. When he was between seven and eight, he recalls, "I received the intelligence that my old master (Anthony) had determined to let me go to Baltimore, to live with Mr. Hugh Auld." Aaron Anthony was Douglass's father, as Douglass suspected and Dickson J. Preston's biography of his early years confirms. By Douglass's as well as Preston's account, Anthony had long since become a hapless and brutal man, though he seems to have favored young Frederick, as did so many other adults, white and black. Here, the thought of Baltimore fills the boy with rapture. He spends the next three days mostly in the creek, "three of the happiest days I ever enjoyed," washing "the plantation scurf" from his body, and readying himself for the new pair of trousers the master's daughter had promised him if he cleaned himself well. "I went at it in good earnest, working for the first time with the hope of reward" (44).

At this point he had no family. His mother, whom he had seen only a few times, and then mostly at night, was dead, and his grandmother, to whom he had been very close, now "lived far off, so that I seldom saw her." He felt no special ties to sisters or brother. With nothing holding him to home, Baltimore loomed as the equivalent of Colonel Lloyd's Great House, and more, since a cousin kept telling him that "even the Great House itself, with all its pictures, was far inferior to many buildings in Baltimore" (*N* 45).

When young Frederick first comes to Annapolis, "it was the first large town that I had ever seen, and though it would look small compared with some of our New England factory villages, I thought it a wonderful place for its size—more imposing even than the Great House Farm!" (*N* 46). The retrospective aside, making "our New England factory villages" the ultimate measure of imposing size, is a telling indicator of how Douglass would progressively redefine his sense of both greatness and "us." His "Baltimore dreams," as he calls them in his revised conclusion to the fight with Covey, bury his acute feelings of deprivation in a vision of happiness uniting white authority, great size, cleanliness, a large loving home, and the possibility of working with the hope of reward.

One can already see the seeds of Douglass's passionate belief in self-reliance and upward mobility. Finally, when he escapes and reaches New Bedford, his Great House dreams become staggeringly fulfilled. "Upon coming to the north," he says, "I expected to meet with a rough, hard-handed, and uncultivated population, living in the most Spartan-like simplicity." Instead, "I found myself surrounded with the strongest proofs of wealth." He saw huge ships, huge warehouses, vast size and admirable bigness on every hand. No one seemed to be poor. Moreover, everyone was hard at work, showing "a sober, yet cheerful earnestness ...a sense of his own dignity as a man." "From the wharves I strolled around and over the town, gazing with wonder and admiration at the splendid churches, beautiful dwellings, and finely-cultivated gardens; evincing an amount of wealth, comfort, taste, and refinement, such as I had never seen in any part of slaveholding Maryland" (*N* 115–116). Wealth, dignity, and big beautiful houses, he discovered, did not have to be the fruits of a plantation system. They could be the aspirations of every man.

Douglass writes with the star-struck zeal of Lincoln Steffens returning from Russia in the early 1920s. He has seen the future, of factories, shipyards, hard work and competition, and it works. A muted theme in the *Narrative* becomes the dominant contrast in his revision for *My Bondage and My Freedom*: how "noiselessly" everyone worked. In the *Narrative*, his observation about the lack of noise confirms his sense of the laborer's "sober, yet cheerful earnestness, ...his own dignity as a man." In *My Bondage*, Douglass launches into an eloquent celebration of a more impersonal form of power: the machine. "There was no loud singing, as in southern ports, where ships are loading and unloading—no loud cursing or swearing—but everything went on as smoothly as the works of a well adjusted machine. How different was all this from the noisily fierce and clumsily absurd manner of labor-life in Baltimore and St. Michaels!" So he continues, for a long paragraph, citing example after example of the quiet efficiency and "scrupulous regard to economy" in the movements of northern workers (*MB* 210–211). A class dynamic shapes his revised perceptions. Released from the contamination of lower-class roisterousness, he unabashedly admires his brave new world of large-scale organization and industrial power.

In the *Narrative*, Douglass's entrance into New Bedford fulfills his simpler artisan dreams of resurrection from bondage to personal dignity and self-respect. He soon finds work—"new, dirty, and hard work for me; but I went at it with a glad heart and a willing hand. I was now my own master.... It was the first work, the reward of which was to be entirely my own" (*N* 117). Before, in Baltimore, he had proudly been "able to command the highest wages given to the most experienced calkers" at the shipyard, $1.50 per day, only to see his master, Hugh Auld, take the money. "I contracted for it; I earned it; it was paid to me; it was rightfully my own;" yet Master Hugh "had the power to compel me to give it up" (*N* 103–104). Now he finds black friends who are free working men, with hardened hands and fine houses. Money becomes his badge of freedom, dignity, and manhood. "I worked that day with a pleasure I had never before experienced. I was at work for myself and newly-married wife" (*N* 117).

III

Douglass's whole sense of latter-day self, in both the *Narrative* and its revision, focuses on manhood; his wife seems an afterthought. He introduces her to his readers as a rather startling appendage to his escape and marries her almost in the same breath (*N* 113). Anna Murray Douglass, who met Douglass at an East Baltimore mutual improvement society, lived out the rest of her life as the stereotypic helpmeet to a public man of force. Her life recalls the old saying that Washington is filled with powerful men and the women they married when they were young. Loving, devoted, and illiterate, she apparently raised objections to Douglass's conduct only when he welcomed his close friend, an unmarried white Englishwoman named Julia Griffiths, into their home. There is no hard evidence that Griffiths and Douglass were more than abolitionist colleagues, though a great deal of accusation came their way from the Garrison camp. In any case, unlike Benjamin Franklin's equally illiterate wife, who was forced to raise his illegitimate son William against her will, Mrs. Douglass finally prevailed. Julia Griffiths left their home in late 1852, after living there for four years.[15]

As Terry H. Pickett has discovered, Douglass also seems to have carried on a long-term relationship with Ottilie Assing, who translated *My Bondage and My Freedom* into German. In a letter to her sister in 1874, she compares her sister's recent marriage with her relationship to Douglass: "The last seventeen years being not married and still living in a union of the deepest mutual affection, more firmly bound than many who are married, without the faintest hope that it might be different, and kept apart by a being incapable of valuing or giving love." At about that time Douglass was urging her to move in with him and his family in Washington, but thoughts of his wife made her balk. In her letters to Douglass, Assing sometimes refers to Anna as "the poor little piece of humanity" or, apparently their joint nickname for her, "Border States." Four years later she writes to Douglass, "Aside from other attractions it is such comfort to be allowed to communicate anything and everything to each other, to confide unconditionally without the least reserve or distrust." She spent many summers with him in Rochester. In 1882 Anna died, and in January of 1884 Douglass married his white secretary, Helen Pitts, twenty years younger than he, over considerable family opposition. On August 21, 1884, in Paris, Ottilie Assing killed herself with an overdose of laudanum.[16]

In *Moral Choices: Memory, Desire, and Imagination in Nineteenth-Century*

American Abolition, Peter F. Walker presents Douglass as a deeply split man, divided between his black mother and white father, struggling to escape not only slavery but his blackness as personified in his mother. He first erases her name from his identity, then all but erases her blackness from his memory of her. In his successive revisions of her portrait, she changes from a sorrowful, toilworn, downcast protector, dependent on white authority, to a mother who made him feel like a prince and who gave him the gift of eloquence. Walker's strongest evidence for Douglass's interior struggle, beyond these revisions, is Douglass's fifty years of reverence for a picture he found in England while looking through James Prichard's *Natural History of Man* in the mid–1840s. He took the picture of a statue, supposed to be Ramses, for his mother. "So for most of his life," as Walker says, "Frederick Douglass apparently found his black mother in the form of a princely man who, as far as the picture showed, may have been white."[17]

Douglass's pride in his Indian grandmother should qualify Walker's assessment.[18] He clearly became more "black," not less so, through the 1850s. Nonetheless, there are deep psychological waters here, and Douglass's emphasis on manhood may have helped him to avoid the plunge.

Despite the various kinds of support given to Frederick as a child, by his grandmother as well as by Thomas and Sophia Auld, despite the continued mothering he received from his wife, and despite the intellectual and perhaps sexual solicitude proffered by a variety of women friends, Douglass argued vehemently and repeatedly for a vigorous self-reliance. Work and politics, not intimacy and emotional exploration, were the proper arenas for a man of force. As Waldo Martin's intellectual biography details, Douglass's unswerving advocacy of middle-class individualism and hard work blocked not only his ability to value intimacy in his self-construction but also his awareness of lower-class black experience.[19]

At its simplest, manhood for him meant the dignity of labor and the Protestant work ethic. It also meant being a self-made man, a topic on which he frequently spoke. "Personal independence is the soul out of which comes the sturdiest manhood," he declared. It is the key to a world where the worker can meet the capitalist on equal terms. "The strife between capital and labor is, here, comparatively equal. The one is not the haughty and powerful master and the other the weak and abject slave as is the case in some parts of Europe. Here, the man of toil is not bowed, but erect and strong. He feels that capital is not more indispensable than labor, and he can therefore meet the capitalist as the representative of an equal power." Waldo Martin tartly summarizes the problems with Douglass's social vision. Douglass's "idealization of the work ethic" not only ignores the dehumanizing effect of industrial work conditions but also presumes that hard work leads to success. The idealization "reflected his deep-rooted commitment to both capitalism and the Protestant work ethic."[20]

It also reflected his commitment to an Emersonian sense of manly heroism. A self-made man, Douglass declared, has "genuine heroism in his struggle and something of sublimity and glory in his triumph." His success benefits all humanity because "it, better than any assertion, gives us assurance of the latent powers and resources of simple and unaided manhood."[21] Douglass liked to praise various heroes whom he considered to be self-made, especially Abraham Lincoln, John Brown, and Toussaint L'Ouverture. Like Thoreau's praise of Brown, the claims articulate an idealized model of himself.

His self-refashioning extends to his four name changes. He kept Frederick as his first name, "to preserve a sense of my identity," the *Narrative* notes. But he shortened "Frederick Augustus Washington Bailey" to Frederick Bailey in Baltimore, then escaped as Frederick Stanley, then became Frederick Johnson in New York (*N* 114–115). Finally, as he says in *My Bondage*, at the suggestion of "my friend, Nathan Johnson, himself a colored man," he chose Douglass from Scott's hero in *The Lady of the Lake*: Lord James of Douglas, "the black one," a paragon of unflinching fortitude in adversity (*MB* 209–210). Leaving behind his mother's name of Bailey, just as he left slavery behind, he renames himself from a manly text. The literariness of his choice itself bespeaks an upwardly mobile self-reliance ambiguously detaching his identity from social bonds.[22]

The manhood expressed through that choice becomes all the more striking if we compare Douglass's successive narratives to Harriet Jacobs's *Incidents in the Life of a Slave Girl* (1861). Here an equally strong-willed and considerably wilier former slave presents a story dense with vulnerabilities, anger, humiliations, and intimate relationships, along with a vital, continuous sense of black community and family ties. The life of "Linda Brent" (Jacobs's pseudonym) takes shape as a series of responses to her master's sexual pursuit. If Douglass seeks freedom and then power, Jacobs seeks freedom intermixed with benign dependence, although expressing increasing ambivalence about her need for others. First, she desperately chooses Mr. Sands as a white gentleman-lover, despite her love for a free black man, to evade the incessant, sometimes brutal advances of Dr. Flint, her master. After having had two children by Mr. Sands, she hides out for nearly seven years. Then she escapes, reunites with her two children and brother in New York, and at last finds herself sold to a loving mistress, Mrs. Bruce, who buys her freedom, half against her wishes, since "Linda" now deeply resents having to see herself as a piece of property. Finally, very reluctantly, she chooses to remain as Mrs. Bruce's servant rather than to secure a home of her own. Where Jacobs's narrative is rich in complex feelings, it lacks the self-centering, self-structuring confidence of Douglass's loner voice as he rises in the world. From first to last, she feels a woman's shame for having children but no husband. From first to last, Douglass defines himself through increasingly heroic separations.[23]

Throughout his three autobiographies, revised as carefully as Whitman's own song of himself, he fashions an idealized self-image of the heroic, upwardly mobile man of dignity and power. Later in his political career, he held to his sense of himself as a model of manly aspiration long after it had become clear to many others that the Republican party was flagrantly using him as a token while abandoning its commitment to black people. Much as Emerson strives to represent an emerging cultural elite in his notion of manhood, Douglass presents his own self-made manhood as the epitome for the potential of his race.[24] He did it; so can every black man.

At the distance of a hundred years and more, the contradictions and limitations of Douglass's ideology are easy to spot. His emphasis on manhood and competitive individualism magnified his own liberation while minimizing the obvious class bias he adopted. If a man did not rise, Douglass liked to assert, he deserved to fall. Moreover, his emphasis on work anticipates Booker T. Washington's later prescription for blacks to become a laboring underclass. Free black men should stay on the land and find dignity in their labor, Douglass said, in opposing the mass black emigration to Kansas in 1879–1881 to flee oppression of every sort in the South.[25] African laziness stifled manly initiative, he implied in his standard speech on self-made men. Many members of the gentility shared that view, from Harriet Beecher Stowe to the "Secret Six," members of Boston's elite who hoped John Brown's raid would rouse servile black men to independence and forcefulness.[26]

Through Douglass's public speeches, especially in his more conservative later years, runs the unmistakable Emersonian note about power and self, together with a simpler allegiance to bourgeois tastes.[27]

Paradoxically, Douglass's passion for manhood also helped to make him an early, unswerving, and ardent feminist, at least of the bourgeois individualist kind. "A thousand times better is it to have a brave outspoken woman by our side than a piece of mincing nothingness," he declared. He seconded Elizabeth Cady Stanton's crucial resolution demanding the vote at the 1848 Seneca Falls Convention, and often affirmed that his work to get that resolution passed by a narrow margin was one of the greatest acts of his life.[28] Strong selves were for him, as for Emerson, proof of the presence of power, and he was much clearer about the possibilities of such power for women than Emerson seemed to be. He died shortly after addressing a feminist convention, where the ladies saluted him by waving their handkerchiefs—an ironic yet complementary close to his boyhood vision of white sails on the Chesapeake. In part feminism proved attractive to him, as Waldo Martin intimates, because it had the right tone: a refined, white, middle-class movement. Feminists also proved to be a crucial constituency for fund raising in the early years after his break with Garrison, when his natural abolitionist constituency recoiled from his newspaper. Nevertheless, Douglass's arguments with Lucy Stone in the 1850s show his profound conviction that slavery and women's oppression were linked issues.[29] Women, too, were blocked from becoming autonomous, forceful selves.

Douglass's earlier sense of manhood as self-respect earned through freedom and hard work has a radical clarity, at least in the context of slavery. His rhetoric of independence taps a more unconscious energy of artisan rebellion as well. "I was born insolent, and have always been insolent," he once remarked. "To be black and insolent in the South means presence of anything like manhood and consciousness of one's humanity."[30] From his youth onward he was a proud fighter, willing and even eager to take on tyrannical men. Douglass's most indelible early memory, he says, is of his probable father, Aaron Anthony, taking "great pleasure" in whipping his aunt for not keeping her sexual favors for master alone (*N* 24–25). Douglass exposes Anthony's brutality, as Whitman more briefly exposes his father's in "There Was a Child Went Forth." Whereas Whitman benignly transcends his father's manhood, however, Douglass first rebels against all such brutal and self-brutalizing men, then elevates himself to manliness of a higher class.

The price Douglass paid, in minimizing his private feelings and his bonds with lower-class blacks, is clear enough. It should be equally clear that Douglass's claims for manhood show his realism about the capitalist middle class. Competition and material success, not kinship ties and craftsmanship, formed the new basis for a man's self-respect, while humiliations of various kinds, especially for a black man, awaited the first display of weakness.

Another distinguished black man, Dr. John S. Rock, a noted Boston physician and the first black attorney admitted to the bar of the United States Supreme Court, underlined the reality with a harsh pungency. In March of 1858, at a meeting commemorating the Boston Massacre, Dr. Rock first attacked whites who say blacks are cowardly and will never revolt. Then, after taunting a clearly sympathetic white crowd with jokes about the physical appearance of whites, he concluded by prescribing a black middle class as the prerequisite for white respect.

> In this country, where money is the great sympathetic nerve which ramifies society, and has a ganglia in every man's pocket, a man is respected in proportion to his success in business. When the avenues of wealth are opened to us, we will then become educated and wealthy, and then the roughest looking colored man that you ever saw, or ever will see, will be pleasanter than the harmonies of Orpheus, and black will be a very pretty color. It will make our jargon, wit—our words, oracles; flattery will then take the place of slander, and you will find no prejudice in the Yankee whatsoever. We do not expect to occupy a much better position than we now do, until we shall have our educated and wealthy men, who can wield a power that cannot be misunderstood. Then, and not till then, will the tongue of slander be silenced, and the lip of prejudice sealed. Then, and not till then, will we be able to enjoy true equality, which can exist only among peers.[31]

Only in the early 1970s, when enrollment of black students in colleges shot up from 2 percent to 10 percent, did Rock's acerbic predictions begin to come true. His sense of what true equality requires in America was as valid then as it is now. It requires "peers" among the dominant power group: "educated and wealthy men, who can wield a power that cannot be misunderstood." In rewriting his description of his fight with Covey, Douglass came to a nearly identical sense of his world. To mix force with dignity is the way to manhood and power as well as wealth.

Douglass's literary self-refashioning is politically realistic, in a more profound sense than Garrison expected or than contemporary critical theory privileges. The antimimetic bias in contemporary criticism, not coincidentally an antibourgeois bias, urges readers to value literature as a self-subverting activity, one which makes us skeptically conscious of the intrinsic alienations of language. The effect of reading Douglass could not be more opposed. As a man who wanted power, he knew what he had to do. Enthusiastically appropriating the dominant cultural code of manly power and dignity in each new white world he sought to master, Douglass reached for social authority with a canny tenacity. If the contradictions in his self-presentations and his rhetoric of self-reliance seem glaringly apparent now, they are the contradictions of the white male culture he had to master to gain a sense of power. More clearly than Emerson's essays, Douglass's successive narrations of his life assure him the status and the ironies of a Representative Man.

5

Two Genteel Women
Look at Men:
Sarah Hale and
Caroline Kirkland

In the first, separatist phase of feminist scholarship during the 1970s, womanhood came close to having a room if not a territory of its own. Manhood, like Freud's ubiquitous Oedipal father, loomed as the universal oppressor, while womanhood seemed the locus of repression, struggle, and potential breakthrough. For a time the polarization between male and female values seemed so complete that any woman who wrote organized, logical, analytical prose could be charged with committing a patriarchy. Books by Dorothy Dinnerstein and Nancy Chodorow tended to associate maleness with impersonality, aggressiveness, and self-repression, while femaleness connoted an idealized sensitivity to relationships and the flux of feelings. More radically, French feminists delighted in making language the terrain for guerrilla gender warfare.[1]

Such polarization rather blatantly replicates the sex role polarities of the nineteenth century, with the difference that the supposedly healthier female values now include carnivalesque aspects of politics and sexuality. More recently, several challenging critiques, especially books by Toril Moi and K. K. Ruthven, have argued against the radical pluralism and exclusivist leanings of the first feminist phase. In their view, manhood and womanhood cannot be understood apart from each other or apart from the historical context generating their often antithetical values. Mary Ryan's study of the middle-class family in mid-nineteenth century New York similarly emphasizes the common aim of male self-reliance and female domesticity to help preserve the family's class status.[2]

In something of that latter-day spirit, the next two chapters ask the question, How did women look at men and manhood? This chapter examines two relatively neglected writers, each self-consciously trying to represent genteel womanhood in the late 1830s and the 1840s. Sarah Hale took over the editorship of the *Lady's Book* (later *Godey's Lady's Book*) in 1837. Two years later, Caroline Kirkland's *A New Home—Who'll Follow?* achieved an instant success as the first "realistic" account of the frontier. For Hale and Kirkland, womanhood was as distant from manhood as Venus is from Mars, though they wished women would keep their distance from Venus as well.

Each writer presumes patriarchal dependence as a given for women. In their view, men are basically money making animals, driven by a need to succeed in business. Kirkland mocks the money making; Hale mocks the animals. With pervasive duplicity, each voice presents genteel womanhood as intimately dependent yet mentally and morally superior. Each also uses class status to alleviate the pain of gender resentments.

This is manhood from the outside. Rarely do we find out how men feel about other men, except in stereotypic family situations. One searches in vain for instances of men's competitive anxiety, rivalry with fathers, fears of humiliation, or hunger for power. Nor do these writers much explore male bonding. Rather, Hale and Kirkland try to express how manhood affects women.

In doing so, they show a much greater class consciousness than we are accustomed to find in canonized male texts of the period. They enjoy speaking collectively, for womankind, or at least for genteel women. Subordinating a great deal of pain, they manifest a buoyantly jaunty optimism about future reform of men (Hale) or a buoyantly satiric adaptability (Kirkland). Each writer extensively employs rhetorical doubles, Hale with the stories she chooses and Kirkland with the tales she tells of other genteel women in the Michigan wilderness, as cautionary tales and mirrors for the pain of dependence.

In the rest of this book, I use my conclusions about genteel womanhood as a base for several arguments. First, while assumptions about patriarchal dependence persist among evangelical women writers of the 1850s (Susan Warner, Harriet Beecher Stowe), the tone of voice shifts from amused superiority to embattled polemic (*Uncle Tom's Cabin*) or embattled self-control (*Wide, Wide World*). Second, the doubling and duplicity characteristic of genteel women's writing continue in the devious, premodernist narrations of Hawthorne and Melville as well as in the impassioned evangelicalism of Warner and Stowe. To compare those four authors, with side glances at Francis Parkman and Richard Henry Dana, can highlight the interdependence of manhood and womanhood as social constructs. Third, the comparison also shows a striking shift from patriarchal to competitive norms for manhood in male writers. Both shifts confirm and extend Anthony Wallace's basic argument in *Rockdale* that by 1850 patrician Enlightenment values were supplanted by a language of middle-class Christian capitalism.

I

Godey's Lady's Book lives on as a symptom to be laughed at. In *Life on the Mississippi*, young Mark Twain enters a decorous lady's house in Arkansas and finds the "chaste and innocuous Godey's Lady's Book" at the center of her parlor display. It was all so genteel, he comments, that there was no bathroom in the house, nor had any visitor ever seen one.[3]

Twain's gibe graphically captures an enduring, partially justifiable assumption about *Godey's*. Undeniably, it encouraged women to be conventionally ladylike at the expense of their bodies and their natural feelings. Sarah Hale, whose astute editorial hand brought the magazine to unquestioned dominance in the 1840s, is now remembered primarily as the author (or plagiarist) of "Mary Had a Little Lamb," the leader of a twenty-year campaign to establish Thanksgiving as a national holiday, and the editor and novelist who, as Ann Douglas mordantly sums up her philosophy, "wished men to become more like women and women to become more like angels."[4]

Once a month, from the early 1830s until the end of the nineteenth century, the variously titled magazine now known as *Godey's Lady's Book* presented women with extravagant pictures of the latest fashions, together with essays and stories designed to teach moral refinement. It was the self-help manual for any woman who wanted to be genteel. After Louis Godey tried and failed to hire Hale from her editorship of the rival *Ladies Magazine*, he bought her magazine and merged it with his, to be assured of her editorial talents. In 1839 Godey could brag to his readers, "Our list now exceeds the combined number of any other three monthly publications." By 1840 *Godey's* would reach 25,000 subscribers, he claimed. Eventually, Hale moved to New York full time, and circulation soared, to 70,000 by 1850, then 100,000 by 1856, reaching 150,000 by the Civil War, a conflict the magazine never mentioned.[5] Throughout this period, the bonds of true American womanhood appear in every aspect of the magazine, from Hale's presumption of conversational intimacy with her readers to the shared fascination with dress, to a great many stories featuring spiritual self-discipline as the remedy for women's painful feelings.

On the surface, *Godey's* seemed to encourage all that was affected and pretentious in American women. J. Richard Beste, an English visitor to Terre Haute, Indiana, in 1851, commented on how deliberately affected American women seemed to be. "The American woman, whether rich or poor, had her rocking-chair and her fan; her simper and her sigh; her whine and her finery." Beste found out to his surprise that these women worked. But they tried to hide that part of their lives. They strove to measure up to the ideal set for them by their men: to be culturally refined, morally superior, and physically ornamental. They would thus be fit emblems of men's success in their work. "The marvel to me," Beste concluded, "is that American men, who are so active-minded themselves, can admire such listless apathy in the other sex. That they do admire it is proven by the fact that the women practice it." For such men and women, the most material symbol of success, besides their houses, was fashionable female attire. To be a lady, one had to change one's dress three times a day.[6]

Toward the end of her first editorial column (January 1837), Hale announced that beauty is woman's calling. "The truth is too glaring to be denied, that all male rational creatures are, in the long run, vile, corrupt, polluted, and selfish. Purity of mind is incompatible with manhood" (3). But women, untainted by "the cares of business," can and must be pure. "We must carry out our plan of the beautiful and appropriate in dress, in poetry, in fiction, in education, till all shall meet like the rays of a star in the centre of its brightness, in the sacred beauty of the Christian character" (5). Men as well as women relished *Godey's* exclusive attention to women's genteel self-image and moral purity, as the editors discovered during the Civil War, when the magazine received requests for subscriptions from the battlefield. Men had been reading it too, all along.[7]

Moreover, the magazine had a certain intellectual cachet. Sarah Hale campaigned voluminously in her columns and in her choice of essays to raise women's intellectual aspirations through education. She instituted a new section, first called "The Lady's Mentor" and later the "Editor's Table," filled with reports on ladies' seminaries, quotations advocating women's education, and book reviews. Women should become educated even in the sciences, she argued, not to enter the public sphere but to be equal with their men and thus better able to improve men's coarser sensibilities.

"I am not advocating what is termed *bluestockingism*," Hale has a sympathetic schoolmaster conclude in her January 1840 lead story, "New Year at Home." "No one can dislike a thorough dogmatical, dictatorial, demonstrating, metaphysically learned lady, more sincerely than I do." With equal firmness, however, Hale has her male protagonist condemn the "fashion-worshipping" that her magazine so ostentatiously abetted: "But it is necessary, if men would improve, that women should be intelligent, and value good morals and great talents above mere wealth and show. The contagion of folly, which a vain, rich, fashion-worshipping, fine lady, scatters around her, like an atmosphere, brilliant but blinding, is more injurious to the morals and happiness of society, than have ever yet been the sophisms of a Wolstoncraft, or Wright, or any of their imitators."[8] Perhaps because of Hale's emphasis on women's education, or perhaps simply because the magazine had such a wide readership and paid well, when Poe published his witty "New York Literati" series in the mid–1840s, he placed the essays in *Godey's*. If not the *New York Review of Books*, it was the *New Yorker* as well as the *Vogue* and the *Ladies Home Journal* of its day.

Above all, *Godey's* mirrored the aspirations and difficulties of women in the new middle class. As Nina Baym has said, the magazine was "programmatically dedicated to advancing the middle class and its values."[9] Class consciousness vies with gender consciousness in its pages. The effect of a great many cautionary tales is to say, "Yes, dear, we know you have problems. Be strong and self-disciplined about your struggling lot, or else you may fall into helpless poverty, like X, Y, and Z. And don't be envious of those aristocratic rich; see how shallow, vain, puffed up, and empty of spunk A, B, and C are when crises come to them, as crises come to us all. God will help you pull yourself through. Your man? Honey, just be glad you have one, and get to work on yourself."

While foreign observers like Alexis de Tocqueville and Michel Chevalier minimized the presence of classes in America, *Godey's* made it very clear that there were the vaguely European rich, the people like us, the simple rustics out on the farms, and the urban poor. What women of all classes shared was the experience of pain through having to depend on men. A true, implicitly middle-class American woman would raise herself from self-pity or, more dangerous, a proud, resentful willfulness, to a self-controlled humility.

To read through just a few issues of *Godey's Lady's Book*—I'll focus primarily on Hale's first year, 1837—is to discover a world of women being done to by men. Men have the money or fail at having money; women have the feelings and fail if they don't have the right ones. Men can be sullen and stern or cold and calculating. Almost invariably even the good men, men of "principle and sense," are preoccupied with business and public affairs, having little leisure for the home. Some women are abandoned for years at a time, and learn not to complain. In the woman's world of love and family, young girls with high spirits and quick tempers have to learn how to govern themselves. They need to find out how to manage the pain of emotional aloneness, and how to break their will of its tendency toward self-destructive rebellion and pride.

Occasionally we meet an actual wife beater, but he tends to be of the lower sort. In the May 1837 issue, for instance, a genderless but genteel narrator tells the story of "The Hospital Patient." She or he follows a crowd to the police station, where a man is being held for beating the woman he lived with. The scene shifts to the hospital, where the dying woman, who obviously loves the man, denies to the police and the crowd that he had beaten her. She holds the man's hand, begs God to forgive *her*, and dies.[10]

The pathos depends on the heroine's absolute suppression of her anger, though the class lines are also very clearly drawn. The pathos also implies a blatant double message: love your man, but be morally superior to the brute. This is female duplicity as Alicia Ostriker defines it: contradictory meanings, both deeply felt. Or as Bonnie G. Smith puts it in *Ladies of the Leisure Class*, a Marxist study of more reactionary bourgeois ladies in middle to late nineteeth century northern France, their fashions and their literature of domesticity expressed rather than resolved their contradictions.[11]

A similar message, with a more conventionally vengeful twist, comes in another story from the February 1837 issue: "The Broken-Hearted," by "M. M." (The tendency for women to sign their stories with initials bespeaks their uneasiness about publication.) Rose Warton, "pure and guileless," falls in love, "and day after day, from the lips of Clifford Delmont, she drank still deeper of the delicious poison, until her very being was bound up in his, though *he* had never breathed the word upon her ear." Then Clifford, after telling Rose he will marry her, marries another woman for her money. Rose slowly languishes and dies, with no hint of anger. She only "faded on—no murmur, no complaint passed her lips." "I have long since forgiven him," she says to a friend on her deathbed; "I am not grieved that my Father calls me early to his arms." She dies, and Clifford Delmont, who follows the funeral, is never again seen to smile. "Disgusted with his heartless wife," he becomes a melancholy, remorseful misanthrope, often prostrating himself on Rose's grave (90–92).

Here are the stark contours of patriarchal dependence. A pure, trusting child-woman becomes "bound up" in a man, who crassly ditches her. Rather than rage at him and cry buckets, she simply fades into the "arms" of her heavenly "Father." While she feels only the helpless acquiescence of a "broken heart," readers can feel the double satisfaction of empathizing with her pain and seeing God's vindictive justice served on the remorseful bounder. Where men do wrong, God can do right. Throughout the trials of love and death, woman's spiritual proving grounds, her self-image stays pure, untainted by the complex vicissitudes of mature feeling.

Most of the stories in *Godey's Lady's Book* have more touches of earthiness and satire in their characterizations. The basic structure of fantasy and feeling, however, remains clear, and clearly double: I am utterly done to, I am utterly superior. The bond with the heavenly Father, which conveys superiority, is the fruition of the broken bond with men on earth. An idealized self joins with an idealized father to condemn the behavior of worldly men.

On the other hand, or with another voice, *Godey's* encourages girls to be content with their dreams of a Mr. Knightly, a fatherly man or an actual father who can protect them against their dangerous and silly puppy loves. As T. S. Arthur puts it directly in a January 1845 story, "Engaged at Sixteen," "A fond, wayward child of sixteen may chance to marry and do well," but only if she meets a fatherly type, "only in case she happen to meet a man of good sense, warm affections and great kindness and forbearance. He can bear with her as a father bears with a capricious child; can forgive much and love much. But give the happiness of such a creature into the keeping of a cold, narrow-minded, selfish, petulant man, and her cup will soon run over. Bitter, indeed, will be her lot in life." This story ends with the selfish husband sending the girl home to her father two years later, carrying her baby. At the age of thirty Anna still lives at home.[12]

Sarah Hale's emphasis on improving men often slides into the same polarity between reverence for paternalism and disgust at male selfishness, though her tone always retains a jaunty optimism about the progress of culture from male grossness to female refinement. Hale's editorial column for May 1837, "Woman the Poet of Nature," puts the case with her usual forceful simplification. After praising English poetry for having responded to female influence to purge itself of "such gross productions as were popular in the age of Swift, or Dryden, and the elder dramatists," Hale launches into a sustained vision of the still purer, still more female-oriented literature of the future. "Purity of taste," she says, is the key. Under its influence,

> the tone of literature, poetry, more especially, will, in every country, become more moral and delicate, refined and perfect. Warlike and bachanalian strains must cease to be sung wherever peace and temperance prevail. Love will always be a theme of exceeding power, but it will be love chaste, steadfast and confiding, not the unholy passion of animal appetite; and in the true and fervent affections of the heart, and the household charities of life will be found themes of exceeding beauty. These are the appropriate domain of woman, which can never become obsolete or exhausted or injurious. (194–195)

After considering the more limited yet "perfect" freedom of women writers as compared with men, Hale concludes with a renewed plea for women to think of love as devotion rather than passion. Since "the feeling of devotion or piety, is inseparable from real genius in a woman, it follows of course, that she could not indulge in any forbidden passion" (198). Let men be the animals, she implies; their day of conquest is passing. In the future, women's "genius" will rule, companionably married to the Father's will.

A generation of feminist critics has exposed the double edge of power and powerlessness in such rhetoric of genteel womanhood. To censure men without doing battle, it appropriates elements of millennial evangelical language, manifest destiny, and a still broader faith in painless progress. To instruct women, however, Hale comes closer to home. Her strictures against giving way to passion turn out to be a lead-in for a remarkable story immediately following the column.

"The Young Wife," by Mrs. Harrison Smith, tells at great length of how a mother's craving for passion leads her astray. First she neglects her children, then she turns from God and her husband, and finally she tries to kill one of her children. A moderately happy ending is tacked on: the child lives, and the bond between husband and wife grows stronger. The vaguely debauched yet brotherly man who had occasioned the wife's passion heads for the Far West, where he dies young.

Readers could distance themselves from this cautionary tale by seeing its moral as the danger of upper-class seduction. From the beginning, the heroine's potential loss of "purity" is associated with "the license allowed to married women in the higher circles, where the European system of gallantry is insidiously undermining the morals, and transforming the simple and rigid forms of our society" (198). The heroine seems much closer to Isabel Archer, however, or perhaps Edna Pontellier. Her innocence about passion, not her worldly sophistication, leads her to succumb unawares to its force. "I am a mystery to myself," the heroine muses, looking at her children. "I feel as if my soul had been sleeping, and that his voice, his look, . . . had roused all its latent powers" (198).

The surprising heart of the story is the narrator's meditation on what makes passion spring alive. The husband, so "virtuous and dispassionate himself—calm and constant in his affections," and in any case preoccupied with business—has little comprehension of the confused struggle in his wife's heart. The wife keeps trying to tell herself that it is simply a sisterlike affection. The narrator tells us that she means her story only "as a warning to those who are not aware of the danger of domesticating young and attractive guests in the bosoms of their families" (200).[13] But the narrator's real focus is on the intrinsic deficiencies of marriage.

"Marriage deprives passion of the fuel which fed its flame," she observes. It removes "all the hopes and fears which prompt the continual effort to please and secure its object," and with them all the "fond, devoted, flattering attentions, so gratifying, not only to self-love, but to our best and tenderest sensibilities." At that point men and women strikingly diverge. "This change inflicts little pain on man. Unceasingly occupied in the business and turmoil of life, various exciting interests afford employment for that moral, intellectual, and physical activity which keeps in motion the human machine. Not so with woman. Love is the main-spring of her existence—when this loses its elasticity and force, the mechanism of the whole being is deranged." Outwardly, Mrs. Smith continues, such a woman "still lives and performs her appointed tasks, faithfully, contentedly, and often cheerfully—but soberly and quietly." Inwardly, however, "a craving void is left in her bosom" (201).[14] This "craving void," a term which Mrs. Smith repeats emphatically a little later on, simply can't be filled by husbands or children. Unwary women therefore may well turn to passion, although "religion alone" can fill the void and regulate the heart."There only can thy fervent nature find an object commensurate with its capacity of loving; an object to fill that craving void which nought on earth can fill" (201).

In a best-selling book some years later, *Reveries of a Bachelor* (1850), Donald Mitchell comes to the same conclusion about men and women. "A man may in some sort tie his frail hopes and honor, with weak, shifting ground-tackle to business, or to the world; but a woman without that anchor which they call Faith, is adrift and a-wreck." A man can look to the public world, to "Fame and Reputation," to solace and ground himself, "but a woman in her comparatively isolated sphere, where affection and not purpose is the controlling motive, . . . where can she put her hope in storms, if not in Heaven?" A quiet desperation, on both sides, impels this insistent lesson. Like Melville's Pip, abandoned on an open sea, a homebound wife faces a domestic version of what her man may be facing in the marketplace: an absolute sense that she doesn't matter, even to her spouse. "The intense concentration of self in the middle of such a heartless immensity, my God! who can tell it?"[15]

But Melville's sense of abandonment is cosmic and self-intensifying, while the woman's is interpersonal and self-stifling. In *Life in the Iron Mills* (1861), Rebecca Harding Davis describes the female solitude that crosses all class lines. Hugh Wolfe, the beaten-down worker with an artist's sensibility, feels kindly toward devoted, misshapen Deborah; "it was his nature to be kind, even to the very rats that swarmed in the cellar." Deborah fully comprehends the lack of "heart-kindness" for her in the man she loves. "And it might be that very knowledge had given to her face its apathy and vacancy more than her low, torpid life. One sees that dead, vacant look steal sometimes over the rarest, finest of women's faces,—in the very midst, it may be, of their warmest summer's day; and then one can guess at the secret of intolerable solitude that lies hid beneath the delicate laces and brilliant smile."[16]

A contemporary self-help manual for men, *The Young Man's Own Book* (1832), offers a curious parallel. It too implies that a man's preoccupation with business leads to an abyss of solitude in genteel marriage. The book's subtitle, "A Manual of Politeness, Intellectual Improvement, and Moral Deportment, calculated to form the character on a solid basis, and to insure respectability and success in life," shows its explicitly genteel frame for success. "Thinking, not growth, makes manhood," the author declares. To the end of improving a young man's thinking, the book stresses a Franklin-like dedication to reading and writing. The book also includes a chapter, "Advantages of Female Society," on refining boorish male manners. "You should treat [women] as spirits of a purer sphere, and try to be as innocent, if not as ignorant of evil as they are; and in assimilating yourself to their purity and refinement, you are most assuredly raising yourself in the scale of intellectual and moral beings," the chapter concludes.[17] Sarah Hale could have put it no better.

With equal emphasis, the next chapter stresses the virtues of early rising. Women, like reading and writing, are means to a business-oriented end. That perspective becomes blatantly evident in the long chapter "Advice on Entering upon Business," in which the choice of a wife takes up a third of the subheadings. A man must "build on [his] own bottom," the author says. Therefore don't marry for money but for the woman's character, though her dowry should be considered. She must be a "good manager" or else "she is no wife for a man of business." Make sure "that she is not surrounded with hungry relations" (176–180).

Above all, remember "that, though most men marry, few live happily." The great dangers in marriage, the author declares, are that a man may become indifferent or a tyrant. "Do not permit yourself to think cheaply of your wife, or neglect her, because you are secure in possession," he advises, continuing to draw on the language of finance. "It is impossible but a woman must be grievously shocked to see the servile lover transformed at once into the tyrant husband. Assure yourself, there are but very few steps between indifference, neglect, contempt, and aversion." At least keep the pretenses afloat, he implies. "Above all things, never let her imagine it is a penance to you to stay at home, or that you prefer any company whatever to hers.... To say the truth, no woman would marry if she expected to be a slave" (182–184).

Faced with the problem of male indifference and tyranny, the author advocates not diminished attention to business but a limited leash for the wife. She should be given discretion "in all trifling matters," for "she will cheerfully forbear interfering in your province, if she finds herself undisturbed in her own." While the separate spheres prevail in the daytime, the husband should preserve the patriarchal unities at night. "Have but one table, one purse, and one bed; either separate, will be attended with separate interests" (183). Remember that your principal goal is to succeed in business and move upward into genteel society. Your wife, if you have chosen well, can help to make you more sociable, less argumentative, more pleasant in conversation, and more elegant in manners. "The very name of an argument frightens a woman, who is commonly sooner convinced by a happy turn, or witty expression, than by any demonstration, or by all the rules of logic. . . . The great secret, with them, is to be amiable without design" (190).[18]

Faced with the problem of women's dependence on men, Hale sometimes adopts a tactic looking very much like design: to be amiable and devious. In May of 1837, for instance, she launches a vigorous campaign to pass a New York law guaranteeing the economic rights of a woman in marriage. (By 1848 the law was passed.) She marshals a great many straightforward arguments against the injustice of forcing a wife to relinquish all her property to her husband. As Hale also takes care to say, however, "it is not to make the wife independent of her husband that we argue this matter upon public attention, but to preserve more indissolubly the union of hearts, by placing the interests of the married pair on the same footing." Then, after chronicling the disastrous effects of present laws on various women, especially poor wives of drunken husbands, Hale startlingly concludes with a ringing affirmation of the wife's stereotypic self-sacrifice. The "self-sacrificing spirit," she says, is "the cement of society. Without these confiding feelings, weaknesses if you will, in the nature of woman, the world would never be humanized and civilized" (212, 214).[19] At the distance of 150 years, the demure veil looks rather transparent.

In the June 1837 issue, too, Hale reprints with obvious approval a stinging defense of female education. "The energies of the female character have seldom been developed; the extent of woman's powers seldom displayed," writes "S.C." "Her situation in life still pre[v]ents the full exercise of her faculties, and not unfrequently renders genius, so worshipped by others, a source only of misery to herself." Such women, "naturally . . . ambitious" because of their "lively and brilliant imagination," see themselves barred from expectations of fame, eloquence, and "high and manly deeds." They feel bound with "chains . . . to the follies and low employments of daily life." And what is the cause? Not any inherent inability, but simply "the voice of *public opin-*

ion." It "is omnipotent, and woman must yield;—the 'little objects of earth, the routine of trifles,' these must become to her matters of interest or her life be passed in bitterness away, and in the vain remembrance of hopes once high but forever fled" (251–252).

A lengthy piece in November 1837, "Thoughts on the Happiness of Woman as Connected with the Cultivation of Her Mind," begins with the conventional presumption of woman's inferiority and dependence: "If a woman would please, let her never study to shine." Man is the "head," the writer (one "B.Y.") continues. Then comes a surprising twist. "If not her superior in intellect, he is unwilling to be thought otherwise." Throughout the piece, a collection of stock formulas about women's dependence, delicacy of feeling, modesty, and refinement, runs an unmistakable note of helpless rage at man's arrogance and power. Woman must not shine, the writer repeats several times, for the simple reason that no man will love a superior woman. Cultivate your mind, therefore, but "veil" it with "that modesty that gives leave to a lesser light to shine." However "lesser" his light, "the pride of man requires that he should be looked up to" (15:204).

The rest of B. Y.'s essay, ostensibly on women's "happiness," compares at length the much more fatiguing and incessant labors of women—"To suffer is indeed the lot of woman!"—with men's "more active employments" and evening "repose" in the home. Nonetheless, his love makes all the difference, the writer intermittently recalls—that and motherhood. "A woman should not aspire to shine, but to please," the writer concludes. Her "cheerful obedience" yields a pleased husband, who forbears from exercising "tyrannically that authority, with which the laws of God and man invest him." Once he dies, and suffering is at its worst, religion can comfort the woman along her "lonely" and "dreary" path (205).

This is not so much duplicity as rather heavy-handed subversion. The effect is to bond women together in a knowing sadness, implicitly depression, since conflict with men seems such an impossibility. Amid the stories of deserted and lonely women, Hale also occasionally publishes sympathetic stories of women who don't marry, such as one by Harriet Beecher Stowe in January of 1840. Stowe presents her heroine's reminiscence by saying, "it was choice, and not necessity, that kept her single.... Aunt Mary was one who had failed in *being pleased*, rather than in pleasing."[20]

For the most part, an emphasis on woman's autonomous possibilities or on the bitterness of being confined to the domestic sphere stays muted in Hale's pages. Instead, she chooses stories that show the pain and solitude of dependence on men while also showing the dangers of pride, ambition, resentment, and passion. Not deviousness but doubleness marks *Godey's* themes. The duplicity carries over to Hale's editorial voice, which simultaneously affirms how superior her readers are to their men and how dependent they must continue to be.

The most flagrant instance of Hale's duplicitous voice comes with her inaugural "Conversazione" in January 1837, as she announces her new leadership and her plans for the magazine. Her first move, under the aegis of Solomon, "the wisest of men," is to disown her power and any intentions for change. "Yes, the wisest of men was right," she begins. "Strictly speaking, 'there is nothing new under the sun.' " Several more paragraphs consider novelty as simply a kind of natural rearrangement and perhaps a slow process of perfection as well. At the conclusion of this general meditation, Hale once again archly invokes a man's authority: "We hope Mr. Richardson, in his 'New Dictionary of the English Language,' will particularly attend to this word, *novelty*—it is a very important word to the ladies: we want the precise meaning" (1, subsequent quotations 1–2).

Only then does Hale present her new *Lady's Book* as an instance. " 'The Lady's Book' has been submitted to this perfecting process." Combined with the *American Ladies Magazine,* of which Hale had previously been the editor, "it comes to the readers of these two periodicals a changed 'Book'—a novelty." Already Hale has promised her readers novelty but no real change, an assertive yet playfully ladylike voice, one readily able to "submit" to wiser men. If she aspires to perfection for her magazine, it will be a humble perfection, announced indirectly and achieved with no danger of presumptuous feminism.

Hale then turns serious. A lengthy paragraph announces her aim to publish the best woman's magazine, building on the essential differences between the sexes.

> It is our aim to prepare a work which, for our own sex, should be superior to every other periodical. To effect this ours must differ in some important respects from the general mass of monthly literature. It must differ, as do the minds of the sexes. This difference is not in strength of intellect, but in the manner of awakening the reason and directing its power.... The strength of man's character is in his physical propensities—the strength of woman lies in her moral sentiments. Man's nature would of necessity be earliest developed, because his physical wants press more tangibly and immediately on his senses than moral

pleasures do on his heart, and being endowed with greater physical strength than woman, her nature would be kept in abeyance till he had found, by experience, that those enjoyments he had sought were imperfect and unsatisfying.

In short, boys will be boys and men will be boy-men, presumably lusting and fighting, until they slowly discover how "imperfect and unsatisfying" these low "physical wants" are compared to "moral pleasures" of the heart.

A contempt for men as they are would be more pronounced if Hale did not immediately invoke her optimism about men as they might be. When a man "turns to the better, holier emotions of his heart, . . . then man's moral faculties are awakened, and he looks to women as indeed a 'help meet for him.' " Companionship with a woman "refines and exalts his nature," in stages ascending from "the household affections" and "benevolent feelings" to "the sentiment of duty" and, finally, reverence for God. Correspondingly, a man's moral awakening makes him "willing that she should enjoy that intellectual cultivation which will increase and diffuse her moral influence."

It all sounds logical and painless, even inevitable. There is no conflict with men here, only a patient optimism about their slow evolution toward appreciating women's virtues. Nonetheless, Hale risks a tart dig at man's animal nature as it currently exists. She quotes Captain Basil Hall, a well-known travel writer, on the woman who formed Sir Walter Scott and " 'did for him the sort of thing which, until some fair hand does for us, we are all bears.' Even so, Captain." The duplicity here is relatively obvious. She defers to the man's position as well as his opinion, while she readily assents to the principle of male bearishness.

Hale directs her more crucial duplicity at women. She wants to join Christian humility with intellectual improvement. The study of mathematics, philosophy, and rhetoric will never be useful to women "in the business of the world—in obtaining wealth, fame, and power," she says. That's fine; such pursuits are crass and low, like utility and business themselves. Instead, "knowledge will discipline her own mind," and help a woman to influence "those she loves." By studying the sciences, "she can increase and serve her empire of the heart." The word *empire* conveys Hale's political agenda. Through education "shall we succeed in advancing Christian morals, and securing national happiness." Rather than be tainted by men's notion of power, the woman's "empire of the heart" requires only moral suasion to ease its way toward taking charge of these rough male beasts, struggling toward mother to be born.

Just as Hale advocates women's public influence through intimacy, she conveys her moral agenda in a tone of friendly conversation rather than high male seriousness. Again she uses a strict sex-role polarity as a foil to set off how crude and boorish men are in their aggressiveness. The new *Lady's Book*, she affirms, "will *not* be polemical, political, philological, philosophical, scientific, or critical—but it will aim to draw forth and form into a pleasant, healthy, and happy combination, the moral uses of all these high sounding pursuits; as the bee, (which, by the way, is a *female*,) succeeds in extracting honey as sweet and pure from the thistle as from the rose, and reaches with as sure an instinct the blossoms of the lofty elm as those of the humble clover." Whether men are "thistles" or "lofty elms," the female bees can buzz within and above their "high sounding pursuits" to extract a purer honey.

Besides, as Hale's half-logical, half-flitting style implies, women have much more fun. "We shall not affect the learned, logical, or profound style; nor yet permit that air of *badinage* which usually resolves itself into satire or coarseness." Instead, the *Lady's Book* will reflect genteel society at its best. "Ours will rather imitate that tone of playful vivacity, intelligent observation, and refined taste, which predominates in the social *re-unions* of the good and gifted." Like her columns, the *Lady's Book* will be "a '*Conversazione*' of the highest character, to which we invite every lady in our land."

Then, arching her voice midway between the high and the cute, Hale gives yet another curtsy to the men who control the power and the purse strings. To gain admittance to her show, presented on the first weekday of every month, "each lady is allowed to introduce as many gentlemen as she thinks worthy the privilege—they, of course, paying for the ticket."

Hale's "Conversazione" continues, declaring the revolutionary potential of America to fulfill woman's genius, but her little joke about the tickets compresses her duplicities into a tidy package. We are all ladies and gentlemen, she implies. Gentlemen, it is true, can act like wild dogs. After all, the silly creatures are men. Beastly as they are, however, they do have the money. We depend on them to pay for our entertainments, just as they need us to "introduce" them to the "privilege" of a lady's refinement. It is all of a piece, isn't it, ladies? Our superiority depends on their inferiority as well as their cash. If we didn't have those puppies to train, how on earth could we feel special except in the dresses that we wear?

II

Dress constitutes no small part of the social comedy in *A New Home—Who'll Follow?* (1839), Caroline Kirkland's witty, often acerbic account of life on the Michigan frontier in the 1830s. Her opening chapter, which she intends as a parable for all "ladies from the eastward world" who may venture into a similar situation, chronicles the disillusionments of her first journey, from the inappropriateness of paper-soled shoes in fording a ditch to her final hapless plunge into a boghole, just as she was inquiring of her husband when she would see their hotel. As she soon finds out, the hotel is only a log house.[21] Chapter 4 presents the hotelkeepers, Mrs. Ketchum and her daughter, Irene, who receive "Mrs. Clavers" (Kirkland's pseudonym) by immediately combing their hair "with great deliberateness" and announcing they will "slick up" by changing dresses for dinner (42–44). Later, observing a local wedding in their new town of "Montacute," Kirkland parenthetically notes that the bride's dress was "not more than three or four years behind the fashion" (101). Throughout, she has a keen eye for the provincial pretensions to fashion pervading this ragbag of people on the make.

Chapter 28 describes Kirkland's inadvertent discovery of what the poorest family in the village does for entertainment. As she pays an unannounced charitable call, she finds the sons and daughters dressed up in ill-fitting finery, with the eldest daughter in a rich silk dress "made in the extreme mode, and set off by elegant jewelry," wrought gold pendants, and elegant gloves. They were clearly preparing for a party, despite their sick father and a house without door, hearth, window, or chimney. Two months later, the eldest daughter dies, presumably pregnant, cooped up in their windowless house during the winter "to elude the 'slow unmoving finger' of public scorn."

Kirkland's own scorn for the Newlands is also unmoved. She frames the chapter with a quotation from Goldsmith: "By sports like these are all their cares beguiled." The chapter concludes with some remarks about how "vicious and degraded" this particular "class of settlers" is. They have left Montacute now, taking their hogs and some neighbors' hogs with them, and good riddance; "I trust we have few such neighbors left" (145–149).

Both the strengths and the limitations of Kirkland's observant sketches can be found in abundance here. While she sees the foibles and the merits of plain folk with what she takes to be a relatively equal eye, her wit depends on a rigorous application of class standards to an egalitarian village. She is the consummate patrician, moving among artisans and farmers. What they see as her pride, she sees as her class superiority. For the most part she restricts her sympathy to other genteel ladies stranded in the wilderness, though even for them she has as much mockery as fellow feeling.

Several tales within a tale present cautionary doubles for Kirkland's wilderness success. Mrs. Rivers, seemingly her best friend and the only person she dignifies with the name of neighbor—at last, she says, "I had a neighbor" (99)—but too sentimental and depressed, has to be taken under Mrs. Clavers's protective wing. "Mrs. B——," who enters with "the step of a queen" but faints when her boy is kicked by a horse, has a face which strikes Kirkland "as one of the most melancholy I had ever seen" (111–113). She too is the depressed wife of a proud and indulgent man, and she too commits the cardinal sin of frontier life: she lets the neighbors see that she thinks them beneath her. Mrs. Beckworth, whose face tells a similar story "of sorrow and meek endurance," had to marry two other men before the penniless man who loved her and whom she loved got up the courage to propose instead of running away around the world (124–136).

As the tales of genteel disillusionment and hapless women's sorrow continue, we also meet a rich panoply of pretentious, gossiping local women. Foremost among them is Mrs. Nippers, epitome of "the talking sex of Montacute" (220). Mrs. Nippers gets her comeuppance in all manner of ways, from other villagers as well as the narrator. In writing this book, however, Kirkland out-gossips her village double and nemesis. While Mrs. Nippers talks of Mrs. Clavers to the town, Mrs. Clavers displays Mrs. Nippers to the world.

Much to Kirkland's surprise, apparently, the people of "Montacute" took her thinly fictionalized portrait extremely amiss. While her adventurousness always outstripped her prudence, as she says of herself (230), to have her *name* be mud was a fate far worse than plunging into a boghole. Eventually she left Michigan and returned to New York, where she settled down to the life of genteel writing and elite literary salons.[22] If Mrs. Nippers and her kind finally won the class war, Mrs. Kirkland's book permanently puts them in their place.

A New Home—Who'll Follow? therefore stands as one of the most flagrant and insouciant instances of the patrician paradigm, surviving and at least temporarily prospering in the American wilderness. It flaunts the class basis for genteel ideas of ladyhood. In keeping with her aristocratic orientation, the complexities of Kirkland's voice and wit depend on a clash between traditional pastoral and antipastoral. Complacent aristocrats arrive among the country roughs seeking self-regeneration or a better life and instead find dullness and pretension, on the one hand, hard work and common sense, on the other. A jaunty optimism leavens Kirkland's sardonic portraits of vulgar peasants and indolent aristocrats with her relish for unpretentious folk, people with generous hearts and plainspoken minds. In her world of "them" and "us," there are salty yeomen among the "them" as well as sugared fops among the "us." More profoundly, she partly dramatizes and mostly preaches her own self-refashioning, from a proud and exclusive fashion plate to an adaptable, cosmopolitan sensibility. By the end of chapter 17 she "had begun to claim for myself the dignified character of a cosmopolite, a philosophical observer of men and things" (102).

Kirkland also enjoys exposing the pretentions of city people to a romanticism and a cliquishness that country life cannot sustain. At times she veers toward cultural relativism, undermining her class allegiances in the name of a common humanity. Much more frequently, she uses her stay in the country to argue the virtues of pastoral retreat for encouraging a more integrated, inclusive patrician vision. In her next-to-last chapter, an explicit homily to her city readers, Kirkland declares that a journey "away from the conveniences and refined indulgences of civilized life" helps wean the comfortable from being "proud, selfish, and ungrateful," much as "occasional privation or abstinence" encourages health. To "the Sybarites, the puny exquisites, the world-worn and sated Epicureans of our cities," she recommends "a course of Michigan." Reduced to "a suit a-piece for herself and her children," any "doll of fortune" or "spoiled child of refined civilization" may discover herself more "a daughter of Eve" than of "that haughty spirit of exclusiveness which is the glory of the fashionable world" (226–227, 229–230).

Kirkland immediately pretends to back away from so direct an assault on what she calls "the rules of the sublime *clique*." Yet most of her cautionary tales have tended toward the same moral, and she now draws it still more stringently. Those in the world of high fashion become straw women for her appeal to more broadly civilized sensibilities. As for the clique, "in acknowledging even a leaning toward the 'vulgar' side, I place myself forever beyond its pale." She twits the "sublime clique" with its "vain-glorious" and "over-bearing . . . superiority," which "forms the usual ground for exclusiveness" (230–231).

So far, so mildly democratic. Yet the overwhelming effect of Kirkland's book is to praise with faint damn the gentility she so assiduously courts, from the mixture of "salvo" and "humble curtsey" at the end of her preface to the pose of "wall flower" with which she bids "an unceremonious adieu to the kind and courteous reader"—her last words. Throughout, she wittily plays with genteel conventions of ladyhood, from the very first sentence of her preface: "I am glad to be told by those who live in the world, that it has lately become fashionable to read prefaces." Mocking fashion, she aligns her voice with the fashionable world—the only world, she agrees, even as she writes from beyond its borders.

Her real salvos, she implies, will be directed partly at sophisticates who question her use of literary materials but mostly at the people of Michigan. Not that the worst will be shown, "pentagraphed from the life." Such horrors do inhabit her journals in great profusion, she says. But published journals "should be Parthian darts, sent abroad only when one's back is turned. To throw them in the teeth of one's everyday associates might diminish one's popularity rather inconveniently." Nonetheless, Kirkland assures her "courteous reader" that what seems the most "unnatural" or "incredible" is "literally true," that only "the most common-place parts" show her invention (31).

From the start, therefore, her voice is double: aggressive darts for her "new home" neighbors, ostentatious deference for her big-city peers. Within that doubleness lies further doubling, as she positions herself above as well as within the world of fashion, while touting the common sense of her new neighbors as they look over her "gimcracks" (76). She is hospitable yet superior to *everybody*, it seems. And that should be the mark of a true lady. Spirited yet demure, or at least demure enough to pass, Kirkland intends her book as a lesson in reducing false pride and increasing real pride. She writes as a self-confessed "mentor" for snobs, to bring her readers, like Mrs. Rivers, toward a more gracious sense of superiority (101).[23] Laced throughout is her belief that true ladyhood can thrive on the egalitarian American frontier, if the lady keeps her will and her wits about her.

The first half of *A New Home—Who'll Follow?* chronicles the slow triumph of that philosophy. Her very title, which seems so clumsy to modern ears, catches the double take of an unprepared genteel lady looking around her in the two hundred acres of unbuilt town which her husband has just bought. Where are my peers? Who will follow me?—who of my sort, that is. Who will share and confirm my status? *Can* I make a home of a place so "homely"?

Within the overt comedy of arrival in the mud, of learning the local language and customs, and of setting up the house, lies the richer comedy of Kirkland's self-refashioning to ensure her double triumph: her social popularity as first lady of the town, and her preservation of a ladyhood unacceptable to everyone below her. First she presents the problem: the impasse between the lady's expectation of deference and the local women's expectations of equality. As Kirkland introduces her home in chapter 1, she immediately addresses the quandary of a lady and her maid taking tea together, "without distinction," as her example of the rampant classlessness that abounds (33–34). Later, on her way to drawing her emphatic moral about not antagonizing the lowly, she recounts the problem of having "a greasy cook-maid, or a redolent stable-boy" as one's "table companion" (87).

Whatever one may think of "our common nature" with such people, the home is where one has to draw the class line. Kirkland fires one servant for too much domestic presumption, and refuses to hire another, the local schoolmistress, because she smokes a pipe (72, 84). Recurrently she is half-humorously appalled at the universal custom of borrowing—one neighbor even wants to borrow another's baby—though everyone feigns self-sufficiency. These people will feel obliged to me despite themselves, she vows (90).

Any true lady can find "many ways of *wearing round*" the habits of her neighbors, Kirkland continues. A lady's "silent influence of example"—her "neatness and propriety, and that delicate forbearance" from encroaching on others—will eventually reform and elevate boorish tastes, even if she has to be "one who sits *all day* in a carpeted parlor, teaches her own children instead of sending them to the district school, hates 'the breath of garlic-eaters,' and—oh fell climax!—knows nothing at all of soap-making" (87). Keep your pride hidden at all costs, Kirkland frequently counsels, since pride is "the bugbear of the western country" (170). But keep to your course, and these lower classes will end up saying admiringly, "sich grand ladies too!" (155).

A New Home—Who'll Follow? has usually been taken as the first notable piece of realism in American fiction.[24] Kirkland herself cues readers in that direction. This book, she repeatedly promises, will introduce city sophisticates to the reality rather than the romance of the frontier. Her realism, however, cannot be separated from her class consciousness, which often reduces her genuinely witty observations to a cloying anxiety about pleasing her absent peers. From the fancy chapter epigraphs, which use English and, occasionally, American texts for mostly ironic commentary on her neighbors, to her pervasive self-consciousness about writing to sophisticated people about a low subject, to her self-presentation as an exemplum for all ladies in the wilderness, Kirkland selects her realism with a lady's-eye view. She is more the Erma Bombeck than the Willa Cather of the frontier. Or rather, she is the Miss Manners of Michigan, since the most characteristic aspect of Erma Bombeck's humor—mothering and children—is almost entirely absent from Kirkland's realism.

Not until the tenth chapter do we learn that she has her children with her (65), though she has introduced her prized greyhound, D'Orsay, long before (54–55). It takes Kirkland another five chapters to mention her three children's names.[25] Either her servants handled almost all the child care, or, what seems more likely, Kirkland's astonishing censorship of her day-to-day domestic realities reflects her deliberate choice to write as a lady, not as a mother. She is intent on speaking collectively, and her "realism" mirrors the perceptions of Michigan that she thinks would interest lady readers. Therefore, she focuses far more on the problem of servants than on the problems and fascinations of children. As the quintessential lady, she only tolerates her children, reserving her love for an aristocratic dog and, most of all, her garden and the flowers of Michigan.[26]

Where is her husband in all this? Where, for that matter, is manhood? Kirkland wants to show how patrician norms of ladyhood can prevail in relentlessly agrarian and artisanal conditions. That she succeeds can be credited partly to her spirited will and partly to the traditional compatibility of patrician and artisan norms. She is, after all, the wife of the man who owns the town. Despite her claims to influencing the morals and manners of the rustics, however, ambitious and competitive men are the real agents of social change. Michigan had become one huge land grab, filled with speculators out for the quick buck.

The nationwide Panic of 1837, brought on by the first wave of rampant and uncontrolled speculation, can be seen in synecdoche here, as the rival town of Tinkerville goes bust before it is built. Mr. Rivers, her lady friend's still more snobbish husband, becomes instant president of the Tinkerville bank, put there by his father-in-law presumably because his gentlemanly pretensions and his aversion to work added a touch of class. This bank, like many others, takes advantage of the General Banking Law, "which allowed any dozen of men who could pledge real estate to a nominal amount, to assume the power of making money of rags" (159–161). In this "magic cauldron" of "bubble-bubble," elegant mansions grew instantly from trees that had not yet been cut down.

"Some thirty banks or more were the fungous growth of the new political hot-bed," Kirkland notes. She also notes the speedy arrival of the Rivers's new furniture and lavish carriage, "covered as closely from the vulgar gaze as a celebrated belle whose charms are on the wane" (161). Then come the ominous visits of the bank commissioners. At last comes the fatal discovery that "our men of power" had filled their vaults primarily with boxes of "broken glass and tenpenny nails, covered above and below with half-dollars, principally '*bogus*.' " So much for Tinkerville. "The distress among the poorer classes of farmers...was indescribable." Soon Mr. and Mrs. Rivers prudently leave for the East. There, "on the spoils of the Tinkerville wild cat," he finally fulfilled his boast to "live like a gentleman" (165–166).

In frontier Michigan a man could buy a great many acres for four hundred dollars and then sell the lot next week as a hundred shares for three hundred dollars each. With visions of founding "a second New-York," "the poor artizan, the journeyman mechanic...staked their poor means on strips of land which were at that moment a foot under water" (62–63). The all-male "madness" of seeing new villages everywhere had persuaded Kirkland's husband to purchase two hundred acres of marginally developed land (34). Envisioning and buying cities fostered an atmosphere of gab, dreams, and sharkishness "where sharp bargains are the grand aim of everybody" (78). While women greet newcomers with "a feeling of hostess-ship...men look upon each one, newly arrived, merely as an additional business-automaton—a somebody more with whom to try the race of enterprise, i.e. money-making" (99). Whereas a woman seeks "that home-feeling," even though her man's "habit of selling out so frequently" makes her search nearly impossible to fulfill, a man "holds himself ready to accept the first advantageous offer," and considers his home or farm "merely an article of trade, and which he knows his successor will look upon in the same light" (53).

The epitome of this new kind of manhood is Mr. Mazard, the gaunt, silver-tongued land speculator who suckers Mr. Kirkland into buying the town. From the first, Mrs. Kirkland presents Mr. Mazard as a fast-talking villain, "into whose clutches—but I anticipate." When she "particularly requested that the fine oaks ... might be spared," those oaks "were the first 'Banquos' at Montacute" to be cut down. Mr. Mazard had an "irresistible" salesman's air, to be sure: an "air of earnest conviction, of sincere anxiety for your interest, and, above all, of entire forgetfulness of his own." As evidence, he encourages the Kirklands to name the town "after the proprietor," though with becoming modesty Mr. Kirkland "referred the matter entirely to me" (41–43). Soon we see Mr. Mazard and her husband forcing the author away from her first ladylike meal, reducing her to tears. Eventually we learn that "Mr. Mazard had absconded; or, in Western language, 'cleared.' " Worse, Mr. Kirkland "had through inadvertence rendered himself liable for whatever that gentleman chose to buy or engage in his name" (88–89). With a sniff about "land sharks," Mrs. Kirkland dismisses the subject, only mentioning in passing that Tinkerville, too, had been another of Mr. Mazard's projects (119–120).

Kirkland's ongoing portrait of her bossy, thoughtful, preoccupied and sometimes helpless husband constitutes her most complex treatment of manhood. Despite himself, Mr. Kirkland fulfills Walt Whitman's credo to be "both in and out of the game." She appreciates him primarily, it seems, because of his deviance from the reigning game of manhood. Though at first he seems just another one of the generic "lords of creation" who sat at the dinner table and "fairly demolished in grave silence every eatable thing on it" (45), Kirkland soon sharply distinguishes her husband from the "men of substance" who ambitiously pursue the hunt for money. When he departs with a group of men who are considering buying another city, she doesn't bother to warn him against the folly, since "he was never very ambitious, and already owned Montacute. He went merely *pour se désennuyer* ... an unconcerned spectator, weary enough of the unvarying theme which appeared to fill the whole soul of the community." She simply tells him to stay out of the water and take care of his spectacles (57).

Occasionally Kirkland mockingly or self-mockingly portrays her husband as the awesome patriarch, preoccupied with business but able to see and punish his wife's many follies from afar. Chapter 19, for instance, begins by extolling the lack of "division of labor" in the country, where "every man ... must be qualified to play groom, teamster, or boot-black, as the case may be; besides 'tending the baby' at odd times, and cutting wood to cook his dinner with." Men of "good sense, good nature, and a little spice of practical philosophy" thrive; men who are "too proud or too indolent" mortify and vex their families. Those general reflections frame a journey taken by Mrs. Kirkland while her husband was away on business. The ensuing incident proves that whatever the division of labor, there is total division of the sexes.

Despite her long familiarity with country ways, she had worn her "silly thin shoes again.... old Broadway habits are *so* hard to forget." As she gets out of the carriage to walk, one of her favorite pastimes, she starts to sink. Suddenly Mr. Clavers appears, in the nick of time. "It seems his high mightiness had concluded by this time that I had been sufficiently punished for my folly, (all husbands are so tyrannical!) and condescended to come to my rescue. I should have been very sulky; but then, there were the children" (108–109).

Kirkland's remarks serve only as a prelude for a more lengthy "lesson" about the folly of a proud and indulgent man they soon meet. Clearly her husband is not *that* sort. True, he has no appreciation of flowers, and he mutely rides on ahead when she starts to sing in the woods (192). But at least he is not taken in by subsequent temptations to speculate, as he was the first time. Of course, he is mostly incompetent at domestic tasks, despite the alleged lack of division of labor. "Oh! for one of those feminine men, who can make good gruel, and wash the children's faces!" (95).

To call these tasks "feminine" gives the game away; she doesn't really mean it. He tries sometimes, and that's enough. Besides, his trying makes her laugh. More important is how she thinks of him among men. There, if he lost most of his shirt, he kept his dignity. If he was gullible, at least he was not rapacious. "My honored spouse—I acknowledge it with regret—" she says, tongue firmly in cheek, "is any thing but 'an enterprising man' " (159).

Here, much more simply than in Emerson, is patrician disdain for the new men on the make. Kirkland dramatizes class conflict on every hand, but her account of the men's sphere portrays a new class as if such men were an old, old story. In the women's sphere she presents the ladies learning about noblesse oblige or simply holding the line against the unwashed plebeian hordes. In the male sphere her husband engages with the new middle class half against his will.

Throughout, Mr. Kirkland's seeming lack of humiliation at having been gulled by Mr. Mazard suggests that for him, as for his wife, these Snopeses are something like Martians. Therefore, only money, not self-respect, can be lost to them. Her own attribution of traditional lower-class status to entrepreneurs may focus her satirical eye, but she misses the social revolution in progress under her nose. Her man is not a zealous competitor, and that negative, along with her triumphant ladyhood, preserves their class status in the wilderness.

Here, equally clearly, is the patrician lady's duplicity about depending on her man. She reveres him and minimizes him, behind a bantering veil. As she prefers not to acknowledge, her sense of ladyhood depends on her husband's ability to prosper among the new middle class. Perhaps for that reason, perhaps because of the simple separateness of their lives, she puts all the men, including Mr. Clavers, to the side. They are givens, to be honored, dealt with, and laughed at on the sly. Kirkland's way of honoring her husband is typically backhanded: she intimates his higher patrician calling by suggesting how little of a man he is in the prevailing mode. While her ambiguous presentation of him satisfies the particular duplicities of being the first lady of Montacute, her more general reflections on manhood and womanhood contain the same unmistakable note of helpless, submerged resentment we have seen in *Godey's Lady's Book*.

On the surface, the second half of *A New Home—Who'll Follow?* has nothing much to do except pad itself out to the length of a book. The essential drama of arrival, self-refashioning, and social triumph has been accomplished. Very aware of her more and more meandering narrative, Kirkland ties it together with a ribbon of self-deprecation. She now frequently charges herself with the usual female sins: digressing, gabbing, gossiping, being disorganized. Her story loiters and wanders just like a woman's mind, she says. She breaks the thread like a bad seamstress.

As she begins chapter 45, for instance, she announces, "I think I have discovered that the bent of my genius is altogether towards digression. Association leads me like a Will-o'-the-wisp. I can no more resist following a new train of thought, than a coquette the encouraging of a new lover." She simply can't "write one long coherent letter about Montacute," Kirkland concludes; "history is not my forte" (220, and see 114, 117–119, 150, 172, 192, 233). Even as she proves she is a much better storyteller than Eloise Fidler, the pretentiously feminine poetess who seeks a man with a euphonious last name, she roundly accuses herself of a generic femininity that incapacitates her for serious narrative.

Embedded in these self-accusations, which are absent from the first half of the book, are some premonitions of *A Room of One's Own*. There Virginia Woolf's much more ironically controlled digressions expose the impersonality, arrogance, and constrictedness of male intellectual

dominance. Kirkland makes something of the same claim for a superiority latent in her self-deprecation, though her sense of superiority
rests more on class than on gender. In one of her first such asides, she
pointedly asks readers not to respond to her "wandering talk . . . this
rambling gossiping style, this going back to take up dropped stitches,"
in "that terse and forceful style which is cultivated at Montacute"
(118).[27]

Montacute's style seems obviously lower class, at least to her. It is
also very male, she recurrently implies. Yet the maleness seems more
good than bad. For every man who brags about being the "boss" of his
wife, we meet two men of whose bossing Kirkland approves. Cora, her
last and lengthy double, develops romance illusions because of a too-
indulgent father (209). Men *should* be firm and patriarchal. When Kirkland tells Mrs. Beckworth's story of being twice deserted by her man,
she portrays the man as a romantic hero who keeps his love aflame
despite her two marriages of desperate convenience.

If Kirkland sniffs at the swaggering husband of the pipe-smoking
school-mistress (91), she delights in the plain-talking, witty man who
continually puts down his shrewish wife—a shrew, that is, until motherhood thankfully softens her (107). Women will gab for hours about
a problem that men will solve in minutes, Kirkland observes, clearly
admiring the men (218–219). If she presents her digressive style as
superior to laconic, uneducated frontier talk, she also presents it as
inferior to the straightforward male modes of good history and terse
logic. As a woman she belittles herself; as a lady she defends her right
to a discourse made up of weavings and adornments.

One could say that Kirkland is simply proving how she has conquered
her pride. Or that she has adopted the traditional rhetorical strategy
of educated women, most brilliantly handled before Woolf by Anne
Bradstreet: run circles around the men with humility. As the price, she
preserves her sense of (quite British) upper-classness by denying anger
and conflict. The second half of Kirkland's book buries resentment under
the arabesque self-image of an increasingly giddy gadabout. Like Poe's
Madeline in "The Fall of the House of Usher," another story about
patricians and the feminine, the suppressed woman returns. Beneath
layers and layers of class complacency, the ample folds of dress within
which she presents herself, a discontented wife and mother is struggling
to articulate herself in terms of gender rather than class.

In at least one sustained moment, a generalized resentment comes
to the fore. Though Kirkland's voice quickly retreats to more conventional duplicity, the passage intimates a stronger critique of manhood

and marriage than she permits herself in the lighthearted presentation of her husband's gullible greed. Seen in this light, her self-accusations act as a compensatory veil for the real drama of the second half: the silenced speech of a mature woman without romance, without society, and without recourse beyond the impersonal solace of class superiority.

Chapter 36 becomes Kirkland's meditation on the differences between young and mature women. The essential condition of women in the wilderness, as she has said several times, is to be left alone most of the day. A young wife, who naturally seeks to please "the old man," can tolerate the isolation. She "forgets the long, solitary, *wordless* day" the moment her man returns. Then "the youthful pair" share a contented dinner with a happiness rivaling that of "England's fair young queen" (186). Kirkland's emphasis on the wife's "wordless day" provides the unspoken frame for "the talking sex of Montacute" (220).[28]

For somewhat older wives, married to men "who have left small farms in the eastward States, and come to Michigan with the hope of acquiring property at a more rapid rate," the situation looks grim. These couples have sold off their first home, "sacrificed the convenient furniture," only to discover "that it kills old vines to tear them from their clinging-places. These people are much to be pitied, the women especially." The man continues to work contentedly, since he has the same work and a fresher "book of nature." But when he comes home, "full of self-gratulation on the favorable change in his lot, . . . he finds the home-bird drooping and disconsolate."

> What cares he if the time honored cupboard is meagerly represented by a few oak-boards lying on pegs and called shelves? His tea-equipage shines as it was wont—the biscuits can hardly stay on the brightly glistening plates. Will he find fault with the clay-built oven, or even the tin "reflector"? His bread never was better baked. What does he want with the great old cushioned rocking-chair? When he is tired he goes to bed, for he is never tired till bed-time.

"Women are the grumblers in Michigan," Kirkland sums up. Their "wearing sense of minor deprivations" contrasts sharply with the man's "conviction of good accruing on a large scale" (187–188).[29]

Among Kirkland's many doubles for herself, her generalized picture of displaced farm wives is the most poignant. Their situation clearly resembles hers, even down to her own "time honored cupboard," which had to do better duty as a corncrib (78). Unlike these women, a true lady must never grumble. Instead of voicing anger, she must set about the task of refining. Farm wives, too, resolve their grumbling in a ladylike way by introducing "those important nothings on which so much depends" (188).

Since "women feel sensibly the deficiencies . . . so they are the first to attempt the refining process." They buy a looking glass or a nice cherry table; they add plants and "a little gate," then some apple trees, lilacs, and currant bushes, "all by female effort." Thus, "if she do her 'spiriting gently,' and has anything but a Caliban for a minister, she can scarcely fail to throw over the real homeliness of her lot something of the magic of [the] IDEAL." Soon Kirkland is celebrating "that freedom from the restraints of pride and ceremony which is found only in a new country . . . the compensating power of the wilderness." By the end of her meditation she has talked herself far away from "the real homeliness of her lot." Now she presents liberty as the source "of the placid contentment, which seems the heritage of rural life" (188–190).

Is she grumbling or is she content? Is she slave or is she free? Chapter 36 retreats from one to the other. Men define women's condition by depriving them of their civilized homes. Women define women's strength by their ability to make "a new home" from intrinsic homeliness or homelessness. Within themselves, too, they refine their ugly, grumbling, helpless feelings into "the placid contentment" of adorning their "lot" with "important nothings." This is what it means to be free from pride and ceremony, which can be reinscribed in the collective fashions of ladyhood. In Kirkland's style, as in the behavior of the farm wives she so eloquently chronicles, being a lady acts as a "compensating power" for the powerless.

Or does it? If a lady's special gift is to pretty up the self-sacrificing disfigurement of her condition, some rancor, indistinguishable from self-contempt, lies in wait far beneath her fashionable style, for only herself to see. Kirkland comes close to acknowledging a certain deliberate falseness in the "realism" of her own style when she says in chapter 30 that she has to veil the truth about these "commonplace people." "Here are neither great ladies nor humble cottagers" to write about, she says, in words paralleling Cooper's remarks about America and anticipating Hawthorne's prefaces. Therefore, "I must try to describe something of Michigan cottage life, taking care to avail myself of such delicate periphrasis as may best veil the true homeliness of my subject" (153). To avail herself of the veil does not quite compensate for the "true homeliness" of a boring, ordinary middle class.

Each lady has been brought to this fallen state, of course, by her man's dream of money and property. But men are men, and in such matters, as Kirkland argues in the context of church squabbles, "it is easier to waive one's rights than to quarrel for them" (170). Quarreling, after all, would instantly reduce her from a lady to a shrew.

III

A New Home—Who'll Follow? differs from *Godey's Lady's Book* in tone as well as genre. Kirkland's jaunty, often sardonic wit contrasts sharply with Hale's conversational pursuit of the moral high ground. As a corollary, Hale makes the Christian religion central to her sense of genteel ladyhood. Kirkland doesn't even introduce the subject of religion until chapter 33, and then only to mock some of the visiting preachers. As she says, "a light work like this" would not be appropriate for speaking of religious matters (170). The difference suggests that Kirkland has a more traditionally upper-class orientation than does Hale, or at least that Hale feels more politically constrained by her growing evangelical constituency. Hale walks the line between the older patrician paradigm represented by women like Kirkland and the new middle-class emphasis on mothering and religious intensity as the basis for self-discipline and social involvement.

Nancy Hewitt's recent study of women's reform movements in Rochester, New York, during the mid–nineteenth century shows five quite distinct and competing groups, ranging from radical Quakers and working-class women to upper-middle-class and patrician women. Of these groups, evangelicalism centered in the upper-middle-class women. Hewitt ties their religious intensity to their upwardly mobile rivalry with the still-dominant gentry.[30] The triumph of the new and upwardly mobile middle class, already signaled in *Godey's* embrace of religious fervor, would come to full literary fruition in Susan Warner's *Wide, Wide World* (1850) and Harriet Beecher Stowe's *Uncle Tom's Cabin* (1852), as my next chapter suggests.

Despite their differences in genre, tone, and perhaps reader constituencies, we can draw several conclusions from taking Kirkland's novel and Hale's magazine together. To compare these two genteel women writers with Emerson and Douglass, each of whom was almost as preoccupied with manhood as Hale and Kirkland were with womanhood, can help to link some issues of class and gender that tend to remain separate in the discourses of both sexes.

My most fundamental conclusion is a very simple one: the two sexes can barely see each other. Emerson and Douglass see a competition for power and dominance everywhere. Their calls to manhood fuse character with freedom and—latent in Emerson, blatant in Douglass—a zest for besting other men, especially men of authority. Hale and Kirkland see manhood as patriarchy, with male dominance as a simple given rather than a complicated struggle.

Though Douglass was deeply committed to feminism, his account of his own self-made manhood reduces women to much the same vague support system as Emerson presumes with his rhetoric of self-reliance. Similarly, though from the opposite end, Hale and Kirkland present men in stereotypic terms as either preoccupied businessmen or generic animals needing to be chastened and polished. Each sex foregrounds its own self-absorptions at the expense of understanding its conflicts, which have a great deal to do with the other sex's conflicts. Women have to be mothers and want to be ladies; men have to be rivals and want to be powerful. The man's "crescive self," as Emerson calls it in "Experience," and the woman's self-deprecation function as inverse fantasy-mirrors of each other.

Here the manly code of hiding one's feelings exacerbates our own historical problem of understanding. A great danger for current feminist criticism lies in taking women's perceptions of patriarchy as the whole of male gender ideology. Patriarchy may well have been women's fundamental experience of men, with fathers and husbands on a continuum of dominance. For men, on the other hand, their domestic authority helped to secure or shore up their self-respect in a world farther and farther away from the small patriarchal shop or farm. If at home they seemed like absentee landlords, their hearts were probably elsewhere, measuring themselves in uncertain competition with other men. Since feelings of fear, humiliation, and inadequacy would be unmanly to voice, they remain as silenced in most men as public ambitions were in most women. Emerson and Douglass permit us to infer a great deal about these male anxieties.

As an equally simple corollary, the men use their gender superiority to transcend class conflict, while genteel women use class superiority to transcend gender conflict. Hale and Kirkland see classes with relative clarity, in part because they use their social status to salve the pain of unwaged gender struggle. Emerson puts class on the periphery of his calls to manhood, even as he taps the competitive jostle of patrician, artisan, and entrepreneurial models. Thoreau and Whitman, in proportion as they felt more deviant from male norms, make class tensions almost invisible.

Of these men, only Douglass discovers and emphasizes class. While Emerson and Thoreau, feeling on the margins of a displaced elite, redefine power as personal and cultural rather than political, Douglass refashions his voice to speak to a broader political base. If Emerson and Thoreau were insiders getting out, or above it all, Douglass was the outsider getting in. The price he pays is an Othello-like exaggeration of gentility suffusing his tone. Similarly, Hale and Kirland constrain their voices to speak collectively, both for and to their female constituencies.

Men such as Emerson, who use fantasies of cultural empowerment to transform their sense of class and sex-role marginality, slip easily into a narcissism equating one's self with the nation-in-the-making. Where women suppress their resentment at men's presumed dominance partly to preserve their class position, Emerson and Whitman—and, more snipingly, Thoreau—variously suppress feelings of rivalry, deviance, humiliation, and dispossession to voice the possibilities of a new class of artist-thinkers, who can join the whole country together just by using their minds to the full. Both the explicit grandiosity of self-empowering and the implicit depressiveness strain against manhood in manly terms.

If Emerson has been canonized and Hale has not, part of the reason has to do with the constituencies they address. Hale addresses leisured middle-class American women who aspire to be ladies—the kind of ladies Kirkland characterizes and caricatures as her audience. Emerson addresses a constituency in the making: a new intellectual elite. While Hale's constituency has fallen by the historical wayside, Emerson's nascent constituency has become institutionalized in the rise of the American university system. Since one of Emerson's great virtues is to make intellectuals feel like liberating gods, we return the favor by exercising our institutional power of syllabus making and our professional power of canon making to put him at or near the head of the American procession.[31]

An institutionalized constituency could not be the whole reason for anyone's primacy, of course, despite some recent conspiracy theories implying the contrary.[32] Emerson can presume upon his privileged maleness and his privileged class to reach for a much greater imaginative range, beyond any constituency in sight. Both Hale and Kirkland write to very specific audiences. They self-consciously attune their voices to their readers' perception of themselves as superior yet dependent. As one result, their voices now seem collectivized and constricted, even inauthentic in the case of Hale, by comparison with Emerson's man-making words.

As attuned to his audience as any woman writer, Douglass rewrites his *Narrative* to reach for a more high-toned self-image. If he speaks far more as a generalized voice of gentility than as the canny, pugnacious power broker he was becoming, Douglass nonetheless remains nearly as adroit as Emerson at speaking to several constituencies at once, tapping various sources of manhood across class and racial lines. The male writers' greater range of voice builds on their greater access to public influence, while the women's narration bespeaks the constraints of an audience not allowed to compete for power.

To contrast Emerson's "American Scholar" with Hale's first "Conversazione," both delivered or published in 1837, may illuminate these issues. Emerson's oration strives to convert men from their pursuit of money, power, and mechanical skill to the pursuit of "the active soul." He also urges the effeminated clergy to restore its connection with "the rough, spontaneous conversation of men" as the proper environment for discovering the connection between thinking and action. When readers as well as writers become creative thinkers, "the discontent of the literary class" will be transformed, and the clergy will be manly again.

Where Emerson calls for a reborn intellectual elite, Hale more accurately assesses the emerging American reading public as largely female and middle class. Though Emerson's rhetoric has been institutionalized in the twentieth century by professors who share Emerson's alienation from bourgeois norms, Hale was far more successful in shaping the values of American readers at that time. Accepting the social divisions that Emerson rebels against, she reflects and encourages a particular female sensibility, one especially suited to the wives of managers, professionals, and entrepreneurial capitalists: well educated but noncombative, superior to men yet self-sacrificing, able to feel as well as think, yet quick to suppress anger, desire, and ambition.

Both Emerson and Hale use religious language and make ultimately religious appeals for conversion, though to opposite social ends. Emerson wants to liberate a Whig manliness through intellectual activity, while Hale wants to define and aggrandize a particular social role for a new class of women. Physically circumscribed yet morally expansive, these women were expected to assume only those powers deriving from dependence, especially the power to influence their men. In that respect Hale laid the groundwork for women to constitute themselves as America's first national political action group. *Uncle Tom's Cabin* would catalyze moral mothers into the most politically effective interest-group agitation the nation has ever known.

One can therefore make a case that the rhetoric of conversion in Emerson and Hale reflects a shared drive to empower disparate audiences. Yet one writer bears rereading, while the other does not. True, my disparagement of writers like Hale could suggest some male bias toward Emerson's high-status alienation. Nevertheless, his current canonization also affirms the obvious: how exciting and innovative Emerson's prose is compared to Hale's deliberate conventionality.

While Caroline Kirkland ultimately looks backward to a traditional sense of class status, which she uses to ward off the pain of dependence, Hale seeks to blend Kirkland's ideal of ladyhood with a more middle-class language of evangelical empowering. The empowering must be felt collectively, rather than personally, and it must be expressed with duplicity, since dependence remains the given. Women must build their moral power on social powerlessness. In practice, Hale's arguments for female education did help to bring about a new, nondomestic role for women, that of schoolteacher. Throughout, however, Hale clothes her narrowly innovative social vision in traditional women's garments. Emerson, by contrast, uses the rhetoric of manhood to spring himself loose equally from the fading, faded language of gentility, from the competitive materialism of the new middle class, and from any specific political program.

To be a man of culture had become an effeminating oxymoron in America well before the Civil War. As the old class base for constituting writers as gentleman amateurs eroded, the self-consciousness of male writers facing a largely female reading public became a matter for public commentary, a decade before Hawthorne's now infamous remark about the "d——d mob of scribbling women." The problem, as a perceptive 1845 essay in *Godey's Lady's Book* emphasizes, had less to do with the tastes of women readers than with the fact that American men didn't read—at least not for pleasure. While the writer perceives the issue clearly, his solution is the conventional patrician prescription of noblesse oblige.[33]

The author of "British and American Monthlies," a hard-hitting comparison of manly British magazines with their feminized American counterparts, is none other than William Kirkland, Caroline Kirkland's husband. This was the man who had seemed so unenterprising and unhumiliated in the midst of the Michigan hustle. Now he argues for the superiority of English magazines because they can count on male readers. Magazines oriented toward men, he says, will emphasize religious, political, and economic controversy. English literary journals can take fire from nonliterary subjects. "This infusion of keen reality gives life and vigor to the whole" (272).

American literary journals, on the contrary, shy away from national controversies, mainly, he says, because "the great *general* questions are more nearly decided among us" (272). No one quarrels over monarchy, separation of church and state, or aristocracy; annexation and tariffs don't compel basic arguments. His list conveniently omits slavery and Indian dispossession, though the omissions might indicate how little those questions vexed most educated northerners before the 1850s. In any case, Kirkland's claim for broad ideological consensus on the virtues of republicanism would certainly be shared by most writers of his day.

Still, the absence of controversy makes for tepid, unmanly fare. An Englishman, he says, "asks for strong reading as naturally as for strong meat." The one bad feature of English periodicals is their endless serialization of sea romances, compared to which American love tales "are the less evil of the two." Having said that, however, Kirkland lays into love tales with an elegant, extended snort: "Love is much less the staple of British magazines than of our own. Whether the cause be that love is more an element in American life, or that our editors, cutting off politics, religion, and, indeed, every thing of a controversial character, have left a narrower field for their contributors, the fact is certain, that the amount of love that floats an American magazine would speedily sink a British one." If American magazines are "more amiable," they lack "strength and variety." If they are fortunately "free from that coarseness" of "the Trollope school," they "professedly aim only to please," not, as the English do, "to instruct and convince on the one hand, or to rail and brow-beat on the other" (272–273).

Kirkland's summation deserves full quotation, both for its pithy contrasts and for an American man's consciousness of female readers and gender polarization in the mid–1840s: "The English magazines are more masculine in character, addressed rather to the understanding than to the feelings. We have little doubt that more men than women read the British monthlies—more women than men our own. Ours have more the air of public amusements—light, graceful, it may be exciting and refining; theirs wear rather the aspect of public business—

eager and contentious, but, withal, strong and impressive." What, then, is to be done? Somehow, the American magazines need "a liberal infusion of *stronger* material." Yet American women readers are notoriously herdlike and capricious, fleeing conflict like the plague. "It is well known that one of our most experienced editors lost a thousand subscribers by a single article which gave the unpopular view of a certain subject" (273).[34]

Kirkland's solution is two-pronged. First, men "of wealth" should subscribe to *"all the best"* journals (his emphasis). If educated, intelligent men would spend fifty to a hundred dollars every year to be "patrons" of American literature, American writing would thrive, since "periodicals offer almost the only chance of compensation to American authors." Second, the best and most established writers should "contribute voluntarily their choicest efforts" for no pay. These pieces would be "gems" for "the connoisseur, . . . yielding their benign power only to the initiated. . . . There would still be room enough for that larger class of writers who must write for pay if they write [at] all" (274–275).

Kirkland's two solutions are of course blatantly elitist. Like his wife, he uses a traditional idea of class to solve a growing problem of gender. Wealthy men should be patrons—they don't actually have to read the stuff—and gentleman amateurs should give their pearls to the swinish marketplace. Both collective actions of the elite would help to improve national taste. Here would be noblesse oblige on a large scale.

Here also, at the end of the patrician hegemony which Caroline Kirkland's novel presumes, we can see manhood nervously pushing beyond its class controls to become a conscious problem. Her husband's essay first raises then avoids the issue of manhood by recourse to elite traditions of privilege. Kirkland's call for patrons among authors and audiences seems a pale shadow of Emerson's cry for more manly readers and writers. Yet it carries something of the same male baggage, while it signals a clear consciousness of the predominance of genteel, middle-class women readers by 1845.

In struggling against these social constraints, male writers of the American Renaissance liberate a great variety of quirky and devious rhetorical energies. To empower their collective dependency, women writers write acres of duplicitous, though more forgettable prose. The contrast between these strategies will shape the rest of this book.

6

Impassioned Women:
The Wide, Wide World and *Uncle Tom's Cabin*

This chapter begins with what may seem a roundabout introduction to classic American literature's Great Divide, the split between popular women's literature and canonized men's texts. Afterward I look in some detail at the first mass-market best seller in the United States, *The Wide, Wide World* (1850). As little Ellen Montgomery ventures into the wide world, so paradoxically constricted by bitter sorrow, her interior journey takes her from passionately resenting her father toward serenely submitting to her future husband, though with oddly centripetal portraits of strong women at the periphery. My analysis differs from some current feminist readings by emphasizing the triumph of patriarchal discourse over initial duplicity in Susan Warner's struggle to interpret and resolve women's suffering.

Warner's impassioned story preaches patriarchal submission and dramatizes solitude; Stowe's impassioned story (1852) preaches and dramatizes how women can triumph over marketplace manhood. The righteous energy of mothers, she shows, can transform their men's "hard Anglo-Saxon" drive for dominance. Both Stowe and Warner assume class hierarchy in their narratives, just as they assume genteel women readers as their primary audience. But gender consciousness displaces class consciousness as their ideological frame for interpreting power, which now seems a matter of male dominance, not social position.

For Warner and Stowe, male dominance is a given. Most men, whatever their class, whether at home or in the world of business, appear interchangeable in their presumptuous insensitivity to women. For men, as male writers portray them, dominance has to be earned through rivalry. As the Ahabs, Hollingsworths, and Westervelts battle it out, the Ishmaels and Coverdales stand off to the side, wavering between self-absorption and mesmerized fascination. They empower themselves as narrators in large part by transforming feelings of unmanly deviance into strategies of deviousness.

If *The Blithedale Romance* becomes the Revenge of the Aesthete though Miles Coverdale's passive-aggressive triumph over the men of force, *Uncle Tom's Cabin* shows how mother love can be the best revenge. Cassy, the ultimate impassioned woman, hoists the ultimate man of force, Simon Legree, by his own gothic guilt for despising his mother. In these contrasting narratives, impassioned women and devious men represent opposite solutions to a common problem: feelings of powerlessness brought on by a new ideology of manhood, which defines male self-worth primarily through workplace competition.

To compare Hawthorne's controlled, guarded, constantly shifting voices with the relatively uncomplicated patrician tone of Francis Parkman's *Oregon Trail* (1849) or Richard Henry Dana's *Two Years before the Mast* (1840) shows a shift from genteel to premodernist narrative strategies. Both Parkman and Dana use class status to fend off anxieties about gender conflicts or, what may be the same thing to them, unmanly breakdown. For Hawthorne, and Melville too, that strategy is no longer available. A parallel shift in women's fiction moves from the pose of amused, adaptable refinement in Hale and Kirkland, at once superior to their men yet dependent on them, to the evangelical passion of Warner and Stowe for conversion. Here models of women's autonomy and feelings of resentment keep breaking through their opposite strategies for subduing a daughter's righteous anger (Warner) or empowering mother's righteous anger (Stowe). My readings of these texts support those feminist historians who emphasize suppressed resentment at the heart of evangelical female piety.

Within and beyond my analyses of various male and female writers looms their basic gender separation. Much complexity follows from the simple conclusion of my last chapter: how different women's experience of men was from men's experience of themselves and each other.

I

Of all the academic committee meetings I've ever attended, one stays most vividly in my mind. It was a meeting of instructors for a required sophomore course in close reading at Rutgers University. We were arguing about a common assignment for chapters 21 and 22—the Colonel Sherburn episode—of *The Adventures of Huckleberry Finn*.

The draft at hand had been written by a well-known specialist in eighteenth-century British prose. He proposed a step-by-step focus on Huck's oddly detached description of the town, the loafers, and their sadistic ways of entertaining themselves. Students would then consider the Boggs-Sherburn episode, so entertaining to the yokels, so disturbing to us, and so noncommittally recounted by Huck. My colleague's goal was to bring students toward an awareness of Twain's ironic narration, especially the Gulliver-like limits of Huck's literalist perspectives, since Huck responds only to what affects him directly and physically.

The draft was brilliantly done, and I still use it in preparing to teach the book. Nonetheless, I wanted more focus on the theme of authority. In particular, I wanted students to consider the circus scene immediately following Colonel Sherburn's facing down of the lynch mob. There, I argued, they could see how Twain inverts the theme of authority. A seemingly drunk man, like Boggs, is not shot down but proves to be completely in control, fooling the ringmaster (to Huck's naïve eyes) and restoring Huck's sense of moral order.

Our discussion became rather heated, at least by academic standards. Finally the eighteenth-century specialist airily waved his hand. "Have it your way," he said. "The dumb ones will write about themes, and the smart ones will write about narration."

It was a superb put-down, of course. Beyond that, it was a superb definition of close reading. Various Americanists glanced furtively at each other around the room, experiencing a belated shock of recognition. If the Trinity, as Eldridge Cleaver once said, is like three-in-one oil, I felt more uneasily triangulated. I was Bottom, exposed as an ass; Miranda, glimpsing a brave new world; and Monsieur Jourdain, discovering that I had been speaking close reading all my professional life without quite knowing it.

Americanists tend to be theme people at heart, several of us concluded later. We felt skeptical of intelligence and irony for its own sake; that kind of formalism somehow seemed, well, too British. We liked the exuberance and risk of taking a stand, affirming a point of view.

Even those of us educated at elite schools had more of the simple middle-class "Go for it!" in our natures. Yet teasing out the ambiguities and ironies, enjoying the play of contrary meanings, appreciating an author's control of voices, was undeniably our stock in trade. The moment remains so memorable for me partly because it gave me such a lucid formula for doing close reading and partly because I felt so deviant from being smart, the prerequisite for high praise in our profession.

I bring up that story here as a way of introducing the vexing chasm in the American Renaissance between popular women's literature and canonized male texts. Reading *The Wide, Wide World* or *Uncle Tom's Cabin* makes me respond powerfully to simple themes: the imperative of self-conversion, the horrors of slavery. To write about that, in our current professional climate, means being dumb. Reading Hawthorne or Melville throws me into the briar patch of devious narrations. To write about that reaffirms my intellectual complexity and elite sensitivity.

A few recent critics, notably Nina Baym and Jane Tompkins, have taken issue with the tendency of academics to value American Renaissance texts for their close-readability, whether of the formalist or deconstructive variety.[1] A more common feminist approach in the last decade, prompted by Sandra Gilbert and Susan Gubar, is to see doubling and duplicity, and thus a sufficient intellectual complexity as well as rebelliousness, throughout nineteenth-century women's literature. My last chapter tries to bring Sarah Hale and Caroline Kirkland into that fold. Despite the exclusivist tendency of some feminist critics, similar narrative strategies are also embedded in the work of various male writers, from Frederick Douglass, as I argued in Chapter 4, to Hawthorne and Melville.[2]

An influential essay by Myra Jehlen, "Archimedes and the Paradox of Feminist Criticism," courageously addresses feminist claims for literary autonomy and the buried issue of quality. Disputing Nina Baym's argument for an independent tradition of women's writing, Jehlen finds not so much a separate territory as "one long border." Moreover, she says, for the most part these women's books are "awful." Women writing in their own image turn out to be writing in the image men have defined for them: sentimental, conformist, self-denying, with murky plots and heavenly visions, high on piety and low on sex. Their plots emphasize moral regeneration, yet without what Jehlen calls "interior life," the essence for her of a real women's tradition. Popular women's fiction should be seen as symptom of the self-suppression exacted by dependence on patriarchy, she concludes. It is a tradition to be superseded, not revered.[3]

Antebellum women's fiction offers much more than sentimentality and religion, to be sure. Fanny Fern, Elizabeth Stoddard, and others conspicuously break the mold Jehlen defines. They are witty, acerbic narrators of women's struggle to escape the prison house of male expectations. As one of Stoddard's minor characters says in *The Morgesons* (1862), "I have a poor lot of roses . . . but some splendid cactuses." The phrase could stand as an epigraph for the novel, or for Fanny Fern's *Ruth Hall* (1855), an exuberantly satiric chronicle of a woman's journey from conventional romance to self-reliance, economic independence, and the pleasures of revenge. Recently Joanne Dobson has made a similar case for E. D. E. N. Southworth's *Hidden Hand* (1859) as well.[4]

Nevertheless, I don't see how anyone who reads Maria Cummins's *Lamplighter* (1854) can deny that Jehlen has scored some palpable hits. To cast the net more broadly, extravagant claims have been made lately for Lydia Maria Child's *Hobomok* (1822), another portrait of a strong heroine who challenges patriarchy. Here the heroine actually marries an Indian and has a child before Mr. Right comes back and Hobomok nobly disappears. To read *Hobomok*, however, or a much better book such as *The Morgesons*, prefaced as they have been with near-canonical praise, has been for me an exasperating and dispiriting experience.[5]

Where Child's prose is almost unrelievedly flat and conventional, Stoddard's at least offers many moments of startling, often malicious wit. In both, caustic observations about patriarchy abound. Satisfactorily reversing Jehlen's formula, each is low on piety and high, if not on sex, then on a more diffusely charged energy, a struggle for self-articulation. With Stoddard, the sea and the tide come to symbolize Cassandra Morgeson's yearning for a boundless self—what Lawrence Buell calls her "drive for self-realization" and autonomy. The men who presume to control her life have no sense of the sea inside them. As her father says to Cassy, "I have been on my guard against that which everyday life might present—a lie, a theft, or a meanness; but of the undercurrent, which really bears you on, I have known nothing" (137).[6]

As Cassy drives about with her father on his business, she discovers that "the sole relation between [men] was—Traffic. Personality was forgotten in the absorbed attention which was given to business. They appeared to me, though, as if pursuing something beyond Gain, which should narcotize or stimulate them" (142). Ambiguously "possessed" from the first sentence, Cassy alternately yearns to be self-possessed, with a room of her own and a Dickinsonian vision that "I must be my own society" (131), or to be swept away in equally Dickinsonian fashion by a strong, alien master who will define her life. As she looks at the sea, "hemmed in on all sides," it seems to her "milky, misty, and uncertain; the predominant shores stifled its voice, if it ever had one" (179). By the end, the sea "wears a relentless aspect to me now; its eternal monotone expresses no pity, no compassion" (252).[7] Such passages evoke the more sustained power of the sea in Kate Chopin's *Awakening*, though with less sensuality and more self-pity.

More frequently Stoddard evokes Emily Dickinson's "My Life had stood—A Loaded Gun" (#754). Explosively Cassy waits in all the "Corners" of her decentered self for some "Owner" to aim her at her mother, sister, and female friends, or any other "Doe" who comes into view. Along with her malice against women she shows a gothic relish for inaccessible, potentially brutal men. After a prickly account of Cassy's early childhood, the first half of *The Morgesons* promises to be a classic bodice-ripper. Charles Morgeson pursues his cousin Cassy with Heathcliffian eruptiveness, while Cassy fends off and reciprocates his passion. A King Kong of a married man, Charles is a newly rich entrepreneur, a brooding, self-made man of force who hits his employees for their own good and loves to break his wild, willful horses. He grows increasingly obsessed with breaking in his willful cousin, whom her hateful puritanical grandfather has already compared to a "skittish" horse (49). Yet Charles also cherishes fragile flowers, to "protect them from my own touch" (81, also 69). Cassy shivers, she dreams of him, she backs away, she responds.

Then—" 'Twas beauty killed the beast"—just as desire seems about to burst into half-incestuous adultery, Charles suddenly dies, killed by his wildest horse as he is trying to save Cassy. This abrupt halt to the novel's only sustained drama has been prefigured by the fate of Cassy's first potential boyfriend, gawky Joe Bacon. His "disgusting" liking for Cassy makes her so "irritable" that Stoddard immediately kills him off with the measles (55–56).

After Charles's death, ostensibly grieving, Cassy opens herself a little toward her mother and her sister Veronica. What seems to be a proto-feminist swerve toward sisterhood, after a good deal of intense hatred between the girls, culminates in Veronica's declaration of love for Cassy, to counter their housekeeper's cynical observation about "sisters that don't love each other" (145, and see 141, where Veronica kisses Cassy's hand). Veronica's outraged declaration plunges her into a near-fatal illness. Cassy's only response: " 'All declarations in my behalf are made to third persons,' I thought" (145). With an odd interior numbness, she quickly retreats from any struggle for female bonding into inter-mittant trench warfare with Veronica and a perfunctory idealization of her mother's selfless love. At last the egregious swerves of plot drive out this reader's involvement altogether, especially after Cassy returns home from a long absence to find her mother placidly sitting in her usual chair by the fire—dead (205–206).

Analytically one can do interesting things with Mrs. Morgeson's death. Cassy's startling sequence of feelingless reactions echoes her hated grandfather's discovery of his dead wife in bed beside him when he woke up one morning. He simply selected a text for the funeral sermon. Subsequently, the only difference in his behavior was "his habit of chafing his hands" (29). Cassy, finding her mother dead, performs three quick actions. First, she picks up the empty inverted cup in her mother's lap and sets it on the shelf. Then, she takes her mother's handkerchief from her "nerveless hand" and "thrust it into my bosom." Finally, she tries to tug off her own gloves. When Veronica comes in, Cassy is still tugging at her gloves. " 'She is dead,' I said. 'I can't get them off.' " Veronica faints, then has hysterics. Cassy watches the scene, and then she goes off to sleep. When she wakes up, she thinks of "Mother!—her goodness and beauty, her pure heart, her simplicity— I felt them all" (206).[8]

Cassy behaves like her grandfather, the heartless patriarch, while her words come from the heart of true American womanhood. In both modes, she poses at the extreme. The more I consider this bizarre scene, the more it strikes me as a teasing game of poses. The daughter's self has been erased long before she erases her mother's.

One could make a *To the Lighthouse* case that such a laconic erasure of mother suggests resentment for a basically loveless and privatized childhood. Blaming mother, or wanting to kill her, becomes displaced into Cassy's protracted fighting with various women, notably Veronica and Mrs. Somers, a much stronger and haughtier mother figure. After all, her father pays much more attention to Cassy than her mother ever does. He at least writes her a letter every few months, while mother sinks into her Bible. Unlike Woolf, however, Stoddard gives readers little access to these undercurrents and little reason to be interested in them. Whatever the possible analyses of such a scene, psychological or sociological, my readerly response is to laugh in disbelief and throw up my hands. Like Cassy, the narrative is a posturing, arbitrary tease, subsiding into a diffuse and bilious narcissism. Neither in voice, plot, nor characterization is there the interior life Jehlen calls for.

In *Hobomok* Child rather simply, if daringly flaunts a daughter's rebellion, then retreats to conventional marriage. In *The Morgesons* Stoddard's zinging one-liners and laconic, elliptical tone finally prove to be equally dependent on the patriarchal family and the patriarchal definition of womanhood she seems to scorn. These novels are "awful" not in Jehlen's absolute sense but in a more frustrating way: they lack commitment to their own energies. At best they offer capricious, arbitrary swerves between rebellion and submission. Their abrupt compressions and discontinuities bring on detachment, at least in me.

A stronger counterargument to Jehlen could claim that the canonized men are not all that different. The need of a Hawthorne or a Melville to be difficult, or intellectually devious, might come in part from similar feelings of quarrelsome dependence not so much on patriarchy as on their provincial readers. My final chapters will analyze their deviousness in somewhat different terms, as a mixture of alienation, rivalry, and deviance from male roles. Where women's writing presumes intense bonds with readers, Hawthorne and Melville solicit, yet deny such bonds.

Elizabeth Stoddard blends passion, malice, and an eerie sense of narcissistic helplessness to portray intense women slowly stifled by small-town conventions of womanhood. Often she momentarily evokes Dickinson's sensibility. After meeting Dickinson in 1870, Thomas Wentworth Higginson began his late-night letter to his wife by saying, "I shan't sit up tonight to write you all about E.D. dearest but if you had read Mrs. Stoddard's novels you could understand a house where each member runs his or her own selves."[9] Yet Dickinson gives us a rich, playful, frightening "interior life," in Jehlen's terms, a life filled with "internal difference / Where the Meanings, are" (#258). Compared to Dickinson's best poems, Stoddard's prose looks like sniping, with little self-exploration.

Hawthorne's deviousness does not take the form of fragmented resentments. Much more guarded than either woman, Hawthorne's "feminine" sensibility—so praised by his contemporary readers—seems at least as calculated as it is dependent. In part the difference has to do with manly self-control. In part, too, Hawthorne could reach for a different audience. The premodernist difficulties of major texts by Hawthorne and Melville presume a potential intellectual elite as audience, perhaps less blatantly than Emerson did in calling for cultural regeneration, but with a similar independence from prevailing social norms.

Women's writing was more rigorously bound to its audience: wives and girls who were afraid to challenge social expectations. Some feared the conflict with men that real autonomy would bring. Many were more diffusely afraid of the stigma brought on by deviance from women's proper domestic role. At least on the surface, still others said they were not only content but eager to be concerned with children and fashions instead of salaried work. Whether leisured or working, happy or unhappy, these were middle-class women who wanted above all else to be, as the reigning phrase put it, polite, refined, and Christian. Melville's wife, for instance, refused to leave her husband in the late 1860s, even though he probably beat her. Various members of her family pleaded with her to leave him, even drawing up plans for her escape. It wasn't love of her husband that kept her home. She just couldn't face the social shame.[10]

Nonconformity was therefore relatively unavailable to women writers, at least those unwilling to brave vigorous public disapproval. An occasional Angelina Grimké, Fanny Wright, or Fanny Fern, ready to take on the slings and arrows of outraged public opinion, could make a sizable public impact. Fanny Fern in particular became magnificently successful as the first female newspaper columnist and a canny feminist satirist for decades. Yet even Margaret Fuller clothed her more sophisticated feminism in the abstracted Emersonian garments of transcendentalism until she went to Europe. Emily Dickinson, who experienced her genius with full force, chose to publish only a trickle of poems. She reserved her impact for a later century.[11]

II

If autonomy terrified and fascinated women, the relatively safe terrain of literary fantasy gave such readers a contradictory mix of satisfactions, allowing them to voice anger at the fathers and husbands who controlled their lives, to see a girl making it on her own, and to see a girl thankfully mastering her anger. Here was the seemingly instantaneous interpretive constituency so avid for *The Wide, Wide World,* the first mass-market best seller in the United States. The story of its 1850 publication is well known. Rejected by publisher after publisher—Harper's reader jotted "Fudge!" in the margin—it was finally accepted by George P. Putnam, who was about to reject it himself when he happened to give it to his mother. "If you never publish another book," she said, "publish this!" Putnam doubtfully complied, printing only 750 copies and forcing Warner to delete the last chapter, in which Ellen marries, to keep the length down. Two years later the novel was moving toward its fourteeth edition. It sold steadily and well for the next half century, moving through sixty-seven reprints to sell over a million copies.[12]

Throughout the novel, Susan Warner portrays Ellen Montgomery as a young girl who has to learn two skills: how to make her way alone in the world and how to curb her too easily excitable passions, which almost always express anger and sorrow. In the long central section, after her heartless father has arbitrarily sent her dying mother to France and sent Ellen to live with his marginally less heartless half sister, Ellen begins to learn how to transform her uncontrollable resentments into patient endurance. Warner frames Ellen's quest for self-mastery with portraits of two very different single women: Mrs. Vawse, a gentle, elderly Christian woman who lives alone on a mountaintop, and Fortune Emerson, Captain Montgomery's sharp-tongued relative.

Born Swiss, Mrs. Vawse had been brought up as the personal attendant to a wealthy young French lady, who married an American and emigrated. Following her to America, where the lady soon died, Mrs. Vawse then married, "and since that time," as Ellen's best friend, Alice, recounts, "she has been tossed from trouble to trouble;—a perfect sea of troubles;—till now she is left like a wreck upon this mountain top." After she lost her mistress, her husband, and her sons, "one after the other," Mrs. Vawse surmounted the wreckage of her life. Now she lives out her days high above the world, with a "beautifully placid" brow, having survived all the "sorrows" and "storms" intimated by its "deep-marked" wrinkles. She is both "truly lady-like," Alice declares, and truly autonomous; "there is not a more independent woman breathing."[13]

Clearly Warner intends Mrs. Vawse as a model for Ellen's conversion from resentment to serenity. The source of her grandmotherly strength, however, is neither a "happy and fulfilled" self-reliance nor matriarchal spiritual power, as Jane Tompkins suggests, but her dependence on Jesus.[14] Mrs. Vawse's quiet contentment with things as they are bespeaks the calm after great suffering—the formal, ceremonious equipoise of freezing and letting go that Emily Dickinson describes in "After great pain" (#341). As Mrs. Vawse tells Ellen, we look to Jesus only when all our dearest friends are taken away (189). Having been pricked and crucified, she settles into her high-peaked house on the mountaintop to remind herself of her childhood in the Swiss Alps, before fate brought her to exile in America.

On the surface her autonomy seems comfortably nourishing to Ellen, even a little comic; she resembles one of Walt Disney's fairy godmothers. Never lonely, she lives not only with Jesus but also with an all-white cow named Snow. After Alice dies, Mrs. Vawse promises to teach Ellen various skills, particularly mending and patching (457), though Ellen's heart is not in her lessons. Mrs. Vawse also helps Ellen to learn French, the language in which they always converse. If her instruction urges Ellen's behavior toward a harmonious blending of self-sufficiency and domestic submission, Mrs. Vawse's example helps to bring that paradox into Ellen's heart as well.

This sweet, solitary lady has learned what Ellen must learn: not self-assertiveness for its own sake, what modern readers might like to prize in her, but the ability to break one's own will. Mrs. Vawse's character teaches Ellen never to be provoked into anger, however justified the anger might be, and always to grasp the secret of unexpressed suffering in even the most aggravating woman's heart. In fact, Alice takes Ellen to meet Mrs. Vawse because both Alice and Ellen need "a lesson of quiet contentment" (188). Ellen especially needs to curb her vehement resentment of her aunt, who seems cast in the role of wicked stepmother.[15] Perhaps Aunt Fortune too, Alice suggests, may be unhappy, "and no one can tell but those that are unhappy how hard it is not to be unamiable too" (184).

Aunt Fortune is also a strong single woman. Significantly, unlike Mrs. Vawse, she has never married. Where Mrs. Vawse has been hurt and thus gentled, Aunt Fortune remains "sharp all over," as Ellen puts it aggrievedly in a letter to her mother (111). Miss Emerson moves weirdly, Ellen says; she walks in jerks and jumps. She also speaks in a "tone of indignant house wifery" (100 and 338: "The ruling passion of this lady was thrift; her next, good housewifery"). Much like the equally sharp Ophelia in *Uncle Tom's Cabin*, she asserts a crisp efficiency. Unlike Ophelia, Ellen's aunt seems filled with resentment rather than zest as she runs her farm. She bustles about officiously and makes demands; she hits the child; she snoops into her niece's letters and keeps some of mother's letters hidden from Ellen for years; she flares up at any sign of Ellen's willfulness or incompetence. Aunt Emerson could be the Lidian Emerson that Gay Wilson Allen describes: "an habitual complainer," a woman no man could love. True, her resentments have some cause: her brother never bothered to notify her when his daughter was coming to stay (99). Nonetheless, the aunt's intrusive harshness looks grossly out of proportion to the misdeeds of an abandoned little girl, vaguely preadolescent, probably ten or eleven though always described simply as "little Ellen."[16]

Such a tormenting mixture of anger and self-reliance, Warner implies, will be the fate of any woman who has not been properly guided by father and husband. A disconnection from fathering ambiguously hovers in the background of Aunt Fortune's incapacity for womanly affection. As Ellen's mother says, she is not her father's sister, "only his half-sister; the daughter of his mother, not the daughter of his father." "I am very sorry for that," Ellen immediately responds. "I am afraid she will not be so likely to love me" (21).

The more immediate joke here, one that Warner fully intended, is embedded in the aunt's name: Miss Fortune Emerson. Any woman would find it a "misfortune" to be an Emerson, self-reliant, taking responsibility for her own life.[17]

Warner's sustained structural pun on Miss Fortune Emerson's name can be taken as a nineteenth-century counterpart to Virginia Woolf's sketch of Shakespeare's sister, in *A Room of One's Own*. But Woolf and Warner go in opposite directions: Woolf toward feminism, Warner toward patriarchy. Warner's cautionary characterization of Miss Fortune represents true American womanhood's heartfelt assent to the supportive role for women implied in Emerson's "nonchalance of boys who are sure of their dinner" or in Frederick Douglass's glorification of self-made men. A boy has to learn how to stride out alone into the world of competition. A girl has to learn how to love, honor, and obey, even when nothing comes back from her man but orders and nonchalance.

Warner's characterization of Aunt Fortune functions partly for local color and comedy. Like Ophelia, she is a stock Yankee character, the crisply obsessive domestic general with no one but Ellen to command. More profoundly, Aunt Fortune's negative characterization illustrates the intense pressure on middle-class women to disown their resentments, or at least to condemn negative feelings as self-disabling. From start to finish, *The Wide, Wide World* chastises women's anger, even as the narrative gives Ellen every right to be angry.

The success of Warner's story suggests the emotional and ideological context for Hawthorne's much more devious narration of *The Scarlet*

Letter, published in the same year. This, too, is a story of a heroine whose initial defiance of patriarchy at last yields to muted submission. On the one hand, Hawthorne's double-tongued narrator enthusiastically agrees with what proper women, which is to say most of his readers, think womanhood should be. Pearl's conversion from anger to tears, at the end of chapter 23, could almost be lifted from Susan Warner, in theme as well as preachiness: "The great scene of grief, in which the wild infant bore a part, had developed all her sympathies; and as her tears fell upon her father's cheek, they were the pledge that she would grow up amid human joy and sorrow, nor for ever do battle with the world, but be a woman in it." That transformation sums up the moral progress of Hester, Ellen, and Miss Fortune, who eventually marries gentle but increasingly masterful Mr. Van Brunt and, as Nancy says of her, lives "quieter" ever after (486). As Nancy continues, "I don't mean she ain't as ugly as ever, you know, but she has to keep it in."[18]

On the other hand, also like *The Wide, Wide World*, Hawthorne's romance evokes the plight of women who hopelessly suffer and sorrow because they depend on men. Pearl, after all, is tearfully kissing a "father" who has never even acknowledged her until that moment, let alone spent any time with her. Though Hester reluctantly gives up her hopes of being a prophet of sex-role equality, her ministrations to other sorrowing women take for granted their shared, continuous burden of unempowered feelings. These women are of only two kinds, the narrator says sympathetically, those "in the continually recurring trials of wounded, wasted, wronged, misplaced, or erring and sinful passion,— or with the dreary burden of a heart unyielded, because unvalued and unsought."[19] Whether through passion or unrequited love, these women live out their lives as wounded discards.

Not for them the jaunty feminist formula of the early 1970s, "A woman without a man is like a fish without a bicycle." Instead, like good readers of Susan Warner, whose sister once said that she wrote *The Wide, Wide World* on her knees, Hester's confidantes have to content themselves with various forms of kneeling, whether weeping, praying, submitting, or simply scrubbing the floor. At best they find some solace in martyrdom, which as we learn earlier for Hester (chap. 5), is "half a truth, and half a self-delusion."[20]

Male dominance and female powerlessness, as Helen Papashvily was the first of many to say about *The Wide, Wide World*, is the basic issue. Ostensibly, however, the issue is how to change women's feelings. As Ellen settles in with her aunt, how the two will humanize each other becomes the essential drama. Can either one learn to love? Can either get beyond her rages and her self-reliance? These questions also shape the middle portions of *The Scarlet Letter*, where Hester and Pearl similarly flounder in untransfigured anger. In the middle of *Uncle Tom's Cabin*, too, Ophelia and Topsy flail away at each other, neither able to love.

For Stowe, little Eva's death provides the answer. The child's Christlike spirit of selfless love redeems Ophelia from her racist disgust and coaxes out her mothering instinct. Topsy will surely bloom into lovingness herself, once she is truly cared for. For Hawthorne, at least in one of his voices, mothering protects Hester from taking radical thoughts too far and softens her toward womanhood again. For Warner, women must grow toward love along more strictly patriarchal lines.

Yet solitude paradoxically defines the inward state of Warner's women. Throughout the novel we focus on Ellen alone. Mothering lies in the girl's vestigial past; marriage beckons in her uncertain future, until the deleted final chapter. While a journey toward marriage dictates the outward shape of Ellen's life, as it should for all girls, woman's essential aloneness shows in the title: not just "the wide world" but "the wide, wide world," awesomely vast to the orphanlike child who carries the reader's sympathies.

III

The Wide, Wide World, therefore, expresses a fundamental duplicity, one well established by recent feminist criticism. Women must yield to patriarchal values; women hate patriarchy. Women must define themselves through marriage and love; women define themselves as alone and hurting. If anything, the reality of powerful men and solitary women seems more starkly humiliating here than in *The Scarlet Letter* or *Uncle Tom's Cabin*, where mothering gives alternative bonds. Ellen's mother offers no protection, strength, or hope, just her often cited, ambiguously pointed counsel that father's will be done, on earth as it is in heaven: "Remember, my darling, who it is that brings this sorrow upon us; though we *must* sorrow, we must not rebel" (12).[21] No wonder the epigraph, from Longfellow, ends with "those realms of Love and Hate."

From the beginning, with strong swift narrative strokes, Warner confronts her heroine with the stock tear-inducing situation of the sentimental novel: the prospect of being separated from her mother, who is dying and has to go to France to prolong her life—at least so the doctor says. Captain Montgomery, who has just lost a lawsuit and seems to be in serious though unspecified financial trouble, agrees. Since he cannot be expected to care for his daughter himself—the issue is not even raised—he will send the child away too. Whether all these decisions are for Mother's health or for Father's peace of mind in the midst of work problems, Ellen doesn't ask. What she does know is that her father cannot be challenged: "She entertained not the slightest hope of being able by any means to alter her father's will. She regarded the dreaded evil as an inevitable thing" (20).[22] With a nice syntactic touch, Warner links Ellen's sense of "the dreaded evil" as much to her father's will as to her mother's approaching departure.

The danger of melodrama looms rather large in the first few chapters. Yet they remain among the most gripping in the novel, in part because Warner quickly multiplies her portraits of insensitive, commanding men. Captain Montgomery, so intrusively blind to the feelings of mother and daughter, gives his orders and disappears, either to sleep "in happy unconsciousness of his wife's distress and utter inability to sympathize with it" or simply to be "away . . . most of the time" (60, 23). Before we meet a bullying clerk when Ellen goes shopping, we see Ellen coping with Mrs. Montgomery's equally authoritarian and much more perceptive doctor, who all but blames Ellen for her mother's worsening health.

Here the narrator's voice mirrors the story's initial duplicity. When Dr. Green enters, he finds "his patient decidedly worse than he had reason to expect." His "sagacious eye" quickly detects the cause: mother and daughter have been working each other up. Since "he had rather taken a fancy" to Ellen, he calls her aside to give her an avuncular lecture on the dangers of exciting patients.

First, "rubbing one of her hands in his," he asks her, " 'What do you think of this fine scheme of mine? . . . this scheme of sending this sick lady over the water to get well; what do you think of it eh?'

" '*Will* it make her quite well, do you think, sir?' asked Ellen, earnestly.

" ' "Will it make her well!" to be sure it will; do you think I don't know better than to send people all the way across the ocean for nothing?' "

Hedging on how long it will take Mrs. Montgomery to be cured, Dr. Green comes to his point: that "my little nurse" Ellen has not done well. "Mrs. Nurse," he says, "I'm afraid you haven't taken proper care of her; she looks to me as if she had been too much excited. I've a notion she has been secretly taking half a bottle of wine, or reading some furious kind of a novel, or something of that sort, you understand?" Suddenly "changing his tone," the doctor gives his orders: "She *must not* be excited . . . You mustn't let her talk much, or laugh much, or cry at all, on any account; she mustn't be worried in the least,—will you remember?" Shaking Ellen's hand as he departs, Dr. Green more coaxingly commands, "All you have to do is to let your mamma be as much like an oyster as possible; you understand? Good-by."

Then we learn what he is really thinking. " 'Poor woman!' said the doctor to himself as he went downstairs (he was a humane man). 'I wonder if she'll live till she gets to the other side! That's a nice little girl, too. Poor child! poor child!' " (18–19).

The mixed signals here abound, both from Dr. Green to the child and from the narrator to us. The doctor is a "sagacious" and "humane" man, we're told. In contrast to her father, he genuinely pities Ellen. It seems quite right, as the next sentence notes, that "both mother and daughter silently acknowledged the justice of the doctor's advice and determined to follow it." Yet the doctor is a patronizing liar, manipulatively fondling the girl and forcing mother away from daughter even though he knows Mrs. Montgomery might not survive the trip. This is patriarchy at its most insinuating. Ostensibly loving, stroking her hand and calling her "Mrs. Nurse," the doctor forces Ellen to forswear her own instincts and to submit blindly to his arbitrary, perhaps wrongheaded decrees. Women, like good children or good oysters, should never open their mouths or their hearts, except when pried open by men.

Framed by these deftly drawn portraits of patriarchy, Ellen's character at first enacts Warner's more subtle drama of acquiescence and resistance. If authoritative men not only rupture mother-daughter bonds but make mother and daughter feel guilty for needing each other, women have no choice but to submit. Ultimately Ellen does submit: she weans herself from mother love, "the strongest feeling her heart knew" (13), to a deeper love of Jesus, who embodies both patriarchal dominance and submissive suffering. Yet Ellen's behavior sharply contrasts with both the helplessness of her mother and the heartlessness of her father. In particular, she takes much more initiative than does her mother, who seems undecided whether to be a dying woman or a fading doormat. If mother must never be excited, Ellen erupts at every opportunity. Moreover, Ellen is not only excitable but resourceful.

In the opening pages, for instance, before making tea for her mother, the little girl stares out the window at the lamplighter—the book's first vision of the wide, wide world. Then Ellen quickly goes to the fire and pokes it, smiling as it lights the whole room. " 'That is something like,' said she to herself; 'who says I can't poke the fire? Now, let us see if I can't do something else' " (10). Already on her own, Ellen has learned how to circumvent parental decrees, without risking direct confrontation, by studying the ways of the world.

Unfortunately, as Ellen inches toward putting her heartfelt trust in her greater Father, that intrepid spark flickers out. Here my reading differs from those feminist readings that highlight subversive subtexts of anger and autonomy or female solidarity. Like Hawthorne's Pearl, Ellen "was a child of very high spirit and violent passions, untamed at all by sorrow's discipline" (63). Unlike Pearl, whose raging passions express the depths of her mother's heart, Ellen's indignant storms spring only from herself. In the more and more relentlessly patriarchal framing of the story, self has to yield. Much less religious than her mother, Ellen has to be brought by slow degrees and various hands toward a genuine submission to Christ, the Lord of Sorrows. Just as several gentlemanly protectors save Ellen from Mr. Saunders, the churlish store clerk, and other social humiliations, so a patriarchal God saves Ellen from her feelings about patriarchy.

John Humphreys, Alice's saintlier brother, whom Ellen will eventually marry, embodies the triumph of the story's Dr. Green side. After all, Dr. Green turns out to be right. Mother does live on for some time, slowly wasting away in France. Meanwhile, self-controlled, serious, and deeply Christian, embodying all the virtues of paternalistic manhood, John applies Dr. Green's sickbed advice to Ellen herself: in general, don't get excited, and specifically, don't read novels. As John's steady hand gains slow control of Ellen's heart, he introduces her first to Parson Weems's life of Washington and then to Bunyan's *Pilgrim's Progress*, which he reads aloud to "my little sister" (367). Soon afterward, in a scene anticipating Charles Morgeson's horsebreaking, Ellen hears of how John whipped and tamed an obstinate horse, patently a symbol for his breaking of Ellen's will (376–377). Though the story scares her at first, she quickly assents to the justice of his seemingly brutal behavior. Her spiritual pride has to experience similar "mortification" (48, 67, 160).[23]

When John saves her from the ubiquitous Mr. Saunders, the contrast between the right kind of man and the wrong kind of man becomes obvious. Mr. Saunders is spiteful, vulgar, lower class, lazy, insolent, a jokester filled with violence. John, soon to be a clergyman, combines the attributes of a wise father with those of a loving brother. His intimacy with Ellen also evokes a grave yet titillating sexuality, in which the commanding man reduces the tearful girl to a respectful, expectant passivity. Kissing her on the lips when they first meet (after she bursts into tears of confusion at the sight of him), and frequently giving her brotherly kisses on the lips thereafter, John provides for Ellen all that Dr. Green might say she needs: a sense of belonging to a loving family, a strong secure faith, and a sanctifying passion. Here at last is a man to lean on, not to fight.

Clearly, as Joanne Dobson nicely puts it, John "educates himself a wife."[24] John expects Ellen to become a girl-woman who will quietly thrill to the Miltonic paradigm, "He for God only, she for God in him." At last, during her long stay in Scotland with her mother's family, now ruled by a blatantly egocentric patriarch, Ellen learns to submit unresentfully to wrongful decrees such as drinking wine or calling Mr. Lindsay father. Though "she was petted and fondled as a darling possession—a dear plaything—" Ellen preserves her secret consciousness that "John's was a higher style of kindness... [and] a higher style of authority too" (538). Finally, when she is about fifteen, Mr. Lindsay takes away a book that John gave her, and Ellen's "war with herself" concludes with a full conversion from resistance to acquiescence. "Ellen threw herself upon her knees; and when she rose up the spirit of pride was entirely broken, and resentment had died with self-justification" (554).

Just as clearly, Ellen's submission to a hierarchy of patriarchal authority does not bring her happiness. Though the book concludes with an implicit promise of marriage, the suppressed final chapter portrays the marriage as a continuing lecture from John on the imperfection of all earthly love. The room he sets up for her to continue her pious studies continues Ellen's solitude. On the one hand she has a room of her own, with luxurious furnishings, lots of time, and her own key. On the other hand, as Jane Tompkins astutely notes, John says the room is "between mine" (573).[25] Now her aloneness harbors neither resentment nor autonomy nor spiritual matriarchy, three hopeful projections of recent feminist criticism. Her tears of helpless rage have yielded to patriarchy with a muted mixture of acceptance and endurance.

Though readers as diverse as Henry James and Gillian Avery praise Warner's attentive evocation of domestic scenes, I prefer the taut duplicity of the first chapters. There, a bad father and a good God make an uneasy symbiosis. There, too, both Ellen and the narrator become half-resisting readers of the patriarchal narrative ultimately imposed to make sense of women's suffering. If *The Wide, Wide World* is a "training narrative," as Tompkins rightly suggests, the training leads women toward masochism, not spiritual empowerment. A diffuse pain supplants direct anger as the source of religious conviction.[26]

Susan Warner's own life shows a similar intensity of submission to both her God and her father. Henry Whiting Warner, a New York real estate investor who lost most of his money in the Panic of 1837, struck at least one acquaintance as "a bigot and everywhere crotchical." So Catharine Maria Sedgwick called him, with a marvelous, though probably unintended sexual innuendo.[27] Not only did Mr. Warner's character and business reverses provide the model for Captain Montgomery, but he appropriated all the money from the book's sales to recoup his losses, apparently with his daughter's consent. Some years later, after she had established herself as a successful writer, Warner switched from Putnam's to a religious publisher, where her patriarchal didacticism found a still more congenial home.

In her life as in her first book, Susan Warner justifies Myra Jehlen's assessment of sentimental women's fiction as a dependent border. *The Wide, Wide World*'s answer to feminist queries about the possibility of empowering women, whether through autonomy, rage, mothering, or influencing men, is None of the Above. Power is simply not one of the cards dealt to Warner's women. It flows to the men, to do with what they will.

A residual patrician sense of class suffuses the book as well. Though Mr. Montgomery seems near bankruptcy, the household still has a waiter as well as a cook. Ellen's kindnesses to Nancy, her bad-girl double, bear a cloying touch of noblesse oblige. In the long, meandering middle chapters, Warner emphatically contrasts Aunt Fortune's provincial doings with the elegant, cultured entertainments at the house of the Marshmans, the local gentry—a contrast entirely in the Marshmans' favor. As Edward Foster says, connecting the Marshmans to the spiritual rectitude of Alice and John, "Their world of perfect manners is the social equivalent of the Humphreys' ideal moral and spiritual realm."[28] In that respect Warner seeks to temper her presentation of patriarchal dominance with a more traditional sense of patrician virtues. Ellen's well-bred manners continually gain her an awed respect from adults, though it seems a bit much that she censures the Marshman children for playing Bible games on Sunday.

The freshness of *The Wide, Wide World*, for me, comes with Warner's stark awareness of how little class status can protect women from authoritarian men. Only evangelical religion can help, primarily by transforming one's rage. On the surface the novel shows some striking similarities to *A New Home—Who'll Follow?* Ellen, too, dirties her white socks when she gets to Miss Fortune's farm (107–108), and she shrinks from the good-hearted but rustic Van Brunt, especially when he bargains with her for a kiss (94, 116). Like Mrs. Clavers, she can't believe such a man would be allowed to eat at Miss Fortune's table (112). Ellen's progress is a spiritual version of Mrs. Clavers's social education, toward the patrician oxymoron of superiority through humility. But Mrs. Clavers doesn't really mean the humility part. We are worlds away now from Caroline Kirkland's jaunty presumption of patrician dominance. Ellen's intensity, piety, and submissiveness, not to mention her indifference to marrying for money, preclude her becoming a lady. Though her room at the end has all the trappings, her mind has been broken.

We are worlds away, too, from the relative indifference of "Mr. Clavers" to economic humiliation. Captain Montgomery seems entirely preoccupied by his financial reverses. In *A New Home—Who'll Follow?* Kirkland relishes more than she resents her man, and she enjoys contrasting him with the other men of the town, primarily because he remains comfortably above the hustle for money. The indifference of Ellen and her mother to Captain Montgomery's straits comes from his indifference to them, not his superiority to his circumstances. If he feels humiliated or disempowered in the world of work, they don't care. All they can see of him is his intensified absences and decrees.

IV

Two years later, *Uncle Tom's Cabin* offered an opposite answer to the same hopeful question, how can women be empowered? Embedding contradictory possibilities of autonomy, rage, mothering, and influencing men, the story responds All of the Above with utopian zeal. Stowe recasts incipient sectional and racial conflicts as a sex-role struggle that any woman can win. Her ability to do so accounts for much of the novel's political impact as well as its narrative ebullience.

At the most obvious rhetorical level, *Uncle Tom's Cabin* insists that what white men do to black people can be changed if men can be brought to feel what any mother feels. "Your heart is better than your head," Mrs. Bird says to her husband, the senator, as he decides to break his own law and help Eliza, the runaway slave. Then, "laying her little white hand on his," she quietly adds, "Could I ever have loved you, had I not known you better than you know yourself?"[29]

Mrs. Bird's demure rhetorical question expresses the book's fundamental view of manhood. Men, as they know themselves, are intrinsically hateful rather than lovable. Senator Bird's political reasonings have been comically prefigured by Black Sam's artful maneuverings, ostensibly to aid Eliza but actually to curry favor with his mistress. He would have pursued his fellow black with equal zest, were it to his advantage. If Sam had been white, Stowe tells us, his "native talent" might have "raised him to eminence in political life,—a talent of making capital out of everything that turned up, to be invested for his own especial praise and glory" (76).

Sam functions as a reflector for a generic white political and economic manhood. Instead of Susan Warner's patrician patriarchy, Stowe emphasizes the acquisitive egotism now flourishing in the marketplace. Later on, Topsy's impish malice similarly reflects the marketplace. "I was raised by a speculator," she tells Ophelia, so she just "grow'd" into a pure self-reliance (242–243). She is Stowe's version of "Misfortune [to be] Emerson." Still later, Sambo and Quimbo faithfully reflect Simon Legree's brutality.

"The love of power is one of the strongest traits of the Anglo-Saxon race," Frederick Douglass declared. Stowe structures her narration of manhood in similarly racist terms. At the top of the manhood scale, secure in his power and social position, Senator Bird seems benignly malleable. Below him, men turn harder and more ruthless. As we move down the scale of men who have heads for business but lack hearts for people, the haplessly genteel Shelby yields to Haley, the more aggressive and vulgar arriviste, who in turn depends on Marks and Tom Loker to do his dirty work. At the bottom we meet marketplace manhood in its most elemental form, Simon Legree, a man whose "bullet head" has left him with no heart at all (334, 336).[30]

Only the men with lots of mother in them, especially Augustine St. Clare, have some potential to transcend their drive for power, and even he remains stymied by his self-pitying cynicism until prompted by his little girl. Lacking pressure from a motherly wife, St. Clare dissipates his flickering zeal for social reform into the "Southern Hamlet" syndrome.[31] Though he interminably argues with his conventionally manly brother about slavery and goes so far as to predict a revolution of the lower classes, he does very little except talk. He doesn't begin to rouse himself from his depressive wit until Eva's death spurs him to ineffectual action. As his last, deathbed word indicates, he still looks to "*Mother!*" for his spiritual salvation (318).

If men cannot change themselves, women can move men from ruling to sympathizing. As Stowe declares of Cassy's sway over Legree, "so it is, that the most brutal man cannot live in constant association with a strong female influence, and not be greatly controlled by it" (403). With Uncle Tom as a manly, yet feminized role model for all his sex, men can be converted to "the gentle, domestic heart" which now characterizes blacks and women, especially blacks. "They are not naturally daring and enterprising," Stowe declares, "but home-loving and affectionate ... naturally patient, timid and unenterprising" (96, 98).

No wonder so many black readers as well as southerners loathe this book. In the mulatto George Harris, any touch of rebelliousness, aggressiveness, or even inventiveness comes from his white father, Stowe assures her readers (111–112), since black men are naturally feminized. From a black woman's perspective, the book might better be called *Aunt Chloe's Cabin Fever*, since Tom is separated from his cabin and his family for most of the story. Belying the book's title, Chloe sadly closes down the cabin midway through. While she eagerly talks of working four or five years to buy Tom back, Tom seems much more interested in saving his various masters and going to heaven than in being reunited with his wife and children.

While blacks have made "Uncle Tom" a byword for servility, feminist critics have idealized Tom, much as Stowe does herself. He is domestic, tender of voice, emotional, nonviolent. Elizabeth Ammons tellingly presents him as the paragon of Victorian heroines and the essence of Christ-like matriarchy. Yet a paternal strain persists in him, long before his name changes from "Uncle Tom" to "Father Tom" (398, 400).[32] In their last dialogue, Chloe desperately accuses him of caring more for his master than for his family: "Sich a faithful crittur as ye've been,— and allers sot his business 'fore yer own every way,—and reckoned on him more than yer own wife and chil'en!" (97). Here, lacking Tom's faith, she resembles Hester Prynne in the forest, trying to make her man think more about their love than about his salvation. Much later, Tom's dying words resemble Dimmesdale's. Perfunctorily invoking Chloe and the children, he breaks out into an ecstasy of indiscriminate, universal love. He dies as "a conqueror," joyously stammering, "Who,—

who,—who shall separate us," not from family but "from the love of Christ?" (421–422).

Chloe sees Tom's Uncle Tomming much more clearly than either her husband or his narrator does, and her stifled irony makes the paternalistic dependence of Stowe's feminism all the more apparent. If Stowe's aim is to attack white men in the name of God and motherhood, rather than to bond with women across class and racial lines, however, *Uncle Tom's Cabin* becomes a genteel white woman's call to arms. The narrative takes Tom away from his cabin and family to conscript him not as a man but as a transcendent "thing," the ultimate nonviolent weapon of Christian love in the war between the sexes. More broadly, Stowe ensures her success with middle-class women readers by representing slavery as an amalgam of white reflectors, motherly male victims, and doughty emblems of female autonomy.

Stowe's attack on manhood extends well beyond exploiting black experience and erasing black community. With more gender fervor than historical accuracy, she depicts northern white men, personified by Simon Legree, as the prime movers of southern slavery. Emerson, oddly enough, partially shared her assessment of what he called "ardent" northern manhood, though he links such men to slavery through their alleged "hatred of labor" rather than through their drive for dominance. New England men "are an ardent race," he muses in his 1847 journal, "and are as fully possessed with that hatred of labor, which is the principle of progress in the human race, as any other people. They must and will have the enjoyment without the sweat. So they buy slaves, where the women will permit it; where they will not they make the wind, the tide, the waterfall, the steam, the cloud, the lightning, do the work, by every art and device their cunningest brain can achieve."[33] "Where the women will permit it": that becomes the key to Stowe's rhetorical strategies and evangelical urgency.

It's no accident that another middle-class women's movement has brought this novel back into favor. Out of print by 1948 and sputtering back to life with the Civil Rights movement, *Uncle Tom's Cabin* soared into the canon on the wings of a new interpretive constituency, feminist teachers who quite rightly see in Stowe's dramatization of slavery a middle-class gender war. From the beginning, Stowe presents slavery not as a peculiar institution of the South but as the most pernicious by-product of what she repeatedly calls "the hard and dominant Anglo-Saxon race" (xxvi). Even mild-mannered Shelby, the gentlest of the hard-hearted acquisitors, comfortably reasons that he could continue to hope for heaven because "his wife had piety and benevolence enough for two" (12). It's all a necessity of the system, he says, lecturing her impatiently about how "women and ministers" should know their place and not meddle with the business of the world (37). The war, then, is between men of business and women of feeling.[34] As Stowe dramatizes various ways that women can win the war, her black characters often seem little more than props and goads to bring male readers to more humane sensibilities.

The dialogue between Augustine and his twin brother Alfred makes the sex-role allegory most explicit. Alfred "was my father's pet, and I my mother's," Augustine tells Ophelia. Alfred grew up in the image of their father, or Ophelia's father, or any father, at least of the New England variety: "a regular old Roman,—upright, energetic, noble-minded, with an iron will." He was able "to rule over rocks and stones, and to force an existence out of Nature" (225–226). Augustine, on the contrary, has the "dreamy and inactive . . . abstract ideality" of his mother, who always wore white, and who filled her life with music, religion, and inexpressible feelings. If he had not separated from her when he was thirteen, he muses, he might have become "a saint, re-former, martyr." As it is, he retains her powerless Christian sympathies for the oppressed, along with "a morbid sensitiveness and acuteness of feeling" (226–229). Real men like Alfred see Augustine as "a womanish sentimentalist" and advise him to write poetry (232). From Augustine's point of view, the real men seem obsessed with hierarchies, boundaries, and mastery. Like all aristocrats, he says, they restrict their sympathies to people of their own class and color, enslaving the lower orders without a qualm (226).[35]

Stowe's explication of the sex-role divide, with St. Clare as her mouth-piece, could be lifted from the pages of Dorothy Dinnerstein or Nancy Chodorow, at least in theme. From their father to Alfred to Alfred's son Henrique, the real men express "that same strong, overbearing, dominant spirit," variously manifested. Father imposed his "inflexible, driving, punctilious" temperament on his five hundred slaves for the sake of "accuracy and precision," employing a brutal overseer from Vermont to ensure that his system worked well (229, 227). Alfred shows the same orientation toward dominance in his pursuit of efficiency and profit, though he muffles it somewhat as a gesture to more democratic times. Henrique, who so shocks little Eva with his brutality toward his horse, continues the manly line.

Unlike Susan Warner, who takes pains to justify John Humphreys's breaking of his obstinate horse, and unlike Elizabeth Stoddard, whose heroine shows ambivalent fascination with her man's struggle for mastery, Stowe quickly aligns her readers with Eva and Augustine. The *"dies irae"* St. Clare prophesies (233), however, turns out to be a day of peaceful conversions instead of wrath and blood. In Stowe's utopian resolution, all forms of social power relations reduce to a battle between womanhood and manhood, with womanhood winning through friendly persuasion. As the kitchen ousts the market, amoral men will yield of their own accord to mothers who know what's best because they feel the most.[36]

Here I part company with feminist critics. Stowe's matriarchal solution seems as simplistic a fantasy as Warner's patriarchal solution to women's oppression. Stowe's dream has considerable feminist exuberance, to be sure. One can draw a straight line from *Uncle Tom's Cabin* to the more explicit conversions of brutal men into feminists at the end of *The Color Purple*, Alice Walker's much more derivative text, now canonized by several new academic constituencies. Like Walker's conclusion or like Stowe's complementary hope that all freed blacks will naturally want to return to Africa, the rhetorical vision of a feminized future evades a great many conflicts. With Stowe, the fantasy also leaves a racist sex-role dichotomy firmly in place. Stowe envisions what Elizabeth Ammons has more sympathetically called a "matrifocal" utopia, explicitly dramatized in Rachel Halliday's Quaker family. In my reading, the utopia rests on a paternalistic base, obscured by millennial expectations.[37]

As a secondary contradiction, Adeleke Adeeko has pointed out, Stowe evades confronting the economic basis of slavery in the South. She strongly implies that slavery persists primarily because these ruthless, dominant, paternalistic businessmen are also incompetent. Shelby has to sell Tom and Eliza because he has "speculated largely and quite loosely" (10). Mr. Harris takes George away from inventing things in the bagging factory because George makes him feel inferior (13–14). Tom takes over St. Clare's managing because his master is "indolent and careless of money" (204). Cassy's master has to sell her and her children "to clear off his gambling debts" (365). As for Legree, his lust for brutality rather than money drives out good sense. Cassy shouts at him, after he has Tom beaten for the first time, "You, who haven't even sense enough to keep from spoiling one of your best hands, right in the most pressing season, just for your devilish temper!" (372).[38]

Such instances of incompetence sometimes undermine Stowe's indictment of insensitive male power, by oscillating between hopes for racial
equality and hopes for more benign paternalist management.

Nevertheless, the book remains vivid and vitalizing, in part because
of its engaging, eclectic contradictions and in part because of its profoundly empowering energy of accusation. Along with Stowe's mainstream conservative feminism run several more radicalizing currents.
If her black characters tend to function as projections of oppressed
middle-class housewives, the slaves' saintly sufferings provided a safe
yet urgent forum for women readers to voice their displaced rage and
to do something about male dominance. Proper ladies could express
their anger as if it were charitable sympathy for the lowly, without any
taint of Marie St. Clare's selfishness. Middle-class wives could aggressively assert their influence, as Mrs. Bird does so successfully, while
maintaining their sense of superiority to the contaminating contentions
of business and politics. Part of the genius of Stowe's narrative strategy,
as I suggested in Chapter 4, is to reaffirm her readers' gentility as she
introduces their sympathies to "Life Among the Lowly." Women readers, therefore, could accuse manhood without acknowledging either
their aggressiveness or, more unconsciously, their rage and their
powerlessness.

Uncle Tom's Cabin specifically empowered northeastern wives to demand an end to compromises with the South, compromises that urban
businessmen might have been disposed to preserve. In that respect this
apolitical book had a staggering political impact. It dramatically accel-
erated sectional conflict, as the dismay of reviewers quickly indicated.[39]
It encouraged northerners to segregate themselves in fantasy as the
Quakers writ large, a self-sufficient community of the righteous, at just
the time when the economy of the Northeast could support its drive
for national dominance. If one accepts David Potter's analysis, the quick
rise of the Republican party and Lincoln's election in 1860 represent
the triumph of sectionalism, certainly at the expense of national unity,
perhaps at the expense of the Northeast's own short-term economic
interests in the urbanizing areas.[40]

Moreover, Stowe's narrative gives ample room for female readers to
identify with plucky, self-reliant women, both black and white. Characters such as Eliza and Cassy, who show all the intrepid resourcefulness
denied to Tom, dramatize the possibilities for women's autonomy far
more energetically than Susan Warner dares to do with Mrs. Vawse's
placid seclusion. Mrs. Shelby, for instance, sighs inwardly when her

husband tries to silence her by saying she knows nothing about business. "The fact was," Stowe remarks, "she had a clear, energetic, practical mind, and a force of character every way superior to that of her husband; so that it would not have been so very absurd a supposition, to have allowed her capable of managing, as Mr. Shelby supposed" (255). It's not surprising to see her capably "straightening" her husband's "entangled web of affairs" after his sudden death (418).[41]

Though the more feminist aspects of *Uncle Tom's Cabin* have been highlighted in recent criticism, their political impact has been unduly minimized. In particular, because Stowe so programmatically depoliticizes racial and sectional tensions, modern critics and historians tend to discount the validity of President Lincoln's alleged comment when he met her in the White House, "So this is the little lady who made this big war." It seems to me quite likely that *Uncle Tom's Cabin* did as much to make the Civil War as Thomas Paine's *Common Sense* did to abet the American Revolution. It forced black sufferings into white readers' consciousnesses, indelibly so, and it made abolitionism socially acceptable for the gentility within prevailing ideologies of class, race, and gender. More ambiguously, despite the book's gestures toward national reconciliation, *Uncle Tom's Cabin* made sectionalism a moral imperative transcending economic gain. Most profoundly, it licensed middle-class women's assertiveness and anger while disconnecting their demonstrativeness from any hint of personal pain or political forwardness.

If Daniel Webster's 1850 compromise to preserve the Union depended on an increasingly fragile patriarchal fantasy, as Eric Sundquist suggests, then Stowe's rhetoric of matriarchy provided a powerful countervailing fantasy.[42] Webster's rhetoric suited the power brokers for a national elite, while Stowe's rhetoric suited the wives of middle-class men now dispossessing that elite from power. Stowe gave the women something to do. If marketplace manhood was the cause, women had to hold men to their shared Christian accounts. Accepting the gender divide, *Uncle Tom's Cabin* shows women how to accuse their men out of love, not anger, and how to bring them across the greater chasm separating the salvation of their souls from the practice of business. When men see how they have been divided from themselves, then women can conquer with open arms.

Along with the transformation of physical male dominance to spiritual female love comes a latent, delightful, Topsy-like malice. Stowe's most ingenious and flamboyant transmutation of anger appears toward the end of *Uncle Tom's Cabin*, when she borrows the madwoman-in-the-attic scenario from *Jane Eyre* to help Cassy terrorize Legree. Cassy's trickery, a piece of pure malice, climaxes Stowe's attack on manhood. In a brilliant essay on the psychodynamics of the female gothic, Claire Kahane argues that the madwoman-in-the-attic theme is a displaced fantasy of what she calls the return of the dead-undead mother.[43] Stowe's empowering variant turns that fantasy toward revenge.

The revenge of the dead-undead mother begins at little Eva's death-bed, when she gives a curl of her hair to each of the weeping slaves (290–291). Much later, Legree's assistant, Sambo, hurries to his master with "a witch thing" that had been tied around Tom's neck. Out of it drops "a silver dollar, and a long, shining curl of fair hair,—hair which, like a living thing, twined itself round Legree's fingers. 'Damnation!' he screamed," and damnation it will be. Little Eva's dead-undead curl reminds him of his mother, whose counsel he had continuously spurned to follow his father's steps and character, "boisterous, unruly, and ty-rannical," in Stowe's familiar sex-role allegory. After he finally "threw her senseless on the floor" and went to sea, he received a letter. "He opened it, and a lock of long, curling hair fell from it, and twined about his fingers. The letter told him his mother was dead; and that, dying, she blest and forgave him" (372–373).[44]

What sounds like a grotesquely self-sacrificing Jewish mother joke is actually generic Mother's opening salvo. Slowly, just as Eva's curl twines around his fingers, so his mother's spirit tightens its loving fingers around his neck. Cassy becomes Mrs. Legree's vindictive vehicle, staging gothic nightmares in his bedroom as part of her escape plan (379). Finally, in "An Authentic Ghost Story," a mysterious figure glides to Legree's bed and touches his hand. Then "a voice said, three times, in a low, fearful whisper, 'Come! come! come!' " (425–426). Already Tom, in a direct parallel with Mrs. Legree's dying words, has forgiven Legree "with all my soul!" and gone to Christ (416). Now Cassy escapes with Emmeline down the road, while Legree's nightmare portends his death and "coming retribution." Soon, "at his dying bed, stood a stern, white, inexorable figure, saying 'Come! come! come!' " (426).

True to the novel's ostensible spirit, Cassy regains her motherly na-ture by reuniting with her long-lost daughter Eliza. Nonetheless, in the duplicitous paradox at the heart of this book about motherly love, Stowe's strongest female character is twice a mother murdering her child. First, anticipating Toni Morrison's *Beloved*, Cassy kills her little baby, to protect him from the horrors of slavery (367).[45] Now, imper-sonating Mrs. Legree, she kills Mrs. Legree's child, a brutal sexual predator. How does she do it? Simply by awakening Legree's guilt about his mother. Just as Christ's second coming will empower the motherly, so mother's second coming will draw every unrepenting bullet head down to hell, whether Legree or the "two old bullets" St. Clare has described earlier (229), his and Ophelia's fathers, or all such manly men.

With such a mixture of malice and matriarchy, with every page pointing a finger at manhood, how could men like this book? George Sand implies a simple answer in her sympathetic 1852 review of *Uncle Tom's Cabin*. The first detail she cites is the incident in which Senator Bird helps Eliza to escape. "This charming episode in 'Uncle Tom' (a digression, if you will) paints well the situation of most men placed between their prejudices and established modes of thought and the spontaneous and generous intuitions of their hearts."[46] In this view, men *want* to be free to feel. Stowe accuses manhood, not men, on their own behalf, to help extricate their own sympathies for black people from their complicity with an exploitative economic system.

That strategy probably accounts for most of the book's conscious appeal to men. Nevertheless, *Uncle Tom's Cabin* belies its gentle, coaxing feminine surface with its relentless indictments of the Anglo-Saxon essence of northern men, their drive for dominance. To consider the little lower layer of the book's appeal to men, we need to move beyond the gender war so well established by current feminist criticism, which my discussion has presumed so far. Not coincidentally, my hypothesis will reinforce my larger thesis about entrepreneurial manhood. In brief, I suggest that men responded to *Uncle Tom's Cabin* with much more empathy than defensiveness because it voiced their own unconscious feelings about marketplace humiliation.

The emotional climax of the book, as Stowe recognized from her first vision of Uncle Tom while she was taking communion in her Maine church, is Tom's beating at the hands of Legree (415–417). A child-man is being beaten, to vary the formulation of Freud's famous essay. The moment starkly evokes one man's brutal dominance and another man's submissive humiliation. The moment also paradoxically confirms the humiliated child-man as more truly dominant and patriarchal. A few pages earlier Cassy calls him, "Father Tom" (398, 400). A few pages later he dies as a "conqueror" (421).[47]

One of the most bizarre reader responses on record can be found in Richard von Krafft-Ebing's case no. 57, the masochist who liked to read *Uncle Tom's Cabin* because the accounts of slave beatings gave him

erections.[48] The perversity of that response, like Leslie Fiedler's interpretation of little Eva's death as a disguised rape, exposes the dynamics
of sadomasochism in Stowe's presentation of entrepreneurial manhood.[49] Just as Warner connects social humiliation to spiritual mortification, Stowe dramatizes these dynamics in Christian, rather than
sexual terms. In doing so, she gives men as well as women a way of
interpreting feelings of worthlessness as potential spiritual power. If,
as I've argued in Chapter 3, competition for dominance and the fear
of being humiliated by a stronger man constitute the ideology of entrepreneurial manhood, then *Uncle Tom's Cabin* may have been so extraordinarily popular with both sexes in part because it was the first
narrative to display humiliation in culturally acceptable and gender-
neutral terms, safely displaced onto blacks rather than little girls and
safely transposed into Christian righteousness.

Why did evangelical Christianity become so intense and powerful as
an interpretive frame for white middle-class experience during this
period? It wasn't simply an ideology to control and discipline the new
working class, as Paul Johnson and others argue. Nor was it primarily
a way of empowering housewives for local activism and moral superiority, as various feminist historians have suggested. Nor was it primarily a way of deflecting, suppressing, and voicing female resentments,
as Barbara Epstein says, though that comes closer to my view.[50] Instead,
or in addition, Christian discourse provided a fantasy of transforming
a beaten-down self into triumphant power, for both sexes, by encouraging an identification with Christ. The fantasy gave both men and
women a way to transcend the very different humiliations brought on
by domestic patriarchy and marketplace competition, without giving
way to helpless anger.

The image of Christ's sorrows, in which Ellen Montgomery takes
refuge after the deaths of her mother and her best friend, clearly shapes
the parallel lives of Tom and little Eva. Each character takes the pain
of others into his or her heart. The novel's two central scenes unmis-
takably present Tom and little Eva as crucified, dying to redeem the
sins and to dramatize the sufferings of others.[51] Eva's decline toward
death begins when she hears of Prue's baby being starved to death for
lack of milk, then of Prue being whipped to death for drinking (217–
222). " 'These things sink into my heart, Tom,' said Eva,—'they sink
into my heart' " (220, also 236). Prue's agonies pierce Eva's heart like
nails. The death of the little "Evangelist" follows as inevitably as Clar-
issa's from being penetrated by the consequences of white men's eco-

nomic desire. While Leslie Fiedler wrongly identifies the rapist as death, he is right, I think, to present sadistic rape as the symbolic cause of Eva's death and transfiguration. At the end, Stowe's one literal rapist is unmanned by Eva's curls, which haunt Legree like pieces of the true cross.

At least two other major texts of the American Renaissance are obsessed with the transformation of social shaming into an image of men being beaten. As I argue in the last two chapters of this book, both *The Scarlet Letter* and *Moby Dick* become increasingly preoccupied with male humiliation. Dimmesdale sinks his guilt into his own body, if not his heart, scourging himself with the whip he hides in his closet. Meanwhile, Chillingworth's malicious drive to possess the soul as well as the secret of his sexual rival turns the middle part of Hawthorne's narration into a sadomasochistic dance of male dominance and potential humiliation, reversed at the end when Dimmesdale ascends to heaven. As Chillingworth then goes limp in defeat, Hester's initial drama of resistance to social shaming seems all but forgotten. More simply and grandiosely, Ahab's rage at having been unmanned by the whale, or by some greater power acting through the whale, goads him to flamboyant, futile postures of dominance.

In my reading, both Ishmael and Hawthorne's narrator deviously collude with their heroes' narcissistic defenses to interpret a suicidal resolution of humiliation as an ambiguous spiritual triumph. One could easily make that case for Uncle Tom as well. But Stowe's narration turns Tom's humiliation into an unambiguous triumph for female values. After Dimmesdale defeats Chillingsworth and ascends into heaven, the narrator fantasizes that the two rivals join there, as their hate becoming love. More desperately, in "The Candles" Ahab's hate becomes a craving to be joined with "pure power." Dissociating Tom from those male mystifications of dominance and submission, Stowe makes Tom's death a duplicitous agent for Christian forgiveness, motherly love, and revenge (in the person of George Shelby) against male power.

An alternative argument, derived from Thomas Haskell, would present the marketplace itself as the change agent for men's sympathies. In two provocative and influential *American Historical Review* articles, Haskell hypothesizes that entrepreneurial capitalism brought about a new cognitive style, one rewarding self-control, the keeping of promises, and the calculation of supply and demand. Such calculations alter men's perceptions of causation and extend their field of moral responsibility. When men start to think slavery might be a remote consequence of their actions rather than a necessary evil, the pressure to abolish it dramatically intensifies, as in fact happened between 1750 and 1850. Challenging theories stressing class interests or ideologies of social control, Haskell sees possessive individualism as a potentially radicalizing precondition for a more comprehensive humanitarianism.[52]

Haskell's argument erases the role of middle-class women, whose absence from the marketplace would preclude them from having an expanded sense of moral responsibility. He relies far more on logic and Nietzsche than on the history of abolition to make his case—his only details come from John Woolman. Even so, despite Stowe's obvious incompatibility with Haskell's thesis, her rhetorical accusations in *Uncle Tom's Cabin* look like the thesis made flesh, or at least the thesis coming to national consciousness. "But who, sir, makes the trader?" Stowe cries, in a passage I've quoted before. "Who is most to blame? The enlightened, cultivated, intelligent man, who supports the system of which the trader is the inevitable result, or the poor trader himself?" (134). You, gentleman reader, Stowe concludes, must act to stop the system perpetuating slavery, the system you keep in motion every day, if you don't want to be damned at God's final accounts.

Haskell's startlingly original claim certainly looks perverse in the contemporary critical forum. To speak any good of the bourgeoisie brings a strong whiff of the hand that feeds us. Many if not most English professors would like to preserve our self-purifying air as connoisseurs of subversion, whether in feminist, Derridean, Bakhtinian, or new historicist variations.

Nevertheless, Haskell's idea about capitalist cognition provides another plausible, though contradictory explanation for why husbands might have taken to Stowe's book almost as readily as did their wives. Perhaps Stowe's vehement indictment of manhood not only voiced men's unconscious feelings about marketplace humiliation but paradoxically extended their sense of power, in two Haskellian ways. First, Stowe idealizes images of male self-control, especially with Uncle Tom. Second, and probably more important, she conveys a vision of how farreaching the market's consequences are and how men can feel responsible for those consequences. In short, *Uncle Tom's Cabin* is not quite as feminized as it looks. Both women's experience of the gender war and men's experience of the marketplace find powerful, contradictory expression in Stowe's narrative, displaced onto slavery.

Stowe's rhetorical fusion of motherhood, passion, and crucifixion had several personal sources. Her own mother died when she was five, and her most beloved child died of cholera in 1849. "It was at his dying bed and at his grave that I learned what a poor slave mother may feel when her child is torn away from her," she wrote in an 1852 letter. "Much that is in that book had its root in the awful scenes and bitter sorrow of that summer." To her outrage at forced separations of mothers from their children Stowe adds a paradoxical undertone of desperation at the slavery of being a mother, constrained by childbearing and child rearing. In letters from the late 1840s her husband, Calvin, implored her to be more available to him sexually; she variously resisted his needs in order to make time for her writing. Stowe's ideology of empowering women through their role as mothers holds together a contradictory mixture of rage, empathy, and accusation under the broad umbrella of a conversion-oriented theology, one obviously indebted to her father.[53]

Beyond its biographical context, the impassioned confidence of Stowe's narration suggests that *Uncle Tom's Cabin* voiced several kinds of shared pain and anger. So too did Susan Warner. For the largely single-sex readership of *The Wide, Wide World*, a girl's humiliations became a woman's humility. In contrast, *Uncle Tom's Cabin* transforms suffering into self-empowering, for both sexes. Warner looks backward, to patrician manners, patriarchal theology, and the patriarchal home, even as all the weight of women's experience burdens her narrative with a muted solitude. Whereas Warner constricts her drama to a child's lonely struggle with resentment, Stowe expansively depicts a wide spectrum of possible energies for women of the new middle class.

At bottom, however, Warner and Stowe think alike about passion. Both writers try to redeem passion from the sexuality appropriated for the word by British romantics, from Byron to the Brontes. What may look from a modern point of view like an ideology of passionlessness is really their return to the older Christian meaning of passion: intense suffering, symbolized by Christ's passion, or crucifixion. Each narrator engages her readers in the work of voicing women's passion, with all the contradictions embedded in women's dependence. Their novels are on the "long border" of male power, as Myra Jehlen puts it, with women's lives embedded in patriarchy and paternalism. Yet they offer the promise of conversion to an inward domain beyond the reach of manhood, where solitude can feel like God's embrace, where rage at men can be transformed into Christian self-control, and where revenge can feel like Christian forgiveness.

For Hawthorne and Melville, who wrote within as well as beyond manhood's reach, rivalry and deviance, rather than dependence, helped to frame their narrative strategies. Faced with an incipient big-business culture, in which men of force were setting postpatrician norms for manhood, these writers evolved premodernist ways of deauthorizing conventional manhood, including their own authority. What look like self-deconstructing stories need to be placed in the context of gender deviance and class dispossession. Returning at last to male views of manhood, my last chapters emphasize the rivalry, deviance, and humiliation latent in male narrative strategies of detachment, self-doubling, and subversive play.

7

Hard, Isolate, Ruthless, and Patrician: Dana and Parkman

Two instantly celebrated texts tell how young patricians can become men in the wide entrepreneurial world of the American 1840s. In *Two Years before the Mast* (1840), Richard Henry Dana, Jr., recounts his journey as a sailor to California and back. Seven years later another "junior," Francis Parkman, Jr., describes his observations and exploits among the Indians, emigrants, and buffalo of the Wild West. Serialized in 1847 and published as a book in 1849, *The Oregon Trail* can be read as an anthropological apprenticeship preparing Parkman for the project he already had in mind, his history of the French and Indian Wars, while *Two Years before the Mast* was written at least in part to establish Dana's credentials as a Boston maritime lawyer. Nonetheless, manly self-fashioning rather than professional ambition constitutes the drama of each narration. As patrician careers lie in wait, the two sickly boy-men launch themselves into a kind of temporary slumming, mixing it up with the real men out there, proving their fearlessness, mastering their bodies and their environments, and then returning to their privileged world.

The norms of manhood which authorize their voices blend patrician sophistication with entrepreneurial ruthlessness. Dana's narcissistic complacency contrasts sharply with Parkman's ironic, often caustic sense of the disparity between reality and his dreams. Yet both men appropriate the entrepreneurial ideology of competitive dominance, along with a more general manly code of self-control, to stifle feelings of humiliation associated with their bodies and their depressed patrician fathers. Together, the two narratives can set the frame within which Hawthorne and Melville try to deauthorize the reigning American norms of self and manly authority.

If the past two chapters can be taken as a diptych of four women looking at manhood, the rest of my book juxtaposes four male writers. Dana and Parkman serve as foils to Hawthorne and Melville, who forsake patrician strategies for coming to terms with feelings of manly inferiority. Like Caroline Kirkland, Dana and Parkman invoke class status while embarking on rites of initiation into more adventurous and physically dangerous modes of manhood. Hawthorne and Melville build their best narrations not from a presumption of elite bonds with their audience but from a self-consciousness of class and gender deviance. Their voices often take on a patrician protective coloring, even as they toy with their readers. They take the literary high ground not to join genteel paternalism with entrepreneurial manliness, as Dana and Parkman do, but to launch sneak attacks on a threatening audience and, more profoundly, to explore threatening aspects of themselves.[1]

I

Dana's story seems much the simpler chronicle of manhood in the making, though ultimately he is both more conventional and more evasive than Parkman. Happily he describes his speedy transformation from a diffident young dandy to the hard, energetic, zestful Anglo-Saxon stereotype Stowe vilifies in *Uncle Tom's Cabin*. Determined "to cure, if possible, by an entire change of life, and by a long absence from books and study, a weakness of the eyes," he discovers that the sailors have no tolerance for weakness: "If I showed any sign of want of spirit or of backwardness, ... I should be ruined at once."[2] Stifling his "fastidious senses" and his longings for "social and intellectual enjoyments," he quickly gets his sea legs and after a bout of seasickness finds himself "a new being.... I felt somewhat like a man" (22, 19, 23).

What he doesn't tell us, as Robert Ferguson points out, is that he went to sea not simply to cure his weak eyes but also to escape his father's depressions.[3] Dana wanted to find a manhood beyond his father's patrician idleness and dependence. His progress in his first two chapters becomes a synecdoche for the rest of his journey. By chapter

11 he and the other four members of the crew have "a pleasant feeling of superiority" over some seasick passengers. "A well man at sea has little sympathy with one who is sea-sick; he is too apt to be conscious of a comparison favorable to his own manhood" (84). At the end of this chapter Dana accomplishes "my first act of what the sailors will allow to be seamanship—sending down a royal-yard," and receives his first "well done" (86). He basks in his fraternity with "hale, hearty men" (84) and also in the approval of the mate, a manlier authority than his father.

The manhood Dana achieves is of two kinds: a personal sense of physical bravery in the face of danger and a national sense of rightful dominance over weaker, idler races or civilizations. Ostensibly, manhood simply means doing one's duty without complaint. "Each one knew that he must be a man, and show himself smart when at his duty" (205). Dana does not explore the submission to patriarchal discipline implied by that definition. Instead, he exults in the crew's collective mastery, especially when competing with other crews of different nationalities. "No vessels in the world go so poorly manned as American and English; and none do so well" (154).[4] A crew of four Americans can best Italian crews of thirty men in every respect save one: the Italians sing so pleasingly. Why? Because "Americans are a time and money saving people" (154), while the Italians and the Spanish seem relatively indistinguishable from Indian men, who "are thriftless, proud, and extravagant, and very much given to gaming" (192).[5]

Dana frequently praises Anglo-American habits of industry, frugality, and enterprise. Dismissing other cultural norms of manhood as hopeless, he eagerly endorses what Martin Green calls "the WASP passions" of prudence and calculation, purpose and resolution. The Spanish have their slaves do all the work (89); the Russians are "a stupid and greasy-looking set" (249). Though John O'Sullivan did not coin the phrase "Manifest Destiny" until 1845, five years after Dana's book was published, Dana's enthusiasm for national expansion and dominance clearly welcomes such a destiny, which presumes the vitality of American manhood. "In the hands of an enterprising people, what a country this might be!" (194).[6]

While appropriating the new middle-class norms of manhood to his sense of himself, Dana also takes care to detach his gentlemanly sensibility from the callousness he sees all about him. Several times he reiterates that at sea a man must never show any sympathy for feelings of fear, homesickness, sadness, and the like, let alone admit any such feelings in himself. "Whatever your feelings may be, you must make a joke of everything at sea," he notes in chapter 5 (46). Otherwise you run the risk of ridicule.

His only extended rumination on the seeming cruelty of this rough-and-tumble manhood amply displays his patrician detachment. The paragraph is worth quoting in full:

> An overstrained sense of manliness is the characteristic of seafaring men, or, rather, of life on board ship. This often gives an appearance of want of feeling, and even of cruelty. From this, if a man comes within an ace of breaking his neck and escapes, it is made a joke of; and no notice must be taken of a bruise or a cut; and any expression of pity, or any show of attention, would look sisterly, and unbecoming a man who has to face the rough and tumble of such a life. From this, too, the sick are neglected at sea, and whatever sailors may be ashore, a sick man finds little sympathy or attention, forward or aft. A man, too, can have nothing peculiar or sacred on board ship; for all the nicer feelings they take pride in disregarding, both in themselves and others. A thin-skinned man could not live an hour on ship-board. One would be torn raw unless he had the hide of an ox. A moment of natural feeling for home and friends, and then the frigid routine of sea-life returned. Jokes were made upon those who showed any interest in the expected news, and everything near and dear was made common stock for rude jokes and unfeeling coarseness, to which no exception could be taken by any one. (278–279)[7]

This passage is usually excerpted as if it stated the brutal truth about how seagoing manhood prevents the expression of "nicer," "natural" feelings. Yet Dana's narrative contradicts his three specific indictments: the pitiless joking, the neglect of the sick, and the sailors' mockery of anything "peculiar or sacred." What Dana seems most concerned about, the sailors' disdain for "sisterly" feelings, his narrative immediately belies.

The paragraph introduces the reading of letters on board, after eighteen months with no news from home. After he reads his own letter, which says all is well, "I could not but be amused" by the spectacle of the poor ship's carpenter, who had married just before leaving Boston and now received no letter from his wife. "He was completely down in the mouth." The sailmaker "tried to comfort him" with advice and tales of his own betrayal by women. Nevertheless, for the next few days the carpenter "was very much dejected, and bore with difficulty the jokes of the sailors, and with still more difficulty their attempts at advice and consolation" (279–281). To be sure, the sailmaker looks rather rough with his commiserations. Nonetheless, the carpenter makes no effort to hide his feelings, and others seem far more sympathetic than the "amused" Dana. Nor does the carpenter lose any respect. Later he becomes the leader of a near mutiny (339–341).

Moreover, when Dana himself takes sick with a bad toothache as they round Cape Horn in perilous seas, the new chief mate for their return voyage orders him to stay below for several days and commands the cook to make a poultice—this, despite the desperate necessity of having all hands on deck to look for ice floes in thick fog and the seeming imminence of either destruction or mutiny. As Dana paraphrases it, the mate says simply "that if we went down, we should all go down together, but if I went on deck I might lay myself up for life" (338, also 328). We have already learned that the chief mate "was 'a man, every inch of him,' as the sailors said" (201). He is tough, a hard driver, extremely competent and forceful, "with a voice like a young lion" (210). Yet in the midst of the utmost danger, the most manly of these real men shows quick practical attentiveness to a sick sailor.

Finally, despite Dana's claim that the sailors mock any peculiarities or any attempt to hold something sacred, they clearly respect him as "the scholar of the company," to the extent of asking him to read to them from a history of England. "I read nearly all day, until sundown," and then into the night with a light they procured from the galley, right through the restoration of Charles the Second. "Many things which, while I was reading, I had a misgiving about, thinking them above their capacity, I was surprised to find them enter into completely" (286–287). Nor do they mock his reading a five-volume romance by William Godwin (183–184). On balance, it seems as though Dana's critique of their manly heartlessness might be more applicable to himself.

Why should that be? No doubt part of the reason is his pique at not being able to indulge self-pity. A more serious reason is his class consciousness, which emerges quite conventionally from time to time, most notably after they reach California and he finds himself on a beach, "positively alone" almost for the first time since he left Boston. Here his language anticipates Hawthorne's sense of himself in "The Custom-House": "My better nature returned strong upon me. . . . I experienced a glow of pleasure at finding that what of poetry and romance I ever had in me, had not been entirely deadened by the laborious and frittering life I had led." Now all the drama of vigorous manhood seems to him like "the play in which I had been so long acting" (157). Earlier, talking to a Spanish father whose daughter had just died, he felt "like

Garrick, between tragedy and comedy" (148). Throughout, Dana holds
quite comfortably to his tastes. For instance, he pointedly enjoys hearing
a falsetto singer, despite the other sailors' disdain (142). In his lengthy
description of a Spanish carnival, he finds the aristocratic waltzing
"beautiful, but, to me, offensive" (267).[8]

At least once the crew's resentment of his class status breaks through,
when hard-tempered Captain T—— (Thompson) threatens to send
Dana back to his previous boat, *The Pilgrim*, from which both he and
the captain have transferred, unless he finds someone to take his place
there. After Dana invokes his connections, the captain decides to send
English Ben, a poor but popular English boy. " 'Oh yes!' said the crew,
'the captain has let you off, because you are a gentleman's son, and
have got friends, and know the owners; and taken Ben, because he is
poor, and has got nobody to say a word for him!' " As Dana acknowledges, "I knew that this was too true to be answered.... The notion
that I was not 'one of them,'... was beginning to revive." He handles
the situation easily enough, by offering six months' wages and all his
spare clothes to any man willing to take Ben's place. Someone soon
obliges, and the tension subsides. Nevertheless, the manly camaraderie
has been disrupted by class consciousness, reinforced as Dana rejoins
"S——, my friend, who... like me, was going back to his family and to
the society which we had been born and brought up in" (295—298).

As a third, more unconscious reason for his evasive heartlessness,
Dana's patrician detachment also bespeaks a narcissistic self-absorption.
While he has a keen eye for characterization and a knack for vivid
narration, *Two Years before the Mast* is curiously deficient in the pleasures
of friendship. Francis Parkman makes Henry Chatillon central to his
narrative as well as to his sense of manly nobility, and Melville's narrators sometimes feel reborn in their affection for the men they admire,
but Dana never allows a need for friendship, or women for that matter,
to touch him in any essential way. He is pleased when others befriend
him, but he admits no more than momentary feelings of ruefulness
when he leaves them. Even his title, as Robert Ferguson notes, signals
his consciousness of how temporary this experience is.[9]

For the most part, Dana's detachment falls within the conventional
bounds of patrician reserve and manly cool, although, as I've suggested,
he seems to project his own lack of sympathetic feeling onto the ship's
code of manhood. In his account of his two most intimate relationships,
however, the detachment seems unnervingly personal. During his four
months in California, he paternalistically delights in the affection of a

little Sandwich Islander, Hope. "Every Kanaka has one particular friend, whom he considers himself bound to do everything for, and with whom he has a sort of contract,—an alliance offensive and defensive,—and for whom he will often make the greatest sacrifices. This friend they call *aikane*; and for such, did Hope adopt me" (167). In return for Hope's attentive services, Dana "used to teach him letters and numbers" (168). Yet the second of Dana's intimate relationships, with a little puppy, seems to touch him more, perhaps because the puppy gave him a still greater feeling of mastery. "In a few weeks, I got him in complete subjection.... I called him *Bravo*, and the only thing I regretted at the thought of leaving the beach, was parting with him" (198). No mention of his trusty Kanaka sidekick at all.

Dana departs without commenting on either Hope or the puppy. Later, briefly returning, he takes a smoke with his Kanaka friends, who "saluted me as the *Aikane of the Kanakas*." Then he adds without further comment, "I was grieved to find that my poor dog Bravo was dead. He had sickened and died suddenly, the very day after I sailed in the Alert" (221). Grief, yes, but no guilt. Is it unfair of me to sense a touch of narcissistic pleasure in his power? The dog died of its grief, making Dana, if not a lady-killer, at least a heartbreaker.

More certainly, he doesn't mention Hope again, despite several opportunities to do so, until he returns once more and finds Hope near death, "wasting away" with an unnamed disease brought by white men. Suddenly Dana's feelings of friendship intensify in a rush. "The sight of him made me sick and faint. Poor fellow!... I really felt a strong affection for him, and preferred him to any of my own countrymen there" (272).[10] Now Dana dramatically contrasts his own affection for the Kanaka with the heartlessness of Captain Thompson, who refuses to allow any medical help (273). "What? a d——d Kanaka?" the captain says, and Dana gloats, "This same man died afterwards of a fever on the deadly coast of Sumatra" (274).

Luckily, the mate is more sympathetic. Dana gets some very strong medicines to Hope, who seems at death's door, then visits him twice more before departing again. Returning nearly three months later, he hastens to see if Hope is still alive. To his surprise and delight, the disease has been checked, though not cured. "I shall never forget the gratitude that he expressed. All the Kanakas attributed his escape solely to my knowledge" (292). Unfortunately, Dana has no more medicine, so Hope's life hangs on the arrival of another ship. Finally, after the ship arrives, Hope "began rapidly to recover." When Dana takes his

last leave of his Kanaka friends, "really, this was the only thing connected with leaving California which was in any way unpleasant. I felt
an interest and affection for many of these simple, true-hearted men,
such as I never felt before but for a near relation" (303).

Dana's language still seems oddly detached: "unpleasant," "interest,"
the generalized stereotyping, the repeated "really." A few pages earlier
he contradicts himself, saying "Not even the last view [of California]
could bring out one feeling of regret" (283). More significant, the tip-
off to what spurs his rush of solicitude comes with Dana's next sentence.
"Hope shook me by the hand; said he should soon be well again, and
ready to work for me when I came upon the coast, next voyage, as
officer of the ship; and told me not to forget, when I became captain,
how to be kind to the sick" (303). There isn't much difference here
between Hope and the puppy. Dana's friendship intensifies so suddenly
because Hope's sickness makes him feel so powerful.

On the surface this passage seems added evidence that Dana maligns
the sailors' code of manhood in saying they neglect the sick. Two of
the three captains involved, one mate, and Dana himself go out of their
way to attend to their dark-skinned employee. But power is the real
issue. If Dana were to admit vulnerable feelings to the crew, his class
inferiors, he would feel humiliated. His solicitude for Hope empowers
his feelings of superiority. To transfer the emotional subtext to a different frame, Hope seems to be the good darky saying, "Oh, let me
work for you again, Massah! Be good to us poor chillun when you's
de boss!"

In Dana's eyes, Hope's sickness transforms him from a forgettable
servant into a memorable rescue fantasy. The Kanaka's helplessness
makes him an eager slave to Dana's need for manhood—not just bravery and duty, not even collective dominance, but a personal feeling of
paternalistic power which views Hope as an utterly dependent yet safely
exotic child. In *Moby Dick* Melville explores the sadomasochistic dynamics of such a relationship, first seductively and benignly with the
mutual dependency of Ishmael and Queequeg, then malignly with
Ahab and Pip in their terrifying symbiosis. Dana contents himself with
simply feeling like a god, or at least a captain, the next best thing.

A great deal of humiliation must be buried under Dana's need for
manhood, if my basic thesis about manhood has any validity. But Dana's
detachment gives us little access to his feelings. Post-Freudian readers
can detect an obvious symbolic progression from his weakness of the
"eyes" to his agility on the "mast." Having overcome his fears of cas-

tration, he can stand erect with any man. That trope tells us nothing of what prompts his fears, though. While the symbolism of manhood hints at *Moby Dick*, Dana wants to demonstrate his prowess, not dive into his mind.

As I have been hinting, I think Dana's relationship to his father is crucial. Yet Richard Henry Dana, Senior, probably appeared the reverse of awesome and castrating. He seems to have been a figure of unmanly, embarrassing weakness and clinging depressions, possessed of conventional literary aspirations. Perhaps the son's problems with his eyes came in part from seeing the spectacle of his father, day after day, and fearing the prospective spectacle of becoming like him. On the other hand, Dana never mentions his eyes after the first paragraph. Nor does he ever disclose the measles that caused his eye problems and forced him to drop out of Harvard. From first to last he seems ashamed of weakness, burying his fears about himself and his father beneath his chronicle of manly prowess.

Dana displaces his feelings about his father in two mystifying ways. He confesses to a strange, inexplicable apathy as he enters Boston Harbor (396), and he shows a great deal of ambivalence about Captain Thompson's authority. Again and again he flares up in suppressed rage against his autocratic captain, whom he snidely calls "my lord paramount" (204, 295). Yet he helps to talk the crew out of their mutiny (340). By the end of the book he defends any captain's right to such authority and implies that captains' excesses are idiosyncratic (404–412).[11] Searching for a self-empowering that preserves his sense of class privilege, Dana ultimately resolves his feelings of manly inferiority through patriarchal and patrician reidentification.

The graphic flogging scene freezes Dana in his ambivalence. For the first ten or so chapters he presents himself as an eager initiate, taking on the sailors' manhood and with it their views of authority. It's a him-against-us world, compounded by the captain's rather comic irascibility. Soon Dana and his patrician messmate successfully petition the captain to shift their berths into the steerage. "We now began to feel like sailors," out from under the eyes of the officers at last. But he and S—— don't want to lose their extra allowance of bread. When they and the rest of the crew go to the captain, he breaks out in an incomprehensible rage, shouting, "I'll *haze* you! I'll work you up! . . . I've been through the mill, ground, and bolted, and come out a *regular-built down-east johnny-cake*, good when it's hot, but when it's cold, sour and indigestable;—and you'll find me so!" Eventually the mate sets the matter right, though "the 'down-east johnny-cake' became a by-word for the rest of the voyage" (66–67).

Unfortunately, the mate of the outward-bound voyage is too much of a Starbuck. He "was a worthy man;—a more honest, upright, and kind-hearted man I never saw; but he was too good for the mate of a merchantman. He was not the man to call a sailor a 'son of b——h,' and knock him down with a handspike" (109). Rejecting a more patrician image of manhood as disfunctional, yet mocking the captain as fatuously angry, Dana retreats to the crew for his ostensible code of manhood. He buries that odd note of desire for an authority figure who can knock him down.

"Wherever the captain is a severe, energetic man, and the mate is wanting in both these qualities," he concludes earlier, "there will always be trouble" (76), and in fact trouble comes. The mate impugns the captain's seamanship. As they quarrel about how to reeve a Spanish burton, the mate says he's right because he was taught by a real sailor. "This, the captain took in dudgeon, and they were at sword's points at once." Taking out his rage at the mate on Sam, the slowest-spoken member of the crew—this is my interpretation, not Dana's—the captain picks a fight. When Sam responds, "I'm no negro slave," the captain says immediately, "Then I'll make you one.... Make a spread eagle of him! I'll teach you all who is master aboard!" (117–118).

Then John, a Swede, identified already as "the oldest and best sailor of the crew" (67), asks why. He too is strung up to be flogged. As the captain himself flogs John, he dances about the deck in sadistic ecstasy, "calling out as he swung the rope,—'If you want to know what I flog you for, I'll tell you. It's because I like to do it!—because I like to do it!—It suits me! That's what I do it for!' " When John cries, "Oh, Jesus Christ!," the captain shouts, "*Call on Captain T——. He's the man! He can help you! Jesus Christ can't help you now!*" (120).

Perhaps as an unconscious rejoinder to these words "which I never shall forget" (120), Dana's final solution to the flogging problem is for the owners to choose captains who have religion (413–414). But that waffly meditation comes much later. For now he simply "turned away and leaned over the rail, and looked down into the water." D. H. Lawrence, who weirdly exults in the flogging as a manly redemption from namby-pambyness, thinks Dana vomits.[12] I think some sort of physical paralysis is more likely. "Disgusted, sick, and horror-struck," he has already argued himself into a mental paralysis. "The first and almost uncontrollable impulse was resistance. But what was to be done? The time for it had gone by. The two best men were fast, and there were only two beside myself, and a small boy.... Bad as it was, it must be borne. It is what a sailor ships for" (119). Everything sounds plausible until that last sentence, which makes Lawrence's relish seem intuitively right, if only for a moment. Then Dana flattens his responses into a patrician's resolve "that if God should ever give me the means, I would do something to redress the grievances and relieve the sufferings of that poor class of beings, of whom I then was one" (122).

Flogging "is what a sailor ships for." A mate should be able to knock a sailor down with a handspike. Under the smooth surface of Dana's patrician initiation into robust American manhood loom the shoals of the entrepreneurial paradigm. While he identifies with the nation's prospective dominance over weaker civilizations and ambiguously supports the captain's tyrannical authority, he touches here on a latent desire to be beaten. Would a beating simultaneously liberate his rage and his desire to be filled up with a strong fatherly self? *Moby Dick* displays these dynamics with suicidal intensity, at least in my reading. Dana barely hints at what may lie beneath his narcissistic pleasure in power: the craving, as he said of his puppy, to be "in complete subjection" to an all-powerful man.

These are irrational waters, however, and Dana is a conventionally rational gentleman. Though he shares some of Melville's psychological dynamics, he takes almost none of Melville's narrative risks. The "maddened temper," of Captain Thompson, so Ahab-like in his insecurity and his obsession with dominance, may well be Dana's double, as Martin Green suggests. Such rage "is the shadow version of that expanded self" Green finds in the nineteenth-century American adventurer.[13] On the other hand, Dana would have had to say only a word and, like John, he would have been flogged himself. If his horror is the outer shell of desire, as I'm perversely suggesting, he keeps that shell securely battened down. Desire never breaks loose from his pose of patrician detachment. Throughout, an identification with the authority of his class blocks his access to the dynamics of manhood.

In the aftermath of the flogging, John, who "was a foreigner and high-tempered, ... talked much of satisfaction and revenge." As for Sam, an American, the flogging "seemed completely to break him down. He had a feeling of the degradation that had been inflicted on him, which the other man was incapable of." Coming from a slave state, he had often entertained the crew "with queer negro stories." Now he "seemed to lose all life and elasticity." For the rest of the voyage he seldom smiled, and often let out "a long sigh when he was alone" (145). Once again, there is no hint of the crew's mockery in the face of such strong feeling. A man has been reduced to slave status, the ultimate humiliation for white American manhood. The captain had succeeded in making him feel like a negro.

Missing the point, Dana simply notes the "remarkable" difference between the two men's responses, ascribes it to their characters, and moves on. As with Caroline Kirkland, his noblesse oblige requires no further exercise of sympathy. Like Kirkland, too, he treats his voyage as a redemptive pastoral, presuming throughout that his natural bonds are with his civilized readers. As he lectures them sententiously midway through, "We must come down from our heights, and leave our straight paths, for the byways and low places of life, if we would learn truths by strong contrasts; and . . . see what has been wrought upon our fellow-creatures by accident, hardship, or vice" (283).

Ostensibly Dana is musing about a young Englishman, mysteriously wellborn and well-bred, with "the latent gentleman about him," who had gone completely native for thirteen months after a shipwreck (283). George P. Marsh had arrived on board "nearly naked, painted from head to foot, and in no way distinguishable from his companions until he began to speak." The natives had given him "two or three wives," and had tattooed him all over, except for his face and hands—there Marsh drew the line. Yet now he departs to be an officer on another ship (229). He falls and he rises, at random.

The "truth" Dana implies by this cautionary example seems to be, Look how "accident, hardship, or vice" can destroy the weaker sort. Such "strong contrasts" should strengthen our resolve to stay at the top. The implication he veils says, There but for my straight and narrow future go I, if George Marsh's "I" exists at all. Critics like to cite Dana's reentry into Boston Harbor, his "face burnt as black as an Indian's" (395). But Dana never lets the Indian get beneath his skin. He settles himself again in Boston, saying "I would not wish to have the power of the captain diminished an iota" (399). For Melville, George Marsh's story might expose the fragility of Dana's attempt to fuse manly and civilized self-images. Analogies to *Typee*, especially to Tommo's fear of being tattooed, abound. For Dana, Marsh is merely "a vagabond" (228), and the Englishman's story, like all the strong contrasts Dana experiences, affirms his hierarchy of high and low.[14]

II

Francis Parkman, Jr., had a great deal in common with Dana. Parkman's father, a gentle Unitarian minister who seems to have been even more depressed than Dana's father, had a nervous breakdown when Parkman was eighteen. After graduating from Harvard Law School, Parkman went west, ostensibly to observe the Indians but also to make himself into a heroic image of manliness beyond his father's psychological weakness. Parkman too developed a disease of the eyes, which incapacitated him for the rest of his life. Kim Townsend's admirable essay "Francis Parkman and the Male Tradition" notes the lack of any physical basis for Parkman's severe symptoms and highlights the self-destructiveness in Parkman's pursuit of a manly self-image. Parkman paradoxically regenerates himself through violence to animals and to himself. Driving himself further into sickness, he proves his manhood as a buffalo killer, a self-image coupling wild physical abandon with rigorous self-control. In the process, he learns to kill symbolically "what was wild and uncontrollable and sickly about himself."[5]

Unlike Dana, Parkman writes with truculent candor about his inadequacies. *The Oregon Trail* is much richer in irony, partly because Parkman doesn't try to make himself appealing. Only twice does Dana get sick, with nausea at the start and with a toothache as they round Cape Horn on the return voyage. Perhaps significantly, the toothache comes in the midst of an incipient mutiny, when ambivalence about Captain Thompson's authority has to be resolved one way or the other. Parkman is sick almost continuously, for weeks at a time. His mordant sense of anticlimax and his sardonic contempt for nearly everyone he meets barely keep his rage in check. Again and again he contrasts his physical state with the manly ideal, personified in his noble and generous guide, Henry Chatillon. "In a country where a man's life may at any moment depend on the strength of his arm, or it may be on the activity of his legs," Parkman was "so reduced by illness that I could seldom walk without reeling like a drunken man, and when I rose from my seat upon the ground the landscape suddenly grew dim before my eyes, the trees and lodges seemed to sway to and fro, and the prairie to rise and fall like the swells of the ocean." He has to dictate his narrative, he says, because of his "deficient eyesight," one of the "remote effects of that unlucky disorder" which brought him so much pain and dysentery on the prairie.[6] Intensify Emerson's sporadic problems with his eyes and bowels, and we have Parkman's day-to-day bondage to his body.

Unlike Dana, too, Parkman presents himself as much more flagrantly a snob. His habitual contempt embraces almost everyone, including himself. Only Henry Chatillon wholly escapes his Thoreau-like eye for the follies and pretentions of men, whether white or red. From the beginning he dissociates himself from "the society of the emigrants" with their strange ways and motives. All the men are either zealous religious doctrinaires or "some of the vilest outcasts in the country" (41–43). Whatever impels them, "whether an insane hope of a better condition in life, or a desire of shaking off restraints of law and society, or mere restlessness, certain it is that multitudes bitterly repent the journey." Dead babies' graves bespeak "the hardihood, or rather infatuation, of the adventurers." The women, he notes with a pithy dismissiveness, seem divided between regret and apprehension (96–98).

Only Parkman travels "from any other motive than gain" (138). What he initially describes as his "tour of curiosity and amusement" (37) does have a purpose: "I had come into the country almost exclusively with a view of observing the Indian character . . . to live in the midst of them, and become, as it were, one of them." His narrative is to be "a record of the progress of this design . . . and the unexpected impediments that opposed it" (168–169). Chief among those impediments is himself. Unlike *Two Years before the Mast*, which progresses from triumph to manly triumph, *The Oregon Trail* recounts one failure after another. Parkman eventually succeeds in joining an Ogallalla village for a time, though he never fulfills his dream of witnessing Indian war ceremonies (184). But this is the narrative of a caustic outsider, first to last. As his encounters with the Indians multiply, his fascination with their physical manhood gives way to sardonic comments on their unmanly character, especially their lack of restraint. Anticipating Marlowe's more ambiguous judgment of Kurtz in Joseph Conrad's *Heart of Darkness* or Hawthorne's ambiguous imagination of Pearl, Parkman writes of "that wild idea of liberty and utter intolerance of restraint which lie at the very foundation of the Indian character" (294). Moreover, Indians don't think. An Indian "never launches forth into speculation and conjecture; his reason moves in its beaten track. His soul is dormant" (152). Only war "saves them from lethargy and utter abasement" (200).[17]

When Parkman meets a white man who has done what Parkman set out to do, "become as it were, one of them" (168), he acknowledges "hardly a feeling in common" (241). Reynal "imitated the Indians in their habits as well as the worst features of their character" (315). Together with Raymond, a man whose owl's face expressed "the most impenetrable stupidity and entire self-confidence" (224), the three men present themselves to the Ogallalla chief as white warriors and allies. In reality, Parkman observes, one "was a coward, another a blockhead, and the third an invalid" (262). When Reynal gazes with him on a long valley amid the mountains, Parkman erases the whiteness of his French companion from his mind: "No civilized eye but mine had ever looked upon that virgin waste" (321). Class has superseded race as the basis for his self-definition.

Holding onto his patrician self-image for dear life, Parkman recurrently recalls his earlier New England existence as "a quiet student of belles lettres" (234), now with the added spice of being able to call Byron "pitiful and unmanly" (351).[18] At first he wonders if he is the same man. Thereafter he invokes New England, or Europe, in the spirit of Dana's "truths by strong contrasts," to remind himself and his readers of his sophistication amid these narrow, bedraggled provincials. He preserves and expands his patrician manhood by grafting frontier skills onto his class status and by heroically mastering his own diseases. He also balances a frank relish for noble Indian physiques with a disdain for tribal culture, which he dismisses as both patriarchal and childish.

Unlike Dana, Parkman disowns patriarchal manhood. For him patriarchy connotes a mindless Indian reverence for their familial and tribal elders (199, 264), an attitude not at all congenial with Parkman's feelings about his father. When Henry Chatillon points to Parkman as their leader, an old Delaware "sententiously remarked: 'No good! Too young!' " and rode away (56). The incident seems to have amused Parkman, who reveres Chatillon as the epitome of manly generosity and grace but detaches himself from any reverence for authority. If Dana, a comprehensively obedient man, subsumes himself by the end in traditional patrician patriarchy, Parkman attempts a more adventurous fusion of patrician disdain with manly individualism. Nor does he show Dana's relish for national expansion and dominance, though he sees the passing of the Indians and buffalo as inevitable.[19] His struggle for mastery focuses more exclusively on himself.

Parkman's real triumph comes not as an observer of Indians but as a killer of buffalo. Most of his narrative recounts a near-comic series of anticlimaxes, a steady onslaught of obstacles, failures, and discouragements. Then, toward the end, he at last achieves what Dana accomplishes in the first few chapters: a sense of heroic bravery, physical dexterity, and manly grace. Even here, Parkman's strict sense of self-definition through hierarchy intrudes. A little earlier he has noted how men are divided in the west: "The human race in this part of the world is separated into three divisions, arranged in the order of their merits: white men, Indians, and Mexicans" (378–379). Presumably women are off the bottom of his chart. Now, in the midst of recounting his daring and skill with the buffalo, he savors the implicit contrast to his bumbling companion Tête Rouge. Yet he also takes care to note the much greater skill of Henry Chatillon, as preeminent in approaching buffalo as Kit Carson is in running them (406).

An analogous hierarchy can be extrapolated from a dialogue midway through Hemingway's *Sun Also Rises*. As Mike implies, Pedro Romero is a bull with balls, Jake Barnes is a bull without balls, and Robert Cohn is a steer. In *The Oregon Trail*, Tête Rouge becomes a scapegoated Robert Cohn, the last in Parkman's long line of stooges. Meanwhile, Parkman's admiration of Chatillon counterpoints his ironic consciousness of his own body's conspicuous inadequacy, much as Ishmael counterpoints his alienated self-consciousness with Queequeg or, in a very different mode, Jack Kerouac with Dean Moriarity in *On The Road*. Chatillon's "manly face was a perfect mirror of uprightness, simplicity, and kindness of heart. . . . He was a proof of what unaided nature will sometimes do." Illiterate, yet with "a natural refinement and delicacy of mind, such as is very rarely found even in women," content with life as he finds it, perhaps overly generous, Chatillon "had not the restless energy of an Anglo-American." Parkman has never "met a better man" (49–50). "Standing erect upon the prairie, almost surrounded by the buffalo," calm and fearless as he shoots one cow after another, Henry Chatillon (Parkman likes to give the full name) looks like Admiral Nelson "on the deck of the 'Victory,' " with the same "sense of mastery" (422–423).

The contrast with Tête Rouge is that of a "jester" to a king. "Henry's face was roughened by winds and storms; Tête Rouge's was bloated by sherry cobblers and brandy toddy. Henry talked of Indians and buffalo; Tête Rouge of theaters and oyster cellars." Henry was "the most disinterested man I ever saw; while Tête Rouge, though equally good-natured in his way, cared for nobody but himself" (424).[20] In the unspoken middle is Parkman, who has struggled out of civilized effeteness and self-absorption to achieve a temporary control of his nerves and his body, but who still lacks Chatillon's natural mastery and natural ease of heart.

Parkman finds his own "contentment of mind" only in the act of killing buffalo patriarchs. Shooting a buffalo bull is unambiguously pleasing, he writes, because the bulls are so astonishingly ugly. "At first sight of him every feeling of sympathy vanishes; no man who has not experienced it, can understand with what keen relish one inflicts his death wound, with what profound contentment of mind he beholds him fall" (418). About shooting other creatures he acknowledges a touch of compassion, though fortunately, as he says several times, the prairie cures men of both "nervous apprehensions" and finicky scruples (128, 246). In a world where "each man lives by the strength of his arm and the valor of his heart . . . the whole fabric of art and conventionality is struck rudely to pieces, and men find themselves suddenly brought back to the wants and resources of their original natures" (106).

Parkman's "original nature," or at least the nature he claims for himself, conforms perfectly to D. H. Lawrence's memorable phrase for American manhood: "hard, isolate, stoic, and a killer."[21] He revenges himself on a particularly aggressive Indian puppy by having it for dinner (258). After killing an antelope, he first measures the distance: 204 paces. Then, "when I stood by his side, the antelope turned his expiring eye upward. It was like a beautiful woman's, dark and rich. 'Fortunate that I am in a hurry,' thought I; 'I might be troubled with remorse, if I had time for it' " (187). Later another antelope's eyes provoke a memorable irony: "His glistening eyes turned up toward my face with so piteous a look, that it was with feelings of infinite compunction that I shot him through the head with a pistol" (235).

For ugly creatures, he feels not a twinge. His ruthlessness extends in fantasy to old Indians. Looking at an "old conjurer" on the lookout, "perched aloft like a turkey-buzzard," Parkman muses how nice it would be to shoot him. "Surely, I thought, there could be no more harm in shooting such a hideous old villain, to see how ugly he would look when he was dead, than in shooting the detestable vulture which he resembled" (225). Later, Parkman becomes more indiscriminate. "For the most part, a civilized white man can discover but very few points of sympathy between his own nature and that of an Indian." After "a few months or a few weeks . . . he begins to look upon them as a troublesome and dangerous species of wild beast, and if expedient, he could shoot them with as little compunction as they themselves would experience after performing the same office upon him" (336–337).

For old Indian women he reserves a special animus. They are "withered witchlike hags" (211), "ugly as Macbeth's witches" (141), "hideous, emaciated" (162). Their looks enrage and disgust him. One "hideous old hag of eighty," with arms like "whip-cord and wire," especially appalls him because she seems to run the place, "screaming like a screech-owl when any thing displeased her" (196). Younger Indian women strike him as either generically pretty or, to the degree that they have personalities, a contemptible drain on their men. Madame Margot, Reynal's woman, sits "from sunrise to sunset, a bloated impersonation of gluttony and laziness" (174).[22] Despite his disdain for Indian culture, Parkman's misogyny exaggerates the Indians' formulaic contempt for "fools and old women." Ironically, his manly idol allows himself much more feeling. When Chatillon's squaw dies, "it was some time before he entirely recovered from his dejection" (191).

For Parkman, his disgust at the witchlike appearance of old Indian women does not extend to killing them, even in fantasy. That would have been unmanly. Nevertheless, Parkman's scapegoating of old women, his relish for young male Indian physiques, and his zest for killing variously express his will to power. That will is not innate, as several contemporary theories have it, but compensatory. Dana's will to power manifests a rather complacent narcissism, at least on the surface. Parkman's will to power suggests what looks like narcissism's opposite, a virulent self-hatred, both denied and vented in his intense loathing of ugliness.

As far as I can make sense of it, he drives his body into sickness to polarize his sense of himself as something contemptible, Emerson's "NOT ME," and something grand, a heroic will to master this self that is not me. He makes his body a pasteboard mask, the visible locus for his feelings of humiliating weakness. Sickness brings his sense of weakness out in the open, where he can disown it and struggle with it to prove his heroism. If Jonathan Edwards used God's authority to break his own will, Parkman used his body to make his will come alive. It was the most intimate arena he could find to transform himself into a lifelong warrior.

Like Dana, Parkman seizes upon conventional manliness to block any further exploration of his feelings. All we know of his childhood dynamics, as Kim Townsend summarizes, is that "his ties to his mother were intimate and strong, his relations with his ministerial father distant."[23] Whatever the sources of his passion for manhood, Parkman goes far beyond Dana in exposing the drive for dominance and the fear of weakness generating their shared code of self-control. He empowers himself with an ideology that blocks every feeling except an

Ahab-like rage, diffused as scorn, and an Ishmael-like longing for manly fraternity.

As with Dana, a passion for manhood also helps Parkman to resolve his conflict between the patrician world he leaves and the entrepreneurial world he enters. Parkman tries to have it both ways. He fashions himself into a new man while retaining some measure of urbane sophistication and detached disdain. Unlike Dana, who chooses a more traditional and self-subordinating mode of adventure, Parkman puts himself at the individualistic edge of his country's expanding economy, partly to observe the losers, and partly to see what it felt like. In his rush to manhood, his animus against old women vents a little of the rage and anxiety otherwise buried as intermittent self-disgust.

William Goetzmann's *Exploration and Empire* makes clear the values of business enterprise generating the frontier spirit. More starkly on the frontier than anywhere else, ambition and enterprise constituted a Jacksonian religion. For Goetzmann the mountain men were really expectant capitalists, who identified their aspirations with the nation's. They saw their personal and collective dominance over the Indians and the land as inevitable. The expectation directed their actions "in countless subtle ways."[24] Active government sponsorship belied the myth of rugged individualism, Goetzmann demonstrates, though as Parkman points out, American companies exerted the real power. Fort Laramie, for instance, was "one of the posts established by the 'American Fur Company,' who well-nigh monopolize the Indian trade of this whole region. Here their officials rule with an absolute sway; the arm of the United States has little force" (150). Collective capitalist dominance, felt as national identification, abetted individualist ruthlessness. As Goetzmann points out, the energy of enterprise was also fueled by an older, patrician dream—to be a landed gentleman.[25] In pursuit of the dream, men found the new ideology of manhood essential to nurture what often must have felt like monomania.

One must above all things be bold and fearless, Parkman reiterates. Never let an Indian sense any hint of weakness, even when a growling puppy nips at your heels (257–258). "If you betray timidity or indecision, you convert them from that moment into insidious and dangerous enemies" (159). Keep "a rigid inflexible countenance," and don't try to be liked (328). Neediness, like weakness, invites attack. Patrician philanthropy dies quickly on the prairie, along with any utopian impulses, he observes tartly more than once, "for from minnows up to men, life is an incessant battle" (341).

Parkman's survival-of-the-fittest philosophy seems stereotypically conventional to us now, looking back at him as we do through the Darwinian codifications of Herbert Spencer and Theodore Dreiser. In the late 1840s, however, Parkman's version of manhood brought the struggle for dominance into patrician parlors, not just as an exotic adventure but as a realistic, if displaced account of what men now had to do to survive and prosper in the business world. Father's depressions were no help. Parkman had to cure himself, with a lifetime dose of entrepreneurial manhood. From any humane point of view the prescription nearly killed him. From his point of view, it gave him access to his will to power, which he exercised in the only way his body could bear, as an obsession with writing powerful accounts of frontier wars, with an emphasis on entrepreneurial men like LaSalle. For him it was a living story: how white men fought to dominate red men, possess the land, and master themselves.

Like *A New Home—Who'll Follow?*, published ten years earlier, *The Oregon Trail* is a survival manual for patricians heading west. Whereas Kirkland advises women to mask their legitimate snobbery and triumph through sophisticated example as well as their husbands' financial resources, Parkman counsels men about the necessity for fearlessness, singleness of purpose, and self-control. As Kirkland presents herself for her women readers, so Parkman becomes for patrician men: a model of how to succeed in a world grossly alien to their values. His model urges a manly heroism, in which will triumphs over incapacity. Only through steadfast will can a man master himself. Then patricians who learn to feel at ease with "the basilisk eye of danger" can once more take command of their uncultured competitors (305). One must beat them by joining them—not the Indians but the patricians' real rivals, the men with the killer instinct.

The Wide, Wide World also provides a lesson in self-help and survival, for dependent girls and women, who had to learn how to stuff their resentments into their spiritual closets. The analogue, in *The Oregon Trail*, is Parkman's recurrent, humiliating sickness. His body keeps voicing the weak and shameful self he continually tries to silence. Unlike Warner's narrative, which blatantly displays the patriarchal oppressiveness Ellen must learn to revere, Parkman's narrative erases the inward trail of his feelings. Yet in some strange unconscious fashion he loves his suffering even more than Ellen loves to cry. "For myself I had suffered more that summer from illness than ever before in my life, and yet to this hour I cannot recall those savage scenes and savage men without a strong desire again to visit them" (460).

Oddly, though Ellen eventually stifles the rage Parkman vents as habitual bile, they share an impulse toward stoicism. More fundamentally, despite their opposite and complementary ideologies of womanliness and manliness, a common loneliness suffuses these two training manuals. Kirkland looks expansively social by comparison. Secure in her family and the village her husband owns, secure too in her class status and her chatty intimacy with her readers, she fends off the wide, wide worlds that Susan Warner's heroine and Parkman himself embrace. On opposite sides of the gender divide, two willful young patricians, orphans in all but name, set out on opposite journeys through domesticity and the frontier. What they share is the struggle to conquer themselves. They do so by reconventionalizing their feelings in the gender ideologies of the new middle class: evangelical womanhood and entrepreneurial manhood. Faced with an inward enormity of unacceptable feelings, both Warner and Parkman flee into the most powerful gender conventions they can find, with loneliness as their conscious price for stifling their discontents.

At the end of Parkman's journey, just before he reaches the wagon trains and the settlements, he sees a lone bull grazing on the prairie about a mile away. After walking toward him, Parkman crawls, then sits about a hundred yards from the buffalo, waiting "till he should turn himself into a proper position to receive his death-wound." The bull "was a grim old veteran," Parkman muses to himself. "He was miserably emaciated.... He looked like some grizzly old ruffian grown gray in blood and violence, and scowling on all the world from his misanthropic seclusion."

The bull trots toward him, but stops about twenty yards away. Then, "for a full quarter of an hour," they look at each other. Parkman sees the history of the bull's battles written in his "large, white scars, which gave him a grim and at the same time a whimsical appearance." Live and let live, the hunter thinks to himself. " 'My friend,' thought I, 'if you'll let me off, I'll let you off.' " But just as the bull "slowly and deliberately . . . began to turn about," Parkman "forgot my prudent intentions, and fired my rifle." The bull spun around "like a top," galloped over the prairie and up "a considerable hill," then "lay down and died." Parkman shoots another bull, his last kill of the trip, then returns to camp (446–448).

The passage anticipates Ishmael's marvelous meditation on Ahab's natural double, the aged and isolated lone whale, who cares for none of his kind. When encountered, "those wondrous grey-headed, grizzled whales . . . will fight you like grim fiends exasperated by a penal gout." But Ishmael's meditation pointedly contrasts their antisocial pugnacity with the caring solicitude of female whales.[26] Parkman remains in a more Ahab-like mode. If the bull evokes war and patriarchy, it also evokes ugliness and physical emaciation. Despicably weak, it is also a noble and generous survivor. As the muted coda to Parkman's trip, the encounter confronts him with a grim, yet whimsical image of his father, his body, and his future self, the residue of generic manhood after innumerable battles for dominance.

All those possibilities are first half acknowledged and then disowned in the act of killing. If the bull backs away, that proves him a coward. Cowards deserve to be shot, and that's that.

The incident has a mysterious resonance, which Dana's narrative nowhere approaches. In the absence of any impulse to think about it, however, a mixture of ruthlessness and projected self-pity takes over. The struggle for dominance allows little introspection and no overt self-pity, to be sure. The struggle to reconventionalize one's feelings allows no self at all. Yet Ishmael floats like an "orphan" at the end of Ahab's quest for self-empowering, while Parkman projects his self-pity into the last buffalo he sees, "a miserable old bull, roaming over the prairie alone and melancholy" (456). To paraphrase D. H. Lawrence's mordant comment about the American passion for nature, absolutely the safest thing for a real man to love is his loneliness.

8

Devious Men: Hawthorne

As my chapter on impassioned women has argued, Warner and Stowe developed evangelical narrations to transform feelings of anger and dependence. Their relatively stable, simple duplicities presume a high degree of sympathy from their readers. They knew their audience, and Stowe often writes as if she and her readers are in the same room. At least once, in a remarkable passage just after Little Eva dies, Stowe concludes her chapter with a collective prayer, in quotation marks, as though Eva's father, author, and readers were all speaking it together.[1] The datedness of these impassioned narrative styles, however they diverge in resolving women's dependence on patriarchy, suggests the common intensity in the writers' engagement with their contemporary female world of love and sentimental ritual.[2]

For Hawthorne and Melville, narrative deviousness helps them transform their feelings of class and gender deviance, not dependence. After briefly considering the two writers together, this chapter focuses on Hawthorne's strategies for arousing then unmanning the reader's will to interpretive power. My readings of several stories and *The Blithedale Romance* emphasize Hawthorne's fascination with malice and humiliation. He enacts that dynamic in his finest narrations even as he critiques it in his characters.

Dana and Parkman try to cure themselves of weak bodies and weaker fathers by embarking on rites of manly passage. They appropriate the

new ideology of entrepreneurial manhood to preserve and enhance
their traditional class status. In reconventionalizing themselves, they
deny the feelings of deviance that Hawthorne and Melville learn to
exploit. Dana and Parkman also presume a bond with genteel readers.
In contrast, the most original fictions of Hawthorne and Melville call
prevailing conventions of self-empowering into question. Their narrations frequently solicit sympathy for deviants. More pervasively, they
quarrel with their readers, sometimes directly in Melville. Sometimes
they explicitly satirize gender codes. Most deviously, especially with
Hawthorne, their narratives induce a will to interpretive power that
the texts then expose and undermine.

Alienated from patrician norms and dispossessed in childhood from
patrician status, appalled and intimidated by the crass forcefulness of
middle-class men, yet unwilling to affiliate themselves with the new
female constituency for culture, Hawthorne and Melville develop narrative ways of pulling the rug out from under the ordinary reader's
rush to sympathy or judgment. Separating the premodernists from the
bourgeois, they coax the knowing few into a complicity of alienated
intellects. Their deviousness extends to deauthorizing their own authority. Ambiguous and contradictory interpretations pop out of their
stories like Thoreau's loon out of Walden Pond. The effect frequently
makes me feel seduced into a sneaky intellectual fraternity yet simultaneously exposed and accused.

Then and now, the struggle to interpret these tales and romances
undermines American norms of selfhood and authority. Hawthorne
and Melville assert the writer's manly individuality not directly, by affirming bourgeois conventions of self-reliance and self-control as Dana
and Parkman do, but deviously, by subverting the reader's interpretive
self-assurance. What does the *A* mean? What does the white whale
mean? Are Young Goodman Brown and Reverend Mr. Hooper right
to see evil in every human heart, or are they neurotic, sadistic, and
sexually terrified of women? Does Bartleby's nameless narrator come
to some awareness of himself through Bartleby, in humane brotherhood or stifled alienation, or does he reveal a false Christian consciousness masking capitalist exploitation?

Is "Ethan Brand" about the dangers of romance—the proud Byronic
isolation of a scornful, heartless intellect—or about the dangers of realism, which reduces both manliness and art to the fellowship of
maimed, crippled villagers? In this "fragment of an aborted romance"
whose last word is "fragments," what about those two self-aborting

images of the artist, the old German Jew with his diorama magnifying the spectators, and the silly old dog chasing his tail? Must the artist cut short his own tale and expose his hairy hand if he wants to keep his own heart alive? Or must the artist abort his quest for the truth of himself if he wishes to entertain his yokel audience? Is "Benito Cereno" a racist story about white innocence vs. black evil, an allegorical story anticipating the Civil War, a malicious theological parable about "A.D.'s" dim-witted complacency as the only route to salvation, a nihilistic story about indeterminacy, or a still more nihilistic story about language itself as a tool of social dominance?

Somehow, to say All of the Above to any of the above leaves me dissatisfied. It forces a contradictory multiplicity into my sense of interpretive authority, and therefore into my sense of myself as a reader. Insofar as I want a feeling of mastery and control over the reading experience, it unmans me. That, as this chapter will argue, is the point.

I

Hawthorne, whom Henry James, Sr., once compared to a rogue in the company of detectives, brings out the detective impulse in readers, only to expose the prying with an ambiguously shaming mirror. Poe thought he had the secret to "The Minister's Black Veil"—"a masterly composition of which the sole defect is that to the rabble its exquisite skill will be *caviare*. The *obvious* meaning of this article will be found to smother its insinuated one. The *moral* put into the mouth of the dying minister will be supposed to convey the *true* import of the narrative; and that a crime of dark dye, (having reference to the "young lady") has been committed, is a point which only minds congenial with that of the author will perceive."[3] In other words, Mr. Hooper's accusation of universal guilt veils a secret crime. Presumably he has impregnated and then killed the young lady whose corpse was said to shudder as he leaned over her body and hastily caught back his black veil.

Sexuality and concealed guilt or at least a fear of sexual intimacy certainly pervades the first half of the story. Despite Hawthorne's ostentatious footnote disclaiming the relevance of a parallel case of guilt, or perhaps because of it, readers are primed to search for evidence of Hooper's secret sin. Post-Freudian readers can easily find its traces in the narration's sly innuendoes, double entendres, and teasing skittishness about sexual desire. As Harry Levin wrote thirty years ago, "The tales are rife with matrimonial fears."[4] *Was* the young lady pregnant? Did she demand marriage?

Then, just as my Poe-like fancies are in full cry, the narrative swerves toward a very different kind of question: not what is the minister hiding behind his veil, but why is everyone afraid to ask him about it? And why does the veil give the minister, a notoriously dull speaker, such awesome power over his listeners? Why does even Elizabeth tremble at its "terrors"?

From D. H. Lawrence to Michael Colacurcio and Philip Young, Hawthorne has inspired a chase for secrets.[5] Like Poe, or like Roger Chillingworth dancing in ecstasy as he discovers what lies on Dimmesdale's sleeping chest, we exult in our sophisticated close readings as we probe to the concealed heart of a Hawthorne story. But just as we feel most complicit with his intelligence and most distinguished from what Poe calls "the rabble," the heart turns out to be a mirror after all, and Hawthorne's parable turns out to be about that kind of reading. Hooper's pointing finger reverses my own. His inscrutable veil—one student, Jorge Navarro, wrote that today Hooper would be wearing "sin glasses"— arouses in me a will to power. My wish to invade his privacy becomes an evasion of myself. At the same time, Hawthorne disowns such an act of malice against his readers by making the minister seem coyly withholding or seductively sadistic. To focus on him both violates and reflects the minister's character. Just as Poe lifts the veil, his face freezes with Hooper's secret smile.

Melville, too, delighted in Hawthorne's deviousness. What he says of Hawthorne's titles has often been applied to the tales: "Some of them are directly calculated to deceive—egregiously deceive—the superficial skimmer of pages." Two of the titles, including "Young Goodman Brown," "did dolefully dupe no less an eagle-eyed reader than myself."[6] A pleasure in being eagle-eyed, yet duped shapes Melville's avid response, at least in his persona as reviewer. More privately, Melville's delight in being deceived yields to the detective. One of Melville's first letters to his new friend trumpets his blatantly projective discovery of "the grand truth about Nathaniel Hawthorne. He says NO! in thunder; but the Devil himself cannot make him say *yes*." Over thirty years later, talking with Julian Hawthorne, Melville mused that he always thought Julian's father had concealed a secret.[7]

Henry James comes closer to my reading when he observes that Hawthorne plays with guilt as with a pigment. In what may be the most quietly subversive moment in *The Scarlet Letter*, the narrator says of

Dimmesdale's hallucinated *A* in the night sky, "Another's guilt might have seen another symbol in it."[8] By that light, any interpretation becomes an act of guilty self-projection. Analysis comes to feel like an act of dominance, very male, heartlessly violating the fragile quasi-female sympathy we should be nurturing in ourselves. Such rhetorical strategies, designed as they are to surprise the reader with his own sinfulness, have a long literary tradition, from Milton through James. Hawthorne's characteristic turn uses the theme of guilt to invite, then indict the reader's aggressive, yet self-revealing gaze.

In so doing, Hawthorne dramatizes the entrepreneurial ideology of manhood he found all about him. Story after story presents conventional manliness as aggressive, insensitive, and murderously dominant. "The Artist of the Beautiful" or "The Birthmark" can stand for many others. From "My Kinsman, Major Molineux" through *The Scarlet Letter*, Hawthorne builds his tales around spectacles of public humiliation, as strong men collectively try to shame weaker, yet nobler individuals. Hester's humiliation pointedly takes place in "The Market-Place." Hepzibah, too, begins *The House of the Seven Gables* with intense feelings of shame at having to enter the marketplace with her wares. Hawthorne's fascination with marketplace humiliation reflects a profound quarrel with the manhood he feels inside himself, so narcissistically needy for self-empowering through malice and cruelty. It also reflects a more superficial patrician disdain for tradesmen.

In his finest stories, the dynamic of dominance and humiliation encompasses narration as well as theme. Making the dynamic central to the act of reading, Hawthorne turns the tables on worldly men of force by inducing an acute desire for premature interpretation. A drive for dominance or to possess a secret brings on a frozen rigidity of self-exposure. The result is a private shaming, though hedged with the mutual safety of ambiguity. Unlike the rhetorical strategy I described in my first chapter, where an "I" invites a textually inscribed "you" to convert from conventional manliness to natural spontaneities, Hawthorne's strategy has a more furtive aim. As detectives sniff and snoop through the underbrush of his tales, he lures them into the open, then humiliates them with their own intellectual prurience.

Ostensibly, of course, he invokes the "I-you" convention quite frequently, as in "The Custom-House." With a becoming modesty he solicits readers to forsake manly rigidity for their more feminine sympathies. His prefaces to the four romances show an increasingly biting need to detach himself from the oppressiveness of ordinary

American experience, so dull and crass and middle class, so strictly confining fiction to probability. Most memorably, to focus Hawthorne's artistic discontents, his preface to *The House of the Seven Gables* symbolically attacks manhood. America breeds readers who want him "relentlessly to impale the story with its moral, as with an iron rod,—or rather, as by sticking a pin through a butterfly—...causing it to stiffen in an ungainly and unnatural attitude." Floating above that destructive, phallic arena, making the most moral soul feel vaguely like a rapist, he teases such readers with the unpinnable butterfly of his fancy.[9]

Hawthorne also teases his readers with a hyperconsciousness about his own intrusiveness, equally manly and violating. Diffidently acknowledging the dangers of egotism in presuming to write about himself at all, he justifies his self-consciousness as the unburdening of a friend who seeks to usher his readers into the frail truths of every human heart. Under the still waters of that persona, which contemporary readers took to be as "natural" as a limpid stream, he baits self-assured readers with his own lack of self-assurance. His vulnerable, unthreatening, feminized voice, controlled and guarded, to be sure, but all the more needy within the bounds of genteel decorum, seems to be saying what Dimmesdale says in the forest: "Be thou strong for me!"[10] Then Hawthorne waits for readers to take the hook.

His two finest tales, in my view, are also the two stories most vexed with contradictory interpretations. "My Kinsman, Major Molineux" (1831) has generated a brilliant array of Freudian explications construing Robin's initiation into adulthood as an Oedipal rebellion and an equally brilliant array of historicist readings arguing for Hawthorne's ironic treatment of "Robinocracy" before the American Revolution. The issue turns on whether readers identify with Robin or see him as a bumptious dupe.[11] "Rappaccini's Daughter" (1844), which I will treat more sketchily, demands to be read as two contradictory stories. Kenneth Dauber briskly sums them up: the innocent girl destroyed by a faithless love, and the dangerous woman enticing an innocent boy.

Here again the historicists have at the psychoanalysts, with the now nearly silenced majority of Christian moralists holding to the hapless middle. Do we identify with Giovanni's sexual fears, do we follow the narrator in disengaging from Giovanni's destructive vanity to affirm Beatrice's purity of spirit, or do we follow Carol Bensick's ingenious historicist counterturn in discovering Giovanni's legitimate fear of syphilis beneath the narrator's transcendental contempt for sixteenth-century empirical science? Bensick's book-length reading of this tale, like Colacurcio's near-book-length reading of "The Minister's Black Veil," celebrates Hawthorne's intent to deconstruct his own narrative authority. His carefully planted details lure the skeptical literary historian on a hunt for Hawthorne's own skepticism about the romantic idealism of his Concord contemporaries.[12]

My reading of both these stories attempts to reconcile psychoanalytic and historicist approaches by setting Hawthorne's devious narrations in a different historical context: competing ideologies of manhood. In Hawthorne's narratives male dominance is partly patriarchal and partly entrepreneurial. "My Kinsman, Major Molineux" differs from almost all his later stories in representing the dangers of American manhood from a patriarchal perspective. With a voice as divided as the face of the man who leads the mob, Hawthorne attempts to resolve the tensions swirling about Robin's initiation into marketplace manhood. Rather heavy-handedly, he presents a traditional authority figure as a victim of mob violence. Much more subtly, he insinuates that upwardly mobile young men are really devils in training. The latter resolution is easy to miss.

At first most readers can't help but sympathize with this young country bumpkin's quest for patrician protection in the big city. As Q. D. Leavis says, "We have to identify our consciousness with the protagonist Robin."[13] After all, we feel as bewildered as he does by the lack of information, since everything comes to us through his consciousness. At the same time, as Freudians rightly emphasize, we feel bewildered in a more detached way by Robin's odd forgetfulness about his mission and by his abrupt pugnacity in response to the mysterious hostility of various townspeople. Though the narrator keeps calling him a "shrewd youth," we begin to wonder about his arrogance and his presumptuous provinciality. In fact, Robin's shrewdness seems to consist largely in being content with obviously inadequate explanations. Instead of worrying and puzzling, he confidently presses on until totally stymied. With each successive reading he looks more and more bullheaded. On first reading, however, we have little choice but to identify with him as he tries to make his way in a near-nightmare world.

If we are extremely alert readers, or rereaders, our bewilderments extend beyond Robin to the narrator. For instance, we might well wonder why the narrator withholds Robin's last name. It takes a good deal of work to figure out that his name is Molineux; most students miss it completely. Here the Freudian reading is compelling, up to a point. The narrator hides the last name because Robin unconsciously wants it that way. He wants to throw off the kinship ties defining his identity up to now. Though he doesn't quite know it yet, he is one of the new men. He and his kind will rise to power in America by over-throwing traditional patterns of deference. A symbolic parricide is in the offing.

On the edge between his need for patrician protection and his con-version to the new middle-class code of self-reliant competition, Robin finally takes sides when he sees his kinsman being tarred and feathered. At first the spectacle of Major Molineux's "overwhelming humiliation" prompts a conventionally tragic response, though the catharsis may be only follicle deep: "Robin's knees shook, and his hair bristled, with a mixture of pity and terror." But as tragedy yields to comedy, Robin joins the crowd. "The contagion was spreading among the multitude, when, all at once, it seized upon Robin, and he sent forth a shout of laughter . . . the loudest there."[4] What looks to Freudians like Robin's unconscious aggression flashes into the open, seemingly without guilt or punishment. As the last line suggests, now he "may rise in the world," without the help of his kinsman. Like a modern-day migrant to urban California, he has no need of a last name. He will be a self-made man, appearing in print one year before Henry Clay coined the term.

Psychoanalytic readings presume, first, that Robin has a self with some depth of feeling, and second, that readers continuously identify with Robin, either consciously or unconsciously. As my intermittently ironic paraphrase has already implied, the narration encourages a strange mixture of empathy and detachment. Freudians tend to dismiss the narrative disengagements as defenses against unconscious parri-cidal wishes, while historicists tend to dismiss Robin as the butt of Hawthorne's political ironies. Or rather, as Michael Colacurcio pro-vocatively puts it, Robin is merely a literary device, part of Hawthorne's "strategy of irony and insult" to lure readers into confronting our own political naïveté. The story debunks and deconstructs the tendency of American typological historiography to personalize politics as an ad-olescent rite of passage. Anyone dumb enough or narcissistic enough to stay with Robin's psychology, Colacurcio implies, has missed both the irony and the insult. Hawthorne's tale is really two deliberately unreconciled stories, about Robin and about political conspiracy, and Robin's shrewdness begins when he discovers he is irrelevant to the political story.[15]

My reading pushes Colacurcio's one more notch toward malice. To see the story as an exceptionally seductive and devious critique of manhood can reintegrate psychoanalytic and historicist perspectives, while preserving Colacurcio's astute sense of narrative ironies. In my reading, the growing impasse between Robin and narrator forces me first to experience Robin's bewilderment as my own. Then I am faced with the guilt and the mourning that Robin never acknowledges. Robin's ability to rise as a new man depends on his serene unconsciousness of having an unconscious. It's as if he is saying, "Who, me? I don't relish anyone's humiliation, and besides, the devil made me do that."

Meanwhile, all the tensions of his initiation into manhood are displaced, first onto the mob leaders and then onto the readers. Ultimately, the narrative calls into question whether Robin's self-made self is a self at all. His aggressive self-possession allows him to *be* possessed, by the new ideology of manhood. For Hawthorne, such a self is the devil's plaything, signaled by the first six meanings of *shrewd* in the *Oxford English Dictionary*, all of which have to do with evil, malice, or the devil's fiery eyes. Not until we get to number 13 do we find the modern meaning of "clever or keen-witted."

Most obviously, the narrative displaces rebellious tensions into the voice of the man with two sepulchral hems and the red-black face of the mob leader. First Robin grabs the coat of a distinguished-looking old man, bows, holds onto the coat, and asks "very loudly" where Major Molineux lives. The gentleman returns anger for presumption—too much so, on both sides, at least for the narrator. The man "answered him in a tone of excessive anger and annoyance. His two sepulchral hems, however, broke into the very centre of his rebuke, with most singular effect, like a thought of the cold grave obtruding among wrathful passions." The man's words brusquely tell Robin to show respect to his betters—"I have authority, I have—hem, hem—authority" (4–5). But his two sepulchral hems put death at the center of the man's claims to authority, claims strangely linked with his "wrathful passions." The narrator's incisive, portentous interpretation establishes an allegorical conjunction of anger, presumption, and death, at odds with Robin's "shrewd" dismissal of the mystery.[16]

Soon Robin encounters a strange double-faced man, whose "features were separately striking almost to grotesqueness." At first Robin simply notices the man's double forehead, bold irregular nose, "deep and shaggy" eyebrows, and glowing fiery eyes, while the man huddles "with a group of ill-dressed associates" (6). When Robin next sees him, the man's complexion "had undergone a singular, or more properly, a two-fold change." One side of the man's face now "blazed of an intense red, while the other was black as midnight," with his mouth in contrasting colors. As shrewd readers might deduce, the man has painted his face. Instead of suggesting that kind of reading, the narrator makes explicit the demonism implied by the first description. "The effect was as if two individual devils, a fiend of fire and a fiend of darkness, had united themselves to form this infernal visage." For the narrator, only devils can explain the erupting political passions in what he calls, with a triple pun, the man's "party-colored features" (11).

When Robin sees the man for the third time, at the head of the mob, his divided face now personifies killing and mourning. In the midst of "a redder light," the man's "fierce and variegated countenance" makes him look "like war personified; the red of one cheek was an emblem of fire and sword; the blackness of the other betokened the mourning which attends them" (15). Here, the narrator practically hands us an Oedipal reading, though couched in pre-Freudian allegory. Anger at authority arouses a terrifying, unresolvable ambivalence, filled with mourning as well as wrath. "The double-faced fellow" and the man with the two sepulchral hems frame Robin's own experience of doubleness, his movement from cathartic grief to laughter when he sees his kinsman's "overwhelming humiliation."

Major Molineux, too, has a double face, curiously like the mob leader's. His ordinarily "strong, square features" have been divided into death and agony: "His face was pale as death, and far more ghastly; the broad forehead was contracted in his agony, so that the eyebrows formed one dark grey line; his eyes were red and wild, and the foam hung white upon his quivering lip" (16). On both sides of the rebellion, adults manifest fearful self-transformations, because rebellion brings on self-dividing feelings. A war for "authority" begets war within selves, with mourning and shame at the center of anger.

At least so the patriarchal narrator construes a rebellion against patriarchy. For him wrathful passions are what a sneeze was in medieval times: an opening through which the devil might possess one's soul. Insidiously the story lures readers toward those passions. Hawthorne's most devious move in his drama of a young man's seduction by demonic forces is to give the narrator a double voice.

In his ambiguous first paragraph, suggesting abuses of power on both sides, the narrator pictures colonial governors as besieged and pitiable middlemen, caught between kings and people. With an appearance of evenhandedness, the narrator allows some legitimacy to the people's anger at English kings, who "assumed the right" of appointment. Nevertheless, he concludes by comparing the people's grievances to a disease. Robin enters a town filled with "much temporary inflammation of the popular mind" (3).

For most of the story, under the press of Robin's confusions, the narrator's quiet identification with authority recedes. Then at the climax, the inflammation metaphor returns in a rush. Robin's laugh comes not from himself in any autonomous sense but from the crowd, whose "contagion . . . seized upon Robin" to make him laugh. Partly for that reason, the rest of the paragraph exults in a giddy sense of collective release. Double faces, death, wrathful passions, and mourning are forgotten as the narrative rises like a balloon into a guilt-free fairy tale. "The cloud-spirits peeped from their silvery islands, as the congregated mirth went roaring up the sky! The Man in the Moon heard the far bellow; 'Oho,' quoth he, the old Earth is frolicsome to-night!' " (17)

The next paragraph pulls me back to earth, and back to an appalling guilt. Insofar as I let myself romp with the cloud spirits, I'm punished for the laugh I was just encouraged to enjoy. "On they went, in counterfeited pomp, in senseless uproar, in frenzied merriment, trampling all on an old man's heart" (17).[17] The relentlessly rhythmic sentence drives home the accusation, first with three harsh adjectives, then with "trampling," which reduces the crowd to cattle, and finally with the heavy spondee of "old man's heart," which compels our pity for the solitary, feelingful major as Robin disappears into the faceless, feelingless mob. Using the first, fairy-tale voice as a setup, the narrator lowers the boom on the reader as well as on the people's will to power.

What has looked like Robin's guilt-free unconscious or his malleable willingness to outdo the winners at their own game now stands condemned as a shared sadistic delight in dominating and humiliating, "trampling all on an old man's heart." Nor does Robin show any concern for his kinsman thereafter. Instead, as Michael Colacurcio sums up, the boy has passed "from the single-mindedness of childhood to the fallen wisdom of adult duplicity."[18] He shows a mature new self, laconic and calculating, with a dry Yankee wit. "I begin to grow weary of a town life, Sir" (17). Such urbane irony and manly self-control will surely be rewarded, as his companion indicates by encouraging him to stay in town for awhile. Shifty and shameless, Robin has become shrewd at last. The narrator's accusation reverberates only in the reader.

Robin's inscrutably kind companion may be the devil himself. In a memorable graduate seminar at the University of Florida, Linde Katritsky and George Williams maintained that position in the face of my incredulity. Their case became plausible to me when they unearthed the associations of "shrewd" with demonism and knavery. As James McIntosh points out, Hawthorne interlaces the tale with allusions to *Midsummer Night's Dream*, in which Puck is identified as "that shrewd and knavish sprite / Call'd Robin Goodfellow." (2.1).[19] At the end, when the gentleman confirms that Robin is "a shrewd youth," the label ironically reverses Robin's lack of shrewdness before. Now he has earned his manhood. Now, implicitly, others in the devil's party will help him along.

True, the gentleman shows no ostensible signs of the devil, unlike his counterpart in "Young Goodman Brown." Nevertheless Robin's rite of passage into entrepreneurial maturity culminates with his laughter at the humiliation of patrician authority. That laughter shows his capacity for being possessed by the new American spirit, what Tocqueville, writing in the same decade, named "the tyranny of the majority." Robin's subsequent success will depend on his willingness to disown his kinsman and sail with prevailing political winds. For the narrator, such undeferential self-reliance is worse than the conformity Emerson would soon disparage. Robin has been claimed by the devil in modern guise, the ideology of self-made men on the make. Such men never look back and never look inward. Instead, they always look a little higher, to see whom they can cut down and trample on.

Hawthorne's story accuses the new men of inhumanity. For him, the mob leader's double face shows the cost to oneself of being possessed by the will to power. The double-voiced narrator brings readers close enough to the demonic contagion for Freudians to join the crowd. Suddenly, he steps back, shaming anyone who might relish trampling on a father figure. Robin's initiation into marketplace manhood makes him a prototype of the new man, admitting only anger and ambition to public self-display. Left with all the conflicting feelings Robin disowns, readers have to choose between aggressive middle-class ambition and empathetic patrician sensibility, Robin or the narrator. Since ambition now seems the first refuge of a scoundrel, I detach myself from Robin and retreat from the mob leader's agonized features. Suitably chastened for my sins of identification, I return to the narrator's patriarchal sympathies, with one key difference. What lingers in my mind is not a reverence for authority but the spectacle of humiliation.

In making that spectacle the climax of his tale, and in using a double voice to shame unwary readers, the narrator comes close to the devilish malice he associates with the new manhood. He protects himself through his own duplicity. He sympathizes with authority figures, quite ostentatiously, just as they lose their authority. Still more deviously, he humiliates readers by indulging, then punishing our pleasure in humiliation.

II

From "My Kinsman, Major Molineux" to "Feathertop," Hawthorne's last story, published over twenty years later (1852), Hawthorne dramatizes manhood as demonic possession, often explicitly. Paradoxically, it becomes one of his most intimate and recurring tropes for his profound fear of losing manly self-control. To let his guard down invites possession or domination, whether by forceful people or by forceful passions, especially rage and desire. What lessens is Hawthorne's patriarchal identification. As he warms to his theme, he becomes more radical than conservative, though always retaining his evasive indirectness. In many of his best stories throughout the 1840s, as in his three romances of the early 1850s, Hawthorne portrays dominating males as if they were rapists, empowering themselves by violating someone weaker. His early concern for patriarchal stability, very much in the patrician mode, yields to a more feminine sense of patriarchal evil, along with a postpatriarchal sense of entrepreneurial manhood as a will to self-empowering through dominance.

"Rappaccini's Daughter" marks a halfway point in Hawthorne's shift from an ambivalently patriarchal perspective on manhood to his mature sense that manhood is a rivalry for dominance. As in other tales of this period, he tries on a sentimental feminization of the narrator as a nonpatriarchal alternative to manhood. But the strategy doesn't work; the story undercuts the narrator's authority. While the narrator canonizes Beatrice, in a lengthier version of the ascent to the cloud spirits at the end of "My Kinsman," the story draws the reader into a vortex of male rivalries, as relentless and inescapable as any vortex in Poe's tales.

As they contend for victory, Giovanni makes himself "potent" with rage as well as the vial, while Rappaccini grows "erect with conscious power" and Baglioni has the last malevolent "triumph." Each man has been poisoned, "from the first," with a fear of powerlessness, the genesis for their common will to power, which drives them toward their common humiliation. (*Tales*, 208–209). Worse, Giovanni's initiation into manhood makes him not simply demonic but vulnerable to being possessed by Rappaccini. With Beatrice as the devious vehicle, Rappaccini's sexualized poisons have been "insinuated" into his body (205). Though the narrator struggles to disengage, his voice takes rivalry to yet another level of triumph and horror.

At first the narrative modulates between two relatively conventional perspectives: a young man's anxious preoccupation with female sexuality and a feminine horror at patriarchy. Despite the narrator's strictures against Giovanni's shallow fancies, we cannot help but share the young man's fascination with Beatrice's voluptuous embrace of her erotic "sister," the shrub, and with the bloom of her own body, "redundant with life, health, and energy; all of which attributes were bound down and compressed, as it were, and girdled tensely, in their luxuriance, by her virgin zone" (190). We also cannot help but share his sense that somehow all the barely restrained sensuality of girl and garden has been created by Dr. Rappaccini's "commixture, and, as it were, adultery . . . the monstrous offspring of man's depraved fancy" (198). The spectacularly sexualized language cannot be bound down and compressed to Giovanni's conventionally voyeuristic sensibility. Clearly the air holds some kind of patriarchal poison. It seems even more oppressive than that in *The Wide, Wide World.*

Carol Bensick thinks syphilis is at the root, while Frederick Crews has detected incest. Though Bensick would probably disagree, the interpretations are quite compatible, if one nudges Crews's implication out into the open.[20] Rappaccini may have raped his daughter, as his name strongly implies. In any case, he has abused her body to give her power. He has enabled her, he exults at the end, "to quell the mightiest with a breath" and asks her, "Wouldst thou, then, have preferred the condition of a weak woman, exposed to all evil and capable of none?" "I would fain have been loved, not feared," replies Beatrice (209). The real poison is manhood: Rappaccini's demonic presumption that power, which for him means doing evil unto others before they can do evil unto you, constitutes everyone's desire. What begins as a young man's fear of female sexuality ends as every man's fear of being powerless.

In the midst of the narrative's slow shift from patriarchy and female sexuality to male rivalry as the locus of poison, the narrator conspicuously disengages from Giovanni. Despite the incontrovertible evidence of a physical threat to the young man, the narrator ringingly endorses Beatrice's spiritual innocence while indicting Giovanni's inability to love. He is shallow and vain, we are told with startling bluntness. More subtly, his narcissism and rage mirror the manhood of the two elder scientists. Like Robin, Giovanni shows through his growing self-possession that he has no real autonomy, only a desire for power and a fear of being toyed with. Much more explicitly than Robin, under his conscious fear of humiliation Giovanni shows an unconscious fear of being penetrated or possessed by another man. His fear intimates his susceptibility.

While Baglioni and Rappaccini vie for the young student as a potential pawn in their scientific combat, Giovanni becomes an unwitting clone of the two men he arrogantly despises. Twice he fearfully avoids Baglioni's penetrating gaze, which he thinks "would look too deeply into his secrets" (196, 202). Giovanni's anger at Baglioni seems as irrational as Baglioni's fear that Beatrice will oust him from his professor's chair. As his fascination with the garden's mystery increases, Giovanni's fear of Beatrice's powers turns toward another kind of fear, both shallower and more intense: the fear of being duped by the elder man. " 'Will you make a fool of me?' cried Giovanni, passionately. '*That*, signor professor, were an untoward experiment' " (196). Like Baglioni, he seeks a competitive edge to ward off his own fears of powerlessness or of acknowledging that he has been possessed.

Like Rappaccini, Giovanni reduces Beatrice to an experiment. Entering the garden as if he were deflowering it, "forcing himself through the entanglement of a shrub that wreathed its tendrils over the hidden entrance" (198), Giovanni immediately out-doctors the doctor. Becoming "calm, and even coldly self-possessed," he "began a critical observation of the plants." On the outside he now looks just like the elder rivals, calm, cool, and calculating. On the inside, mirroring them again, he boils with rage. Unlike theirs, though, his rage boils over. Still young, he lacks their mature self-control and their purposeful malice. Erupting at Beatrice, their common scapegoat, he cries out one of the most memorably antiromantic lines in American literature: "Let us join our lips in one kiss of unutterable hatred, and so die!" (207).[21]

In the ironic "upshot" of their rivalry, each man stands exposed at the end as a killer. Baglioni, who thinks of Giovanni as a means to "foil" and "thwart" (204) his adversary, gives him the vial of Benvenuto Cellini. Implicitly, Carol Bensick has demonstrated, Baglioni has filled the vial with what he thinks is a cure for syphilis.[22] Sure that he will win,

Baglioni then allows himself a "chuckling" respect for Rappaccini, as if grateful for the competitive challenge: "But, let us confess the truth of him, he is a wonderful man—a wonderful man indeed" (204). The real men are now in their element. After Giovanni administers Baglioni's vial to counter Rappaccini's poison, the three men can fairly be accused of having killed Beatrice together, in the process of trying to best each other.

Baglioni has the last, heartless, half-gloating word: "Rappaccini! Rappaccini! and is *this* the upshot of your experiment?" His "tone of triumph mixed with horror" serves as the ironic epitaph for all three men, bound together now by their symbiosis of triumph and horror. The dead body of their victim turns their struggle for dominance into a mutual semipublic humiliation. Meanwhile, though the narrator flirts with encouraging our sympathy for Giovanni's experimentation, by the end he has thoroughly converted to Beatrice's view of Giovanni: "O, was there not, from the first, more poison in thy nature than in mine?" (209). The two concluding rhetorical questions are really accusations against manhood.[23]

In suggesting that Giovanni himself may have syphilis from his Naples days, Carol Bensick deflates the metaphoric force of Beatrice's accusation.[24] Bensick's skeptical reading of the narrator ends up returning to Giovanni as the locus of feelingful perception or at least of fear. It's certainly true that the narrator simplistically polarizes and allegorizes interpretation to blame Giovanni. Beatrice becomes all spirit, love, purity, and selfless womanhood, while Giovanni comes to represent the body, hate, contamination, selfish manhood, and the lurid intermixtures of his narcissistic fancy. As Kenneth Dauber's fine reading of the two contradictory stories argues, no amount of narrative hectoring can wholly dispel Beatrice's threatening poison.[25]

One could even argue that right up to the end she expects Giovanni to die, "so to let thee pass away," as she puts it euphemistically (207). On the other hand, through Beatrice the narrator offers us an oasis of purity and blame. It would resolve the tensions very nicely if we could agree that Beatrice's sexuality, like her death, was caused by poisonous maleness. While contamination unnervingly persists on every side, the narrator resolutely tries to shift the balance of fear and loathing from womanhood to manhood, which, "from the first" shapes Giovanni's "nature."

And yet, and yet. Given the narrator's indictment of this shallow young man, almost no one except Carol Bensick wants to return to Giovanni's point of view. Yet Bensick's reading voices a sophisticated discomfort with the narrator's evasive spiritual simplicities. Steven Mailloux thinks a truly moral reading of the tale can begin only when we become skeptical of the narrator's holistic allegorizing. For Nina Baym, the story would be better off without the narrator, since his "intervening, prosy . . . commentary" can't control the story's fictional and symbolic material.[26] Though the narrator's point of view seems much more straightforwardly rendered than in "My Kinsman, Major Molineux," the impasse between narrator and story seems all the more unresolvable. The drama as well as the commentary clearly condemn manhood, in both its patriarchal and its rivalrous guises. Yet the only alternative is a womanhood stripped of body, sexuality, and anger, presented in what look suspiciously like anemic cliches. If my response is any guide, the reader puts the story down feeling utterly baffled, horrified at all three men yet unable to trust the narrator's pat moralizing.

My own reading of the story finds two levels of deviousness. On the surface, as I have already been arguing, the narration first entices us toward Giovanni's seemingly legitimate fears, then exposes him as a junior version of Rappaccini and Baglioni. To the degree that we continue to identify with his need for self-empowering, we share his shaming as a killer. The manly wish to take control, whether of the garden and the girl or of the story, leads to humiliation, while an intuitive trust in Beatrice's spiritual purity leads to salvation. Not coincidentally, once we let ourselves be led by the feminized narrator, we can accuse all the men with a clear conscience.

At the little lower layer of deviousness, Hawthorne undermines his narrator's feminized authority by making his affirmations sound like accusations. Even as we want to believe in Beatrice's innocence, the narrator's intrusive judgments and prissy piety invite distrust. Unlike "My Kinsman," the story offers no patriarchal resolution of its tensions. Nor does it dismiss the new men as devils in disguise. Instead, the narrator's holier-than-thou pontifications, especially his growing scorn for Giovanni, implicate him in the struggle for power. At the friezelike finale he becomes the unspoken fourth man, standing higher than Baglioni. While disowning his own maleness to celebrate Beatrice's purity, he uses her purity for another turn of the screw. With a snooty rancor belying his allegorical disengagement, the narrator takes the feminine high ground for its rhetorical artillery. Like the rest of them, he exploits Beatrice to give himself the ultimate triumph mixed with horror.

If feminization represents just another strategy for humiliating men of power, then "Rappaccini's Daughter" brings male readers into a morass of fears and rivalry from which there is no way out, except to stifle one's discontents with the narrator. D. H. Lawrence was right: under the blue-eyed darling lurks a trickster.[27] Under the trickster lurks someone with a terrified vulnerability to male invasiveness. Both the vulnerability and the malice enable Hawthorne to dramatize entrepreneurial manhood from the inside.

As Gloria Erlich points out, "Rappaccini's Daughter" is strikingly autobiographical in at least one crucial respect. Hawthorne's uncle Robert Manning, the dominant male in his childhood, was not only a successful businessman but also the most famous pomologist in America, with an extraordinary collection of fruit trees, including over a thousand varieties of pears. Domineering, decisive, and often censorious, he energetically controlled the raising of his sister's children.

Conventional Oedipal models simply don't apply here, Erlich rightly observes, since Hawthorne's father, a sea captain whom the boy barely knew, died in Dutch Surinam when Hawthorne was only four. Nevertheless, as with Emerson, it would be wrong to follow Quentin Anderson's lead and see only the writer's ache for an absent father. Erlich's fine critical biography is the first to emphasize Uncle Robert's central role in Hawthorne's life and art, and in his sense of manhood. Early on, the boy "learned the power of weakness, a way of manipulating his manipulators in order to create a psychic space" for himself. Yet he internalized the manliness he resisted. "Nathaniel's passivity and indolence appeared especially unmanly in the presence of Robert Manning's energetic capabilities, not only to the uncle but to the boy himself."[28]

One could say that Hawthorne's narrative strategies point toward "un-Manning" such a man, or such a man in himself. Forceful, attentive, and severe with young Nathaniel, the uncle evoked in the boy a lifelong ambivalence—a concealed rebelliousness, yet also a profound self-distrust about his deviance from manliness. Throughout his life, Hawthorne tried to succeed both as an artist and as a man among real men. His work as surveyor of customs and as consul in Liverpool, together with his campaign biography of his friend Franklin Pierce, balance his mature productivity as a romancer. Except perhaps for Melville, whose need for intense friendship seems to have been quietly blocked, Hawthorne's closest friends were men like his uncle, not literary types. Yet his tales tend to portray such men as heartless monsters. At the end of his life, apparently with the clear knowledge that he was dying, Hawthorne baffled his family by leaving home to die on a journey with Pierce, the former president, his old and manly friend.[29]

If such bonds helped him firm up his self-control, his art gave partial voice to his fears. Hawthorne's horror of male invasiveness may have a yet more intimate biographical dimension. Uncle Robert made Nathaniel share his bed for many years, until his handsome young nephew went to college, even though the Manning household was not crowded during Hawthorne's adolescence.[30] In a speculative footnote to *Nathaniel Hawthorne in His Times*, James Mellow apologizes for doing the usual thing, hunting Hawthorne's secret, then offers his candidate: "I would suggest that he may have been subjected to homosexual assault or seduction, perhaps by his Uncle Robert, during the period when the two were sleeping together."[31]

The horticultural associations for several of Hawthorne's villains, as Mellow notes, might support the connection. So, too, might the frequent portraits of spiritual rapists, who threaten men as well as women, as Hawthorne's characteristic way of dramatizing male dominance. The worst sin in *The Scarlet Letter*, Dimmesdale says, is for his housemate Roger Chillingworth to have "violated, in cold blood," the sanctity of Dimmesdale's heart. In *The House of the Seven Gables*, Jaffrey's "evident purpose of forcing a passage" to Clifford and his larger "hot fellness of purpose, which annihilated everything but itself," manifests the rapacious maleness of old Colonel Pyncheon, who "had worn out three wives, and, merely by the remorseless weight and hardness of his character in the conjugal relation, had sent them, one after another, broken hearted, to their graves."[32] In *The Blithedale Romance*, Coverdale experiences Hollingsworth's attempt to possess his heart with sensations eerily foreshadowing the pole Hollingsworth later sticks through Zenobia's breast.

Gloria Erlich concludes that if an actual homosexual assault had occurred, then Hawthorne would have felt free to rebel more directly. Instead, given Uncle Robert's "probity and self-discipline" as well as the sneakiness of Hawthorne's attacks against him, she thinks it more likely "that the sin was in the fantasy of the nephew rather than in overt acts of the uncle."[33] Despite the reasonableness of Erlich's discussion, I like Mellow's idea. The threat of homosexual rape seems much more central to Hawthorne's narrative tensions than does homosexual desire, which seems more relevant to Melville's narrative deviousness.

As feminists say of rape in general, the threat of homosexual rape has more to do with power than with desire. Or rather, it has to do with manhood: a way of empowering oneself through someone else's humiliation. Whatever Hawthorne's personal fears and desires, he finds in the spectre of spiritual rape a spectacular trope for dramatizing the entrepreneurial will to power. On the surface, he condemns the solitary egotism induced by manhood, as in "Ethan Brand," one of his last stories (1851). Below the surface, rivalrous men experience a fearful, demonic intercourse. When the dull-witted Bartram is alone with Brand, "heart to heart," he feels "a throng of evil shapes" flow between their breasts, all but possessing him to start down the same road toward the Master Sin (*Tales*, 234).

III

In the three romances of the early 1850s, Hawthorne takes his exploration of manhood beyond "Rappaccini's Daughter," with its not quite believable sentimentalization of Beatrice, and, for that matter, beyond "Ethan Brand," in which little Joe provides a tenuously feminized alternative to the real men who reject Mother Earth and brotherhood alike. Now Hawthorne risks a stronger if intermittent identification with female subjectivity, especially in Hester Prynne. At the same time, his covert fascination with men competing for power moves his narrations toward intimate dramas of rapelike humiliation, far beyond the controls of patriarchal or patrician authority. Conventional manliness becomes a cage of iron, barred from within, where egotism twists into frightening perversions of desire. For Chillingworth or Jaffrey Pyncheon or Westervelt, demonic possessiveness seems indistinguishable from a relentless will to control and violate.

Hawthorne frames the prison house of manhood with what looks at first like a clear allegiance to feminine values. Especially in *The Scarlet Letter*, the fragile rose at the opening of Hester Prynne's story clearly beckons the reader toward Hester's side, challenging the spiky masks of authority within which men shut up their womanish needs and feelings as well as their deviant women. Yet Hawthorne's subversions of manly power and authority, including his own narrative authority, lead to an exceptionally evasive self-deconstruction in his narrators.

Under his relatively obvious condemnation of heartless male egotists in his three major romances, Hawthorne simultaneously dramatizes two contradictory stories: a woman's struggle for strength and autonomy within patriarchy, and the rivalry of several men for dominance. The latter story—whether it takes the form of Chillingworth vs. Dimmesdale, Jaffrey Pyncheon vs. Clifford, with Holgrave as triumphant observer, or Hollingsworth and Westervelt and Coverdale in a competitive triangle—slowly stifles the independent strength of Hester, Hepzibah, and Zenobia. As male rivalry takes center stage, the narrators disengage from their heroines. At once sympathetic and judgmental, involved and aloof, sentimental and punitive, they put up a fog of ambiguities, ironies, self-consciousness, and multiple points of view to screen their covert participation in the men's struggle for narcissistic self-empowering. My next chapter indicts the narrator of *The Scarlet Letter* along those lines.

In *The Blithedale Romance* (1852), a ubiquitously malicious story of impassioned women and devious men, Coverdale assiduously ferrets out the ruthless rivalries for power beneath everyone's claims to brotherhood. Priscilla and Zenobia become rivalrous pawns as the men struggle for dominance over each other. Ostentatiously fleeing the warfare he sees all about him, Coverdale indirectly triumphs over both Hollingsworth and Westervelt through a catty withdrawal into class-linked dandyism. His triumph seems fraudulent even to himself.

"I hate to be ruled by my own sex," Coverdale says to Zenobia in "Eliot's Pulpit." "It excites my jealousy, and wounds my pride. It is the iron sway of bodily force which abases us, in our compelled submission."[34] Earlier and later, however, Coverdale confesses that he has fallen in love with Hollingsworth. Unlike Westervelt, this man of force also has a woman's capacity for tenderness. He makes the intensely self-conscious and alienated narrator feel befriended and cared for rather than challenged in rivalry.

"Hollingsworth's more than brotherly attendance gave me inexpressible comfort," Coverdale muses about his sickness. "Most men," he continues, "have a natural indifference, if not an absolutely hostile feeling," toward the sick, the injured, and the weak, "amid the rude jostle of our selfish existence." This "ugly characteristic of our sex ... has likewise its analogy in the practice of our brute brethren, who hunt the sick or disabled member of the herd from among them, as an enemy" (66). Like Frederick Douglass in his 1855 revision, Coverdale fully understands that real men, including himself, scorn weakness. He is astonished that this hairy man of iron doesn't try to humiliate him, as any normal man would do.

But love between men can go only so far. When Hollingsworth appeals to Coverdale to join his cause, Coverdale reports his sensations as if he were being raped by the man's "rigid and unconquerable idea" (147). It was "as if Hollingsworth had caught hold of my heart, and were pulling it towards him with an almost irresistible force.... Had I but touched his extended hand, Hollingsworth's magnetism would perhaps have penetrated me with his own conception of all these matters" (150). Coverdale's language foreshadows Zenobia's fate, as Hollingsworth's rigid pole strikes Zenobia's breast with its "iron hook," which Coverdale feels as if it smote his own breast, and lifts her dead body to the surface of the river (239). Terrified of being "penetrated" by this strong, tender man's "conception," Coverdale precipitously flees Blithedale to rejoin the "swinish multitude" (47), after saying good-bye to the pigs (158–159).

Throughout, Coverdale portrays intimacy as a "veil" for power relations. Westervelt's mesmeric control of Priscilla as the Veiled Lady becomes the narrator's recurrent symbol for the dangers of enslavement lurking in any entangling domestic alliances. He thinks of intimacy as a strangling "knot" (41, 170) leading even so strong a character as Zenobia to suicide. Better to be a self on a hill, solacing one's self-esteem with a voyeuristic aestheticism and a residual sense of class superiority.

At least three recent critics have argued that Coverdale secretly killed Zenobia.[35] While I don't think the argument quite holds up, I sympathize with the impulse to make it. As Hollingsworth, Coverdale, and Silas Foster stand over Zenobia's body, Foster having supplied the pole and Coverdale having traced the trail, the scene echoes the end of "Rappaccini's Daughter," where three men stand branded as killers. By then I am so thoroughly disenchanted with Coverdale's voice that I wouldn't mind seeing him accused of a crime. At least then he might be forced out into the open. Self-absorbed and heartless, cloyingly malicious and intrusive, guarding his vulnerabilities while probing for everyone else's, he justifies all the criticisms the other characters make of him. "Miles Coverdale is not in earnest, either as a poet or a laborer," Hollingsworth announces (90). Coverdale laughs at any enthusiasm, including his own, another companion remarks (39). Zenobia accuses him of "following up your game, groping for human emotions in the dark corners of the heart" (220). When he suggests "Utopia" as the name for their community, the proposal "was unanimously scouted down, and the proposer very harshly maltreated, as if he had intended a latent satire" (62).

Coverdale's entire narrative is a not-so-latent satire, belying its devious claim to being a "Romance." Antiromantic from the start, Coverdale mocks the pretensions to egalitarian brotherhood suffusing their communal experiment. Relentlessly he exposes the class hierarchies and marketplace dynamics at the heart of their effort to escape social inequality and "selfish competition" (46). He mocks himself as well, not simply for being a minor poet but for trivializing feelings. He is well aware of his incapacity to love. From the very first scene, when Old Moodie accosts him, he gets angry with anyone who seems to need him, whether it's Priscilla, Westervelt, or Hollingsworth. He can't feel anything deeply except malice and humiliation, and he knows it. Terrified of losing control, either through passion or bondage, he likes to empower himself with his "keen, revengeful sense of . . . insult" (173). He particularly likes to pick on people still weaker than he, especially Old Moodie and Priscilla, "making my prey of people's individualities, as my custom was" (105). Without malice, he feels "impotent to regulate" his thoughts (167).

With Priscilla in particular, all his malice comes to the fore. When she first enters their company and starts to cry, Coverdale smiles. "Perhaps it showed the iron substance of my heart. . . . Hollingsworth's behavior was certainly a great deal more creditable than mine" (56). Once, when she falls down, he sheds a tear for her, but only because she makes him feel protective (95). Later, sequestered within his impenetrable tree-hermitage, he blithely sends her an unspoken message: "Say that if any mortal really cares for her, it is myself; and not even I, for her realities,—poor little seamstress, as Zenobia rightly called her!— but for the fancy-work with which I have idly decked her out!" (120).

More than a snob's fancywork lurks in the "turret" of Coverdale's mind. Keenly attuned to any slight, real or imagined, he is hyper-aware of being at or near the bottom of the Blithedale friendship ladder, and he takes out his narcissistic frustrations on the "poor little seamstress." Nobody loves me, he says, in one self-pitying version after another. Even as he speaks of love, he translates it into hierarchies of dominance. The question that fitfully preoccupies him is, Why aren't I number one? Why am I only a Greek chorus, number three or four?[36]

When he sees Hollingsworth becoming first with both Priscilla and Zenobia, he can't bear it any longer. Out of "some petty malice" and "a foolish bitterness of heart," he vengefully tries "to come within her maidenly mystery" and "take just one peep beneath her folded petals" by talking to Priscilla of how happy Hollingsworth and Zenobia look together. Though Coverdale's conscious malice makes Priscilla a compensatory scapegoat, he resentfully hungers not for her but for the position and attention given to his rival, now "engrossing every thought

of all the women, and leaving his friend to shiver in outer seclusion."
When even Priscilla spurns him, he "strolled moodily homeward," ironically thinking of Hollingsworth's "huge egotism" (142–143).

   Like Giovanni, Coverdale sexualizes nearly everything he sees. Yet
his sexualizing impulses veil his need for self-empowering. His voyeurism fragments bodies into objects to be possessed. In particular, he
sexualizes Zenobia to demean her passion, and thus her power. When
he first takes inventory of Zenobia's physical attributes, he passes from
her clothes to "one glimpse of a white shoulder. It struck me as a great
piece of good fortune that there should be just that glimpse" (42). The
glimpse becomes a commodity, a "piece of good fortune," as separable
as money or one of Priscilla's purses from any sense of intimacy or
subjectivity. Later he speaks of Zenobia's heart, "which must at least
have been valuable while new" (100–101), and still later he lingers over
her drowned body, as if it were a "marble image" or statue, with rigid
arms, clenched hands, bent knees, and wounded breast (239–240).[37]

   Coverdale's penchant for visual fragmentation does more than establish his pose as detached voyeur. It solaces his strongest feeling, his
fear of humiliation. In the city, outraged at Coverdale's attempts to
pry and interfere, Zenobia lets loose a withering blast at what lies beneath his pretentions to dutiful concern: not desire but "Bigotry; self-
conceit; an insolent curiosity; a meddlesome temper; a cold-blooded
criticism" (182). She goes on, directly humiliating him, then dismissing
him as shallow, skeptical, and selfish. "Thus excluded from everybody's
confidence," he says, feeding his depression with a lame pun, he seeks
out Old Moodie, someone to whom he can still feel superior (185).
After a leisurely survey of the saloon, very much in the manner of the
Dutch realist painters, he finally "recognized his hand and arm" (188).
Young Moody, meeting Old Moodie, fragments the man almost out of
habit. Neither quite realizes how much they mirror each other as "men
of show."[38] Each man has become a vaguely criminal creature of artifice,
turning people into dismembered, possessable objects.

   Again like Giovanni, Coverdale hates above all to be made a fool of.
His aggressive voyeurism reverses his feelings of vulnerability to humiliation. "The greatest obstacle to being heroic is the doubt whether
one may not be going to prove one's self a fool," he announces at the
start (38). That fear surges up most vehemently when Zenobia asks
him why he never fell in love with Priscilla. "In society," she continues,
matter-of-factly exposing the reality of class consciousness behind
American claims to equality, "a genuine American never dreams of

stepping across the inappreciable air-line which separates one class from another." But why should that prohibition have continued at Blithedale? " 'There were other reasons,' I replied, 'why I should have demonstrated myself an ass, had I fallen in love with Priscilla.' " Then he smoothly changes the subject (182).[39] To lower himself to the level of the poor seamstress would make him lose class status in society; he accepts that as a given. Additionally, even at Blithedale, for him to love anyone would put Coverdale in that person's power, implicitly making him "an ass."

What then are we to make of his egregious last line, which hangs like a guillotine over each re-reading? One can't explain it away by saying Hawthorne may have added it as a last-minute sop to E. P. Whipple.[40] Coverdale's extravagant, theatricalized claim to have been in love with Priscilla makes sense in two contrary ways. First, it seems so blatant a lie that it exposes both Coverdale and his narrative as a fraud. Coverdale's penchant for confession turns out to be another form of his self-preoccupied evasiveness. Continually obtruding his self-consciousness to make himself number one in our eyes, if in no one else's, he at last forces our credulity to the breaking point. He has truly demonstrated himself an ass, casting himself in the role of an unrequited lover after all his previous snobberies, self-indictments, and dismissals of Priscilla make such a role impossible.

Second, and contradictorily, Coverdale's confession might be true, if we twist "love" toward the only context he can imagine for it, power relations. Loving Priscilla satisfies his need for dominance, this time vicariously. For one thing, Priscilla has received Old Moodie's money, so she has suddenly shot up in status. Much more important, just as Jane Eyre tends a stricken Rochester, Priscilla now watches like a "guardian," with "a veiled happiness" (246) over a limp and defeated Hollingsworth.

As Coverdale has previously confessed, once directly and several times indirectly, his passions have always centered on Hollingsworth, for whom the book was almost named. "I loved Hollingsworth, as has already been enough expressed," he says early on (92). Hollingsworth, more than reciprocating, avows love to his friend: " 'Coverdale,' he murmured, 'there is not the man in this wide world whom I can love as I could you. Do not forsake me!' " (149–150). These words, Edwin Haviland Miller has persuaded me, may well have been spoken by Melville to Hawthorne.[41] In any case, they prompt Coverdale's terror of being penetrated and possessed. Fleeing his love for Hollingsworth, he nonetheless hints at a strong "secret" analogy between Zenobia's passion for the former blacksmith and his own (228).[42] Now, at long last, his lover and rival has been reduced through guilt to "a childlike or childish" (246) dependence on Priscilla, who had depended on them all. The most threatening man of force has become weaker than the weakest.

Coverdale's confession of love for the wife veils his declaration of triumph over the husband. At that level, "I was in love with Priscilla," shorn of the stammering capital letters, should be translated as "I loved how Priscilla dominated Hollingsworth." An earlier scene prefigures that translation. Directly after Zenobia's passionate indictment of Hollingsworth's manhood, Coverdale hopes that Priscilla would disobey the shaken man's command to "come." "Yes; the strong man bowed himself, and rested on this poor Priscilla! O! could she have failed him, what a triumph for the lookers-on!" (225). Coverdale's malicious hope for "triumph" through Hollingsworth's defeat anticipates his "love" for Priscilla's protection of her husband's "self-distrustful weakness" (246).

At a more profoundly ambivalent level, Coverdale's malicious sense of glee at his rival's humiliation becomes the safest of submissions to the man he still loves, especially now that Hollingsworth has become so "depressed" and nonthreatening. Coverdale's "love" is a passive-aggressive bonding both to Priscilla's new power and to her "deep, submissive, unquestioning reverence" for her husband (246). Moreover, he risks nothing, since they are married.

At a still more veiled and confused level, Coverdale's declaration may reveal the most buried aspect of his feelings, his desire not for dominance but to be humiliated. The only time he had ever felt a twinge of desire for Priscilla came directly after his "petty malice" toward her. For the first time, "with true feminine imperiousness," she dismissed him. "It provoked me; yet, on the whole, was the most bewitching thing that Priscilla had ever done" (143). In retrospect, most of Coverdale's behavior throughout his story seems to be courting humiliation in one form or another. Now his love for Priscilla might be translated as an identification with Hollingsworth's fate. In any case, the last line freezes his voice in a moment of public ridicule. Bidding farewell to the reader with a lie that is not a lie, he hangs the lingering label of "ass" on his feelings, as if that summed himself up.

But finally, who cares? Coverdale's voice induces an enormous excess of unsympathetic analytic attention directed his way. He forces me to become as voyeuristic and prying as he is, just to figure him out. Once again Hawthorne has lured me into the vortex of manhood, translating any intimacy into power relations. To extricate myself, I try to humiliate Coverdale. Yet what if that's what he really wants? He himself admits that his "intercourse" with "worldly society at large," personified in his mind by Professor Westervelt, has made him ambiguously "responsive" to Westervelt's "sceptical and sneering view" (120–121).[43] Does he have a self at all? Or is he, like Robin, a mirror for the manhood he thinks he despises?

Coverdale bashing is great sport, at least for contemporary critics. Curiously, nineteenth-century readers—even Henry James—did not think the book was at all ironic at Coverdale's expense.[44] They saw both the narrator and the narrative as patently autobiographical. The striking disparity between nineteenth-century and late twentieth-century readings of Coverdale represents the most extreme version of the problem we have been confronting in all Hawthorne's narrations. Coverdale's voice probably represents Hawthorne's own views, his own self-deprecating sensibility. Yet the narration undercuts its authority with punitive ironies recoiling on both writer and reader.

My own way beyond the Coverdale impasse, after satiating myself with dissecting him, is to read *The Blithedale Romance* as the male version of *Uncle Tom's Cabin*, both published in 1852. Stowe's narrative purports to be an impassioned account of the evils of slavery, while Hawthorne's narrative veils a satire of utopias in the deceptive garments of romance. They converge as sex role allegories, each attacking manhood. Coverdale is a dandified version of an ideology of manhood refracted in every other male character as well. Despite his self-presentation as a patrician aesthete, his voice and behavior express the marketplace manhood from which he and his "brothers" try to detach themselves. While the self-humiliating narrator solicits both sympathy and contempt, Zenobia's great speeches voice the most impassioned indictment of American manhood to be found in any writer of the American Renaissance, male or female. Then she slavishly dies for love.

Both *The Blithedale Romance* and *Uncle Tom's Cabin* expose marketplace manhood as heartless, egotistical, and driven to dominate. In each book, the last becomes first: a powerless and feminized Priscilla/Tom triumphs over a hard, coarse, and all-powerful Westervelt/Legree. Any man untouched by womanhood is a villain, melodramatically so. Although Westervelt is dressed with a "well-ordered foppishness," Coverdale's first vision of him abstractly parallels Tom's first vision of Legree, intermingling sexuality, aggressiveness, and lower-class associations. Westervelt's "masculine style" has a "hard, coarse, forth-putting freedom of expression," including "the naked exposure of something that ought not to be left prominent" (111–112). Besides that protrusive "something," Westervelt has possessed Zenobia. Even worse, "every one of his brilliant grinders and incisors was a sham" (114–115). The last touch distinguishes Coverdale from Tom, since the dandy ironically sees sham in everyone but himself. Nevertheless, Hawthorne's self-reflexive ironies counterpoint Stowe's impassioned sentimentalism, with the evils of manhood as their common theme.

Each book also replicates the culture's gender contradictions, in opposite ways suiting the writers' opposite gender socializations. Stowe's advocacy of maternal values veils a contradictory spectrum of alternative female possibilities, from Eliza's autonomy to Cassy's revenge. Yet full-fledged autonomy is never a permanent option for women, except perhaps for Mrs. Shelby's briefly acknowledged success as a widow. The mothering role also generates a great deal of ambivalence. After independent Ophelia discovers the natural mother in her, Cassy talks of killing her baby without a qualm. While neither rage nor autonomy surfaces as a full-voiced possibility, Stowe builds duplicity into her impassioned vision of womanhood triumphant through dependence.

In the male sphere, Coverdale disengages from marketplace rivalries, while reinscribing the rivalries in his own fascination with dominance and humiliation. Taken together, the five male characters represent an allegory of marketplace competition in the midst of a utopian community. Silas Foster, the traditional farmer, thinks of nothing but day-to-day tasks and how to increase their competitiveness. With stolid Yankee grimness he keeps disenchanting their bubble of romance with the reality of the market. Westervelt represents the new managerial class, all control and facade, while Hollingsworth represents the artisan turned entrepreneur and moral speculator. After the former blacksmith triumphs over Westervelt to possess the veiled lady, he takes over as the prime villain, dumping Zenobia when Priscilla suddenly gets Zenobia's wealth. If Coverdale reduces Zenobia to her body, Hollingsworth reduces her to her money. Old Moodie, the source of Zenobia's fortune, had long since tried to reduce her to a showpiece, in his own "man of show" image. For every man except Silas Foster, women become commodities, used to prove one's power.[45]

Coverdale and Old Moodie represent what D. H. Lawrence called "the disintegrated gentry,"[46] ousted from power by the new men, Wes-

tervelt and Hollingsworth. Both men are also impotent, petulant narcissists, capable at best of Coverdale's half-mocking hope for "one crime
apiece!" (49, and 192–193 on Old Moodie's unspecified crime). Hollingsworth recurrently tries to make a man of Coverdale, hoping to
take "the nonsense and fancy-work" out of him (89) and transform
him into "a man of sobriety and earnestness" (147). Join me, he says,
and instead of "languor and vague wretchedness" or "aimless beauty,"
"there shall be strength, courage, immitigable will—everything that a
manly and generous nature should desire!"(149). By the end, Hollingsworth's manly and generous nature has been exposed as heartless capitalist exploitation, with innuendoes of rape. Hawthorne drives home
the point, symbolically, when Hollingsworth appropriates the farmer's
pole to hook Zenobia's body. In this allegory of manhood, men are all
alike, as Coverdale occasionally declares, and the ripples of humiliation
have no end.

Unlike the women in "Rappaccini's Daughter" or even *The Scarlet
Letter*, a woman in *The Blithedale Romance* can speak with unduplicitous
anger of the male will to power. "Thus far," Zenobia says to Coverdale,
"no woman in the world has ever once spoken out her whole heart and
her whole mind." Women feel throttled, "as with two gigantic hands
at our throats!" (137). Where Coverdale leers at what he takes to be
her exhibitionistic sexuality, Zenobia defines herself not through desire
but through anger and bitterness. "When really in earnest, particularly
if there were a spice of bitter feeling, she grew all alive, to her fingertips"
(43). As she walks with Westervelt, she looks "alive with a passionate
intensity,... not love, but anger, largely intermixed with scorn" (121).

Zenobia's anger magnificently erupts in her great speech against
Hollingsworth's egotism: "Are you a man? No; but a monster! A cold,
heartless, self-beginning and self-ending piece of mechanism!... Nothing else; nothing but self, self, self!" (224). She sees the paradox of his
manhood very clearly: on the outside an enslaving of others to prove
one's control, and on the inside an empty, heartless mechanism driving
the narcissistic show. Implicitly, her speech applies to all four rivals for
power. Three have already possessed her, Old Moodie, Westervelt, and
Hollingsworth, each looking for a showpiece. Then the fourth caps the
showmen's rivalry by marketing her in his narrative. What each man
takes for his "self, self, self" is a piece of capitalist mechanism, fueled
by the only passion that makes a man feel real, the competition for
dominance. "Thus the track of an old conventionalism was visible on
what was freshest from the sky" (39).

The narrator undercuts Zenobia's anger with his very traditional sense of woman's natural role as wife and mother. "Did you ever see a happy woman in your life?" she rhetorically asks Coverdale. "How can she be happy, after discovering that fate has assigned her but one single event, which she must contrive to make the substance of her whole life?" Immediately sexualizing her frustration, Coverdale leeringly responds that "by constant repetition of her one event, [a woman] may compensate for the lack of variety" (82). Earlier he has wondered whether Zenobia has consummated "the great event of a woman's existence" (70), so ambiguously poised between sex and marriage.

At the very end, after her death, he pays sentimental lip service to the "nonsense" and "miserable wrong" of having "the success or failure of woman's existence . . . depend wholly on the affections, and on one species of affection, while man has such a multitude of other chances, that this seems but an incident." With judicious feminine empathy he blames woman's dependent condition on "masculine egotism" (245), while he breathes a masculine sigh of relief that Zenobia became such a weak, conventional, dependent woman after all. His analysis also allows him to gloat at Hollingsworth's guilt without seeing any relevance to his bachelor self. His own priorities for women have long since been made clear. Early on, Coverdale frames his portrait of Zenobia's "magnificent" energies by twice noting that she was a very bad cook (68, 72).

For Coverdale, the prospect of a woman's autonomy would be nearly as unthinkable as the prospect of a man's single parenting. In his view, Zenobia is bitter for two reasons. First, her "eccentricity and defiance" come from a bad marriage, to Westervelt, who can't respond to her "passionate womanhood" (122). Second, she was hopelessly warped in childhood because "she lacked a mother's care." No father could supply the lack. "With no adequate control, on any hand (for a man, however stern, however wise, can never sway and guide a female child), her character was left to shape itself" (198).

In Coverdale's list of a father's virtues, sternness comes first. It's no accident that the conventional "papa" he witnesses in a city window kisses his little girl while pulling his little boy's ear (165). Nor does it strike him as odd that in their games young girls are "incomparably wilder and more effervescent than boys," who play by the rules rather than their fancies. Faced with severe male controls from the start, "young or old, in play or in earnest, man is prone to be a brute" (95). He could be echoing Sarah Hale. The difference is that Coverdale

imports these generalized feminine cliches about manhood to accuse
his fellow men, and himself, without being the least bit interested in
rousing himself from his exterior complacency and interior
competitiveness.

Zenobia's dead body graphically displays the unresolved tensions of
Coverdale's narrative. While he does his best to reduce her to a statue,
her anger still evades his grasp. "Her arms had grown rigid in the act
of struggling, and were bent before her with clenched hands; her knees,
too, were bent, and—thank God for it!—in the attitude of prayer." He
seizes on that "hope" for her knees. "She knelt, as if in prayer. With
the last, choking consciousness, her soul, bubbling out through her lips,
it may be, had given itself up to the Father, reconciled and penitent."
Even as he speculates, his fascination with her bubbling lips undermines
his pious patriarchal framing. Then, against his will, he comes back to
her anger. "But her arms! They were bent before her, as if she struggled
against Providence in never-ending hostility. Her hands! They were
clenched in immitigable defiance. Away with the hideous thought!"
(239–240).

The demonic doubleness of the new men in "My Kinsman, Major
Molineux" has now been vested in Zenobia, much more sympathetically.
She carries the burden of rage and patriarchal assault, with a passion
that overflows the bounds of Coverdale's timorous, prying conventionality. The drowning scene remains by far the most memorable to every
reader, in part because of its shocking physicality. While Coverdale
almost fulfills his private utopian fantasy of seeing Zenobia with her
clothes off, he also indulges an unconscious fantasy of mutilation.
Meanwhile her death mutely indicts the manhood to which her life
submitted. Her doubled-up body brings out a welter of contradictory,
unresolvable responses: male voyeurism, male guilt, feminist disap-
pointment, and a riveting empathy with the rage of dependent women.
As with Hester, however, we can sympathize unreservedly with Zenobia
only when she is safely stowed as a victim.

Later, after failing in his sanctimoniously patriarchal wish to bury
Zenobia at the base of Eliot's pulpit, Coverdale lingers on the fate of
her body with a brutalizing condescension. Nature will be kind to "the
tuft of ranker vegetation that grew out of Zenobia's heart," he muses,
as to any "crop of weeds." After all, he moralizes, "It is because the
spirit is inestimable that the lifeless body is so little valued" (248). If
"her mind was full of weeds," as he had concluded long before (68),

and her body is "rank," what's left? To the last, like the narrator of "Rappaccini's Daughter," he claims to "value" only a woman's spirit while capitalizing on her rich and fascinating sexuality.

The power of Zenobia's rigid doubleness, joining prayer and defiance, goes far beyond any narrative moment in *The Wide, Wide World*. It stunningly articulates women's self-dividing feelings about the sex-role divide. Yet Warner's book makes a stronger emotional impact. Hawthorne's makes me feel like Coverdale: bored, annoyed, titillated, and analytically aggressive. Coverdale's self-consciousness is a book-long double bind. He continually demands that his readers both mock him and sympathize with him. Floating among postures of malice, narcissism, and voyeuristic detachment, he weaves a complicated knot of emotional evasiveness. His narrative is much more fun to analyze than to read.

In my next chapter, I consider Hawthorne's most compelling narrative, *The Scarlet Letter*, which similarly oscillates between conventions of manhood and womanhood. Paradoxically, the third-person voice gives Hawthorne a way of steadying the text's contradictions. It permits him a greater range of sympathies and mutes his self-reflexive ironies. Though the narrator edges toward Coverdale's fascination with male narcissism and male rivalry, he does not continually force a man's ironic self-consciousness to center stage. Instead, he grants his heroine a sustained amplitude of sympathy before he, too, does her in.

9

Mrs. Hawthorne's Headache: Reading *The Scarlet Letter*

When Hawthorne read the end of *The Scarlet Letter* to his wife, it "broke her heart and sent her to bed with a grievous headache—which I look upon as a triumphant success!" His Chillingworth-like tone belies his own feelings. Ostensibly his "triumphant" sense of professional satisfaction depends on breaking a woman's heart and mind, much as his narrative pacifies the heart and mind of its heroine. But Hawthorne's "success" also depends on evoking great sympathy for female suffering. Several years later he vividly recalled "my emotions when I read the last scene of the Scarlet Letter to my wife, just after writing it—tried to read it, rather, for my voice swelled and heaved, as if I were tossed up and down on an ocean, as it subsides after a storm." As Randall Stewart notes, "Hawthorne was not in the habit of breaking down." This scene and the shaking sobs that overcame him at his dying mother's bedside "are the only recorded instances of uncontrolled emotion" in Hawthorne's life.[1]

Mrs. Hawthorne's headache is a rare moment in the history of American reader responses. It reveals not only a spouse's ambiguously painful reaction but also the author's incompatible accounts of his own first reading. Both responses seem deeply divided: one with a splitting headache, the other with a split self-presentation. If we accept at face value the goal announced by Hawthorne's narrator in the first paragraph of "The Custom-House," to seek a self-completing communion with his readers, his quest to discover "the divided segment of the writer's own nature" ends in frustration. Both Hawthorne and his most intimate sympathizer experience inward turmoil and self-controlled withdrawal. As several first readers commented in print, Hawthorne's romance left them with similarly intense and unresolved feelings—of sadness, pain, annoyance, and almost hypnotic fascination.

The Scarlet Letter's strange power over its contemporary readers derives from its unresolved tensions. What starts as a feminist revolt against punitive patriarchal authority ends in a muddle of sympathetic pity for ambiguous victims. Throughout, a gentlemanly moralist frames the story so curiously as to ally his empathies with his inquisitions. Ostensibly he voices Hawthorne's controlling moral surface, where oscillations of concern both induce and evade interpretive judgments. Yet his characterizations of Hester and Chillingworth bring out Hawthorne's profoundly contradictory affinities with a rebellious, autonomous female psyche and an intrusive male accuser. The narrative's increasing preoccupation with Dimmesdale's guilt both blankets and discovers that fearful inward intercourse. D. H. Lawrence's directive to trust the tale, not the teller, rightly challenges the narrator's inauthentic moral stance.[2] But that becomes a complicating insight, not a simplifying dismissal. In learning to see beyond Hawthorne's narrator, readers can see what lies beneath the author's distrust of any coercive authority, especially his own. Though the narrator sometimes seems quite self-consciously fictionalized, he functions less as a character than as a screen for the play of textual energies.

The plot establishes incompatible centers of psychological power: Hester's fierce private passion, at once radically independent and voluptuously loving, and Chillingworth's equally private rage to expose, control, and accuse. These centers have surfaced in modern criticism as feminist or psychoanalytic responses to the text. The narrator's voice acts as a safety valve, releasing and containing feelings in socially acceptable ways. His very self-conscious relation to his readers, whom he frequently appeals to and fictionalizes, both abets, displaces, and conceals his story's unresolved tensions.

The narrator also mirrors the limits of his contemporary American reader's toleration for strong subjectivity, especially anger. As Trollope noted, "there is never a page written by Hawthorne not tinged by satire." The narrator of *The Scarlet Letter* skillfully intermingles earnest appeals for sympathy with mocking exposure of rage, distanced as cruelty.[3] His tolerance for human frailty, his addiction to multiple interpretations, and his veiled hints of self-disgust deflect his fear that anger destroys a lovable self. In claiming that art should veil self-exposure, he invites both sympathy and self-accusation. He is a Dimmesdale who doesn't quite know he is a Chillingworth.

Several nineteenth-century readers sensed Chillingworth's ascendancy in the narrator as well as his narrative. Trollope and Henry James both noted with some surprise that the romance was a hate story, and James speaks of Hawthorne's constant struggle between "his evasive and his inquisitive tendencies."[4] Anne Abbott felt "cheated into a false regard and interest" by Hester's seeming suffering and Dimmesdale's seeming faith, because Hester's pride destroys her Christian character, while Dimmesdale's suffering becomes "aimless and without effect for purification or blessing to the soul." "A most obstinate and unhuman passion, or a most unwearying conscience it must be," she continues, "... but such a prolonged application of the scourge." Finally, the man whom Hawthorne considered his most astute critic, E. P. Whipple, concluded that the narrator's tendency to "put his victims on the rack" establishes an uncomfortably compelling despotism. Though the morbid suffering appalls sensible readers, he said, they yield despite themselves to "the guidance of an author who is personally good-natured, but intellectually and morally relentless."[5]

The narrator is protected by his duplicitous stance from full exposure, as he half admits. The rhetorical strategies that can give his reader a headache preserve his good name. Yet under his interpretive equivocations, unresolved conflicts about anger, authority, male rivalry, and female autonomy continuously impel the contradictions in his voice as well as his story. A close reading of *The Scarlet Letter* along these lines, as I try to offer here, raises the possibility of using formalist methods to explore the text as an expression of conflicts both in the author's feelings and in contemporary gender conventions. My reading also argues that the narrator's attempt to transcend his narrative's conflicts not only stifles his heroine's subjectivity but implicates him in an exceptionally narcissistic resolution of male rivalry. Just as the narrator's allegorizing hand slowly clamps down on his story's symbolic possibilities, so his increasing complicity with Dimmesdale's triumphant humiliation drives Hester and Pearl toward womanhood.[6]

I

A surprisingly aggressive feminist interpretation seems self-consciously mandated as the storytelling begins. The narrator's first sentence deflates church and state to "steeple-crowned hats," and the first paragraph associates those hats with the iron spikes on the prison door. As the next paragraph explains, the colony's patriarchs have appropriated "the virgin soil" for graves and a prison, while stifling their utopian hopes with a grave distrust of human nature. Hats and "sad-colored garments" blend with the "beetle-browed and gloomy front" of the prison in a shared exterior gloom.[7] Inwardness has been shut up and spiked, along with youthful hopes and the virgin land.

The narrator's implicit symbolic advocacy becomes overt with his presentation of "a wild rose-bush," growing beside "the black flower of civilized society." The prison is massive, forbidding, even "ugly"; the rose bush brings out feminine delicacy and "fragile beauty." It also promises to awaken the body to imaginative life. It "might be imagined" to offer fragrance to a prisoner, "in token that the deep heart of Nature could pity and be kind to him." Perhaps, the narrator muses, this rose bush "survived out of the stern old wilderness, so long after the fall of the gigantic pines and oaks that originally overshadowed it." Without pinning himself down, he allegorically intimates that patriarchs will die while tender flowers endure.

Or perhaps, he continues, the rose bush sprang up under the footsteps of "the sainted Ann Hutchinson"—the adjective lets loose his anti-Puritan, even papist bias—as she walked through the prison door. In either case, his interpretive alternatives evoke a woman's triumphant survival beyond her towering, glowering elders, or at least her stubborn public opposition. As new elders die the natural death of Isaac Johnson, the first dead Puritan patriarch, they will retreat to "the congregated sepulchres" that define their eternity as interchangeably as their gravity defines their lives, while the rose and true womanhood may persevere toward a more naturally blossoming future.

Taking a final swerve from patriarchal authority by abdicating his own, the narrator refuses to "determine" which alternative should hold. Instead he presents the rose to his reader, since it grows "so directly on the threshold of our narrative, which is now about to issue from that inauspicious portal." With a lushly symbolic self-consciousness the narrator has established a broad array of sympathies joining feminism, nature, youth, the body, and imaginative life. This associational array opposes patriarchal oppression, which doubly oppresses itself. The narrator's rhetorical strategies awaken reader expectations as well as sympathies. When Hester walks through the prison door, she will "issue" as the narrative itself, with all the hopes embodied in what is now the reader's wild red rose.

Yet Hester also walks forth into narrative hopelessness. With a hand even heavier than his heart the narrator suddenly imposes his gloomy end on her brave beginning. He tells us that the rose may "relieve the darkening close of a tale of human frailty and sorrow." That portentous phrase shuts the door on her wild possibilities as massively as the prison door dwarfs the rose. His plot will undercut the hopes his voice has just raised. His other alternative, that the rose bush might symbolize "some sweet moral blossom," seems deliberately anemic beside the contending passions his introduction promises. The narrator's sudden deflection from the rose's prospects suggests his fatalistic alliance with the prison's "darkening close." His narrative will be both, inextricably. He opens and shuts the door.

What seems here to be only a slight discomfort with the rose's radical implications eventually becomes an ambivalent inquisition into the dangers of Hester's lawless passion. The narrative issues forth as Chillingworth as well as Hester. Chillingworth's probing brings out the reader's powers of psychological detection while Hester's character encourages feminist responses. At once rebel and inquisitor, the narrator falsely joins these poles in a mystifying voice-over. He implies that the law can be transcended through Dimmesdale's growth through pain toward spiritual purity or softened through Hester's growth through pain toward maternal sympathy. At the bottom of both those transfigurations, his narrative inflicts pain. To the degree that we can also perceive the narrator's voice as an "issue," we can locate the inquisitorial self-display in his still more mystified "sweet moral blossom" of being true to oneself.

Hester Prynne's first gesture, to repel the beadle's authority (43), refocuses narrative sympathies. Her radical feminism goes further than Hyatt Waggoner's sense of her as a champion of the oppressed and beyond Nina Baym's various arguments that she champions the private imagination.[8] In chapter 13 she goes so far as to imagine the "hopeless task" of building the whole social system anew, changing sex roles so completely that both womanhood and manhood will become unrecognizable to themselves. It seems an extraordinary instance of negative capability that Hawthorne, who forbade his daughter to write because it was unfeminine, could imagine the most radical woman in nineteenth-century New England, even retrospectively. Though his narrator several times interjects that Hester's mind has gone so astray only because her heart "had lost its regular and healthy throb" (120), his abstracted, fitful cavils seem to heighten our sense of her sustained independence.[9]

Like Zenobia's question whether any woman is happy, Hester's meditation about the "race" of women can still leap off the page for modern readers: "Was existence worth accepting, even to the happiest among them?" She has long since decided this question for herself "in the negative" (120). Later, from her radical freedom of fresh perception, she sees all social institutions "with hardly more reverence than the Indian would feel for the clerical band, the judicial robe, the pillory, the gallows, the fireside, or the church" (143). Not even Melville, with his more impulsive extremes of negation, offers such a laconic, liberating list. For Hester the comforts of fireside and church grow from the punitive powers of the clergy and judiciary, as interlocked and equivalent institutions.

As we've seen in Hawthorne's stories, such self-reliance is more than dangerous; it's potentially demonic. Yet Hester's rebellious autonomy shields two very different kinds of loving. Why is it, the narrator asks in chapter 5, that Hester doesn't leave Boston? She could go to Europe, where she could "hide her character and identity under a new exterior," or she could enter the forest, "where the wildness of her nature might assimilate itself with a people whose customs and life were alien from the law that had condemned her." In rejecting both these ways of abandoning herself, whether to a civilized mask or to diffused natural passion, Hester consciously chooses to define her "roots" as her "chain." Her identity is the sin so "galling to her inmost soul." But the clear separation of outer sin from inner soul shows how unrepentant her desire remains. She becomes the jailer of a fearful secret: her dream of "a union, that, unrecognized on earth, would bring them together before the bar of final judgment, and make that their marriage-altar, for a joint futurity of endless retribution." I don't think any commentator has noticed the sacrilegious force of the hope that really impels her: to be united with Dimmesdale forever, in hell. A Dantesque fantasy of condemned love "struggled out of her heart, like a serpent from its hole" (61).[10] It terrifies her more consciously self-reliant conceptions of herself.

For the narrator, Hester's passionate loving, like Chillingworth's no less passionate hating, leaves the self wide open to demonic possession. Whether loving or self-reliant, Hester is going to hell. Yet her dream of a love forever framed by patriarchal punishment also allows the narrator to present her as more victim than rebel. She is a woman more sinned against than sinning. Moreover, she is a mother as well as a woman in love. Her daughter's existence providentially prevents her from becoming a radical prophetess like Anne Hutchinson. The narrator observes that mothering, like knitting, fortunately "soothes" Hester's tendency toward conflict. In the task of educating Pearl, "the mother's enthusiasm of thought had something to wreak itself upon" (120).[11] To reduce her ideas to an "enthusiasm" ready to be "wreaked" shows the narrator's bias. As a solitary, victimized woman Hester can rethink all social relations, but as a mother she has to nurture conventional womanhood, in herself as well as her daughter. As Dimmesdale says to John Wilson in chapter 8, the child "was meant, above all things else, to keep the mother's soul alive" (85). The narrator recurrently echoes the minister's sense of this "softening" charge: "Providence, in the person of this little girl, had assigned to Hester's charge the germ and blossom of womanhood, to be cherished and developed amid a host of difficulties" (120). The narrator veils his ambivalence about Hester's intellectual independence and her passionate desire by reinforcing what Nancy Chodorow has called "the institution of mothering" as the cure for all her ills.[12]

A less ambivalent narrator would see himself as part of his heroine's problem. Hester is far from liberated, even inwardly, despite her extraordinary perceptiveness about social repression. She avoids any struggle for public power except to preserve her conventional role as mother. Her only public heroism is to refuse to speak. She realizes that her winning advice to Dimmesdale—"Preach! Write! Act! Do anything, save to lie down and die!" (142)—applies to men but not to herself. Yet she does not realize how grossly inadequate a man Dimmesdale turns out to be, as lover, parent, and friend. While the narrator seeks to shift Hester's ground from radical thought and sexual intimacy to more acceptable maternal love, Hester's tenacious affirmation of her continuously punished union holds fast despite increasingly glaring flaws in her man as well as the man who tells her story.

One scene in particular becomes a graphic paradigm of the forces converging to bring her strength within the sphere of Dimmesdale's self-absorbed struggle for redemption. In "The Child at the Brook-Side" Pearl stands across the brook from the two lovers, deliberately disregarding Hester's anxious pleas to come to them. When Hester tries to coax her across by saying that Pearl will have twice as much love as before with Dimmesdale beside her, the child fixes her eyes on her mother and the minister "as if to detect and explain to herself the relation which they bore to one another." Then, "assuming a singular air of authority, Pearl stretche[s] out her hand, with the small forefinger extended." With "piercing shrieks," she stamps her foot and "burst[s] into a fit of passion," her finger seeming to point at Hester's bosom, which now lacks the scarlet letter. Dimmesdale, never one to relish strong feelings, erupts with the immemorial plea of a father bent on adult matters: "Pacify her, if thou lovest me!" (149–150).

As with any key scene, the incident focuses larger issues. To demand that Hester pacify Pearl if she loves him implies, most immediately, that Dimmesdale will continue to avoid the role of parent himself. Hester has to accept his abdication as part of loving him. More subtly, Dimmesdale's "if" is both a bargain and a threat. He can measure Hester's love for him by her success or failure in disciplining Pearl. Dimmesdale's habit of mind here reflects town values of authority and accounting, what the narrator satirizes in "The Custom-House," rather than wilderness intimacy. It is one of the narrator's more sympathetic cues, here and elsewhere, that we know Hester by her first name and Dimmesdale by his last. Using her first name encourages intimacy with her freedom from her husband, and from other imposed self-definitions, while the near impossibility of calling him "Arthur" indicates his anxious conformity to inherited social codes.[13]

The scene also prefigures Hester's own accommodation to those codes. The narrator already has taken some care to assert that Pearl is Hester's hidden nature. She is a classic female double, in terms that Sandra Gilbert and Susan Gubar have made familiar. She embodies the lawless passion and impetuous rages constrained in her mother. Nevertheless, as Hester senses from the first, her disturbingly alien "imp" enforces society's punishing judgment, felt in the letter's own imperiousness.[14] To pacify these contending elements in Pearl, Hester reassumes the scarlet letter. That acceptance of Pearl's pointing finger means accepting love defined in Dimmesdale's terms, as a self-pacification.[15] After all, Pearl's punitive conformity makes her Dimmesdale's child and double as well.

As the story continues, Dimmesdale becomes the primary agent for Hester's change from perceptive radical to sad-eyed sympathizer. In their forest colloquy, for instance, Hester seems not to notice that the minister prefaces her heretical claim to their wilderness "consecration" by comparing their "sin" to Chillingworth's "blacker" sin. His mind still hovers anxiously in a hierarchy of sin, guilt, and violation. Equally symptomatic, his first response to her urgent assertion of mutual consecration is "Hush, Hester!" (140). For him to rise and say he has not forgotten, as he then does, avoids confronting the impasse between his sense of violation and her sense of holiness. His association of intimacy with violation also connects him to the narrator. The very first paragraph of "The Custom-House" both solicits and denies the possibility of "perfect sympathy" between writer and reader by associating knowledge of "the inmost Me" with veils and violation(6–7).

A comprehensive fear of being exposed to male rage, from within and without, generates Dimmesdale's self-accusations. His obsessive guilt for a moment of consummated desire masks a deeper reluctance to expose aspects of himself that might displease authority. Relentlessly his fear brings on Chillingworth's assault, while his pain becomes a mystified accommodation that internalizes Puritan authority as self-punishment.

Overtly the narrator disengages himself from Dimmesdale's morbid self-scrutiny. He accuses the minister of selfishness, egotism, and cowardice, while presenting Dimmesdale's closet self-flagellations as bizarre. Yet the narrator frequently locates the sources of both art and truth within Dimmesdale's "anguish." When the minister speaks publicly, as he does several times "in tongues of flame," his eloquence becomes analogous to the writer's "power . . . of addressing the whole human brotherhood in the heart's native language." Such eloquence must "gush" with "its own throb of pain" (104). For the narrator, all art seeks ways of sharing that pain, without full self-exposure. "The only truth, that continued to give Mr. Dimmesdale a real existence on this earth," the narrator concludes in chapter 11, "was the anguish in his inmost soul" (107). This anguish, he explains a few pages later, is not guilt but "all the dread of public exposure" (112).[16]

Twice in the narrative Dimmesdale allows flashes of anger to break through, and twice the feelings subside to a guilty sadness. In chapter 10 the minister suddenly demands of Chillingworth, "But who art thou, that meddlest in this matter?—that dares thrust himself between the sufferer and his God?" He rushes from the room with "a frantic gesture." Then, after secluding himself for several hours, he makes "the amplest apologies" to "the kind old man" for the "violence" of his "unseemly outbreak of temper." As Chillingworth calculates, manipulating his anger is a "step" toward exposing "the hot passion of his heart!" The physician's cool malice toys with the minister's heated wrath to show the dangers of self-exposure. "As with one passion, so with another!" Chillingworth says to himself (101).

When Hester tells Dimmesdale that Chillingworth is her husband, her lover explodes with rage. Now the frightening extremes of his anger disturb the narrator as well as Hester. Suddenly imposing a hierarchical interpretive frame, the narrator associates violence, blackness, and intermixture with the Devil's "portion": "The minister looked at her, for an instant, with all that violence of passion, which—intermixed, in more shapes than one, with his higher, purer, softer qualities—was, in fact, the portion of him which the Devil claimed, and through which he sought to win the rest. Never was there a blacker or a fiercer frown, than Hester now encountered. For the brief space that it lasted, it was a dark transfiguration." Dimmesdale's "lower energies" yield, but only because he "had been so much enfeebled by suffering." "Woman, woman, thou art accountable for this!" he cries, again invoking the town's habit of punitive accounting. "I cannot forgive thee!" But when Hester throws her arms around him with "sudden and desperate tenderness," he allows his forgiveness to emerge, "out of an abyss of sadness, but no anger." Her mothering restores him to his better self, and saves him from his dark demonic transfiguration. God, they agree, should be the punisher (139–140). The narrator's recoil from his character's rage diminishes Dimmesdale's passion to guilt and constricts Hester's passion to tenderness. Each character has been safely reconventionalized.

Outwardly Hester seems to have long since accepted her "stain," a taint that at last precludes any role for her as prophetess (185). In some respects, as Nina Baym and others have emphasized, her compromise compels the townspeople to soften their harsh views of her. Her "power to do," when she restricts it to the "power to sympathize," makes "the world's heavy hand" ordain her a Sister of Mercy, her last papist transfiguration (117). At the end Hester returns to Boston to live out her life as a quiet force for sympathy if not immediate change, invigorating other despondent women with the hope of some future prophetess.[17]

Under her womanly behavior, Hester's real passions remain buried except for one last try. On the scaffold with her lover, she desperately resurrects her secret dream of union in hell: "Shall we not meet again? ... Shall we not spend our immortal life together? Surely, surely, we have ransomed one another, with all this woe!" Once again she claims that their relationship can be "ransoming" in its own terms, though now through the more equivocal authority of martyrdom.

Characteristically, Dimmesdale's first response again is "Hush, Hester, hush!" He has set his "bright, dying eyes" on higher spiritual possibilities for himself. As he cites God, soul, reverence, and the impossibility of "an everlasting and pure reunion," his language shows an ascendant selfishness. Hester, willing to sacrifice her purity for his love, finds her love sacrificed for his purity. Once again she is abandoned, as Roger Prynne had abandoned his wife for almost two years, as her lover abandoned both her and her daughter for much longer. The men in her life have maintained their intellectual or spiritual self-control by rejecting intimacy. The last she hears from her lover's lips is not her name but "Praised be his name! His will be done! Farewell!" (181).[18]

Her experience here finally does to Hester what Dimmesdale demands for Pearl in that scene by the brookside. It pacifies her. Her capacity to love diminishes to a tender mothering, the defeated residue of a passionate equality. Pearl's own change toward tenderness, when she kisses the minister on the scaffold, has been foreshadowed by several narrative admonitions about her dangerous lack of "heart." Now Pearl gains her narrator's praise for returning to femininity. Her tears, beyond anger at last, indicate her "pledge" that she will no longer "do battle with the world, but be a woman in it" (181). Similarly, Hester realizes that her future prophetess must never be stained with sin, shame, or even a lifelong burden of sorrow. Secretly she still preserves her "consecration": "Here was *yet* to be her penitence" (185, my emphasis.) Ambiguously, though she takes up the letter of her own free will, she has not yet repented. Does she ever repent? Does she ever assent that her lifelong sorrow is also a shame and a sin? We never know. Instead, mutely accepting the conflation of town with narrative values, she takes on all the traditional female roles: nurse, seamstress, mother, helpmeet, confidante, and tender heart. There, she ministers to the sorrows of other women who loved too passionately or were never loved at all.

Several critics, notably Nina Baym and Michael Colacurcio, have found in the ending at least a partial fulfillment for Hester.[19] That may be true in terms that the town can recognize. Nevertheless, it seems to me that the narrative ponderously thwarts the twin sources of her rebellious strength: her tenacious desire and her fierce mind. More specifically, the narrator breaks his explicit promise of reunion with Dimmesdale.

As the minister assures Pearl on the midnight scaffold, all three will stand together "At the great judgment day!" The narrator, too, sees them illuminated in "the light that is to reveal all secrets, and the daybreak that shall unite all who belong to one another" (112). But Dimmesdale's revelation leads to eternal separation, not reunion. In the procession he had seemed "so unattainable in his worldly position, and still more so in that far vista of his unsympathizing thoughts, through which she now beheld him!" (170). Now, the narrator's final words bury Hester's hopes in a permanent gloom, nervously commented on by the most sensitive early reviewers and symbolized by her tombstone's engraving of red based on black, a "device" which to the narrator sums up his story. That tombstone is all that unites the two graves, whose dust, as the narrator at last concludes, "had no right to mingle" (186). After the child who danced on Isaac Johnson's grave in chapter 10 (98) is reduced to tears, the narrator escorts Hester to her "darkening close" among the congregated sepulchres (40). Her life has been a motherly survival among imprisoned possibilities.

II

A narrative that begins by challenging patriarchal punishment ends by accepting punishment as a prelude to kindness. From Anthony Trollope to Frederic Carpenter and beyond, the ending has disturbed many readers who like Hester's spirited subjectivity. As one critic noted in 1954, "unlike his judicial ancestor, who consigned a witch to the gallows with an undismayed countenance, Hawthorne would have sprung the trap with a sigh. If one were the witch, one might well wonder wherein lay the vital difference."[20]

Though my reading continues that tradition, I question whether the narrator represents all of Hawthorne. While he provides a safely overarching frame of moral values to which both Hawthorne and his audience could consciously assent, the narrator's evasive mixture of sympathy and judgment also provides a safe way of going beyond socially responsible norms to investigate dangerously attractive interior states of mind. From the first paragraph of "The Custom-House" Hawthorne presents his "intrusive author" as a solicitous, sensible, yet receptive interpreter whose movement from torpid business surroundings to a romantic sensibility opens the door for Hester's story. The scarlet letter takes the narrator beyond his own more satirical accounts. Its meanings "streamed forth from the mystic symbol, subtly communicating itself to my sensibilities, but evading the analysis of my mind" (28).

A tension between sensibility and analysis persists through the narrative. The power of authority to take the shameful measure of vulnerable subjectivity terrifies the narrator. Yet he seems equally terrified of the heart-freezing isolation inherent in aggressive autonomy. Fleeing coercive authority, including his own, he defines himself simply as an imaginative re-creator of Surveyor Pue's manuscript and imagines Hester's rebellious self-reliance with sustained flights of empathy. Fleeing self-reliance, he chastises Hester's pride and relentlessly accuses Chillingworth's self-possessed malice. For him passionate subjectivity seems always vulnerable to demonic invasion. Chillingworth's own invasion of Dimmesdale's soul manifests the devil's entry into the scholar-physician. Perpetually oscillating between subjectivity and authority, the narrator dodges being pinned down to one mode or the other. To commit himself either way might expose his fearful cruelty of heart or his equally fearful vulnerability to violation.[21]

His solution, for both himself and his heroine, is the fluidity of sympathetic relationship. He strives to "stand in some true relation with his audience," fictionalizing his reader as "a kind and apprehensive, though not the closest friend." Without such a relation, he says, "thoughts are frozen and utterance benumbed" (7). The metaphor comes close to self-exposure. Seeking a nonthreatening communication that protects him from real intimacy, he indicates his fear of a solidifying self-possession. The audience has to warm the intrinsic coldness of his heart and tongue.

Similarly, the coldness of Hester's radical speculations must be warmed by her mothering heart. "A woman," he concludes, "never overcomes these problems by any exercise of thought"; they can be solved only by letting the heart "come uppermost" (120). Having established Hester's radical potential, the narrator now undercuts her force by dramatizing her transformation back to lovability, not toward public combat. The "magic touch" to bring about her "transfiguration," as he says earlier (119), sets the second half of the narrative in motion. She vows to redeem Dimmesdale from his own weakness and his malevolent tormentor. She will accomplish "the rescue of the victim" from her husband's power (121).

Why the sudden swerve toward selfless liberation of a man whom, even near the end, she can hardly forgive for deserting her? As the narrator says so empathetically in one of his last oscillations, "Thus much of woman was there in Hester, that she could scarcely forgive him, . . . for being able so completely to withdraw himself from their mutual world; while she groped darkly, and stretched forth her cold hands, and found him not" (170). Yet here, nine chapters earlier, she resolves to rescue her self-absorbed lover. In part the narrator advocates a maternal sympathy that can subdue Hester for her own good.

More deeply, by both investigating and identifying with the victim, the narrator encourages a Chillingworth-like interpretive mode intensifying punitive perceptions of guilt and sympathetic throbs of pain, on all sides. In its latest form this mode has become psychoanalytic detection of the Chillingworth-Dimmesdale relationship.

It seems obvious to post-Freudian readers that Chillingworth's revengeful penetration into Dimmesdale's bosom constitutes the climactic moment of physical intimacy in the story. His intrusive, sadistic rape first awakens protracted throbs of pain, then culminates in the "moment of his ecstasy," when his discovery of what lies on the sleeping minister's chest sends Dimmesdale into a "shudder" and Chillingworth into a "ghastly rapture" of riotous gestures (102). The sexualization of revenge accompanies the desexing of love. More broadly, the narrator's overt language of sympathy frequently masks his fascination with the violation of inward spheres. Various readers have noted that Chillingworth bears the same relation to Dimmesdale that Pearl often has to Hester: the unrestrained underside of socially conforming energies.[22] Dimmesdale's self-preoccupied guilt, to take this view further, licenses Chillingworth's rage for penetration, possession, and violation, even as it recalls the minister's own moment of violation in the past. In the psychological allegory to which the narrator seems increasingly disposed, guilt invites malicious intrusion. In terms of my gender paradigms, a fascination with male dominance and humiliation displaces a potentially feminist vision of patriarchy.

The narrative itself becomes a further stage for contrary energies, as Richard Brodhead's fine discussion of its mixed modes indicates. After establishing initially intense sympathies with Hester's resolute integrity and defiant creativity, it moves toward framing her, in several senses. It also induces a covert fascination with violating her inwardness and humbling her strength. This drama is displaced from Hester to Dimmesdale. The sexuality of victimization and the intellectualized control of rage move Hester's subjectivity toward the margins of Hawthorne's romance.

Psychoanalytic readings tend to suppress Hester's struggle for autonomy; like Chillingworth, they pry into Dimmesdale. Both Frederick Crews and John Irwin, the two most prominent psychoanalytic investigators, assume the role of detective on the trail of a narcissist. Crews presents the story primarily as the narrator's ambiguously ironic relation to Dimmesdale's libidinal repression, while Irwin's implicitly Lacanian reading finds narcissistic mirroring doubled and redoubled throughout the text. But Dimmesdale's growth from narcissism to sublimated independence, like the narrator's ironic pursuit, is a flight from feeling. In seeing either Freudian desire or Lacanian absence at the heart of the text, Crews and Irwin mistake the narrator's defenses for narrative truths.[23]

Anxiety about anger, a more fearful passion to him than sexual desire, generates the narrator's incompatible fascinations with Hester's independence and Chillingworth's malice. Both these frozen stances intimate anger, in opposite ways. Because Chillingworth's rage has its base in intimacy, unlike Hester's more generalized social rebellion, he is punished far more severely by the narrator, who makes the cuckolded husband his prime villain. For the narrator anger and desire are the same thing: low, base, the devil's plaything. They lead to violence and violation, not love. Yet his idea of love is finally a mystified self-projection. In affirming sympathy as the key, he defines it as the capacity to complete one's divided self without undue self-exposure, from the first paragraph of "The Custom-House" to the last pages of the story. That narcissistic definition avoids acknowledging conflict as part of intimacy. In fact it avoids otherness altogether, because for the narrator otherness brings a terror of unloving regard—a "horrible ugliness" of self-exposure, Dimmesdale says at the height of his own rage at Hester, "to the very eye that would gloat over it!" (139–140). In rigidifying Chillingworth's anger as possessive malice the narrator controls that terror as allegory, while in reducing Hester's more complicated subjectivity to maternal sympathy he diffuses that terror as romance.[24]

By the end of the story both Dimmesdale and the narrator release emotions only through an ascension of words that nobody quite understands. Dimmesdale's new power of unclear statement, in his sermon and his confession, mirrors a broader narrative mystification of pain as the source of eloquence and transfiguration. From an initial appreciation of Hester's strength and fascination with Chillingworth's power, the narrator has moved toward exalting Dimmesdale's weakness. The minister's diffuse anguish displaces Hester's clearheaded suffering. Through insistent narrative framing, his masochism becomes the scaffold for self-magnifying transcendence, culminating in the narrator's advocacy of spiritualized male narcissism as the way to complete one's divided self. Spectacularly inverting the entrepreneurial paradigm, Dimmesdale gains a sudden dominance over Chillingworth by flaunting his self-humiliation.

Dimmesdale's feminized pain also brings some traditional male rewards. Though he forsakes his own fatherhood from the moment of
conception, he ascends to meet his heavenly father after receiving a
weepy kiss from his daughter, whom he barely has time to acknowledge
before his death. Pearl's childhood is an extreme instance of the absent
father and the overpresent mother so basic to American middle-class
society and experienced by Hawthorne in his own life. Considered as
an American dream, Dimmesdale's success is made possible by his flight
from woman and child. He has no distractions from his work, and he
can exercise to the full his intellectual powers. He makes an extraordinary social impact, gains respect as a public and private adviser, and
after a satisfactory dark night of the soul, he gains his final reward of
celestial approval. Meanwhile Hester, like a good mistress, remains
bound to her child, her duties, her isolation, her marginal status, and
her hopeless dreams of union.

The narrator's astonishing corollary to Hester's decline into sympathy unites Chillingworth, Dimmesdale, and himself in a loving ascension. After Dimmesdale spurns Hester to gain an uncontaminated
integration for his purified maleness, we are asked to imagine him
united in heaven not just with God but with Chillingworth as well. In
the middle of the story the narrator oddly interpolates that "hatred,
by a gradual and quiet process, will even be transformed to love," if
new irritations of hostility do not impede the process (116). At several
other points he implies that rage and desire fuse as violent passion, a
demonic strangeness erupting within oneself. Now the narrator inverts
the devil's work. He takes the ability to transform hate into love as his
final test of the reader's tender capacities.

Asking his readers to be merciful to Chillingworth, he wonders
"whether hatred and love be not the same thing at bottom." Each
supposes "intimacy and heart-knowledge." Each needs dependence.
Each dies if the object withdraws. "Philosophically considered, therefore, the two passions seem essentially the same, except that one happens to be seen in a celestial radiance, and the other in a dusky and
lurid glow. In the spiritual world, the old physician and the minister—
mutual victims as they have been—may, unawares, have found their
earthly stock of hatred and antipathy transmuted into golden love"
(183–184).

The passage still seems to me the strangest in all of Hawthorne.
Transforming devilish rage into divine love, it takes Dimmesdale's hierarchy of high and low to its highest extreme. If the narrator hesitates

to assert their fanciful union as spiritual fact, he has no qualms about describing them as "mutual victims." Victims of each other, or victims of Hester? Anne Abbott cited this passage as a prime example of Hawthorne's "mistborn ideas" and asked "if there be any firm ground at all" here. Yet she also mused, in some perplexity, that Hawthorne seems to share that "doubt."[5] Her reaction is quite right, for the passage substitutes loving victims for strong selves in conflict. Its several levels of meaning bring the reader's contrary responses to their final suspended inversion.

The possibility of spiritual union in heaven joins the two whose intercourse on earth comes to center the story: revengeful father and violated/violating son. The cuckold and the lover rise together to an all-male paradise, while Hester mutely returns to Boston. The narrator's fantasized embrace of father and son gives a more openly Oedipal dimension to the classic American fantasy, first described by Leslie Fiedler, of two men in flight from strong women. Moreover, the transmutation suggests an integration of the male self as well, if only in coupling two sides of a self-falsification. Intrusive sadism and guilty vulnerability come together at last, released from any pressure to come to terms with anger, love, or fear.

Most significantly, the union occurs not in the plot but in the narrator's relation to his audience. He sets his readers a last challenge: can you take your sympathy that far? In asking readers to sympathize with Dimmesdale and Chillingworth as "mutual victims" and to imagine hate transmuted into golden love, the narrator brings himself into that embrace, with his reader as witness. All three male voices, ironically at odds on earth, escape together, free from sexuality and emotional conflicts, and free from genuine intimacy.[26]

This narrative flight, like all the narrator's extremes, doesn't last. Returning to earth, he sympathetically concludes with Hester's solitude, not Dimmesdale's transcendence. Part of the narrator's strategy for reconciling conflicts is to condemn fixity of any kind, physical or spiritual. If rigidity seems fearfully demonic, associated with anger and the lower parts of the soul or body, flexible sympathy becomes the narrator's vague placebo. This tactic allows him momentary participation in his contradictory extremes, but it also establishes multiple authorial interpretations as a shifting medium for the plot. His self-dramatizing ceaselessly pacifies and resurrects his plot's tensions, while deflecting attention from his punitive plotting to the sympathetic puppeteer.

Pearl represents what most needs pacification: her rebellious impulses toward creative autonomy and her aggressive impulses to detect and accuse. Dimmesdale, far from being the "true self" of the romance, unites two weak contemporary gender strategies to fend off strong subjectivity. He embodies a male accommodation to public role and a female sense of self as vulnerable victim. If Pearl joins contradictory strengths, Dimmesdale joins fragile defenses. Slowly, gently, implacably, the narrator's voice quells these polarized versions of anger and authority through his rhetoric of sympathy and his intimacy with what he often calls Dimmesdale's "tremulous" voice. His feminized hero, a dimmed valley even in his name, becomes both the narrator and the object of his inquisition.

In the narrator's increasingly Oedipal allegory, a regressive, inquisitorial family triangle of cruel, impersonal father; kind, despairing mother; and tortured, triumphant son all but drives out early expectations for Hester's adult subjectivity against public patriarchy. A sadomasochistic symbiosis of father and son becomes a vision of transcendent, victimized love. Yet the narrative insistently returns to its latent subversion of male inauthenticity. Hester's integrity mutely survives. If Pearl ceases to do battle with the world, she finds a wider world unimaginable to Boston, or for that matter to the narrator himself, whose Salem roots "have intertwined themselves" with his own nature (12). This is as close as he comes to directly acknowledging his Chillingworth side. At the same time, his presentation of himself gives access to strong subjectivities beyond his conscious accommodations.

A psychoanalytic focus on anger and dependence might illuminate Hawthorne's biography here, especially if complemented by an analysis of the polarized sex-role expectations so basic to his time. Hawthorne's remarkable empathy with a solitary woman and his fear of an unloving other insinuated into his own psyche probably have their contradictory sources in his ambivalent ties to his mother, whose death helped to impel Hester's creation, and his fearful resentment of Robert Manning, as my last chapter suggested.[27] The contradictory intensities of those bonds probably impel the narrative oscillations, while the basic plot reflects an obvious Oedipal guilt for having possessed a woman whose husband strangely disappeared.

On another level, the complexities of narrative dissociation in *The Scarlet Letter* have as much to do with Hawthorne's canny relation to his audience as with his uncanny relation to himself. In conforming to his audience's expectations for a morally comfortable narrator, Hawthorne fictionalizes himself so as to partially undermine his own characterization. His fragmenting empathies outstrip the narrator's growing alliances with Dimmesdale's self-centering scrutiny and Chillingworth's intrusive detection. He seems fully aware that his readers will accept Hester only while she suffers for her sin; as no fewer than three reviewers remarked, the narrator avoids the dangers of "the French school" by making his heroine satisfactorily miserable.[28] Yet though he silences Hester with values he and his audience hold dear, he makes his readers uncomfortable with those values. If his intensifying focus on male dominance and humiliation helps to suppress Hester, he also leaves readers dissatisfied with the narcissism of Dimmesdale's manly salvation. His narrative continuously invokes and undermines prevailing conventions of womanhood and manhood.

When he at last offers his "sweet moral blossom," it turns out to be a version of Dimmesdale's anguish over self-display. "Among many morals which press upon us from the poor minister's miserable experience, we put only this into a sentence:—'Be true! Be true! Be true! Show freely to the world, if not your worst, yet some trait whereby the worst may be inferred!' " (183). Like Dimmesdale's public stripping, this is the hesitant exhibitionism of a disembodied Salem Flasher, who encourages his readers to imagine his worst while showing their own. He assumes that his readers share with him not only a self worth hating but also the ambivalent desire to detect, to be detected, and to stay respectably hidden. From "Young Goodman Brown" onward, a mutual revelation of guilty subjectivity constitutes Hawthorne's idea of true sympathy, true community, and true interpretation. Just as passion feels like demonic intrusion, any self-exposure brings on further accusation. Now Hawthorne invites both sympathy and accusation by reducing Hester's story to "the poor minister's miserable experience." Uneasy lies the tale that wears that crown.

Finally, however, *The Scarlet Letter* takes readers beyond its narrator and his imagined audience. Dimmesdale's guilt, like the narrator's, conceals a dependence on public authority for his sense of self and a fear of passion, especially rage. But Hawthorne's romance evokes strong subjectivity in opposition to dependence of any kind. Throughout, like an anxious referee, the interpreter's voice strives to rise above the fray. Trying to sympathize, judge, and reconcile, he imposes the masks he wants to lift. Yet while the storyteller oscillates between guilt and decorum, his story brings out a much more risky inwardness, whose unresolved tensions sent Mrs. Hawthorne to bed and Hester to a deeper solitude. Hester's epitaph suitably blazons forth her red strength against her black background. By contrast, the narrator's epitaph could be the remark he addresses to "the Minister in a Maze": "No man, for any considerable period, can wear one face to himself, and another to the multitude, without finally getting bewildered as to which may be the true" (154). In accommodating his voice to conventions of manhood and womanhood, the public authority of his own time, Hawthorne's narrator blends with Boston's "congregated sepulchres" (39), while Hester's life continues to speak with embattled vitality.

10

Ahab's Queenly Personality: A
Man Is Being Beaten

This last chapter explores the pain more than the pleasure of the text. *Moby Dick* makes many readers feel as though they are swimming for their lives. Robert Zoellner begins his impassioned study of the novel by saying that he wrote his book "in sheer self-defense."[1] Students and critics alike often seem drawn against their wills into Ahab's vortex of desperate, narcissistic rage. At the same time the narration encourages readers to float free of Ahab's mad quest, as Ishmael seems to do. I, for one, feel more comfortable with Ishmael's depressive yet resurgent fluidity of mind than with Ahab's mesmerizing coerciveness. Ahab's grand, stagey voice bullies me into empathizing with his heroic mastery of pain. He tasks me, he heaps me with helpless awe as he transforms himself into the ultimate Representative Man, avenging humiliation for readers and crew alike. Yet I also shy away from this tranced, demonic killer. I feel repelled, or worse, bored by his self-inflating paranoia, and jolted by his shocking inhumanity.

Psychoanalytic perspectives tend to reduce my awe and discomfort to a more manageable, if unconscious empathy with a victimized little boy. Ahab and Ishmael split underlying out-of-control feelings, especially anger, helplessness, and vulnerability. Social perspectives tend to take a safe distance from feeling by emphasizing Melville's ironic control over a basically political allegory.[2] Most readers, I think, oscillate between the two modes, as does this chapter. Like Ishmael I'm swept away, I gain control, I'm swept away again. I relish Ahab's madness as vital truth, really vital manhood, a very rhetorical self-empowering in the face of cosmic insult. Yet his madness also glaringly represents everything most life-hating in that same quest for power.

For the past thirty years many critics have found a way to rescue Melville's narrative from his sadomasochistic hero. Faced with the seductive pain of reading Ahab's story, critics focus on the storyteller. Some argue that Ishmael slowly disengages from Ahab's destructive quest. He discovers a life-affirming buoyancy through rhetorical play, imaginative fraternity, and peaceful interdependence.[3] Others emphasize the creative indeterminacy of Ishmael's narration, as opposed to the tyrannical rigidity of Ahab's self-petrifying perceptions.[4]

This chapter tries to return the book to Ahab and to explain my discomfort in reading his story. I argue that Ishmael and Ahab are doubles of a self that loathes itself. Ishmael's oceanic disappearing act covertly parallels his captain's journey from rage to suicide. Twinned in their desire to be beaten, Ishmael passively turns humiliation into fantasies of fraternity, while Ahab flaunts the bad aggressive self who deserves a whipping. Both sides of this doubling flee the feelings locked up in self-loathing.

The idea of Ahab as Ishmael's deep self is not new. Several critics have seen Ahab's narcissistic anger and self-pity lurking under Ishmael's depressive reveries about abandonment and his manic fantasies of fraternal merger.[5] What may be more controversial is my claim that *Moby Dick*'s unstable intensities of voice are both seductive and evasive. To voice feeling, for Ishmael and Ahab, is to experience pain. Their beating fantasies both express and displace a deeper self-loathing, expressed primarily as a craving to be dominated by unloving power.

Many readers have felt the narrative's seductiveness, and a few have voiced their sense of inauthenticity. In a 1907 letter, Joseph Conrad memorably dismisses *Moby Dick*: "not a single sincere line in the whole 3 vols of it." Michael Davitt Bell is the only recent critic I'm aware of who stresses the narrative's evasiveness. There's "something defensive in all of this," Bell says. For him, both Ahab and Ishmael evoke simultaneous, contradictory fears of the self's violence and the self's nonexistence.[6]

To take Bell's terms further, Ahab and Ishmael think of themselves as both potentially violent and periodically nonexistent to evade a more threatening contradiction in feelings: they fear and crave being dominated by a stronger man. Ishmael's recurrent emphasis on orphaned isolatoes abandoned by a heartless stepmother universe is an inflatable flotation device for escaping his shipwreck of feelings about men beating down men. At the center of the wreck, Ahab struggles for absolute dominance—over his crew, over his malevolent God, and perhaps over his still more malevolent self. Like Hawthorne's Jaffrey Pyncheon, he wants to feel nothing in himself but pure power. By the end, however, he experiences power as just that: a nothing, a lack, a vacuum craving to be filled. Pip suddenly surfaces as the psychological center for both Ahab and Ishmael, a needy little boy who begs his sadistic father-God to walk all over him. As I have already suggested, Dana shows a touch of that fantasy in his response to the flogging he witnesses. Now, much more flagrantly, the aggressiveness that Ishmael hides and Ahab parades at their respective entrances turns out to be a mask for ecstatic yet terrified passivity. If God's right worship is defiance, as Ahab says in "The Candles," his unvoiced plea says, Hit me again, Daddy. Tell me I exist in your omnipotent, uncaring eyes.

Readers are right to feel torn between empathizing with a victimized little boy and relishing Melville's political ironies. But *Moby Dick* has much more to do with the basic contradictions and pressures of entrepreneurial American manhood than with the specifics of American politics. Melville exposes the chaos of narcissistic needs and fears in the American middle-class marketplace—the same marketplace that drove his patrician father to bankruptcy, insanity, and perhaps unconscious suicide. *Moby Dick* is obviously a man's book, about a man obsessed with avenging his shattered manhood. Melville himself told a woman correspondent not to read it.[7] Strangely, however, both Ahab and his narrator discover that the threat of being beaten awakens two stereotypically feminine responses to male power: Ahab's voracious desire and Ishmael's wifely submission. Ultimately, the novel's confused psychological depths simultaneously mystify Melville's personal narcissistic trauma and invert the gender ideologies from the novel's social surface: the sex-segregated world of American capitalism in its most predatory individualistic phase.

I

In the first third of *Moby Dick*, Ishmael's embrace of Queequeg and his awe of Ahab signal several contradictory flights from deep depression.

Announcing his "hypos" in the first paragraph of "Loomings," he links them vaguely to his stepmother and the marketplace. Unlike Francis Parkman's simpler fascination with Henry Chatillon, which Melville praised in a review of *The Oregon Trail*, Ishmael's delight in Queequeg's Noble Savage primitivism has a triple edge.[8] It expresses a fantasy of homoerotic dependence, releasing him from his self-disgust; an initiation into artisan fraternity, releasing him from city alienation; and a thumb in the eye for white, civilized, Christian readers who hug tight their landsmen identities, so dependent on hierarchies of race, gender, and class.

Quite ostentatiously and melodramatically, as he faces the prospect of sleeping with a cannibal, Ishmael's hypersexualized anxieties circle toward castration fears. No one likes to sleep two in a bed, he keeps saying—especially if it's the landlord's wedding bed, where their son "came near breaking his arm." When Ishmael pokes his head through Queequeg's poncho, so "shaggy and thick, and I thought a little damp," the sight terrifies him: "I tore myself out of it in such a hurry that I gave myself a kink in the neck" (27–28).[9] These and other evocations of sexual fear culminate in the spectacular image of Queequeg leaping into their bed with a tomahawk between his teeth.

Within moments, Ishmael has cozied up to his bedmate, and by the end of the night he feels like Queequeg's wife. His parade of anxieties has been a comic setup, to tweak the reader's expectations about manliness. A rather stagey terror yields to a stereotypically feminized domesticity. The sex role reversal complements Ishmael's jauntiness about preferring Queequeg's pagan rituals to his own "infallible Presbyterian Church" (54), or his cavalier subversion of the reader's patriotic iconography in calling Queequeg "George Washington cannibalistically developed" (52). Throughout this sequence, Ishmael's self-presentation is a rhetorical construct designed to mock the racial, religious, and sexual assumptions of his readers. The mockery looks more ingratiating than aggressive. His sentiments for Queequeg affectionately parody a best seller of the previous year, *Reveries of a Bachelor or A Book of the Heart* (1850).[10] By example Ishmael draws conventionally manly readers toward fraternal fluidity, dismantling the snug little social boxes they take for their identity.

So far the narration displays some relatively comfortable, if subversive strategies for reader conversion—the "I-you" conventions that I sketched in my first chapter. Most readers, from the book's first reviewers to contemporary college students, feel quite pleasurably at ease with this section. Just as Ishmael espouses a most intimate fraternity, however, his fear of unloving intimacy destabilizes the narrative once more. While his anxious anticipation yields to surface feelings of chumminess, his sensations in Queequeg's embrace evoke renewed fear, this time without any touch of comic irony. The Counterpane dream brings back his latent anxiety about castration, this time in the memory of being punished by his stepmother for climbing up a chimney.

First he was sent to bed supperless, he recalls. Then he awoke to feel his hand being held by a nameless, unimaginable phantom. As at least one reader has suspected, that phantom may have been no more than Ishmael's worried stepmother, sitting by his bedside to reassure him. But Ishmael gives us no access to reassurance or to a caring image of female parenting—not yet. Instead, he subverts his own wifely bonding with a genuinely terrifying image of being possessed by a vague, unloving power. "Take away the awful fear," he says, and the sensations were the same as he now feels in Queequeg's embrace (33).[11]

As a brawny harpooneer, Queequeg is a consummately self-reliant craftsman, strong of body and serene of mind. "He looked like a man who had never cringed and never had had a creditor" (52). Beneath the facade of his patrician slumming with this idealized artisan, Ishmael shows an impulsive eagerness to be gripped by a strong man's dominance, whether Queequeg's or Ahab's—the stronger the better. His homoerotic chumship, here and elsewhere, veils a masochistic passivity and a fascination with the spectacle of men being humiliated by manlier men. From the beginning he relishes images of men being beaten: the hapless sub-sub-librarian, whom he rhetorically kicks himself (2); the thumpings and punchings he has accepted from old sea captains, which he rationalizes as the "universal thump" that makes everyone a "slave" (15); his first kick from Peleg (95); the kick from Ahab that begins Stubb's merman dream (115–116); and the reaping away of Ahab's leg by Moby Dick (159–160). The prospect of Moby Dick's final assault becomes the fixed fate from which all of Ishmael's improvisations stray like giddy thoughts at a hanging.

At one level, Ishmael's narrative exposes the craving for dominance and the fears about being beaten that underlie the conventional American rhetoric of freedom and individualism. At a more confused and primal level of feeling, his narrative exposes not fear but a *craving* to be humiliated and thus to be passively fused with manly power. With Queequeg, Ishmael's loving, submissive response temporarily suspends his preoccupation with being assaulted—but only momentarily. The Counterpane dream brings back his terrified wish. While he masks his passive expectation of sexual assault as a giddy chumminess, his suppressed fear of the man who holds him fast has turned into desire, which in turn strangely evokes a feeling of having been possessed by power, stripped of its gender or any human facade.

Wishing to be bound to a man much stronger than himself, yet pursuing "that story of Narcissus, . . . the key to it all," Ishmael goes to sea to escape and find the self writ large as Ahab: an uncontrollable fusion of aggressive and suicidal impulses. Ishmael presents his hypos as the norm. All around the city, he says, "stand thousands upon thousands of mortal men fixed in ocean reveries." Why? Because they "are all landsmen; of week days pent up in lath and plaster—tied to counters, nailed to benches, clinched to desks." Such men, slaves to an anonymous urban marketplace, gaze at the water like Narcissus, Ishmael says (12–14). Seeking and fleeing the phantom of himself, Ishmael affixes himself to Ahab's quest to avenge his manhood. If Ishmael is a manhood junkie, Ahab will be a manhood pusher.[12]

At the same time, Ishmael recurrently defines manhood as an invulnerable spiritual integrity beyond Ahab's will to dominate. He claims for vanquished men like Starbuck and himself not just the solidarity of victims but an individual dignity triumphing through passivity. He floats the survival of artisan democracy—a democracy of sub-subs—on the coffin of manlier men. Whether he calls it the "Divine Inert" (129), an "insular Tahiti" (236), or the "mute calm" at the heart of his "tornadoed Atlantic of my being" (326), he continually recurs to an untouchable, inviolable inner core as the best refuge from the world's blows.

Perpetually evading conflict with other men, Ishmael turns his passive responses to prospective humiliation into fantasies of manly fraternity, especially when he speaks of Starbuck's upcoming defeat. The narrative, he intimates, may well tell of Starbuck's inability to withstand Ahab's "spiritual terrors." But were his story to tell of "the complete abasement of poor Starbuck's fortitude," "scarce might I have the heart to write it." Such a defeat would bring on nothing less than "the fall of valor in the soul." Nevertheless, even if we should see such a spectacle, we could take heart. As compensation, he says, we would discover an "immaculate manliness . . . so far within us, that it remains intact though all the outer character seem gone; bleeds with keenest anguish at the undraped spectacle of a valor-ruined man." We should throw our "costliest robes" over such a man, hiding "any ignominious blemish"; our own manhood should bleed with empathetic pain (104).

What is doing the bleeding? Something has been taken away outside:

the "outer character seem[s] gone," the valor-ruined man is an "undraped spectacle." These innuendoes look like euphemisms for castration. Yet the syntax poises the bleeding midway between castration and crucifixion. It's the "immaculate manliness," still "intact," that "bleeds with keenest anguish," and looks on the loss of manhood with horror and pity.

Ishmael's devious transition to a tragic yet redemptive Christ launches him into a still more confusing non sequitur. If the prospect of Starbuck's humiliation has been raised only to be disowned, the promised spectacle of unmanning becomes still more exposed, yet hidden by Ishmael's rhetorical robes, which suddenly clothe "the stumped and paupered arm" of artisan democracy with royal manhood. The "meanest mariners, and renegades, and castaways" will become manly champions like Cervantes and Andrew Jackson (104–105), beloved of God himself, through Ishmael's empowering narration. If robes fail, rhetorically or otherwise, then—as Ishmael says in the first chapter—our response to the universal thump should be to rub shoulders all around (15). If that fails there is always heaven, where cowards can strike unsplinterable glasses instead of splintered hearts (2, also 53).

In *White-Jacket* (1850), published just a year before *Moby Dick*, the narrator's passionate plea to abolish flogging anticipates Ishmael's sense of artisan manhood and entrepreneurial shame. Four men have been caught fighting, and five hundred sailors have to watch them receive the lash. The spectacle leads Melville, or his protagonist, to reflect on how some men can retain an "untouchable" feeling of "innate dignity" even as their bodies are scarred for life. Such a feeling "is one of the hushed things, buried among the holiest privacies of the soul." But what if the soul bleeds as well as the body? "What torments must that seaman undergo who, while his back bleeds at the gangway, bleeds agonized drops of shame from his soul!" "In the name of immortal manhood," the next chapter concludes, let the floggers feel the lash on their own backs.[13]

At one level Melville simply continues the mounting attack on naval flogging begun by Dana. Michael Rogin and more recently Richard H. Brodhead have brought out many of the social and psychological contexts for these rhetorical assaults on traditional disciplinary practices.[14] Melville explicitly addresses legislators and state authorities in his celebrated conclusion to chapter 36. There he invokes America as a new Israel, its citizens as "the peculiar, chosen people" who should be the "pioneers" and "the advance-guard" into the future, not slavishly beholden to tyrannical practices of the outmoded past (506). I suspect that his gratuitously paradoxical finale—"national selfishness is unbounded philanthropy"—may reflect his inability to address legislators in their own language without insinuating some parodic contradictions.

Even so, Melville's preoccupation with shame and manhood takes him beyond conventional pleas for reform and beyond conventional connections to slavery or to domestic uses of the rod. Later, after a black man has been scourged, White-Jacket discovers to his horror that he is about to be flogged himself, for not following orders he had never been given. Despite his terror, he curiously intensifies Captain Claret's wrath by not doing the customary thing, "obsequiously" touching his hat at every sentence he addresses to the captain. Instead, as Captain Claret vows to flog him, White-Jacket plunges into vivid fantasies of hurling himself and the captain overboard, to mutual death. As in Ishmael's first paragraph or in Ahab's life, White-Jacket's fantasy fuses suicide with aggression against tyrannical authority. These "wild thoughts" give him a strangely acute sense of his body. "My blood seemed clotting in my veins; I felt icy cold at the tips of my fingers, and a dimness was before my eyes.... I can not analyze my heart, though it then stood still within me" (643–645)

Then White-Jacket's self-inspection eerily takes on the tones of Ishmael's narrative, as if Ishmael were a passive, instinctive Ahab.

> But the thing that swayed me to my purpose was not altogether the thought that Captain Claret was about to degrade me, and that I had taken an oath with my soul that he should not. No, I felt my man's manhood so bottomless within me, that no word, no blow, no scourge of Captain Claret could cut me deep enough for that. I but swung to an instinct in me—the instinct diffused through all animated nature, the same that prompts even a worm to turn under the heel. Locking souls with him, I meant to drag Captain Claret from this earthly tribunal of his to that of Jehovah, and let Him decide between us. No other way could I escape the scourge.... The privilege, inborn and inalienable, that every man has, of dying himself, and inflicting death upon another, was not given to us without a purpose. These are the last resources of an insulted and unendurable existence.

At this melodramatic point, just before his thoughts turn into action, White-Jacket finds himself saved from flogging by two shipmates who intercede. Fraternity keeps his manhood intact, and the little lower layer of insult and humiliation recedes.

Manhood's claims surface just once more, in comic form, during the massacre of the beards. Otherwise White-Jacket keeps himself rather prissily under wraps, as his name implies. His sententious ending— "There are no mysteries out of ourselves" (768)—becomes Ishmael's portentous beginning.[15] As Ishmael contemplates Starbuck's fate, his more equivocal attempt to invoke artisan chumship and passive spiritual dignity springs from the same horror of self. What can't be borne is the prospect of watching a soul bleed shame when humiliated by tyrannical authority.

II

Why is it that Ahab never has to flog anyone? Because his words lash them to his own spiritual "mysteries" as if they were the common cause. In White-Jacket's terms, he seeks to empower "my man's manhood" as the "last resource" of "an insulted and unendurable existence." If Ishmael's sense of passive fraternity rises like Bulkington's spirit from abject defeat, to Ahab such friendship seems just a sop for losers. All of himself rides on his last fight. His quest is not for an artisan's sense of craft, dignity, and community or for Ishmael's oscillation between fantasies of artisan fraternity and civilized mind play. Instead, he seeks a revenge that will restore the only sense of himself that matters: the will to power. Whatever "the almost frantic democracy of those inferior fellows" (133), only dominance survives at the top.

Ahab's monomania focuses a general male sense of helplessness. He claims to be empowered with a representative, redemptive mission to avenge all those who have been unmanned and who therefore feel simultaneously enslaved and murderous. For the first two-thirds of his story Ahab has been manhood at the cutting edge—what D. H. Lawrence, another such man, called "the last phallic being of the white men."[16] Everything with him has been manly rage and rivalry. Ahab's passion for dominance is the obsession of nineteenth-century American men, the complement to female hysteria, which has so much to do with women's feelings of powerlessness.

Hysteria, a word originally derived from "wandering womb," was the label so often applied to a woman's helpless succession of vacillating, decentered emotional states. The emotional decentering frequently found physical expression in partial paralysis, convulsions, and choking seizures. Doctors would sometimes operate on women to try to find their wandering wombs and cut them out.

Monomania, a label that came into usage in the 1820s, hitched its own wagonload of male anxieties to the star of entrepreneurial competition. As Michael Rogin says, "it was the disease specific to a society of uprooted and driven men."[17] In Ahab's case, he feels possessed by overmastering evil and talks about it as if he were a cosmic prisoner. But his voice bristles with competitive fire. "I'd strike the sun if it insulted me," Ahab says to the crew in "The Quarter-Deck." All greatness, he insists, is built on the "fair play" of rivals in combat, "jealousy presiding over all creations." Ahab's confusion of jealous rivalry with greatness anticipates Harold Bloom's equally American sense of strong creativity by 120 years. Not even fair play is Ahab's master, he says. "Who's over me? Truth hath no confines." His wild, exultant, metaphysical claims bring Starbuck to "enchanted, tacit acquiescence" (144). "Who's over me?" is Ahab's fundamental question, just as "Who aint a slave?" (15) is Ishmael's.

Ahab's monomania inflates the emerging middle-class ideology of manhood. His fair play of masterless, jealous rivals is entrepreneurial capitalism on a cosmic scale, reflecting at least two entrepreneurial modes of power: a will to exploit fluid resources and a will to dominate weaker men.[18] Disdaining the actual marketplace, Ahab voices the metaphysics of manhood and humiliation under the pasteboard mask of profits. In his monomania he becomes an exaggerated prototype for the male behavior pattern that helped ensure the worldwide dominance of American industry. He not only inherits Miltonic and Byronic patterns of pride but anticipates what has come to be known in America as the type A personality: the hard-driving, finger-drumming, aggressive, and insensitive executive, whose life so frequently ends its heartlessness in a heart attack. If we take literally Ishmael's blood-and-thunder imagery for his captain's body, Ahab's life seems to be one continuous heart attack, as he strives to "burst his hot heart's shell" upon Moby Dick (160). He could represent every workaholic whose anger explodes at home. Birthing the narcissistic phantoms that consume him, with no life except in his quest for mastery, he thinks of his body as he thinks of any subordinate—at best a "craven mate" (458).

For Ishmael, Ahab is an awesome impossibility: a manly Christ in a feminized age. Ishmael despises the womanish Christ of today, the "soft, curled, hermaphroditical" Christ who has been "most successfully embodied" in Italian paintings. There, the savior's brawny powers have been reduced to "the mere negative, feminine one of submission and endurance, which on all hands it is conceded, form the peculiar practical virtues of his teachings" (315). Ordinary people, curiously like Ishmael's readers, who live on "the evangelical land" (193), endure ordinary lives of faith, fear, and subjection. Faced with what both he and Ishmael think of as womanish submission on every side, Ahab takes on the hopeless burden of saving everyone's manhood. He will conscript and kill their bodies to save their souls. Even Starbuck wants his manhood to be saved. Only once does he openly bristle at Ahab, when he mistakenly thinks his commander has called him a coward (458). To the end, what Starbuck fears most is the conventional man's humiliation, not dying but dying "in a woman's fainting fit" (467).[19]

Yet Ishmael also sees Ahab as a machine or puppet. What makes Ahab run? Ahab's crazy purpose, Ishmael says in "The Chart," has "a kind of self-assumed, independent being of its own" (175). By the end Ahab himself suspects that his obsessive drive may have enslaved him. Right before "The Candles," Stubb hears him mutter, "Here some one thrusts these cards into these old hands of mine; swears that I must play them, and no others" (413). Sometimes Ahab wonders if his "intense thinking," the essence of his spiritual power, has made him not a "Prometheus" (175) but a puppet, heartless and driven, without any inward existence. "What is it," he asks in "The Symphony" as he responds to the joyous mothering of the air, "what cozening, hidden lord and master, and cruel, remorseless emperor commands me; that against all natural lovings and longings, I so keep pushing, and crowding, and jamming myself on all the time; recklessly making me ready to do what in my own proper, natural heart, I durst not so much as dare? Is Ahab, Ahab? Is it I, God, or who, that lifts this arm?"(444–445). Already he seems half-joined with Fedallah, like lord and slave or shadow and substance, Ishmael says; "both seemed yoked together, and an unseen tyrant driving them" (439).

Clearly Ishmael wants readers to think of Ahab with equal and contradictory sympathies. He is "a mighty pageant creature" (71), hopelessly trying to redeem our manhood; he is a passive victim of some unseen tyrant. But pity for Ahab's helplessness, like awe for Ahab's tragic fight, accepts the growing mystification of feeling, especially of rage and pain. The narrative magnifies Ahab's rage, disconnects rage from any human object, and disowns the rage by attributing it to a mysterious nonhuman source figured forth in the whale. By the end Ahab's "bold and nervous lofty language" (71) has completely disconnected his will to power from its social base in entrepreneurial rivalry or from White-Jacket's terrified rage at being degraded by human tyranny. For Ahab the feeling of power has become a sadomasochistic fusion. He stands exposed, in Robert Zoellner's felicitous phrase, as an Ugly Narcissus.[20] To anticipate my conclusion, Ahab is the bad self of an unloved child, the self who deserves a whipping. Ahab rages to be beaten by an enormous symbol of both the father's and the mother's power, a sperm whale and a milk-white breast, at once mutilating and abandoning.[21]

After losing his "leg" trying to plunge his "six inch blade" into the whale (159–160), Ahab pursues the symbol of his potency, now felt as alien, malicious, and inhumanly potent. In Ishmael's eyes, Ahab's quest becomes, first, an epic of hopeless manly courage, then, a strange blurring of boundaries between two raging antagonists. Ahab comes to look more and more like the whale: a pleated forehead, a concentered purpose, a malicious intelligence, a ruthless spiritual power. Meanwhile the whale comes to look at least as much like a wandering womb or a malevolent breast as a castrating penis. The narrative's earlier emphasis on the social power of boss over slave gives way to Ahab's self-engendered idea of power as vindictive otherness and projected rage, balanced with Ishmael's scattered metaphors of power as bad mothering.

These confusions surface in Ahab's self-consciousness after he has a second brush with near-castration. Furiously rejecting the goofy fraternity of Captain Boomer and Dr. Bunger, Ahab storms back to his ship, where he twists his leg as he commands the pilot to steer more inflexibly. Only then does Ishmael relate that Ahab had sequestered himself so long at the start of the voyage because his groin had been "stake-wise smitten, and all but pierced" (385).[22]

While ordering his new leg, Ahab voices what seems to be an appealing new ability to dissociate himself from his rage. First he exuberantly yet self-critically commands a giant man to be made in his own image, fifty feet high, all brains and no heart, and no eyes—just "a skylight on top of his head to illuminate inwards." Then he asks a blatantly paranoid question: whether some intelligent, heartless otherness may be inhabiting the carpenter, the leg, or perhaps even himself (390–391). Shortly thereafter, Ahab's reveries about a dying whale take him still further away from his rage, toward a death wish.

Just as power seeks greater power, he implies, so the whale has sought the sun in vain. But now the ocean welcomes the dying whale. She rocks it in her dark nether regions of death and "unnamable imminglings." If Ahab ostensibly invokes the ocean's aid to battle the powers of the air, his stately musings take him beyond the man's world of rivalry to a deeper, queenly world of self-dissolution. "Oh, thou dark Hindoo half of nature, who of drowned bones hast builded thy separate throne... thou art an infidel, thou queen." Ahab thanks his "infidel queen" for having "suckled" him, and he easefully imagines abandoning himself to her embrace (409–410).

So seductive is the depressive self-mothering of his death wish that we forget why the whale is dying. Ahab has killed it. Not only has he killed it, but he is "soothed," Ishmael says, by the whale's death. Moreover, after musing about death as a dark nursing queen, Ahab forces the crew of his whale boat to stay all night by the dead whale, while the other three crews return to the *Pequod*. Lying all night by his whale-queen, and rocked all night by his ocean-queen, the crazed killer sleeps with his victim while he and Fedallah talk of death and hearses.

The renewed threat of symbolic castration takes Ahab first toward a manic self-criticism, then to a paranoid disowning of himself, and finally to a fantasy of self-dissolution that denies any aggressiveness of his own. These confusions set the stage for Ahab's discovery of his "queenly personality." In "The Candles," Ahab's growing sense of himself as less and less alive, more and more a victim, veers from the language of paranoid monomania to the language of hysterical desire.

The change from manly rage to the pose of female hysteria comes when Ahab realizes for the first time that he is about to be beaten. The discovery transforms rage to desire. In "The Candles," his rhetorical fireworks function in at least three contradictory ways: to flaunt his masochistic craving, to intensify his domination of the crew, and to expose the absence of self binding Ahab to the power he defies. Paradoxically, as readers precipitously detach themselves from his demonic delirium, his wild and whirling words coerce the crew's mesmerized submission. Still more paradoxically, his words implicitly acknowledge that he will lose, that he is driven, and that he is already dead inside.

III

"The Candles" takes place in a storm so intense that the lightning rods at the ends of the masts start to burn with an eerie, mesmerizing flame. The crew stands stupefied. Up in the rigging some men "hung pendulous, like a knot of numbed wasps from a drooping, orchard twig."

Meanwhile, their captain reaches out his left hand and grabs hold of the links to the lightning rods. It seems a demonic parody of Benjamin Franklin's kite experiment.

Then, as if to parody American race relations as well, Ahab plants one imperial foot on the tawny back of the Parsee who kneels in front of him. He sticks up his right arm, fixes his "upward eye" on "the lofty tri-pointed trinity of flames," and announces that he is a woman. "In the midst of the personified impersonal, a personality stands here.... the queenly personality lives in me, and feels her royal rights" (416–417).

It's a startling line, especially when it stands by itself. At this point in the story I've become impatient with Ahab's majestic uproar of metaphysical brag and flailing desperation. Yet almost nothing prepares me for the gender change. Moreover, his announcement is strangely ambiguous. It's not *his* personality, but "*a* personality," a queen that "lives in me," as if Ahab's brain were her castle. He now equates his "me" with the outer shell, the "personified impersonal," within which some queenly stranger "stands...and feels her royal rights." What these rights are, he doesn't say. Nor is it clear how he/she can "feel" a "right." All we can say with certainty is that he now thinks of his defiance as female. While his rigid manly stance seems to be petrifying into a mask for the personified impersonal, a woman takes command of his feelings. More seems to be at stake here than simply proving he's not a coward.

Ahab's queenly personality lives in him only for a moment. Then it vanishes from his self-consciousness, with no reappearance. Critics have never known quite what to make of it. It stands like a lighthouse on a nonexistent island. Faced with such an unnerving self-dislocation, Melville scholars tend to let the line rush by as an odd, quirky gust in the midst of a basically theological storm.[23] But God, Lucifer, and Gnostic heresy are more pretext than text. The "queenly personality" line seems so memorable, and so anomalous, because it brings to the surface the gender inversion latent in the story's beating fantasy.

What are the queen's royal rights? Astonishingly, it appears, to wed and bed the king, her hateful husband, in slavish desire and helpless defiance. "I now know thee, thou clear spirit," Ahab declaims to the fire, "and I now know that thy right worship is defiance.... I own thy speechless, placeless power; but to the last gasp of my earthquake life will dispute its unconditional, unintegral mastery in me" (416–417). Ahab simultaneously "owns," or acknowledges, the fire's power over

him ("Who's over me?") and "owns," or possesses, that power within
him. Fire and queen are both inside him, yet alien and mutually hostile.
The rest of Ahab's wild speech tries to couple them. With an extravagantly artificial blending of gothic melodrama and Elizabethan solil-
oquy, his queenly defiance becomes the first step in a hysterical dance
of seduction. First his manhood, then his queenliness yield to his desire
to be ravished by the power he hates and hallucinates.

Come to me, Ahab cries to the fire as he clutches the links. "Come
in thy lowest form of love, and I will kneel and kiss thee; but at thy
highest, come as mere supernal power" (417). He, or she, wants to feel
electrified, or electrocuted, by something that "comes" into the body.
Emily Dickinson phrases it with more deference in the second of her
"Master" letters: "I wish with a might I cannot repress—that mine were
the Queen's place."[24] Dickinson is wistfully wishing, not imperiously
demanding, but the desire is the same: to be possessed by an all-
powerful lover, spirit, and father. Ahab's spiritual lover-father, however, is as abstracted, hateful, and heartless as he is. The closer he gets
to intimacy with power, the more his pleading sounds like the impersonal conventions of drugstore romance.

Warner Berthoff sees in the "curiously abstractive" ascendancy of
Ahab a loss of the "strong, sure, humorous, masculine poetry" in Ishmael's earlier narration. Now Melville plunges into "a state of self-
conscious uncertainty, violently compensated for in the writing." Hershel Parker more sardonically suggests that Melville may have been
going crazy.[25] Berthoff is right to see a close connection between Ahab's
speeches and the uncontrollable parody of women's fiction and conventions of womanhood in *Pierre*. But his assumption that masculine
prose is healthy creativity misses the point of Melville's eruptive uncertainty. Defiance has become exposed as a pasteboard mask for slavish
adoration. The exuberant rush of manly words has become a desperate
desire to be raped by the unloving otherness of pure power. Ahab's
queenly claim to royal rights becomes a lover's self-abasement, which
in turn yields to a new and still more intimate fantasy. He is now the
child-bride and offspring of pure power. "Oh, thou clear spirit, of thy
fire thou madest me, and like a true child of fire, I breathe it back to
thee" (417).

Ahab shows most of the conventional nineteenth-century symptoms
of hysteria here: theatricality, fragmented discourse, vivid momentary
emotions, a sense of being swept away, a deeper sense of oneself as
uncontrollable. But this is not classic female hysteria. "For the most

part," writes Amariah Brigham in 1840, "hysteria occurs in young and middle aged females, of delicate constitution, indolent habits, and highly susceptible nerves." The symptoms consist of "sighing, sobbing, laughing or weeping, with a feeling of stiffness and suffocation about the throat." Females are much more liable to hysteria, Brigham continues, because "the duties of a mother are so peculiar, requiring patient, long-enduring self-immolation in the discharge of them." Therefore women need "a more delicate and susceptible brain and nervous system, . . . endowed with sensibilities to which men are strangers."[26]

One could read Nancy Chodorow's *Reproduction of Mothering* as a psychoanalytic and sociological gloss on how a mother's "self-immolation" leads to the "more delicate and susceptible" sensibilities that bind women to the mothering role. Carroll Smith-Rosenberg has argued that hysteria is really an infantilized response to a contradiction in the social roles expected of young middle-class American women in the nineteenth-century: first to be wooed and idealized, then to be stifled and forgotten as wife and mother. Jean Strouse speaks of Alice James's hysteria as an escape route from conflicting imperatives and incompatible states of being: safe and boring domesticity vs. dangerous public self-assertion; woman as frail vessel, woman as emotional volcano. In *Women: The Longest Revolution*, Juliet Mitchell argues that hysteria in the nineteenth-century was "the battleground on which women and men fought in an unconscious, pre-political manner." As a spontaneous protest, it struggles and fails to revalue characteristics debased by male obsessionality.[27]

Of these analyses, Mitchell's comes closest to Ahab's state of mind. He certainly is not afflicted with contradictory or discontinuous role expectations. But he does start to experience a desire for fusion, previously blocked by his obsession. Moreover, Ahab now imagines his quest for revenge as a queenly struggle against and for all-powerful maleness. Some abstract paternal power has seduced and abandoned him, leaving an abject passivity at his core.

To evade his horror at the passivity he is discovering in himself, Ahab appropriates woman's desire in the conventional male terms for hysteria, terms later literalized by Freud. As Woody Allen recounts in *Zelig*, Zelig broke with Dr. Freud because Freud wanted to restrict the concept of penis envy to women. *Moby Dick* is the most extravagant projection of male penis envy in our literature. Ahab glimpses what could be a feminist interpretation: "woman" signifies an embattled yet helpless victim of the power she craves and hates, while "penis" signifies the most intimate symbol of power. In the midst of his momentary feminization, however, Ahab is still possessed by the bond between power and manhood. Feelings of rage, fear, and desire have to do only with his hallucinated rivalry for dominance, not with human intimacy or nurturance. What might look like Ahab's sudden empathy with female struggle, or a homosexual queen coming out of the patriarchal closet, turns out to be more male power seeking in a masochistic mode.

Ahab's speech appropriates conventions of women's hysteria as men defined its causes. What every hysterical woman wants, said knowledgeable men, is good sex. What her unconscious wants, Freud would add later, is her father and a penis. Emerson puts the conventional nineteenth-century view of women quite bluntly, after reading through the papers of his late friend Margaret Fuller. "The unlooked for trait in all these journals to me is the Woman, poor woman: they are all hysterical. She is bewailing her virginity and languishing for a husband. 'I need help. No, I need a full, a godlike embrace from some sufficient love.' &c. &c."[28] Ahab wants a godlike embrace from some sufficient hate, the only feeling he consciously acknowledges inside himself.

This want is both homoerotically intense and abstractly phony. As Gertrude Stein remarked in a different context, there is no there there. Instead, Ahab is shifting poses every moment, with absolute intensity, from an absolute lack of self. He is being spoken by the ideology of manhood that has possessed him. Weirdly, Ahab's obsession with manhood has flipped into the resentful yet hungering powerlessness of true American womanhood.

Acting out his hysterical desire, Ahab now becomes melodramatically suicidal. He clutches the links; St. Elmo's fire shoots through his body. Demonic Franklin becomes a demonic Calvin, experiencing an unholy rape of the spirit by "Lucifer" himself. Ahab's grotesque, self-pitying images of blindness and beheading now evoke King Lear with a strangely stilted majesty of castration agony: "mine eye-balls ache and ache; my whole beaten brain seems as beheaded, and rolling on some stunning ground." Yet he wants more. He wants to be penetrated again and again, with still more "javelins" coursing through his "beaten brain" (417).

Just as Ahab shrieks what seems to be flamboyant masochism fused with homoerotic desire, another Ahab disowns his desire to be beaten. "There's that in here that still remains indifferent," he interjects a little earlier. Now he obscurely associates his heart's strange inertness with the "puzzle" of his inward mother, as absent to him as Lear's wife is absent from the play. "But thou art but my fiery father; my sweet mother, I know not. Oh, cruel! what hast thou done with her?" One might say rather cynically, the same thing Ahab seems to have done with *his* queenly personality: absorbed her into himself, to be exploited and forgotten.[29] Yet the absence at the center of himself, momentarily felt as a female presence, makes him see that something has already been possessed and beaten down.

A stereotypically male competitiveness reasserts its royal rights. "I know that of me, which thou knowest not of thyself, oh, thou omnipotent," he gloats. "There is some unsuffusing thing beyond thee," Ahab says, which dominates power just as power dominates Ahab. Omnipotence, too, is enslaved, empty, and mechanical. The fire, too, is a "foundling" (417). At the simplest level of rivalry, the best defense is a good offense. Therefore Ahab attacks by calling God a bastard, since God doesn't know his own father.

At another level Ahab simultaneously flaunts his aggressive desire while universalizing his self-pity. He shows his behind to the Political Father, in Roland Barthes's ambiguous phrase, while presenting himself in Ishmael-like terms as a cosmic orphan.[30] Nonetheless, the accusation about doing away with mother contains a hint of frantic truth. Ahab senses that the drive for the feeling of power has destroyed any capacity for real feeling and real intimacy. The heartless bully is a lost little boy. The moment such feelings emerge, he transposes them into the hostile circlings of dominance and submission.

Like a classic hysteric, Ahab has presented himself rhetorically as a flaming queen and a passive victim whose desires have been scripted. More and more he thinks of himself as the latter, an errand boy for some alien, demonic force that drives him on. His voice becomes a babble of poses, a gothic Lear on the outside, "indifferent" at the core. While Ishmael disowns his body's submissiveness by floating off into the vapors of philosophical indeterminacy, where he covertly deconstructs the reader's expectations for a consistent voice and a continuous plot, Ahab both worships and defies the experience of being beaten that he discovers again and again under his rage for dominance.

At the center of his beating fantasy sits an unholy trinity: a queenly personality, a perhaps murdered mother, and an inability to feel. Instead of trying to uncover their secrets, he climaxes his hysterical dance of seduction by claiming to "read" a father who is pure dominance, pure submission, and pure text. Wholly spoken now by manhood, Ahab's extravagant textuality culminates in ritualized verbal ejaculations: "With haughty agony, I read my sire," he crows. "I leap with thee; I burn with thee; would fain be welded with thee; defyingly I worship thee!" (417). At that instant, with a spectacular sexual displacement, Ahab consummates his desire to be possessed. His harpoon, lashed to the lifeboat "in its conspicuous crotch," bursts into flame.

IV

At this point readers may well be objecting that I take Ahab's language too seriously. Certainly this scene—and it is a scene—has climactic rhetorical intensity, but it looks like flimflam and hokum. Ahab sounds melodramatic, abstracted, incoherent, literary, and pretentious. Besides, as John Seelye has pointed out to me, St. Elmo's fire is as safe as a kitten to carry about. The whole affair has been staged by a verbal magician to manipulate his crew.

Yet why does he speak just that way? Why all this strange flaming queenliness? If it looks like rant, it also looks like what Newton Arvin once called the "tiger-pit" of Melville's repressed emotions. If Ahab's language seems grotesquely empty of real feeling, as Neal Tolchin has implied, its hypertextuality allows a safely distanced response to contradictory states of mind.[31] The captain of the good ship *Manhood* discovers that he has been sailing toward the ultimate in manly humiliations, a desire to be homosexually raped. Simultaneously, he discovers his own inauthenticity. Much earlier, Ishmael muses that Ahab's will to power is an "unbidden and unfathered birth" in which his mind ceaselessly experiences a "blankness" while a self-created "vulture" ceaselessly feeds upon his heart (175). Born of humiliation, this monomaniac will is not his own but is perpetually birthed in him by the gender conventions flaring out in his words.

A contrary argument might say that Ahab's queenly defiance turns homosexual pleasure into homophobic pain or terrorism. One could easily situate Ahab's speech in the "paranoid Gothic" tradition sketched by Eve Kosofsky Sedgwick, for instance. To borrow from her analysis of a quite different text, Ahab's "abjection" voices himself as a woman to desire a man: "identifying hatingly with [the queenly personality,] he hatingly throws himself at the man who seems to be at the fountainhead of male prestige." Or, at the little lower layer, one could borrow from Vivian Pollak's analysis of Emily Dickinson's psyche to say that Melville's self-loathing suppresses and transforms his fear of homosexual desires. Or one could do a Lacanian turn here—the whole of *Pierre* invites such a turn—and say that Ahab has just discovered his hysterical desire to be possessed by the symbolic phallus, a desire based in lack.[32] Ahab's craving for the phallus evades confronting his raging identification with the hysterical female.

My problem with all these readings is that Ahab's rhetoric seems so empty, and he half knows it. Ahab has become a grandiose convention of entrepreneurial manhood whose desire for greater manhood burns all the hotter as he, or she, or it, becomes dead to human feelings. He flips into the abject underside of his desire for dominance, a desire to be beaten or raped, as a desperate strategy for keeping his intensity of purpose alive. But he is being spoken by otherness now, not a symbolic name of the Father but a social construction of gender. What looks like a homoerotic desire to be raped mystifies his growing awareness of nonself, or petrification of feeling. More obviously it mystifies his use of all this metapsychological-theological discourse to control his crew. Finally, to reverse Pollak's argument about Dickinson, it mystifies what I take to be the heart of Melville's homoeroticism: not desire but self-loathing.

A personal analogy may make my argument look more plausible. When our son was four years old, a new family moved in next door. That afternoon the neighbor's daughter, a year older than Trevor, had a spectacular tantrum, flipping about like a break dancer on their driveway. Trevor and I watched, fascinated and horrified. Later that day, for reasons I have forgotten or repressed, Trevor became furious at me. As I tried and failed to stop his screaming, I became conscious that he was flailing about in bizarre new ways. It was the neighbors' daughter, I suddenly realized. In the midst of going absolutely out of control with rage, off the wall and over the cliff, he was trying out her moves.

A much more paranoid version of that doubleness is what I see in Ahab here or, more precisely, in Melville's imagining of Ahab. One could call it childish or narcissistic or manipulative, to be sure. It does look homosexual, if taken half seriously. Yet it's also a primal experience of feeling one's voice being constructed, in this case by manhood. Ahab begins in rivalrous rage at what he takes to be humiliation. Now, as his fated defeat comes near, I suspect that Melville turned to Lear, perhaps unconsciously, to try on a new style of madness to empower his hero. As Ahab puts on Lear's "Hysterica passio"—"this mother," as Lear calls it, that "swells up toward my heart"—to see how it fits, queenly anger astonishingly becomes a desire to be impregnated by a malevolent god.[33] Much more benignly, Ishmael relishes fetal images for the mind.

Analogously, Melville all but directly announced in "Hawthorne and His Mosses" that he had been impregnated by Hawthorne, to whom he dedicated *Moby Dick*. In words that only nineteenth-century writers could respectably declare, Melville proclaims through the mask of his Virginian, "this Hawthorne has dropped germinous seeds into my soul. He expands and deepens down, the more I contemplate him; and further, and further, shoots his strong New-England roots into the hot soil of my Southern soul" (rpt. 548). Ahab's "Candles" speech transposes that fantasy from homoerotic to paranoid desire.

Beyond his discussions of paranoia and homosexual desire, Freud offers several insights into Ahab's wish to be "welded" with his hostile maker. In "A Child Is Being Beaten," he discusses the child's fantasy of being beaten by an authority figure. For Freud the fantasy indicates a displaced incestuous desire for the father as well as a wish for the father to punish a rival. The child experiences sadistic pleasure under a masochistic veil. Using Freud's essay, Michael Rogin discusses the flogging scenes in *White-Jacket* as a masochistic fantasy of reparation "in which the aggressive child replaces his victim under the scourge."[34]

Freud's essay may well illuminate Melville's feelings about his older brother Gansevoort, very much his father's darling. Nevertheless, I think the more basic dynamics have to do with an evasion of self-loathing through masochistic passivity. In his last theoretical essay, Freud concludes his "Analysis Terminable and Interminable" by speaking of the two most intractable problems he found in his patients: "the wish for a penis in women and, in men, the struggle against passivity."[35] Ahab combines the two. Like one of Freud's hysterics, Ahab wants to be seduced, or knows he already has been, by his hateful father. What Freud would call Ahab's "rebellious over-compensation" breaks down into passivity and a desire for fusion. Mixing rebellion and seduction, Ahab finally gets his desire, if only momentarily and symbolically: his father's penis of pure power, a spirit-spout blazing from the tip of his harpoon. But Ahab, like Dora, perhaps seducing and perhaps seduced, speaks with several tongues. As his rage veers toward hysteria, he also discovers the absence of feeling in his circle of rage and desire. Here Freud, because of his own patriarchal code of manhood, mistakes passivity for unconscious desire, not the evasion of feeling that I take it to be.

From a social and political point of view, Ahab's seemingly suicidal behavior looks manipulatively fake. His hallucinated union with his supernatural conqueror simultaneously whips up his defiance and evokes sympathy for him as martyred victim. More simply, Ahab's melodramatic ploy to electrocute himself proves very useful as a way of keeping everyone else terrified of him. When Ahab sees his harpoon leap into flame, he waves it about "like a torch." His action immediately stifles the crew's "half mutinous cry." "Petrified," they fall back and run from him "in a terror of dismay" (418). Similarly, Ahab flourishes his flaming torch song, ostensibly wooing pure power to enhance his dominance.

Later Starbuck, for one, will come very close to killing him. It is clear to everyone on the boat, even Pip, that their captain has gone over the top. Yet everyone stifles his anger and fear to empathize with Ahab's anger and pain. So, for the most part, do the readers who have followed him this far, half mesmerized by his quest, while aware that his quest has less and less to do with any human sense of either power or feeling. Hamlet-like, Starbuck stares at his sleeping captain, fingers the loaded musket, and thinks that Ahab is about to become "the wilful murderer of thirty men and more." But he can't pull the trigger. It isn't just Starbuck's rational allegiance to human and divine law that stops him. It's also Ahab's voice, speaking inside the mate's mind even while Ahab sleeps—a voice that "say'st the men have vow'd thy vow; say'st all of us are Ahabs" (422).

Ahab's madness gains allegiance and credibility, or at least awed submission, not because he makes sense but because he shouts the stresses of manhood with a shaman's intensity. In granting psychological authenticity to his woe, however, we accept his metaphysical aggrandizement of manhood, which for Ahab means dominating or being dominated, as the only interpretive frame for subjective experience. If "self" becomes the inscription of a sadomasochistic boss-slave intercourse, then Ishmael's decentered fluidity of voice becomes the only alternative for the survival of the mind.

We also accept Ishmael's appropriation of mothering to nurture his self-deconstruction, while Ahab appropriates a queenly personality to voice his defiant desire to be beaten. Ishmael's appropriation is much more seductive and long-lasting. The buoyancy of an orphan dependent on faceless maternal care becomes the survivor's alternative to Ahab's tyrannical quest. Especially toward the end of *Moby Dick*, Ishmael mutes his attacks on "the step-mother world" (443) and celebrates maternal love in a variety of ways: not just in the exuberant sexuality and regressiveness of "The Grand Armada" but in many quiet images of nurturance at the margins of Ahab's quest, such as the contrast between the lone bulls and the loving concern of female whales (330), the account in "The Life-Buoy" of seal dams who have lost their cubs (429), or "the devious-cruising Rachel" that picks up orphaned Ishmael in the epilogue (470). These mothers, like Ishmael, are victims.

A perhaps more feminist reading would argue, as Robert Zoellner has, that Ishmael moves from Ahab's male consciousness of power as dominance to a perception of relational female powers in the ocean, the whale, the self, and language. Female powers give birth to a womb-like, fluid creativity that regenerates rather than destroys. This model of noncompetitive power has been popular in recent feminist theories as a celebration of patriarchal subversion and free play. Certainly Melville indulges a similar vision of creativity, and critics like Zoellner, Joyce Sparer Adler and others are right to emphasize Ishmael's narrative countermovement.[36]

In my reading, Ishmael's images of loving maternity constitute a powerfully seductive erasure of conflicted feelings. His recurrent fantasy of bereft mothers solacing bereft children indulges a narcissistic self-pity that veils his narcissistic rage. Just as Freud mistakes passivity for desire, one could use more current psychoanalytic theory to mistake Ishmael's metaphors of separation and abandonment for his fundamental feelings. Rather, I see them as sentimentalized props appropriated from women's fiction.

Susan Warner begins *The Wide, Wide World* with the drama of a child separated from her mother by a heartless father. Harriet Beecher Stowe builds the rhetorical impact of *Uncle Tom's Cabin* on the same device, the separation of child from mother. Under her much more controlled emphasis on salvation through good mothering, Stowe's narrative shares a strange central fantasy with *Moby Dick*: Uncle Tom, like Ahab, is a man being beaten. Moreover, as Nina Baym has pointed out, *The Wide, Wide World* is the feminine counterpart to *Moby Dick*, in that each narrative "focuses so quickly and exclusively on the issue of power and how to live without it."[37] For both Warner and Melville, good mothering is a vestigial sentimental fantasy meant to solace powerless victims.

More generally, whether found in Ishmael's fancy or in recent feminist theory, defining women's powers as birthing, mothering, and intimacy or imagining woman's creativity as a self-decentering babble of tongues perpetuates nineteenth-century sex-role polarities in inverse form. The result: a tightening of the bond between public power and male narcissism. That bond continues to depersonalize women as mothers and body-objects in an idealized and apolitical mode.

V

To gain some measure of clarity on *Moby Dick's* seductive mystifications, one has to look through the text to social context in two ways—toward Melville's family and toward American gender ideology. The confusion of feelings in *Moby Dick* has profound personal roots in the narcissistic injuries of Melville's early life.

Beneath Ishmael's manic-depressive rush of words and Ahab's abstracted posturings of rage, the two characters share a terrifying craving for humiliation. They reflect Melville's need to expose and punish a self felt as very, very bad. Both Ahab's narcissistic grandiosity and Ishmael's oceanic evaporation are evasive strategies to split feelings of fearful need, joined again as raging fusion with an unfeeling tyrant.

What were Melville's narcissistic injuries? Here I will risk some simplified speculations. Both his genteel father, a New York clothing importer, and his social-climbing mother seem to have been preoccupied with social appearances. His father put enormous faith in kinship, family responsibility, and family image. Most biographers see him as benevolent, caring, and concerned for his children, though Edwin Miller emphasizes his use of the rod. Herman's mother, on the other hand, seems to have been quite bossy. She also seems to have been frequently depressed, especially in Herman's early years. Family legend has it that when she wanted to take a nap, she would place her eight children on stools around her bed, where they would sit immobile until she woke. Then she would release them to their play.[38]

Herman was the classic second son, a pale shadow of their firstborn, Gansevoort, whom both parents adored. Gansevoort was their dream of family success. They thought of Herman, when they thought of him at all, as dull, amiable, and docile. In response Herman seems to have made himself compliant and invisible, especially with his father, an ineffectual businessman whom Herman apparently idealized. He was a good boy, his parents said—a little dumb, but sweet.

Then Allan Melvill went bankrupt. The family moved from New York to Albany; he went bankrupt again. Returning from a desperate midwinter business trip, Allan walked across the ice floes of the Hudson River in $-2°$ weather, and died in a raving frenzy two weeks later. Herman had just turned twelve.

At the end of *Moby Dick* Ishmael is rescued in place of a twelve-year-old boy, after watching Ahab destroy himself in a crazed fight to prove his manhood. Neal Tolchin argues that Melville's entire creative career shows a struggle to work through his blocked mourning for his father. Ahab's last visible moment, as he is whipped out of the boat by a rope around his throat, looms in a passage from *Redburn* that biographers like to quote: "I must not think of those delightful days, before my father became a bankrupt, and died, and we removed from the city; for when I think of those days, something rises up in my throat and almost strangles me."[39]

Melville's mother now turned coldly Calvinist. Changing their name by adding an *e*, to dissociate the family from her husband's shame, Maria Melville froze her rage, especially when she discovered that Allan had probably fathered an illegitimate child, who visited the Melvills with her mother to ask for more money. Beyond that shock, Maria was faced with the simple facts of his death and their impoverishment. In her haughtiness, which Melville so maliciously portrays in *Pierre*, Maria saw Allan's death as God's ruthless judgment on his damned soul.[40] As the end of *Moby Dick* approaches, Melville similarly shifts Ahab's characterization. First depicted as a mixture of Paul Bunyan, Prometheus, and a crucified Christ, Ahab goes to his self-destruction attended by an increasingly heavy-handed language of demonism. At the same time, Ishmael intensifies sympathy for Ahab as a helpless victim, joined with the devil to be beaten by fate and God.

The fascination with watching an insanely raging man being beaten to death satisfies several contradictory fantasies: to see Gansevoort being punished by Melville's father, to feel himself fuse with his idealized father, to bear witness to his father's beating at the hands of the market, and perhaps, if one accepts Edwin Miller's version of Melville's childhood, to kill a father "chiefly known to me"—as Father Mapple says of God—"by Thy rod" (51). More deeply, dramatizing Ahab's demonic self-destruction may have been Melville's most intimate way of complying with his mother's rage while voicing his need for tenderness from his father.

The incessant talk of abandonment and abstracted rage in *Moby Dick* hides a more fearful resentment. Melville once said to a niece that his mother hated him. At the heart of Ahab's heartlessness lies a deep, stone-dead coldness, an absolute zero of self. As Ishmael's Counterpane dream intimates, such a state can be brought on by a mother's loathing for any noncompliant feelings and behavior.

Harry Stack Sullivan incisively illuminates what he calls "The Malevolent Transformation" of the child's need for tenderness in such family situations. The malevolence emerges, he says, when children find that their need for tenderness leads to an experience of being hurt. "A particularly ugly phase of this is found in cases in which the mother is very hostile toward the father." The mother therefore explains the child's expression of malevolence—really the perception that he lives among enemies—"by saying that he is just like his father." An "even more subtly destructive" phase occurs when "malevolence has come about because the mother is malevolent toward the child." Then the child feels profoundly ugly inside, with a rage mirroring his mother's assessment of him.[41]

Loathing, not abandonment, is the core of the mother's response. In "Letter for Melville 1951," while praising Henry Murray's psychological understanding of Melville, Charles Olson similarly assesses Maria Melville's unloving presence at the center of Melville's feelings. Murray loves Melville, Olson says, and knows him as a doctor should,

> a family doctor, how
> his mother stayed inside him, how
> the compact came out hate, and what
> this kept him from, despite
> how far he travelled.[42]

The way from imposed self-loathing to the Lacanian abyss of self-decentering is through abandonment and rage. Julia Kristeva brilliantly voices the abysses of maternal loathing in *Powers of Horror*. Like Melville, too, Kristeva abstracts her feelings from the anxiety of intimacy and recasts them as power relations. There, any experience of subjectivity is felt with paradoxical paranoia as an experience of being dominated.[43]

Fleeing the terrifying resentment at his own centerless center, Ishmael becomes vital and invisible by fusing himself with contradictory aggressors: the ocean, a "masterless" bad mother, which "like a savage tigress . . . overlays her own cubs" (235); the whale, in all its milky malice of phantom narcissism; and Ahab, in his noble yet doomed assault against cosmic forces felt as both omnipotently paternal and diffusely maternal. To join passively with any potential aggressor, whether Queequeg or Ahab, whether oceanic mother or a still more abstracted Fate, becomes Ishmael's way of being beaten. Ahab rages for manly self-empowering, to fight such humiliation. Yet his quest for revenge takes Ahab toward deep thinking, which is really the pursuit of truth, which is really the discovery of cosmic malevolence, which is really self-loathing. Turned toward self-pity, that loathing becomes the fated helplessness of a beaten man, a "captive king" on a "broken throne" buried far beneath the "spiked Hotel de Cluny" of his noble warrior facade (161). Turned toward philosophy, it becomes what Melville calls a "Calvinistic sense of Innate Depravity and Original Sin, from whose visitations...no deeply thinking mind is always and wholly free" (540, "Hawthorne and His Mosses").

The structuring fantasy in *Moby Dick* is to watch a man being beaten. It has two sources: Melville's personal narcissistic trauma, which recasts helpless resentment as a raging desire to be punished by a godlike, yet malevolent father-mother, and Melville's depth of intuition about the code of entrepreneurial manhood, which made men like his father so fear humiliation. Unlike Allan Melvill, Ahab rejects the market out of hand. But Ahab participates wholeheartedly in the underlying dynamic of the new capitalist class: the one-against-the-universe struggle for dominance. He *has* been possessed, by a drive that turns against himself. Ahab's imperial self is an imploding star, as Walter Herbert has said, sucking every human feeling into the black hole of manhood.[44]

By the end, Pip the coward has become the story's emotional "conduit" (433). Use me, Pip says to his master; "do ye but use poor me for your one lost leg; only tread upon me, sir; I ask no more, so I remain a part of ye." "Weep so, and I will murder thee!" Ahab replies; "have a care, for Ahab too is mad" (436). "One daft with strength, the other daft with weakness," the old Manxman has already noted. "But here's the end of the rotten line—all dripping, too. Mend it, eh? I think we had best have a new line altogether" (428).

The new line never comes. What makes *Moby Dick* so exhilarating is its extravagant plunge into the manly American mind: its zest for exploration, its awe at pain, its rapture at the hunt for whales and ideas, its craving for dominance and fluidity all at once. Toward the end, however, the narrative starts to expose both the pain and the scripted conventionality of manhood. A stark passivity belies Ahab's rhetorical posturings, while the narrative's tightening vortex of dominance and humiliation, malevolence and helplessness, circles inexorably toward the final beating. There the bad self exits as hapless victim.

In Ahab's last act of aggression, the king-turned-spear-carrier gives up the spear. He throws his harpoon; the harpoon hits Moby Dick.

But the rope runs foul. "Ahab stooped to clear it; he did clear it; but the flying turn caught him round the neck, and voicelessly as Turkish mutes bowstring their victim, he was shot out of the boat, ere the crew knew he was gone" (468).

Ahab's quest for manhood ends in the passive voice: "he was shot out of the boat." The tyrannical shouter dies as he inwardly lived, incapable of speech. Here is hysteria's most classic symptom, what Amariah Brigham called "a feeling of stiffness and suffocation about the throat." His life ends in a choking seizure. At that moment, carried away by his bond to power, Ahab may have sensed what it felt like to be voiceless and terrified, an emotionally battered child-bride of the nineteenth-century.

Or is it Melville's last devious twist to compel our own trancelike bond with the bully as victim?

It's not enough to subside into Ishmael's whalelike view of things, and regard both possibilities "with equal eye" (314). That's evasive, frustrating, mocking, even maddening. Yet it's where his narration comes to rest. To go further, we have to look through the text to the social origins of feelings about power and powerlessness. Where power is felt as narcissistic compensation, there can never be enough. What remains in the ripples of powerlessness is Ishmael, afloat on the mystery of himself, telling a story of men pursuing a demon beyond themselves. That demon, I have been arguing, is manhood. As the most searing exploration of manhood in the American Renaissance, *Moby Dick* bears full witness to the aspirations and terrors of American men at midcentury, and bears partial witness to Melville's personal pain.

Notes

Introduction

1. James Joyce, *Ulysses*, end of Nestor Episode 2. See *Ulysses: A Critical and Synoptic Edition*, prepared by Hans Walter Gabler et al. (New York: Garland, 1984), 1:69.

2. Frank Lentricchia, *After the New Criticism* (Chicago: University of Chicago Press, 1980), 349–351; Geoffrey H. Hartman, *Criticism in the Wilderness: The Study of Literature Today* (New Haven: Yale University Press, 1980), 291. On the next page, however, Hartman accuses historians of "making a compact with the social sciences," clearly more contaminating than the reverse tendency of English professors to succumb "to our innate purity complex."

3. Henry James, *Hawthorne* (Ithaca: Cornell University Press, 1956, 1st pub. 1879), 2.

4. Nina Baym, "Melodramas of Beset Manhood: How Theories of American Fiction Exclude Women Authors," *American Quarterly*, 33 (Summer 1981), 123–139.

5. An essay by Barbara Foley, "From New Criticism to Deconstruction," *American Quarterly*, 36 (Spring 1984), 44–64, perceptively discusses the enduring appeal of Charles Feidelson, *Symbolism and American Literature* (Chicago: University of Chicago Press, 1953), despite, or because of, its flight from history into language. Yet the brilliance of Feidelson's book or of Richard Poirier, *A World Elsewhere: The Place of Style in American Literature* (New York: Oxford University Press, 1966), comes in part from the critic's room to respond to American Renaissance language play in its own terms. In reviewing Michael Rogin, *Subversive Genealogy: The Politics and Art of Herman Melville* (New York: Knopf, 1983), among other studies, Richard Brodhead crisply illuminates the problem of reductiveness involved in trying to apply any historical frame to these texts. See *Nineteenth-Century Fiction*, 38 (September 1983), 214–219.

6. For example, Sean Wilentz, *Chants Democratic: New York City and the Rise of the American Working Class, 1788–1850* (New York: Oxford University Press, 1984); Nick Salvatore, *Eugene V. Debs: Citizen and Socialist* (Urbana: University of Illinois Press, 1982).

7. Catherine Gallagher, *The Industrial Reformation of English Fiction: Social Discourse*

and Narrative Form, 1832–1867 (Chicago: University of Chicago Press, 1985), 267: "The politics of culture ... is one very significant component within a larger ideological battle between the gentry, with its allies in the intelligentsia, and the industrial middle class, a battle that was handily won by the gentry. Their ideological victory, it seems, contributed to the decline of England as an industrial power."

8. I realize these remarks invite a more comparative study than the one I have written. Gallagher's *Industrial Reformation of English Fiction* opens the door for a sophisticated comparative study, if one accepts my presumption that in the Northeast the new middle class won while in England the new middle class lost. The Anglo-American continuity has been variously stressed by Nicolaus Mills, Edwin Eigner, William Spengemann, and others, while Michael Davitt Bell's *Development of American Romance: The Sacrifice of Relation* (Chicago: University of Chicago Press, 1980) implicitly reaffirms the distinction between American romances and English novels. No one to my knowledge has emphasized the impact of male gender ideology in comparative terms, though Robert Weisbuch's fine recent study foregrounds the rivalry of American writers with their English counterparts. See Weisbuch, *Atlantic Double-Cross: American Literature and British Influence in the Age of Emerson* (Chicago: University of Chicago Press, 1986). On the English side, Norman Vance, *The Sinews of the Spirit: The Ideal of Christian Manliness in Victorian Literature and Religious Thought* (Cambridge: Cambridge University Press, 1985), discriminates among varieties of moral manliness, though without much analytical depth.

For ample evidence of American writers' patrician backgrounds, see Mary Kelley, *Private Woman, Public Stage: Literary Domesticity in Nineteenth-Century America* (New York: Oxford University Press, 1984), and the appendix to Lawrence Buell, *New England Literary Culture: From Revolution through Renaissance* (Cambridge: Cambridge University Press, 1986), 375–397. Buell's book emphasizes "the symbiosis of respectability and deviance" (15) as writers responded to the moral expectations of the Unitarian-Whig orthodoxy in Boston.

9. See, for instance, David G. Pugh, *Sons of Liberty: The Masculine Mind in Nineteenth-Century America* (Westport, Conn.: Greenwood Press, 1983), which defines manhood primarily in terms of anxiety about women. For a more general study, see Peter N. Stearns, *Be a Man! Males in Modern Society* (New York: Holmes, 1979). Joseph H. Pleck, *The Myth of Masculinity* (Cambridge: MIT Press, 1981), usefully emphasizes manhood as a socially imposed role, not an innate psychology, and questions the psychoanalytic tendency to Blame Mother. See esp. 108–114, 157–158. See also *The Making of Masculinities: The New Men's Studies*, ed. Harry Brod (Boston: Allen & Unwin, 1987), for an eclectic introduction, and Walter J. Ong's more essentialist and sociobiological *Fighting for Life: Contest, Sexuality, and Consciousness* (Ithaca: Cornell University Press, 1981).

10. Alfred Habegger, *Gender, Fantasy, and Realism in American Literature* (New York: Columbia University Press, 1982).

11. Quentin Anderson, *The Imperial Self: An Essay in American Literary and Cultural History* (New York: Vintage, 1971), 51–58, also 15–16 on failed fathers.

12. David Leverenz, "Manhood, Humiliation, and Public Life: Some Stories," *Southwest Review* 71 (Autumn 1986), 442–462.

13. Whitman's remark to Traubel is quoted by David S. Reynolds, *Beneath the American Renaissance: The Subversive Imagination in the Age of Emerson and Melville* (New York: Knopf, 1988), 108, from Horace Traubel, *With Walt Whitman in Camden* (New York: Mitchell Kennedy, 1915), 1:223. Cf. Emerson's journal, September–October 1845: "In Spenser (Book III Canto XI) is the Castle of Busyrane on whose gate is writ Be Bold, on the second gate, Be bold, be bold, and the inner iron door, Be not too bold." *Emerson in His Journals*, ed. Joel Porte (Cambridge: Harvard University Press, 1982), 347.

Chapter 1. "I" and "You" in the American Renaissance

1. Quoted by Richard Bridgman, *Dark Thoreau* (Lincoln: University of Nebraska Press, 1982), 284–285. See Gay Wilson Allen, *Waldo Emerson: A Biography* (New York: Viking, 1981), vii–viii. Richard Lebeaux, "Identity Crisis and Beyond: Eriksonian Perspectives on the pre-Walden and post-Walden Thoreau," in *Thoreau's Psychology: Eight Essays*, ed. Raymond D. Gozzi (Lanham, Md.: University Press of America, 1983). Justin Kaplan, *Walt Whitman: A Life* (New York: Simon and Schuster, 1980), 198–201. Both Kaplan and Paul Zweig, in *Walt Whitman: The Making of the Poet* (New York: Basic, 1984), connect the genesis of *Leaves of Grass* and the assumption of the name "Walt" to Whitman's complicated relationship with his father, who died the week *Leaves* was published.

2. Edwin Haviland Miller, *Melville* (New York: George Braziller, 1975), 65; Randall Stewart, *Nathaniel Hawthorne: A Biography* (New Haven: Yale University Press, 1948), 1.

3. Stephen Greenblatt, *Renaissance Self-Fashioning: From More to Shakespeare* (Chicago: University of Chicago Press, 1980), emphasizes self-fashioning as a reciprocal, contradictory language process "at the point of encounter between an authority and an alien" (9). His chapter on Thomas Wyatt and manhood is especially relevant, esp. 154–156, 160, on dominance, passivity, and doubleness.

4. F. O. Matthiessen, *American Renaissance: Art and Expression in the Age of Emerson and Whitman* (London: Oxford University Press, 1941). As Kermit Vanderbilt recounts in *American Literature and the Academy: The Roots, Growth, and Maturity of a Profession* (Philadelphia: University of Pennsylvania Press, 1986), 471–480, Matthiessen's canon-making and now canonized book had a tortuous and difficult beginning. Solicited by Norton in 1929, the book was rejected a decade later by Norton and Houghton Mifflin; Oxford accepted it only if Matthiessen would pay for one third of the publication costs, about $1,000. Norton's letter of solicitation invited Matthiessen to write a literary history "from the new social and historical angle," since "American literature has become a stepchild of the English Literature Departments" (471). Note the lack of a capital letter for American literature. At one point, during his late 1930s leave to finish the book, Matthiessen plunged into a deep depression, prefiguring his later suicide. Harry Levin suggested the title (478).

5. *Emerson in His Journals*, ed. Joel Porte (Cambridge: Harvard University Press, 1982), 391; William Charvat, *The Profession of Authorship in America, 1800–1870: The Papers of William Charvat*, ed. Matthew Bruccoli (Columbus: Ohio State University Press, 1968), 241. According to Charvat, *The Scarlet Letter* sold 10,800 copies in its first five years, 25,200 in its first twenty. *Moby Dick* sold only 2,500 copies in its first five years, and only 465 more in its first 20. On Emerson and *Uncle Tom's Cabin*, see Matthiessen, *American Renaissance*, 67. Donald E. Pease, "Melville and Cultural Persuasion," in *Ideology and Classic American Literature*, ed. Sacvan Bercovitch and Myra Jehlen (Cambridge: Cambridge University Press, 1986), 384–417, argues that Matthiessen's book helped to establish a "Cold War" reading of *Moby Dick* in which Ishmael's freedom survives Ahab's totalitarianism.

6. Wright quoted by Celia Morris Eckhardt, *Fanny Wright: Rebel in America* (Cambridge: Harvard University Press, 1984), 172; Alexis de Tocqueville, *Democracy in America*, ed. Phillips Bradley (New York: Vintage, 1945; 1st pub. 1840), 2:219. See also various selections in *Ideology and Power in the Age of Jackson*, ed. Edwin C. Rozwenc (New York: New York University Press, 1964), e.g., Michel Chevalier, 27–28; George Hooker Colton, 48–52; and Francis J. Grund, 257–261. A fine study emphasizing the middle-class roots of the American work ethic is Daniel T. Rodgers, *The Work Ethic in Industrial America, 1850–1920* (Chicago: University of Chicago Press, 1978).

7. Longfellow's speech is quoted in James R. Mellow, *Nathaniel Hawthorne in His Times*

(Boston: Houghton Mifflin, 1980), 34–35. Emerson records Wordsworth's observation in his journal for August 28, 1833, *Emerson in His Journals*, 113–114. Both Charvat, *Profession of Authorship*, and Michael Davitt Bell, *The Development of American Romance: The Sacrifice of Relation* (Chicago: University of Chicago Press, 1980), emphasize the social deviance of the romancer's role.

8. *Emerson in His Journals*, 369; Margaret Fuller, "American Literature, Its Position in the Present Time, and Prospects for the Future," 1846, reprinted in *Margaret Fuller: American Romantic* ..., ed. Perry Miller (Garden City, N.Y.: Anchor Books, 1963), 245. For a comprehensive account of the New England transcendentalists as social reformers, see Anne C. Rose, *Transcendentalism as a Social Movement, 1830–1850* (New Haven: Yale University Press, 1981). Rose tries to rescue transcendentalists from charges of being too apolitical by emphasizing both their social perceptiveness and their examples of moral integrity. But their principled opposition to getting organized remains a key problem.

9. Channing quoted in Bell Gale Chevigny, *The Woman and the Myth: Margaret Fuller's Life and Writings* (Old Westbury, N.Y.: Feminist Press, 1976), 89; *The Letters of Margaret Fuller*, ed. Robert N. Hudspeth (Ithaca: Cornell University Press, 1984), 3:141–142. See also Annette Kolodny's chapter on Fuller in *The Land before Her: Fantasy and Experience of the American Frontiers, 1630–1860* (Chapel Hill: University of North Carolina Press, 1984), 112–130, esp. 124–129 on Fuller's sense of male exploitation on the frontier.

10. Sarah Josepha Hale, *Northwood, or Life North and South* ... (New York, 1852; 1st pub. 1827), quoted by William R. Taylor, *Cavalier and Yankee: The Old South and American National Character* (Garden City, N.Y.: Anchor, 1963), 111. The governor of Michigan is quoted by Julie A. Matthaei, *An Economic History of Women in America: Women's Work, the Sexual Division of Labor, and the Development of Capitalism* (New York: Schocken, 1982), 104.

11. *Emerson in His Journals*, 368, 412; "Worship" in *The Conduct of Life* (New York: A. L. Burt, n.d.), 178, 188, 212, 206.

12. Charvat, *Profession of Authorship*, esp. ch. 2; Robert A. Ferguson, *Law and Letters in American Culture* (Cambridge: Harvard University Press, 1984), 279–280; Lawrence Buell, *New England Literary Culture: From Revolution through Renaissance* (Cambridge: Cambridge University Press, 1986), 429–430 (citing several critics on "authorship and symbolic femininity"), also 53–54 on women as producers and consumers while men consolidated the power of canon formation.

13. James Fenimore Cooper, *Notions of the Americans*, chaps. 23, 24 (1828), accessibly excerpted in *The Norton Anthology of American Literature*, 2d ed., ed. Nina Baym et al. (New York: Norton, 1985), 1:764–766, 769, 773; Matthiessen cites Hawthorne, *American Renaissance*, 225; Tocqueville, *Democracy in America*, 1:273, 275 ("freedom of opinion does not exist in America" because of "the perpetual utterance of self-applause" by the tyrannical majority and the consequent ostracism forced on those who deviate from the norms). On parallel problems faced by American artists, see Neil Harris, *The Artist in American Society: The Formative Years, 1790–1860*, 2d ed. (Chicago: University of Chicago Press, 1982). Harris's argument (xi–xii) that artists used conceptual abstractions in sculpture "or the neutrality of landscape in painting" as "refuge for the dissenting yet dependent creator" (xii) has many parallels with Michael Davitt Bell's sense of how writers used the genre of Romance. See also his discussion of transcendentalism, 172–186.

14. *The Letters of Herman Melville*, ed. Merrell R. Davis and William H. Gilman (New Haven: Yale University Press, 1960), 128, 134. Throughout my book *Moby Dick* will appear with no hyphen, except when I cite or quote the work of critics who use the hyphen. See the first note to chapter 10.

15. Bell, *Development of American Romance*, 35. For a study of antibusiness bias in American literature, see Emily Stipes Watts, *The Businessman in American Literature* (Athens: University of Georgia Press, 1982). She also emphasizes the lack of institutions for

supporting fine arts (27–30).

16. Hawthorne to William D. Ticknor (January 19, 1855), *The Centenary Edition of the Works of Nathaniel Hawthorne: The Letters, 1853–1856*, vol. 17, ed. Thomas Woodson et al. (n.p.: Ohio State University Press, 1987), 304. David S. Reynolds usefully corrects misperceptions about the rise of women writers; only between 1784 and 1810 did women writers come close to parity with men (41 percent to 44, the rest being issued anonymously). For 1830–1860 the proportion of female-authored volumes fell to 23 percent while male-authored volumes rose to 57 percent. *Beneath the American Renaissance: The Subversive Imagination in the Age of Emerson and Melville* (New York: Knopf, 1988), 338.

For a useful review of the scholarly controversies concerning popular women's literature, see Mary Kelley, *Private Woman, Public Stage: Literary Domesticity in Nineteenth-Century America* (New York: Oxford University Press, 1984), 345–347. In *Novels, Readers, and Reviewers: Responses to Fiction in Antebellum America* (Ithaca: Cornell University Press, 1984), Nina Baym stresses the function of women's literature as a mode of social control (e.g., 53–54, 98–100, 170–171, 257–258). Baym also makes various acerbic remarks about professors who like complexity and hostility rather than pleasure and geniality in their reading (e.g., 54, 194–195, 247). Jane Tompkins argues that Hawthorne's canonization reflects the politics of a cultural elite from the start. See her *Sensational Designs: The Cultural Work of American Fiction, 1790–1860* (New York: Oxford University Press, 1985), 3–39. On the politics of canonization, see also the essays by Jane Tompkins, Jonathan Arac, and Donald E. Pease in *The American Renaissance Reconsidered*, ed. Walter Benn Michaels and Donald E. Pease (Baltimore: Johns Hopkins University Press, 1985). Arac's essay focuses on Matthiessen.

17. Walter Benn Michaels, "*Walden*'s False Bottoms," *Glyph*, 1 (1977), 132–149. Michaels argues that *Walden*'s contradictions necessarily make readers feel "wretched" and "nervous," because they aim at a "literary anarchy" that breaks down any dependence on authority.

18. Melville, "Hawthorne and His Mosses" (1850), reprinted in the Norton Critical Edition of *Moby-Dick*, ed. Harrison Hayford and Hershel Parker (New York: Norton, 1967), 549. All citations of *Moby Dick* are to this edition.

19. Bell, *Development of American Romance*, passim. See also Edwin M. Eigner, *The Metaphysical Novel in England and America: Dickens, Bulwer, Melville, and Hawthorne* (Berkeley: University of California Press, 1978). Eigner is especially useful on narrative uses of hostility to the reader. Michael T. Gilmore, *American Romanticism and the Marketplace* (Chicago: University of Chicago Press, 1985), emphasizes the opposition of truth to the marketplace in American Renaissance writings, but with a more social than metaphysical sense of how marketplace issues continually return.

20. For contemporary responses to Hawthorne and Melville, see *Hawthorne: The Critical Heritage*, ed. J. Donald Crowley (New York: Barnes & Noble, 1970); *The Recognition of Herman Melville: Selected Criticisms since 1846*, ed. Hershel Parker (Ann Arbor: University of Michigan Press, 1967); also Hugh W. Hetherington, *Melville's Reviewers: British and American, 1846–1891* (Chapel Hill: University of North Carolina Press, 1961).

21. Nina Baym, "Melodramas of Beset Manhood: How Theories of American Fiction Exclude Women Authors," *American Quarterly*, 33 (Summer 1981), 123–139. Baym reviews the major male paradigms, here associated with R. W. B. Lewis, Richard Poirier, Quentin Anderson, Sacvan Bercovitch, Michael Davitt Bell, and Leslie Fiedler, respectively.

22. These female paradigms are associated with Barbara Welter, Ann Douglas, Kathryn Kish Sklar, Carroll Smith-Rosenberg, and Nina Baym, though with much overlap and interplay. See again Kelley's review of the literature, *Private Woman, Public Stage*, 345–347. The best study of women's culture in the context of bourgeois capitalism focuses not on the United States but on northern France: Bonnie G. Smith, *Ladies of the Leisure*

Class: The Bourgeoises of Northern France in the Nineteenth Century (Princeton: Princeton University Press, 1981). Another powerful study is Barbara Leslie Epstein, *The Politics of Domesticity: Women, Evangelism, and Temperance in Nineteenth-Century America* (Middletown, Conn.: Wesleyan University Press, 1981). On the other side, two fine studies emphasizing women's uses of religion for social empowerment are Nancy Cott, *The Bonds of Womanhood: "Woman's Sphere" in New England, 1780–1835* (New Haven: Yale University Press, 1977); and Mary Ryan, *Cradle of the Middle Class: The Family in Oneida County, New York, 1790–1865* (Cambridge: Cambridge University Press, 1981). A recent social history by Nancy A. Hewitt discriminates among women reformers along class lines. See Hewitt, *Women's Activism and Social Change: Rochester, New York, 1822–1872* (Ithaca: Cornell University Press, 1984).

23. On Howells and James as "sissies," see Alfred Habegger, *Gender, Fantasy, and Realism in American Literature* (New York: Columbia University Press, 1982). The best study of the uncertainty of the (male) American writer's role and audience from the 1830s through the American Renaissance is still William Charvat's *Profession of Authorship*; he emphasizes changing class dynamics. See also Charvat's *Literary Publishing in America, 1790–1850* (Philadelphia: University of Pennsylvania Press, 1959).

24. See W. Daniel Wilson, "Readers in Texts," *PMLA*, 96 (October 1981), 848–863, for a useful summary and codification of reader-response terms, especially fictive, characterized, and implied readers.

25. Emerson's lines are from the first draft of what becomes "Merlin I"; see his *Journals and Miscellaneous Notebooks*, ed. Ralph. H. Orth and Alfred R. Ferguson (Cambridge: Harvard University Press, 1971), 9:168. I am indebted for this reference to Albert J. von Frank.

26. Tompkins, *Sensational Designs*, 122–146. See also Alice C. Crozier, *The Novels of Harriet Beecher Stowe* (New York: Oxford University Press, 1969), 3–33, for an earlier emphasis on Stowe's evangelical frame. My text of *Uncle Tom's Cabin or, Life Among the Lowly* is the Harper Classic edition (New York: Harper & Row, 1965), 131–134.

27. Stowe's farewell to her reader is quoted by Eric J. Sundquist in his Introduction to *New Essays on "Uncle Tom's Cabin,"* ed. Sundquist (Cambridge: Cambridge University Press, 1986), 10. Robyn Warhol has sharply contrasted female narrative techniques of engagement with male techniques of distancing; see "Toward a Theory of the Engaging Narrator: Earnest Interventions in Gaskell, Stowe, and Eliot," *PMLA* 101 (October 1986), 811–818, and her responses in the March and May 1987 *PMLA* Forums.

28. Thoreau, *Walden and Civil Disobedience*, Norton Critical Edition, ed. Owen Thomas (New York: Norton, 1966), 1–5.

29. Sacvan Bercovitch, "Horologicals to Chronometricals: The Rhetoric of the Jeremiad," *Literary Monographs*, 3, ed. Eric Rothstein (Madison: University of Wisconsin Press, 1970), 122. J. Lyndon Shanley, *The Making of "Walden"* ... (Chicago: University of Chicago Press, 1957), analyzes Thoreau's extensive revisions, though he doesn't discuss the epigraph.

30. On Thoreau's excremental wordplay, see especially Michael West, "Scatology and Eschatology: The Heroic Dimensions of Thoreau's Wordplay," *PMLA*, 89 (October 1974), 1043–1064. Richard Poirier connects Thoreau's "excremental vision" to issues of relinquishment and possession as well as self-transformation; see *A World Elsewhere: The Place of Style in American Literature* (New York: Oxford University Press, 1966), 88–90.

31. Gilmore, *American Romanticism and the Marketplace*, 35–51, quotations 35, 37. Robert Weisbuch acerbically criticizes "Higher Laws" for disrupting Thoreau's exemplary, atemporal American persona with a "neurotic," "trivial and tortured" personal self. *Atlantic Double-Cross: American Literature and British Influence in the Age of Emerson* (Chicago: University of Chicago Press, 1986), 238–240. In "Thoreau's Enterprise of Self-Culture in a Culture of Enterprise," *American Quarterly*, 39 (Summer 1987), 231–251, Leonard N. Neufeldt emphasizes Thoreau's quarrel with the pressures of business enterprise. He

reads *Walden* as an attempt to redefine *business, commerce, profit,* and other such words in terms of literary vocation and self-culture rather than business.

32. Here I implicitly take issue with Carolyn Porter's emphasis on reification in *Seeing and Being: The Plight of the Participant Observer in Emerson, James, Adams, and Faulkner* (Middletown, Conn.: Wesleyan University Press, 1981). Gilmore's emphasis on humiliation seems to me closer to Thoreau's hidden fears. Richard Lebeaux emphasizes Thoreau's "quiet desperation" in response to his family dynamics, especially to his weak and financially troubled father (*Young Man Thoreau* [Amherst: University of Massachusetts Press, 1977], 4, 29–58). In a spirited interchange with Raymond D. Gozzi, Lebeaux argues that Thoreau wanted to challenge and surpass his father, whereas Gozzi takes a more orthodox Freudian position on Thoreau's lifelong Oedipal conflicts. (See *Thoreau's Psychology,* ed. Gozzi, 26–27 and passim.) Gozzi's discussion of Thoreau's father notes that Henry felt "unmanned," as he wrote in his journals, by shops and other town associations connected with his father (3–4). In *Young Man Thoreau,* Lebeaux has a superb discussion of the fire Thoreau set off in the woods in April 1844, the social humiliation that prompted his retreat to Walden Pond (209–213, quotations 209–210). Lebeaux suggests that at some unconscious level Thoreau wanted to start the fire, as a contradictory expression of his hostility toward the townspeople and also as self-punishment (212).

33. Eliot's review is quoted in the Norton Critical Edition of *Walden,* 265.

34. Emerson, "Thoreau," *Selections from Ralph Waldo Emerson,* ed. Stephen E. Whicher (Boston: Houghton Mifflin, 1957), 381.

35. D. H. Lawrence, *Studies in Classic American Literature* (Garden City, N.Y.: Doubleday, 1951; 1st pub. 1923), 33.

36. *Moby-Dick,* 139–140, 192–193. I am indebted to Sam Kimball for alerting me to the masturbatory aspects of "The Mast-head." See Robert K. Martin, *Hero, Captain, and Stranger: Male Friendship, Social Critique, and Literary Form in the Sea Novels of Herman Melville* (Chapel Hill: University of North Carolina Press, 1986), 74–75. Here I disagree with Robert Weisbuch's *Atlantic Double-Cross,* which argues that Ishmael begins "so stuffed with self-contradictions as to appear ultimately bogus," then relaxes in his contradictions, transforming "aggression and death into love and buoyed life" (255).

37. Lawrence, *Studies in Classic American Literature,* 179. Here I disagree with Donald Pease, among others who argue that Whitman's voice is more fluidly incorporative or shamanistic. In "Blake, Crane, Whitman, and Modernism: A Poetics of Pure Possibility," *PMLA,* 96 (January 1981), 64–85, Pease finds the "you" of "Song of Myself" to be not a separable reader but the beginning of a process transforming the ego of poet and reader into an "interlocutive process" or a "confluence of self and other." In *Visionary Compacts: American Renaissance Writings in Cultural Context* (Madison: University of Wisconsin Press, 1987), 108–157, Pease argues that Whitman is trying to recover a common self for the masses (115). I see Whitman's voice as more rhetorically self-conscious of distances.

Various recent critics have been developing Roger Asselineau's original insight that Whitman seeks to integrate his country's divisive politics with his voice. See, for instance, Herbert J. Levine's essay in *American Literature,* 59 (December 1987), 570–589, "Union and Disunion in 'Song of Myself,' " which emphasizes Whitman's suppression of anger at slaveholders, capitalists, and politicians to create a serene self embodying the Union. Levine teases out the tensions in that self-representation, especially Whitman's use of synecdoche and metonymy for artisanal and erotic union, while metaphor struggles with differences. In *The Ecstatic Whitman: Literary Shamanism and the Crisis of the Union* (Columbus: Ohio State University Press, 1986), 67–94, George B. Hutchinson argues that Whitman's "shamanic" voice in "Song of Myself" seeks to revitalize and cure the nation by creating a truly democratic audience. Urbanization and capitalism as well as the Civil War are the impending national dangers (10–11). As C. Carroll Hollis argues, Whitman may have wanted to sound like a shaman or prophet, but he doesn't subordinate himself as such a voice requires. See Hollis, *Language and Style in "Leaves of Grass"* (Baton Rouge: Louisiana State University Press, 1983), 79–81, 104–105.

38. Emerson quoted in Gay Wilson Allen, *Waldo Emerson* (New York: Viking, 1981), 580.

39. Albert Gelpi, *The Tenth Muse: The Psyche of the American Poet* (Cambridge: Harvard University Press, 1975); Sandra M. Gilbert, "The American Sexual Poetics of Walt Whitman and Emily Dickinson," in *Reconstructing American Literary History*, ed. Sacvan Bercovitch (Cambridge: Harvard University Press, 1986), 123–154, esp. 129–130 and 144–148 on Whitman's use of "male" genres to empower his voice. As several critics have noted, the first edition of *Leaves of Grass* all but plagiarizes the cover design from Fanny Fern's best seller, *Fern Leaves from Fanny's Portfolio* (1854); see Gilbert, 136, and Reynolds, *Beneath the American Renaissance*, 403.

40. Jeffrey Steele, *The Representation of the Self in the American Renaissance* (Chapel Hill: University of North Carolina Press, 1987), 67–99. Steele emphasizes a tension between phallocentric self-expansion and "threatened dismemberment" not only in "Song of Myself" but in Whitman's poetic career (93). Reynolds, *Beneath the American Renaissance*, 509–516. Reynolds's similar argument for Ishmael as a b'hoy (463–466, 543–544) seems more forced. See also Habegger, *Gender, Fantasy, and Realism*, 124–125, linking Whitman's persona to the Rip Van Winkle tradition of "easygoing" male vernacular opposing refined and refining ladies.

41. I am using the 1855 edition, ed. Malcolm Cowley (New York: Viking, 1959). Whitman added "and sing myself" to the first line much later, weakening it considerably by emphasizing his voice's literary connection to epic poetic traditions (iambic pentameter, Vergil's "Arms and the man I sing," Homer's "Sing, Muse") at the expense of the first version's direct challenge to the reader. For a similar critique, see Paul Zweig, *Walt Whitman: The Making of the Poet* (New York: Basic, 1984), 167–168. Gilbert's essay argues that both Whitman and Dickinson resisted gender conventions as well as literary conventions by writing "not-poetry" rather than poetry as their age defined it (128–130).

Ivan Marki, *The Trial of the Poet: An Interpretation of the First Edition of "Leaves of Grass"* (New York: Columbia University Press, 1976), celebrates the first edition by reading it through the opaque lens of Whitman's preface. Marki's study minimizes the poet's relation to "you" except in fear or insecurity. He sees the poem as an interior monologue, "by a man profoundly alone" (115), who "turns 'outward,' to his audience, only as a last resort in moments of greatest insecurity and crisis" (137). In *The Ecstatic Whitman*, Hutchinson, too, argues that Whitman's visionary ecstasies take him away from consciousness of his audience in "Song of Myself." He reads all of sections 26–38 as a prolonged shamanistic ecstasy, for instance, where I read section 32 in particular (on animals) as a blunt mockery of those "demented with the mania of owning things" (82–85).

Hollis, in *Language and Style*, discusses at length Whitman's extraordinary stress on "you" throughout the years 1855–1860 (88–123) noting that Whitman's later revisions weaken his "forceful directness" and eliminate "the challenging question or riddle to push the audience to self-examination" (113). He suggests that readers may well feel talked down to when Whitman paradoxically tries to bring us toward democratic selves with his "somewhat autocratic attitude" (100). In *Atlantic Double-Cross*, Weisbuch deftly contrasts Whitman with Wordsworth, whose *Prelude* establishes an enclave of private friendship. Whitman's "you" functions simultaneously as soapbox oratory "and the reader's own inner voice" (231).

42. David Cavitch reads the ending quite differently. In *My Soul and I: The Inner Life of Walt Whitman* (Boston: Beacon, 1985), 70, he argues that the last lines fulfill the promise of the opening lines, "what I assume you shall assume," by both subordinating the reader and reversing "his preemption of other peoples' identities through most of the poem." Now "he surprises us in the end by making us absorb him." For a sophisticated reading

of Whitman's "I" as two speakers, "one timid, gentle, frequently disconsolate, the other large, all-inclusive, affirming," in relation to contemporary politics, see Mitchell Robert Breitwieser, "Who Speaks in Whitman's Poems?" in *The American Renaissance: New Dimensions*, ed. Harry R. Garvin and Peter C. Carafiol (Lewisburg, Pa.: Bucknell University Press, 1983), 121–143.

43. Pollak, "Whitman and Dickinson," in *American Literary Scholarship: An Annual/1986*, ed. David J. Nordloh (Durham: Duke University Press, 1988), 71; Cavitch, *My Soul and I*, 83; Zweig, *Walt Whitman*, 36–39, also 128–143, where Zweig connects Whitman's ambivalent rivalry with his father to the poem's implicit class warfare against polite literature. Rejecting a role as man of letters, Whitman returns to working-class roots and celebrates his father's fading artisan world, while in life he took over his father's role in the family, writing *Leaves of Grass* while his father was dying in another room. On Whitman's complicated identification with his seemingly placid but perhaps narcissistic mother, see especially Cavitch, 8–10 and passim; also Kaplan, *Walt Whitman*, 61–63, 85, and 15: "The fictive hero of Whitman's poetry was the sexual athlete and swaggerer, 'one of the roughs,' not Whitman himself, 'a great tender mother-man.' " Cavitch emphasizes Whitman's vulnerability to his mother's "threatening self-centeredness" (e.g., 96).

An excellent recent study explicating Whitman's poetry in the context of the ambivalent resistance of urban artisans to industrial capitalism is M. Wynn Thomas, *The Lunar Light of Whitman's Poetry* (Cambridge: Harvard University Press, 1987). Thomas discusses Whitman's use of "you" for complex social criticism and illuminates Whitman's "I" as an idealized adversarial transformation of possessive individualism, partly by his "perfect imitation" of it in a noncompetitive mode (40). Thomas also beautifully highlights Whitman's techniques for frustrating possessive readers.

44. Leslie Fiedler, *Love and Death in the American Novel*, rev. ed. (New York: Stein and Day, 1966). On homosexual desires in Melville, see Edwin Haviland Miller, *Melville* (New York: George Braziller, 1975); in Thoreau, see *Thoreau's Psychology: Eight Essays*, ed. Raymond D. Gozzi (Lanham, Md.: University Press of America, 1983), esp. Walter Harding's fine essay "Thoreau and Eros," on Thoreau's sublimation of guilt for latent homosexuality (145–157). On Whitman's reception by English homosexuals, see Eve Kosofsky Sedgwick, *Between Men: English Literature and Male Homosocial Desire* (New York: Columbia University Press, 1985), 201–217.

45. Hawthorne, *The Scarlet Letter*, second Norton Critical Edition, ed. Sculley Bradley et al. (New York: Norton, 1978), 27, 20–21, 22. Further references are included in my text.

46. John T. Irwin, *American Hieroglyphics: The Symbol of the Egyptian Hieroglyphics in the American Renaissance* (New Haven: Yale University Press, 1980), 269–284 on "The Custom-House." Irwin interprets Hawthorne's account of his beheading and his change from patriarchal to feminine sensibility as a self-castration that is an ironic revenge against his Puritan fathers.

47. Stephen Nissenbaum, "The Firing of Nathaniel Hawthorne," *Essex Institute Historical Collections*, 114 (1978), 57–86.

48. Sandra Sawyer, in a Spring 1986 class at the University of Florida.

49. Joel Porte, *Representative Man: Ralph Waldo Emerson in His Time* (New York: Oxford University Press, 1979), 75–78.

50. For a subtle account of the risks and contradictions in Emerson's tone of voice at the start of "Nature," see Richard Poirier, *A World Elsewhere*, 60–70. Poirier focuses on issues of possession and relinquishment. Carolyn Porter, in *Seeing and Being*, 104–107, emphasizes the self-beheading alienation intrinsic to the transparent eyeball image.

51. On Emerson's skating, see Rose Hawthorne Lathrop, *Memories of Hawthorne* (Boston: Houghton Mifflin, 1897), 53. The reminiscence, by one of Hawthorne's daughters, implies a good deal about the literary as well as physical styles of the three men: "One

afternoon, Mr. Emerson and Mr. Thoreau went with [Hawthorne] down the river. Henry Thoreau is an experienced skater, and was figuring dithyrambic dances and Bacchic leaps on the ice—very remarkable, but very ugly, methought. Next him followed Mr. Hawthorne who, wrapped in his cloak, moved like a self-impelled Greek statue, stately and grave. Mr. Emerson closed the line, evidently too weary to hold himself erect, pitching headforemost, half lying on the air." Longfellow's remark is quoted by Larzer Ziff, *Literary Democracy: The Declaration of Cultural Independence in America* (New York: Viking, 1981), 56.

52. Emerson, *Journals and Miscellaneous Notebooks of Ralph Waldo Emerson*, ed. William H. Gilman et al. (Cambridge: Harvard University Press, 1965), 5:391. Cf. *JMN* 5:336–337, also Thoreau's account of his self-doubling in the midst of his chapter "Solitude": "With thinking we may be beside ourselves in a sane sense. . . . [I] am sensible of a certain doubleness by which I can stand as remote from myself as from another. However intense my experience, I am conscious of the presence and criticism of a part of me, which, as it were, is not a part of me, but spectator, sharing no experience, but taking note of it; and that is no more I than it is you. When the play, it may be the tragedy, of life is over, the spectator goes his way. It was a kind of fiction, a work of the imagination only, so far as he was concerned. This doubleness may easily make us poor neighbors and friends sometimes." *Walden*, 90–91.

53. Gilmore, *American Romanticism and the Marketplace*, 35–51; Walter Benn Michaels, "Romance and Real Estate," *Raritan*, 2 (Winter 1983), 66–87, also in *The American Renaissance Reconsidered*, 156–182. See also Brook Thomas's fine recent study *Cross-Examinations of Law and Literature: Cooper, Hawthorne, Stowe, and Melville* (Cambridge: Cambridge University Press, 1987).

Chapter 2. The Politics of Emerson's Man-Making Words

1. Jonathan Bishop, *Emerson on the Soul* (Cambridge, Mass.: Harvard University Press, 1964), 6; James Russell Lowell, "Emerson the Lecturer" (1871), reprinted in *The Recognition of Ralph Waldo Emerson: Selected Criticism since 1837*, ed. Milton R. Konvitz, (Ann Arbor: University of Michigan Press, 1972), 45; Emerson to Thomas Carlyle, in *The Correspondence of Emerson and Carlyle*, ed. Joseph Slater (New York: Columbia University Press, 1964), 185. Of the readers who have helped me with this chapter, I am especially indebted to Frederick Crews, Tanya Gregory, T. Walter Herbert, Jr., and Cecil Jones.

2. Eric Cheyfitz, *The Trans-Parent: Sexual Politics in the Language of Emerson* (Baltimore: Johns Hopkins University Press, 1981), 10. See also a fine review of the Library of America edition of Emerson by Paul Berman in *Nation*, November 19, 1983, 513, 515.

3. See Edgar Branch's essay, " 'The Babes in the Wood': Artemus Ward's 'Double Health' to Mark Twain," *PMLA*, 93 (1978), 968–970. On Western responses, see Bishop, *Emerson on the Soul*, 154–155; also Mary Kupiec Cayton, "The Making of an American Prophet: Emerson, His Audiences, and the Rise of the Culture Industry in Nineteenth-century America," *American Historical Review*, 92 (June 1987), 597–620.

4. Bishop observes that Emerson's special audience consisted of young men in search of an identity at variance with social expectations. See *Emerson on the Soul*, 146–150.

5. Cheyfitz, *The Trans-Parent*, 84, also 83–96. Larzer Ziff, *Literary Democracy: The Declaration of Cultural Independence in America* (New York: Viking, 1981), discusses writers and marketplace dynamics, e.g., 56–59.

6. Emerson, "Historic Notes of Life and Letters in New England," *Works*, ed. Edward W. Emerson (Cambridge, Mass.: Riverside Press, 1883), 10:311. I'm indebted to Evelyn Barish for this reference, and to her essay, "The Moonless Night: Emerson's Crisis of

Health, 1825–1827," in *Emerson Centenary Essays*, ed. Joel Myerson (Carbondale: Southern Illinois University Press, 1982), 1–16.

7. Joel Porte explores Emerson's "spermatic" eloquence; see *Representative Man: Ralph Waldo Emerson in His Time* (New York: Oxford University Press, 1979), esp. 215–217, 233–247, 276–279. For the journal entry, see *Emerson in His Journals*, ed. Joel Porte (Cambridge: Harvard University Press, 1982), 271. Further references from this volume will be included in the text as *EJ*. *The Journals and Miscellaneous Notebooks of Ralph Waldo Emerson*, ed. William H. Gilman et al. (Cambridge: Harvard University Press, 1960–), will be noted as *JMN*.

8. The quotations are from *The Collected Works of Ralph Waldo Emerson*, ed. Robert E. Spiller et al. (Cambridge: Harvard University Press, 1960–): *CW* 1:53, 64, 53, 65, 2:29, 43, 41, 50, 1:80, 88, 92.

9. John Jay Chapman, "Emerson," in *The Selected Writings of John Jay Chapman*, ed. Jacques Barzun (New York: Farrar, Straus, and Cudahy, 1957), 166, 201–202, reprinted in Konvitz, *Recognition*, 110, 116–117.

10. See Harold Bloom, *Agon: Towards a Theory of Revisionism* (New York: Oxford University Press, 1982), and his Introduction to *Ralph Waldo Emerson*, ed. Bloom (New York: Chelsea House, 1985), 1–11; also Richard Poirier, "Writing Off the Self," *Raritan*, 1 (Summer 1981), 106–133; and Cheyfitz, *The Trans-Parent*, passim.

11. James quoted by C. Hartley Grattan, *The Three Jameses: A Family of Minds* (New York: New York University Press, 1963), 43–44: "I used to lock myself up with him in his bedroom, swearing that before the door was opened I would arrive at the secret of his immense superiority. . . . It turned out that any average old dame in a horse-car would have satisfied my intellectual rapacity just as well as Emerson."

12. Bishop, *Emerson on the Soul*, 153–154, 44–45. For John Morley's response, see Konvitz, *Recognition*, 77. The elder James's letter is reprinted in Ralph Barton Perry, *The Thought and Character of William James* (Boston: Little, Brown, 1935), 1:51. John McAleer, in *Ralph Waldo Emerson: Days of Encounter* (Boston: Little, Brown, 1984), cites a January 1850 entry in Bronson Alcott's diary: "The best of Emerson's intellect comes out of its feminine traits, and were he not as stimulating to me as a woman and as racy, I should not care to see him and to know him intimately nor often" (21–22).

It's striking that women such as Annie Fields and Virginia Woolf, while experiencing extraordinarily strong responses to Emerson's voice and mind, don't indicate any associations to conventional femininity. Field's response can be found in *Ralph Waldo Emerson: A Profile*, ed. Carl Bode (New York: Hill and Wang, 1968), esp. 78 and 86; Woolf reviewed Emerson in the *Times Literary Supplement*, March 3, 1910, 69–70. I'm indebted for this last reference to Celeste Goodridge.

13. Cheyfitz, *The Trans-Parent*, 103, citing James Elliot Cabot's observation that people were uncomfortable with Emerson's public speaking because "people like a preacher who has made up his mind." James McIntosh notes that Emerson's model of the mind resembles a New England town meeting; see "Emerson's Unmoored Self," *Yale Review*, 65 (1976), 238. Emerson did have a brief quasi-political career, serving on the Concord school board in the mid-1830s.

14. Barbara Packer, *Emerson's Fall: A New Interpretation of the Major Essays* (New York: Continuum, 1982), 19–20, 122. See also Bishop, *Emerson on the Soul*, 151–157, on Emerson's modesty and self-annihilation in the discovery of common powers, also 130–142, on the aggressive-yielding doubleness in his tone. In *A World Elsewhere: The Place of Style in American Literature* (New York: Oxford University Press, 1966), 68–69, Richard Poirier makes similar observations about the tensions between relinquishment and possession in Emerson's voice.

15. *EJ* 125–126 (July 1834). In *Seeing and Being: The Plight of the Participant-Observer*

in Emerson, James, Adams, Faulkner (Middletown, Conn.: Wesleyan University Press, 1981), Carolyn Porter extensively discusses Emerson from a Marxist point of view, in the context of reification. Her sense of his resistance to and replication of bourgeois ideology has many parallels with my argument here; see 38–39, 58–61, 91–118. It seems to me, however, that class and gender relations are more fundamental than man-thing relations.

16. Packer, *Emerson's Fall*, 96; Porte, *Representative Man*, 257–266, 292, though Porte tends to shift his discussion to sexual issues. See also Ziff, *Literary Democracy*, 15–30.

17. *EJ* 350 (Nov. 1845–March 1846). Stephen Whicher rightly uses this entry as a coda for Emerson's prose in his influential textbook *Selections from Ralph Waldo Emerson: An Organic Anthology* (Boston: Houghton Mifflin, 1957), 406.

18. I'm indebted to Kathleen O'Connell for calling this passage to my attention. See Michael T. Gilmore's account of Emerson's ambivalent and changing responses to the new capitalist market, "Emerson and the Persistence of the Commodity," in *Emerson: Prospect and Retrospect*, ed. Joel Porte (Cambridge: Harvard University Press, 1982), 65–84; also Carolyn Porter's *Seeing and Being*, 58–61.

19. Porte suggests that "The Divinity School Address" uses antinomian language to overthrow a book Emerson's father had written on Anne Hutchinson, while the first paragraph of "Nature" uses hidden biblical allusions to accuse murderous fathers. The paragraph "is laced with more anger than we are normally willing to hear." (76). Later Porte highlights Emerson's account of the severity of his father in forcing the boy into the ocean. "Fear, shame, and anger are thoroughly mixed in this account," Porte concludes, and those feelings abet "a cripping habit of self-consciousness and self-questioning that threatens to paralyze the will" in Emerson's early adult years (156, also 97–104). David Robinson differs from my view in minimizing Emerson's rebellion and stressing Emerson's continuity with his father's ministry. See *Apostle of Culture: Emerson as Preacher and Lecturer* (Philadelphia: University of Pennsylvania Press, 1982), 38–40, 45, 50, 184–185.

20. Gay Wilson Allen, *Waldo Emerson: A Biography* (New York: Viking, 1981), 4, 10, viii, 58.

21. Ibid., 117, 73, 264, 266.

22. On Emerson's diseases, see Cheyfitz, *The Trans-Parent*, 49, 113; and Allen, *Waldo Emerson*, 189–190, for discussions of diarrhea. See also Barish, "The Moonless Night," 1–16.

23. Allen, *Waldo Emerson*, 22.

24. Ibid., 114, also 39.

25. Ibid., 118–119, 22.

26. Cheyfitz, *The Trans-Parent*, 161–163. Gay Wilson Allen is exceptionally hard on Mary Moody Emerson, deploying a tone of patronizing mockery completely absent from his discussion of William's equally crazy demands. He says she had "an overcharged ego" imbued with resentment (18) and that masochism may be the real secret of her "pathological" asceticism. He believes "this frustrated anchorite" hated her body and launched herself into all manner of harsh, unpredictable, and eccentric behavior (20–24). Evelyn Barish has unearthed a strange and revealing early fantasy of Emerson's concerning a witch figure who has some of his aunt's attributes; see Barish, "Emerson and 'The Magician': An Early Prose Fantasy," *American Transcendental Quarterly*, 31 (1976), 13–18, and her expanded discussion in "Emerson and the Angel of Midnight: The Legacy of Mary Moody Emerson," *Mothering the Mind: Twelve Studies of Writers and Their Silent Partners*, ed. Ruth Perry and Martine Watson Brownley (New York: Holmes, 1984), 218–237, which presents the aunt as more of a muse. See also Phyllis Cole, "The Advantage of Loneliness: Mary Moody Emerson's Almanacks, 1802–1855," in *Emerson: Prospect and Retrospect*, 1–32.

27. Allen, *Waldo Emerson*, 4–6.

28. Whicher, *Selections*, 335.

29. Here I differ from John Peacock's sense that Emerson's dialectic is more genuine than mystifying. See his essay "Self-Reliance and Corporate Destiny: Emerson's Dialectic of Culture," *ESQ*, 29 (1983), 59–72. On the conversion of the elite to power as a conventional upper-class fantasy, see Daniel Walker Howe, *The Political Culture of the American Whigs* (Chicago: University of Chicago Press, 1979), 25–32. In *An American Procession* (New York: Knopf, 1984), e.g., 47, Alfred Kazin emphasizes Emerson's concern with power but doesn't probe the issue. Michael Lopez explores romantic ideas of power in "'Transcendental Failure: 'The Palace of Spiritual Power,'" in *Emerson: Prospect and Retrospect*, 121–153.

30. *JMN* 9:17, cited by Leonard Neufeldt in *The House of Emerson* (Lincoln: University of Nebraska Press, 1982), 108. Emerson, who had extravagantly admired the "genius" of Whig senator Daniel Webster, felt bitterly betrayed after Webster endorsed the Fugitive Slave Law in 1850. His anger at the perversion of manly oratory took him toward polemics and anarchy, to the dismay of friends like Longfellow. See McAleer, *Days of Encounter*, 509–513, 521–528; also Chapman, *Selected Writings*, 177; and for a fine comparative analysis of Emerson's and Thoreau's views of Webster, Neufeldt's *House of Emerson*, 101–121. For a thoughtful analysis of Emerson's 1854 attack on Webster, see Gertrude Reif Hughes, *Emerson's Demanding Optimism* (Baton Rouge: Louisiana State University Press, 1984), 117–125.

31. Whicher, *Selections*, 220, 337.

32. Ibid., 316. David Porter has a fine close reading of transformations in "American Scholar," in *Emerson and Literary Change* (Cambridge: Harvard University Press, 1978), 210–214.

33. See, for instance, Mary Ryan's critique of Paul Johnson and Anthony Wallace, *Cradle of the Middle Class: The Family in Oneida County, New York, 1790–1865* (Cambridge: Cambridge University Press, 1981), 103–104. Also see Karen Halttunen, *Confidence Men and Painted Women: A Study of Middle-Class Culture in America, 1830–1870* (New Haven: Yale University Press, 1982), for a cultural study of the impact of economic change at this time. The best study of working-class formation in the United States is Sean Wilentz's *Chants Democratic: New York City and the Rise of the American Working Class, 1788–1850* (New York: Oxford University Press, 1984). See also Paul E. Johnson, *A Shopkeeper's Millennium: Society and Revivals in Rochester, New York, 1815–1837* (New York: Hill and Wang, 1978); Anthony F. C. Wallace, *Rockdale: The Growth of an American Village in the Early Industrial Revolution* (New York: Norton, 1978); Joseph F. Kett, *Rites of Passage: Adolescence in America, 1790 to the Present* (New York: Basic, 1977); Nancy Cott, *The Bonds of Womanhood: 'Woman's Sphere' in New England, 1780–1835* (New Haven: Yale University Press, 1977).

34. Kett, *Rites of Passage*, 107–108, where he discusses character as "an internal gyroscope"; Ryan, *Cradle of the Middle Class*, 153. Ryan juxtaposes the new stereotype of the self-made entrepreneur with the privatized domesticity of the female, 147–155. In *The Bonds of Womanhood*, 20–25, 70–74, Nancy Cott sketches the conditions within which, as she says, "women's self-renunciation was called upon to remedy men's self-alienation" (71). Halttunen's *Confidence Man and Painted Women* emphasizes what she calls the "liminal fluidity" of America's transition from rural to urban experience. Mary Cayton, "Making of an American Prophet," astutely discusses Emerson's appeal to the commercial classes as a representative of culture. In "'Put God in Your Debt': Emerson's Economy of Expenditure," *PMLA* 103 (Jan. 1988), 35–44, Richard A. Grusin intriguingly suggests that Emerson's "gift" of self-reliance is a "potlatch" to "humiliate us" by putting us in his debt (42).

35. Gordon Wood, *The Creation of the American Republic, 1776–1787* (New York: Knopf, 1972), 562. See also Richard Hofstadter, *The American Political Tradition and the Men Who*

Made It (New York: Knopf, 1948), esp. chaps. 1–4. Jonathan Bishop, in *Emerson on the Soul*, notes that "the pleasures of the Emersonian tone are at their best when the speaker fronts the enemy and borrows one or another of his idioms to make his point . . . taking over some part of the businessman's or farmer's world to make a metaphor of it" (134).

36. Bishop, *Emerson on the Soul*, 48, 85. In "Emerson's Unmoored Self," James McIntosh discusses isolation and self-decreation as the other side of "those moods when we think of ourselves as unmoored, abstracted, in a condition of potency" (239).

37. In *The American Narcissus: Individualism and Women in Nineteenth-Century American Fiction* (New Brunswick: Rutgers University Press, 1984), Joyce W. Warren forcefully critiques Emerson's disdain for social relations (23–54). Warren's feminist approach too simply allies Emerson with American individualism and misses the passionate, conflicted intensities in his struggle with manhood. But her analysis of Emerson's relationship with Lidian is very perceptive, and her conclusions parallel mine in many respects. See also Amy Schrager Lang's fine chapter on Emerson's uses of womanhood to complete his manly ideal and save men from the dangers of self-reliance, in *Prophetic Woman: Anne Hutchinson and the Problem of Dissent in the Literature of New England* (Berkeley: University of California Press, 1987), 137–160.

38. Allen, *Waldo Emerson*, 8. "Psychologically, and perhaps subconsciously, Emerson was striving for emotional invulnerability," Allen says later (226–227).

39. See Bishop, 44–45, 181–187, where he sensitively connects Emerson's "teasing" of women to a latent aggressiveness. Chapman, *Selected Writings*, 189–190, connects Emerson's dread of emotion to "the lack of maternal tenderness characteristic of the New England nature." McAleer, in *Days of Encounter*, emphasizes but doesn't explore Emerson's affection for his mother; see 19–27, 536–537.

40. It has by now become a convention, embedded in psychoanalysis and surfacing in movies like *Shoot the Moon*, that rage against mother deprivation voices authentic male feeling. The convention perpetuates male manipulations of anger to keep women in a mothering role that soothes men's self-hatred while supporting solitary ambition. Both depressive and ambitious postures evade interpersonal feelings while nurturing a self born of rivalry and detachment.

41. Emerson, "Philosopher," vol. 9 of *Emerson's Complete Works*, ed. Edward W. Emerson (Boston: Houghton Mifflin, 1883), 314; Erik Ingvar Thurin, *Emerson as Priest of Pan: A Study in the Metaphysics of Sex* (Lawrence: Regents Press of Kansas, 1981), 128–129. Thurin links the poem to Richard Crashaw's "Satan." As Thurin shows, Emerson associated power, heaven, and intellect with the male principle, while seeing woman as more earthbound and relative, associated with tragedy and mortality. Women at best are undeveloped men, whereas male genius embraces womanhood in its androgyny (61–75 and passim). For a complementary analysis see Lang, *Prophetic Woman*, 137–160.

42. *Correspondence of Emerson and Carlyle*, 320; Allen, *Waldo Emerson*, xii.

43. See Porte, *Representative Man*, 195, 185; Whicher, *Freedom and Fate: An Inner Life of Ralph Waldo Emerson* (Philadelphia: University of Pennsylvania Press, 1953), 111–122; Packer, *Emerson's Fall*, 148–179, quotation 150.

44. A May 1843 journal entry gives more bite to the association of woman with devil. "In every woman's conversation & total influence mild or acid lurks the *conventional devil*. They look at your carpet, they look at your cap, at your saltcellar, at your cook & waiting maid, conventionally— to see how close they square with the customary cut in Boston & Salem & New Bedford" (*EJ* 306).

45. Whicher, *Selections*, 334. See especially Joel Porte, *Representative Man*, 198–199, on the passage about the "born again" traveler. As Porte says, "The reader who does not respond well to this passage will probably never be an Emersonian, because the excited shift of mood and the spontaneous exfoliation of joy out of literally nothing are among the best surprises Emerson has to offer."

46. In " 'Put God in Your Debt,' " 38–40, Grusin links Emerson's "chilling" language

here to his problems with bank stocks from 1841 to 1844.

47. Ellen Tucker Emerson, *The Life of Lidian Jackson Emerson*, ed. Delores Bird Carpenter (Boston: Twayne, 1980), 128–129, 146, 155. Gay Wilson Allen simply notes of Lidian that "she was an habitual complainer" (*Waldo Emerson*, 437). Joyce Warren, in *American Narcissus*, 201, more empathetically concludes, "Marriage, for Lidian, meant total subordination of her personality and made her into a chronically ill nonperson."

Emerson's sense of "the vitriolic acid of marriage" (*EJ* 308) is mirrored and intensified in a letter of John Milton to his most intimate Italian friend, Carlo Dati, in which Milton writes of his "frequent grievings over my own lot." Where Emerson dismisses marriage as a trap and an illusion, Milton rails against his intimate domestic relations as what he calls the necessity of useless neighborhood, "the sense, namely, that those whom the mere necessity of neighborhood, or something else of useless kind, has closely conjoined with me, whether by accident or by the tie of law, they are the persons, though in no other respect commendable, who sit daily in my company, weary me, nay, by Heaven all but plague me to death whenever they are jointly in the humor for it, whereas those whom habit, disposition, studies, had so handsomely made my friends, are now almost denied me, either by death or by unjust separation of place, and are so for the most part snatched from my sight that I have to live well-nigh in a perpetual solitude" (James Holly Hanford, *John Milton, Englishman* [New York: Crown, 1949], 131).

48. Emerson, "Illusions," in *The Conduct of Life*, vol. 6 of *Works*, ed. Edward Emerson, 299, 305. Cf. *EJ* 392–393 (September 1848).

49. For a passionate reading of "Experience" that could not be more opposed to mine, see Gertrude Reif Hughes, *Emerson's Demanding Optimism*, 35–65. Hughes nicely teases out Emerson's pervasive ventriloquism, as she calls it, while arguing that Emerson's initial "bitterness and even resentment" at his loss of power yields to a complex affirmation of hope, using "limitation and reduction to effect expansion" (41, 62–63). See also Leonard Neufeldt, *House of Emerson*, 219–230, arguing for Emerson's growing skill as an artist of muted and modulated affirmation, transcending his sense of being victimized by his materials. Sharon Cameron, in "Representing Grief: Emerson's 'Experience,'" *Representations*, 15 (Summer 1986), 15–41, forcefully foregrounds Emerson's inability to allow grief direct expression. She argues that Emerson converts his emotional dissociation to "the dissociation that facilitates power" (25). His essay's "brutality" prohibits grieving and insists on isolation and rootlessness, she concludes. In *Emerson's Fall*, Packer vigorously defends Emerson's ruthless resiliency of mind. Agreeing with James M. Cox that Emerson actually feeds on death, she suggests that readers "resent him for springing back with renewed force" rather than being "crippled by his losses" (52).

50. The journalist is N. Willis, quoted by Chapman, *Selected Writings*, 185. Nick Salvatore's prize-winning biography, *Eugene V. Debs: Citizen and Socialist* (Urbana: University of Illinois Press, 1982), shows that Debs's appeal to industrial workers lay in his ability to invoke American traditions of manliness, not European traditions of socialism. Debs's calls to manhood both transcended and blurred the social perceptions of his working-class audiences, much as Emerson's did for the new middle class and the children of old gentility. Also see Nina Baym, "Melodramas of Beset Manhood: How Theories of American Fiction Exclude Women Authors," *American Quarterly*, 33 (1981), 123–139.

Chapter 3. Three Ideologies of Manhood, Four Narratives of Humiliation

1. John Von Neumann's "min-max" or minimax theory comes from his mathematical analysis of game strategy. It was popularized by others, who derived from it the idea that corporations function not to maximize profit but to minimize maximum loss. See John Von Neumann and Oskar Morgenstern, *Theory of Games and Economic Behavior* (Princeton: Princeton University Press, 1953), 153–155 ("the Min-Max type"); and for

a more accessible proof, Andrew Colman, *Game Theory and Experimental Games: The Study of Strategic Interaction* (Oxford: Pergamon, 1982), 273–280. My emphasis on humiliation might complement Norbert Elias's analysis of self-regulation and shame in advanced industrial societies. See Elias, *The Civilizing Process*, vol. 2: *Power and Civility*, trans. Edmund Jephcott (New York: Pantheon, 1982).

2. *The Life and Speeches of the Hon. Henry Clay*, ed. Daniel Mallory (New York: Van Amringe and Bixby, 1844), 2:31. For Franklin's account of America's "general happy mediocrity," which is so congenial to artisans and which puts a premium on hard work rather than social status, see his "Information to Those Who Would Remove to America" (1784), widely reprinted. On self-made men and the spirit of enterprise, see Rush Welter, *The Mind of America, 1820–1860* (New York: Columbia University Press, 1975), 129–162; Irvin G. Wyllie, *The Self-Made Man: The Myth of Rags to Riches* (New Brunswick, N.J.: Rutgers University Press, 1954); and John G. Cawelti, *Apostles of the Self-Made Man* (Chicago: University of Chicago Press, 1965).

3. On the introduction of "middle class" as a term in the 1830s, see Karen Halttunen, *Confidence Men and Painted Women: A Study of Middle-Class Culture in America, 1830–1870* (New Haven: Yale University Press, 1982), 29. Myra Jehlen, *American Incarnation: The Individual, the Nation, and the Continent* (Cambridge: Harvard University Press, 1986), argues that the middle-class ideology of liberal individualism encourages collective possession of the land as if the land incarnated the ideology. While some of her close readings are very suggestive, Jehlen presumes middle-class triumph from the earliest settlers onward.

4. Henry James, *Hawthorne*, introduction by Tony Tanner (London: Macmillan, 1967; 1st pub. 1879), 61; F. O. Matthiessen, *American Renaissance: Art and Expression in the Age of Emerson and Whitman* (London: Oxford University Press, 1941), 72, 235–236, 270–271.

5. See, for instance, Edward Pessen, *Jacksonian America: Society, Personality, and Politics*, rev. ed. (Homewood, Ill.: Dorsey Press, 1978). In "Social Structure and Politics in American History," *American Historical Review*, 87 (December 1982), 1290–1325, Pessen argues for a six-level class structure, measured largely by wealth (1293), though by other indicators as well, with little movement across class lines. In his rejoinder, Robert Wiebe rightly remarks that Pessen really believes in a two-level class structure, the rulers and the ruled (1326–1327), despite the lack of nationally connected elites during the mid-19th century. As Wiebe says, "No portion of United States history poses more complicated problems in class analysis than the half-century from approximately 1825 to 1875" (1328). In another rejoinder, Michael Katz finds Pessen woefully out of date, using 1940s-style sociology to present class as a thing instead of a relationship (1332). Katz urges that we call the middle class the "business class."

6. Jackson, "Farewell Address" (March 4, 1837), *The Statesmanship of Andrew Jackson*, ed. Francis Newton Thorpe (New York: Tandy-Thomas, 1909), 511. The best history of Jacksonian confusions and resentments remains Marvin Meyers, *The Jacksonian Persuasion: Politics & Belief* (Stanford: Stanford University Press, 1960).

7. A prominent Marxist study of the rise of bourgeois individualism in 18th- and 19th-century America is Elizabeth Fox-Genovese and Eugene D. Genovese, *Fruits of Merchant Capital: Slavery and Bourgeois Property in the Rise and Expansion of Capitalism* (New York: Oxford University Press, 1983), which defines politics as "the relations of class power at the heart of historical process" (159). While the book remains exciting as a big-picture polemic, it scants immersion in historical details. It also slights what for me is a fundamental problem about such class analyses: how the middle class experiences power not as collective domination but as individualized antagonisms. A more sophisticated and detailed neo-Marxist study is Bruce Laurie, *Working People of Philadelphia, 1800–1850* (Philadelphia: Temple University Press, 1980). Laurie usefully discriminates among three

different working-class cultures, using religion as a key index of differentiation. He depicts the antebellum elite as continuously mercantile, however, solidifying their power as a class by 1850. See 11–30 on formation of working-class cultures.

8. Sean Wilentz, *Chants Democratic: New York City and the Rise of the American Working Class, 1788–1850* (New York: Oxford University Press, 1984), 11. Nick Salvatore, in *Eugene V. Debs: Citizen and Socialist* (Urbana: University of Illinois Press, 1982), similarly emphasizes the presence of artisan ideals of manhood in American radicalism, though Salvatore is much clearer about the limitations of the artisan tradition. In *Working People of Philadelphia*, 197–203, Laurie connects continuing worker deference with evangelical Protestantism. Cf. George B. Hutchinson, *The Ecstatic Whitman: Literary Shamanism & the Crisis of the Union* (Columbus: Ohio State University Press, 1986), 18: "The class whose habit Whitman donned for the frontispiece of his first edition was undergoing a deeply-resented loss of status and filling the ranks of nativism and revivalism."

9. Gordon S. Wood, "Ideology and the Origins of Liberal America," *William and Mary Quarterly* (July 1987), 635, 640. For a discussion of the clash between mobile, undeferential new men and elite expectations of hierarchy, a phenomenon beginning before the Revolution and intensifying in the 1780s, see Wood, *The Creation of the American Republic, 1776–1787* (New York: Norton Library, 1972), 476–479, 498–499, 562.

10. Walt Whitman, *Leaves of Grass*, 1855 ed., ed. Malcolm Cowley (Harmondsworth, Eng.: Penguin, 1976), 73; William Charvat, *The Profession of Authorship in America, 1800–1870: The Papers of William Charvat*, ed. Matthew J. Bruccoli (Columbus: Ohio State University Press, 1968), 61–62. Charvat continues: "In the thirties the real class animus was not between the 'haves' and the 'have-nots.' So far as the writers and intellectuals were concerned, the struggle was between their own homogeneous patrician society and a rising materialistic middle class without education and tradition, who were winning cultural and economic power and changing the tone of American life" (64). See also Larzer Ziff's extension of Charvat in *Literary Democracy: The Declaration of Cultural Independence in America* (New York: Viking, 1981), 98. For Ziff, class struggle "does not form an important conscious part" of their outlook, though the elite writers saw "the new power of the prospering middle class" everywhere. Rather, writers from patrician backgrounds (Emerson, Hawthorne, Melville) sought "yeoman allies (Thoreau, Whitman)" against materialism, while, more profoundly, they explored the nature of the unfixed self. Finally, the appendix to Lawrence Buell's *New England Literary Culture: From Revolution through Renaissance* (Cambridge: Cambridge University Press, 1986), 375–397, makes the almost uniformly patrician background of New England writers unmistakable.

11. Carroll Smith-Rosenberg, *Disorderly Conduct: Visions of Gender in Victorian America* (New York: Knopf, 1985), 86. See also Halttunen, *Confidence Men and Painted Women*, 195: "Sentimentalism offered an unconscious strategy for middle-class Americans to distinguish themselves as a class while still denying the class structure of their society, and to define themselves against the lower classes even as they insisted they were merely distinguishing themselves from vulgar hypocrites."

An excellent 1985 review essay by Stuart M. Blumin, the historian who first emphasized the prevalence of downward mobility in antebellum Philadelphia, makes a strong case for studying middle-class formation beyond a traditional Marxist framework. Despite the obvious divergence between nonmanual and manual work, or commercial and mechanical interests, and despite the intensification of ambition among clerks and businessmen, "there is very little evidence from the nineteenth century that the middle class was emerging as a conflict group or as a self-conscious social group." Instead, it was "most likely to express awareness of its common values and beliefs as a denial of the significance of class." See Stuart M. Blumin, "The Hypothesis of Middle-Class Formation in Nineteenth-Century America: A Critique and Some Proposals," *American Historical Review*, 90 (April 1985), 316–317, 309. Blumin believes the new middle class should be seen as an intermediate, rather than dominant class, defining itself paradoxically through an ideology of social atomism and focusing its energies on work, not political power.

12. A recent comparative study of Boston and Charleston during this period implicitly challenges my paradigms by finding little class conflict in Boston, especially between a mercantile elite and entrepreneurial-capitalist interests. *The Web of Progress: Private Values and Public Styles in Boston and Charleston, 1828–1843* (New York: Oxford University Press, 1985), by William H. Pease and Jane H. Pease, concludes that Charleston had much more class stratification and a traditional patrician disconnection of manliness from labor. While Boston had continuing "disharmony" and "tension" between mechanics and artisans, on the one side, merchants and manufacturers, on the other, the Peases do not find class conflict nearly as strong as a shared belief in the work ethic and upward mobility, among all groups of Boston men (27–28, 222). Significantly, fewer than a quarter of all corporate directors in Boston had upper-class standing or cared about being citizen-leaders. Men gained social and self-respect primarily through attending to work and profits, more than through social status or public power (38–39, 82, 114–116, 169 on Boston's "homogeneous culture").

I think the Peases overstate the city's ideological homogeneity. Also their sense that older elite values have already given way to the new middle-class orientation toward work as the measure of manhood (these are my terms, not theirs) shows both the ascendancy of middle-class values and the transformation of class issues into individual competition. For a study much more in line with my sense of class conflict, though not of who won, see Ronald Story, *The Forging of an Aristocracy: Harvard and the Boston Upper Class, 1800–1870* (Middletown, Conn.: Wesleyan University Press, 1980). Story argues that Boston's elite became self-consciously a triumphant "Brahmin Aristocracy" after the Civil War, in dialectical response to pressures from middle- and lower-class antagonisms. See xiv, on entrepreneurial accumulation vs. elite values; also 135–159, and 164–165. For a study putting class struggle at the center of a somewhat earlier period, see Charles G. Steffen, *The Mechanics of Baltimore: Workers and Politics in the Age of Revolution, 1763–1812* (Urbana: University of Illinois Press, 1984). Steffen emphasizes the politicization of mechanics during this period, their clear connections to Methodism and their shifting alliances with the Republican party.

13. In *The Decline of American Gentility* (New York: Columbia University Press, 1973), Stow Persons explores what he calls the "traditional emphasis on obligation and personal responsibility" as basic to a gentry sense of manliness (286). The gentry's "heavy burden of cultural responsibility" (292) mixed idealism with internalized discipline, especially for elite writers. Unlike Myra Jehlen in *American Incarnation*, Persons connects "the rise and fall of liberal individualism" to "the life span of gentility in the mass society" (301). See Edwin Harrison Cady, *The Gentleman in America: A Literary Study in American Culture* (Syracuse: Syracuse University Press, 1949), a leisurely defense of gentlemanly values of character, courtesy, social obligation, and moral idealism against the crass materialism of the lower orders, from the Puritan "theocratic gentry" (17) through Emerson and Howells. On the persistence of the gentry's code of manhood in the South, see Bertram Wyatt-Brown, *Southern Honor: Ethics and Behavior in the Old South* (New York: Oxford University Press, 1982).

Steffen, *Mechanics of Baltimore*, challenges the presumption of elite dominance, at least in Baltimore before 1815, when mechanics' class consciousness was aroused. In *Forging of an Aristocracy*, Story defines the changing ideology of upper-class identity in response to pressures from below: "The focus of responsibility shifted from village, region or sect, as in agrarian society, and from self or nuclear family, as in petit bourgeois society, to clan, peerage, and institution, as befitted an evolving upper class" (164). A fine recent study of how republican values united patrician and artisan readers of *The New-York*

Magazine in the 1790s is David Paul Nord's "A Republican Literature: A Study of Magazine Reading and Readers in Late Eighteenth-Century New York," *American Quarterly*, 40 (March 1988), 42–64.

14. See Paul E. Johnson, *A Shopkeeper's Millennium: Society and Revivals in Rochester, New York, 1815–1837* (New York: Hill and Wang, 1978); and Anthony F. C. Wallace, *Rockdale: The Growth of an American Village in the Early Industrial Revolution* (New York: Norton, 1978). Wallace in particular analyzes the connections between the gentry's Enlightenment values and its economic base in mercantile capitalism and village shops.

15. Royall Tyler, *The Contrast* (1787), most accessible in *The American Tradition in Literature*, 5th ed., ed. Sculley Bradley et al. (New York: Random House, 1981), 416.

16. Cathy N. Davidson, *Revolution and the Word: The Rise of the Novel in America* (New York: Oxford University Press, 1986), 213; Buell, *New England Literary Culture*, 337.

17. Tyler, *The Contrast*, 403.

18. Ibid., 431–432; Davidson, *Revolution and the Word*, 212–215, also Buell, *New England Literary Culture*, 337–343, on later transformations of Jonathan.

19. Alexander Hamilton, James Madison, John Jay, *The Federalist Papers*, ed. Clinton Rossiter (New York: New American Library, 1961; 1st pub. 1787–1788), 78–79. For a broader argument about the European elite's sensitivity to the dangers of class conflict and its hopes that capitalism might channel individual passions into the socially safe desire to make money, see Albert O. Hirschman, *The Passions and the Interests: Political Arguments for Capitalism before Its Triumph* (Princeton: Princeton University Press, 1977).

20. *Federalist Papers*, especially Hamilton's paper no. #35, 214–216. Steffen, *Mechanics of Baltimore*, xiii, finds Hamilton's enthusiasm "as much wishful thinking as dispassionate analysis." Nonetheless, Federalists such as James Fenimore Cooper's father commandeered votes in the old seigneurial manner well into the new century. See Richard Slotkin, *The Fatal Environment: The Myth of the Frontier in the Age of Industrialization, 1800–1890* (New York: Atheneum, 1985), 83, quoting the elder Cooper as telling a citizen at the polls, "You cannot know how to vote as well as I can direct you."

21. *Federalist Papers*, 322.

22. Salvatore, *Eugene V. Debs*, 10. His context is schools. For a study connecting the elite's emphasis on deference and civic purpose with its neoclassic literary values, see Robert Ferguson, *Law and Letters in American Culture* (Cambridge: Harvard University Press, 1984), e.g.,75–76.

23. Salvatore, *Eugene V. Debs*, 23–24. On Whitman's artisan roots, see especially M. Wynn Thomas, *The Lunar Light of Whitman's Poetry* (Cambridge:Harvard University Press, 1987). Eric Foner traces the complex intermingling of artisan ideas of freedom and individual competition in several books; see, for instance, *Tom Paine and Revolutionary America* (New York: Oxford University Press, 1976), connecting Paine's celebration of free labor to an artisan class, though with complex tensions in artisan roles (28–45); also Foner's *Politics and Ideology in the Age of the Civil War* (New York: Oxford University Press, 1980), a collection of essays on republicanism, abolitionism, and the ideology of free labor.

My emphasis here differs from Steffen's argument for class struggles, in his *Mechanics of Baltimore*, though his analysis may reflect an urban context. Steffen also stresses the artisan values of industry, sobriety, and discipline, suggesting that such values helped as "psychological defenses" against insecure livelihoods and the threat of "a lower-class subculture" with antithetical values (262–263). A recent essay by Amy Bridges challenges the link between artisan values and working class formation. She argues that the American working class originated in ethnic urban groups, as an alien minority. See "Becoming American: The Working Classes in the United States before the Civil War," in *Working-Class Formation: Nineteenth-Century Patterns in Western Europe and the United States*, ed. Ira

Katznelson and Aristide R. Zolberg (Princeton: Princeton University Press, 1986), 157–196.

Another book emphasizing the decline of artisan culture as a complex system of paternalistic or "fatherly" education is W. J. Rorabaugh's *The Craft Apprentice: From Franklin to the Machine Age in America* (New York: Oxford University Press, 1986). See esp. chap. 7, "The Machine Age," 131–156, on the incentives to capitalization and entrepreneurial competition which helped to destroy artisan pride of craft.

24. Tyler, *Contrast*, 414. A little earlier (411), Jonathan describes a theater audience who "stampt away, just like a nation." T. Walter Herbert, Jr., illuminates Melville's "gentleman-beachcomber" narrative as part of "the complex psychology of a failed patrician." See *Marquesan Encounters: Melville and the Meaning of Civilization* (Cambridge: Harvard University Press, 1980), 149–191 on *Typee*, quotations 160, 155.

25. Whittier, "Democracy" (1st published in November 1841 *Democratic Review*), in *The Complete Poetical Works of John Greenleaf Whittier*, ed. Horace E. Scudder (Boston: Houghton Mifflin, 1894), 351–352; Jay Fliegelman, *Prodigals and Pilgrims: The American Revolution against Patriarchal Authority, 1750–1800* (Cambridge: Cambridge University Press, 1982). Fliegelman argues for an "antipatriarchal revolution that would replace patriarch with benefactor, precept with example, the authority of position with the authority of character, deference and dependence with moral self-sufficiency" (210). The particular changes he details so tellingly seem less "antipatriarchal" than shifts of attitude within patriarchy. On the tensions between independence and filial deference, especially in traditional patriarchy, see Philip Greven's first book, *Four Generations: Population, Land, and Family in Colonial Andover, Massachusetts* (Ithaca: Cornell University Press, 1970).

26. Whitman, *The Early Poems and the Fiction*, ed. Thomas L. Brasher (New York: New York University Press, 1963), 124–125, 152, 157, 212, 181, 239, 174. I am indebted to Herb Levine for suggesting *Franklin Evans* to me. Whitman's plot is much more bizarre and arbitrary than I have sketched here; it includes a defense of slavery.

27. *Benjamin Franklin's Autobiography*, Norton Critical Edition, ed. J. A. Leo Lemay and P. M. Zall (New York: Norton, 1986), 17, 24–25, 46. In discussing Franklin and Edwards in *The Language of Puritan Feeling: An Exploration in Literature, Psychology, and Social History* (New Brunswick, N.J.: Rutgers University Press, 1980), 225–238, I develop a similar view of Franklin, though from a perspective more psychological than social. For a broader view of father-son tensions in seventeenth-century artisan families in New England, see Robert Blair St. George, "Fathers, Sons, and Identity: Woodworking Artisans in South-East New England, 1620–1700," in *The Craftsman in Early America*, ed. Ian M. G. Quimby (New York: Norton, 1984), 89–125. St. George argues that extensive first-generation mobility, which eased father-son conflicts much as Franklin's did, all but disappeared in the third generation's tight, rural family cohesion. For an essay emphasizing Franklin's ambivalence and guilt more than I do, see Hugh J. Dawson, "Fathers and Sons: Franklin's 'Memoirs' as Myth and Metaphor," *Early American Literature*, 14 (Winter 1979/80), 269–292.

In *Craft Apprentice*, 3–15, Rorabaugh emphasizes how Franklin's brother exploited him, though he then blames Franklin's autobiography for teaching apprentices that running away can be richly rewarded. Franklin, he concludes, did more than anyone else to destroy the artisan institution of apprenticeship (15). A similar nostalgia pervades his anecdotal book, though he usefully emphasizes the entrepreneurial aggressiveness that artisan institutions could not hold in check.

28. Mary Kelley, *Private Woman, Public Stage: Literary Domesticity in Nineteenth-Century America* (New York: Oxford University Press, 1984), 297, 392 n. 23. On Lemuel Shaw, see the Genoveses, *Fruits of Merchant Capital*, 345; also Michael Paul Rogin, *Subversive Genealogy: The Politics and Art of Herman Melville* (New York: Knopf, 1983), 18, 36–37, also 99–101, 141–143 on Shaw and slavery; and especially Leonard W. Levy, *The Law*

of the Commonwealth and Chief Justice Shaw (New York: Oxford University Press, 1957), e.g., 303–336, on how Shaw helped to "channel and legitimize social change" (305) toward entrepreneurial individualism, anticipating regulatory capitalism. For a fine, incisive study of the interplay between Shaw's decisions and Melville's fictions, see Brook Thomas, "The Legal Fictions of Herman Melville and Lemuel Shaw," *Critical Inquiry*, 11 (September 1984), 24–51, expanded in *Cross-Examinations of Law and Literature: Cooper, Hawthorne, Stowe, and Melville* (Cambridge: Cambridge University Press, 1987), 93–112, 164–250.

29. Mary Ryan, *Cradle of the Middle Class: The Family in Oneida County, New York, 1790–1865* (Cambridge: Cambridge University Press, 1981), 236; Herman Melville, *Pierre Or The Ambiguities*, ed. Harrison Hayford et al. (Evanston, Ill.: Northwestern University Press, 1971), 9.

Henry Clay's 1832 speech defending tariffs argues that tariffs are one way of managing the dangers of unchecked competition. "Of all human powers operating on the affairs of mankind, none is greater than that of competition. . . . It resembles the meeting of the mountain torrent, grooving, by its precipitous motion, its own channel, and ocean's tide. Unopposed, it sweeps every thing before it; but, counterpoised, the waters become calm, safe, and regular." Clay, *Life and Speeches*, 2:37.

30. Ryan, *Cradle of the Middle Class*, 155 on male and female roles, 220 on sons as early strangers to mothers, also 178–184 on the new middle class's emphasis on self-control. Joseph F. Kett, *Rites of Passage: Adolescence in America, 1790 to the Present* (New York: Basic, 1977), esp. 121 on self-denial, 127, 161 on relation between discipline and bureaucracy, 172 on conflict between new modes of discipline and older expectations for independence and autonomy.

31. Ryan, *Cradle of the Middle Class*, 210; 184, also 238 on fear of falling into lower class, 169–171 on education rather than property as family legacy to children. On "career" see Raymond Williams, *Keywords: A Vocabulary of Culture and Society*, rev. ed. (London: Fontana, 1983), 52–53.

32. George Stigler is quoted, with evident relish, by Gary Hart, *A New Democracy* (New York: Quill, 1983), 46. A letter from Jerry James to the *New York Times*, Sunday, September 28, 1986 (sec. E, p. 24), notes that Lombardi did *not* say "Winning isn't everything; it's the only thing." In a 1953 John Wayne movie, *Trouble along the Way*, Wayne plays a once-great football coach fired for making illegal payments to his players. His social worker daughter quotes him as saying what is usually credited to Lombardi. James cites the real Lombardi remark.

On the spirit of "Try again! Go ahead!" see Welter, *Mind of America*, 131. For Fanny Wright's remarks, see Celia Morris Eckhardt, *Fanny Wright: Rebel in America* (Cambridge: Harvard University Press, 1984), 99. A recent book reflecting entrepreneurial assumptions of battle and dominance is Peter F. Drucker, *Innovation and Entrepreneurship: Practice and Principles* (New York: Harper & Row, 1985).

33. Cotton Mather, *Magnalia Christi Americana*, Bks. 1 and 2, ed. Kenneth B. Murdock (Cambridge: Harvard University Press, 1977; 1st pub. 1702), 273–359, quotation 279. See Kenneth Silverman, *The Life and Times of Cotton Mather* (New York: Harper & Row, 1984), 162–165. For Silverman, who recurrently emphasizes Mather's own suppressed anger, Mather's portrait of Phips represents the minister's ambivalent accommodation to "the new epoch of commercial enterprise, imperial expansion, and perriwigs" (165). I am indebted to John Seelye for suggesting Mather's account to me. See Seelye, "The Clay Foot of the Climber: Richard M. Nixon in Perspective," in *Literary Romanticism in America*, ed. William L. Andrews (Baton Rouge: Louisiana State University Press, 1981), 118–124. In *Cotton Mather and Benjamin Franklin: The Price of Representative Personality* (Cambridge: Cambridge University Press, 1984), 153–170, Mitchell Robert Breitwieser argues that the Phips biography functions as "a kind of national park" for Mather (160), giving him a wish-fulfilling excursion from his filiopietistic Puritan self into vicarious

identification with a fat, hedonistic hothead, Franklinesque and self-fathered as well (163–165). Breitwieser also stresses the complementary "blankness" under Franklin's more rebellious self-fashioning, producing a self calculated to function as capital (18, 262, and passim).

34. Ryan, *Cradle of the Middle Class*, sees the new middle class as composed primarily of professionals and clerks (146), not entrepreneurs. However, she emphasizes that an entrepreneurial attitude was necessary for survival: "The corporate, collective aspects of the household economy and the master artisan's retinue of journeymen and apprentices had by the 1850s become overwhelmed by the imperatives of maximizing individual gain in a competitive market" (153, also 154). Ryan also argues that mothers tried to socialize middle-class children to reproduce "the usual array of petit bourgeois traits—honesty, industry, frugality, temperance, and, preeminently, self-control.... the model child was infused not with the spirit of a daring, aggressive entrepreneur but with, rather, that of a cautious, prudent small-business man" (161). This argument seems too simple to me, on two counts: it confuses what mothers wanted with how their children turned out, and it presumes very strong maternal socialization even though, as Ryan shows elsewhere, sons were removed from maternal influence quite early.

On the other hand, Stuart Blumin finds the "joiner" impulse as strong as competition among entrepreneurs ("Hypothesis of Middle-Class Formation," 335). The Peases, too, in *Web of Progress*, discuss the tensions between those who promoted competition and those who worried that too fierce a competitiveness would lead to " 'violent and spasmodic effort' rather than the 'patient and moderate labor' by which the prudent workman succeeded." (113). At the very least, we can see a great deal of ambivalence here concerning competitiveness vs. more traditional models of hard work.

35. Wilentz, *Chants Democratic*, 380. Cf. Smith-Rosenberg, *Disorderly Conduct* (90–108), which analyzes the violence and sexuality in the Davy Crockett myth as a reflection of "the marginality of Jacksonian men poised between economic classes and socially acknowledged institutional niches: the sons of artisans, suspended between the hope of emerging as successful entrepreneurs and the fear of sinking into the industrialized and unskilled work force" (99).

36. Emerson, "Napoleon; or, The Man of the World," in *Representative Men*, vol. 4 of *Emerson's Complete Works*, ed. Edward W. Emerson (Boston: Houghton Mifflin, 1883), 214, 239, 218, 241, 216. On 229 Emerson muddies the class issue somewhat by calling Napoleon an "organ" of "the industrious masses."

37. Melville, "Bartleby the Scrivener: A Story of Wall Street" (1st pub. 1853), in *Herman Melville: Selected Tales and Poems*, ed. Richard Chase (New York: Holt, Rhinehart and Winston, 1950), 109, 119, 130. There are a great many analyses of Bartleby and the narrator as split or double selves, neither able to acknowledge anger and alienation, though some see Bartleby as the radically individual self that the narrator would like to be. A superb Marxist reading of the story in its Wall Street setting is Stephen Zelnick, "Melville's 'Bartleby': History, Ideology, & Literature," *Marxist Perspectives*, 2 (Winter 1979/80), 74–92. See also Thomas, "Legal Fictions of Melville and Shaw," 34–39, and his chapter on "Bartleby" in *Cross-Examinations*, 164–182; and Robert Shulman, *Social Criticism and Nineteenth-Century American Fictions* (Columbia: University of Missouri Press, 1987), 6–27, on the narrator as "a gentry version of possessive individualism" and Bartleby as an urban office worker who rejects "the dominant class hegemony" from within (18, 27, also 15).

38. Raymond Williams, *Culture and Society, 1780–1950* (Garden City, N.Y.: Anchor, 1960); Carolyn Porter, *Seeing and Being: The Plight of the Participant-Observer in Emerson, James, Adams, Faulkner* (Middletown, Conn.: Wesleyan University Press, 1981), esp. 9–20, 62–88; Myra Jehlen, "New World Epics: The Novel and the Middle-Class in America," *Salmagundi* (Winter 1977), 49–68, reprinted in *Ideology and Classic American Literature*, ed.

Sacvan Bercovitch and Myra Jehlen (Cambridge: Cambridge University Press, 1986), 125–144. See also Jehlen's introduction, 1–18. A fine critique of the implicitly conservative politics in Charles Feidelson's *Symbolism and American Literature* (Chicago: University of Chicago Press, 1953) is Barbara Foley, "From New Criticism to Deconstruction: The Example of Charles Feidelson's *Symbolism and American Literature*," *American Quarterly*, 36 (Spring 1984), 44–64.

39. Michel Chevalier, *Society, Manners, and Politics in the United States: Letters on North America*, trans. T. G. Bradford (1839), ed. John William Ward (Ithaca: Cornell University Press, 1961), 418–419; Tocqueville, *Democracy in America*, ed. Phillips Bradley (New York: Vintage, 1945; 1st pub. 1835), 1:288. Porter, *Seeing and Being*, 19–21, adapting Louis Hartz's thesis about American liberalism, argues that the absence of feudal institutions unleashed the full force of capitalist expansion and consequent social atomism.

40. For a subtle, evocative account of the fate of the artisan work ethic in industrialization, see Daniel T. Rodgers, *The Work Ethic in Industrial America, 1850–1920* (Chicago: University of Chicago Press, 1978).

41. On the rise of a managerial class after 1850, see Alfred D. Chandler, Jr., *The Visible Hand: The Managerial Revolution in American Business* (Cambridge, Mass.: Harvard University Press, 1977). Chandler argues that managers, not entrepreneurs, made the rise of big business possible and that the managerial class rose despite political and public hostility (484–498) and despite the rhetoric of American individualism. This class, which did not exist in 1840, was the key to coordination of what Chandler calls multiunit business enterprise. After 1870 the entrepreneurial quest for personal dominance, personified in Chandler's study by Jay Gould (141–164, 199–203) often hurt more than it helped the management of risk.

42. Hawthorne, *The House of the Seven Gables*, ed. Seymour L. Gross (New York: Norton, 1967; 1st pub. 1851), 7, 23, hereafter cited in the text by page number.

43. From a somewhat different perspective Eric J. Sundquist discusses Holgrave's covert affinities with both Jaffrey and the narrator, as he "cultivates" the Pyncheons for revenge and mercenary gain. See *Home as Found: Authority and Genealogy in Nineteenth-Century American Literature* (Baltimore: Johns Hopkins University Press, 1979), 123–142, esp. p. 129–130.

44. Walter Benn Michaels, "Romance and Real Estate," *Raritan*, 2 (Winter 1983), 66–87. Michaels also argues that in marrying wealth, Holgrave defuses the threat posed by a transient underclass (71, 77, 75). The analysis is extremely suggestive, though, like the narrator, Michaels sometimes confuses mercantilist property rights with capitalist dynamics. See also Brook Thomas's two chapters on *House* in *Cross-Examinations*, 45–90, exploring the narrator's conservative use of legal concepts.

45. See Carolyn L. Karcher, *Shadow over the Promised Land: Slavery, Race, and Violence in Melville's America* (Baton Rouge: Louisiana State University Press, 1980), 128–143, esp. 136 on "Southern Hamlet," a term from William R. Taylor's *Cavalier and Yankee: The Old South and American National Character* (Garden City, N.Y.: Anchor, 1963). See my discussion of Stowe's St. Clare, in Chapter 6. Karcher also discusses Babo as Iago, 141.

46. Melville, "Benito Cereno," *Selected Tales and Poems*, 90, 5, hereafter cited in the text by page number.

47. Eric J. Sundquist's dazzling discussion of the story illuminates how the narrator "moves silently in and out of [Delano's] point of view." "The razor of Melville's narrative plays about the mind of Delano just as Babo's razor plays about the neck of Don Benito, regulating in a ritual of suppression the rebellion of recognition that threatens to occur at any moment." "Suspense and Tautology in 'Benito Cereno,'" *Glyph* 8 (1981), 109, 119. See also Sundquist's historical essay, "'Benito Cereno' and New World Slavery," in *Reconstructing American Literary History*, ed. Sacvan Bercovitch (Cambridge: Harvard University Press, 1986), 93–122, esp. on white fears of black barbers (112). For another useful

discussion of contexts in black history, see Jean Fagan Yellin, "Black Masks: Melville's 'Benito Cereno'," *American Quarterly*, 22 (1970), 678–689, reprinted in *The Intricate Knot: Black Figures in American Literature, 1776–1863* (New York: New York University Press, 1972), 215–227. For the story's implications about the authority of American law, see Thomas, "Legal Fictions of Melville and Shaw," 26–34, and *Cross-Examinations*, 93–112.

48. For an essay connecting Delano's "inquisition" of Don Benito to American expansionism, a Manifest Destiny continuing Catholic Spain's earlier expansionism, see Allan Moore Emery, " 'Benito Cereno' and Manifest Destiny," *Nineteeth-Century Fiction* 39 (June 1984), 48–68. An excellent study of how the narrative's racism induces reader discomfort is Kingsley Widmer, *The Ways of Nihilism: A Study of Herman Melville's Short Novels* (n.p.: California State Colleges, 1970), 59–90. Widmer also notes the "homoeroticism" in the master-slave bond and the "rape-paranoic fantasies" embedded in the story's false consciousness (68–69, 89–90).

49. Richard L. Ochberg, *Middle-Aged Sons and the Meaning of Work* (Ann Arbor: UMI Research Press, 1987), e.g., 77–80. In emphasizing paternal humiliation as a dynamic for several American Renaissance writers, I am disagreeing with Quentin Anderson's argument that every classic male writer with the exception of Cooper had an absent or weak father in his childhood. See *The Imperial Self: An Essay in American Literary and Cultural History* (New York: Vintage, 1971).

50. Thoreau, "A Plea for Captain John Brown" (1859), reprinted in *Thoreau: People, Principles, and Politics*, ed. Milton Meltzer (New York: Hill and Wang, 1963), 171, 173, 181, 182, hereafter cited in the text by page number.

51. Richard Lebeaux, *Thoreau's Seasons* (Amherst: University of Massachusetts Press, 1984), 323–332. Lebeaux connects Thoreau's "Plea" with his need to preserve his ego-ideal of wildness, purity, autonomy, and heroism, as opposed to the responsible, businesslike head of household he had become (324–326), and also with surrounding journal entries about autumnal ripening. While Lebeaux writes movingly of Thoreau's presentiments about his own death and nicely connects the "Plea" to the 1844 fire Thoreau set, he minimizes the incendiary anger in concluding that "Thoreau seems to be reaching for a wise serenity, a vision of his life cycle" (330).

52. William Howarth, *The Book of Concord: Thoreau's Life as a Writer* (New York: Viking, 1982), 177–179; Richard Bridgman, *Dark Thoreau* (Lincoln: University of Nebraska Press, 1982), 245–250; also Lebeaux, *Thoreau's Seasons*, 323–332.

53. See Meg McGavran Murray, "Thoreau's Moon Mythology: Lunar Clues to the Hieroglyphics of *Walden*," *American Literature*, 58 (March 1986), 15–32. Murray discusses the various ways that Thoreau finds restorative, unthreatening mothering in the woods, though with recurrent ambivalence, as manifested in the 1844 fire. See also Richard Lebeaux, *Young Man Thoreau* (Amherst: University of Massachusetts Press, 1977), 31, 36–40, on Cynthia Thoreau's strong-willed ambitions for her children.

54. Lawrence Buell, *Literary Transcendentalism: Style and Vision in the American Renaissance* (Ithaca: Cornell University Press, 1973), 299. Alice Miller, *Prisoners of Childhood: The Drama of the Gifted Child and the Search for the True Self*, trans. Ruth Ward (New York: Basic, 1981), is an eloquent psychoanalytic account of the effects of a mother's narcissistic resentments on gifted children. More politically, a passage from Jonathan Dollimore, *Radical Tragedy: Religion, Ideology and Power in the Drama of Shakespeare and His Contemporaries* (Brighton: Harvester Press, 1984) illuminates both Thoreau and the "world elsewhere" of classic American criticism: in *Coriolanus*, "the ethically unified subject of a world elsewhere allows us to transcend the political and social realities foregrounded in and by the dislocated subject in this one" (229).

55. On Thoreau's receptivity to Grahamism, see a vivid essay by James Armstrong, "Thoreau, Chastity, and the Reformers," in *Thoreau's Psychology: Eight Essays*, ed. Raymond D. Gozzi (Lanham, Md.: University Press of America, 1983), 123–139.

56. Paul Zweig, *Walt Whitman: The Making of the Poet* (New York: Basic, 1984), 39, also 41–42 on Whitman's pervasive idealization of mothering. Another poem in the 1855 edition, "I Sing the Body Electric," briefly celebrates femaleness as stereotypic submissive mothering (sec. 5), then moves to a lengthier celebration of maleness as "action and power": "Scorn becomes him well and appetite and defiance become him well, / The fiercest largest passions... pride is for him" (sec. 6). Here Whitman idealizes his father's passions rather than detaching himself from their threat. M. Wynn Thomas, *The Lunar Light of Whitman's Poetry* (Cambridge: Harvard University Press, 1987), puts Whitman's father in the context of class defeat: he alternated "between the kind of morose sense of isolation that drove many of his class to drink" and a rudimentary working-class solidarity. He seemed surrounded by "the air of social failure and defeat... as if he had never quite, to the very end, got the hang of entrepreneurial capitalism." (29). In the brief real estate boom of the early 1850s, Walt employed his father and two brothers as carpenters (34).

57. I am borrowing this insight from Agnieszka Salska, *Walt Whitman and Emily Dickinson: Poetry of the Central Consciousness* (Philadelphia: University of Pennsylvania Press, 1985), 104. More generally I am indebted to Brenda Gordon, whose seminar essay on various responses to this poem both prompted and helped to clarify my own responses, and to Herb Levine for several discussions about Whitman.

58. Two relatively lengthy psychoanalytic commentaries are by Edwin Haviland Miller, *Walt Whitman's Poetry: A Psychological Journey* (Boston: Houghton Mifflin, 1968), 27–32, and Stephen A. Black, *Whitman's Journeys into Chaos: A Psychoanalytic Study of the Poetic Process* (Princeton: Princeton University Press, 1975), 61–66. Miller's evocative analysis nicely stresses the associative links in the early part, though he and I disagree about the poem's ending, which for him is "perhaps rationally unconvincing" but emotionally satisfying, especially in its circular restoration of a womb-Eden idyll through nature (31–32). Later, Miller emphasizes the lack of real intimacy in Whitman's vision of selfhood and love, in this poem as in others (34–40). Black also argues that the ending converts the world into a cradle. In his view, Whitman leaves doubts and confusions unallayed: "he does not learn anything about his identity" (62). As I do, Black emphasizes the poem's ostensibly transcendental, actually regressively narcissistic, defenses against Oedipal conflict (63–66).

A recent essay by Helen Vendler, "Body Language: *Leaves of Grass* and the Articulation of Sexual Awareness," *Harper's Magazine* (October 1986), 62–66, celebrates "There Was a Child Went Forth" as the poem that introduced her to the Whitman beyond the braggadocio myth: the Whitman who could be "delicate, ethereal, noiseless," and who had "invented an oceanic American rhythm unknown to English verse" (65). She offers a more extended reading of the poem's movement toward distance and solitude in "Whitman's Placing of the Aesthetic in Two Early Poems: 'There Was a Child Went Forth' and 'The Sleepers,'" *Delta*, 16 (1983), 19–32. I am indebted for this reference to Herb Levine.

Betsy Erkkila and Robert Shulman offer recent political readings. Erkkila, "The Federal Mother: Whitman as Revolutionary Son," *Prospects*, vol. 10, ed. Jack Salzman (Cambridge: Cambridge University Press, 1985), 423–441, traces how authoritarian male figures menace images of female liberty and familial union in various poems and links national fragmentation to aggressive commercial maleness (431). Shulman, in *Social Criticism and Nineteenth-Century American Fictions*, 125–133, also links the father to "a masculine, self-reliant market society" (129), though Shulman believes the father transmits those values to the child, who is left in a marketplace without cohesion.

59. Mitchell Robert Breitwieser, "Who Speaks in Whitman's Poems?" in *The American Renaissance: New Dimensions*, ed. Harry R. Garvin and Peter C. Carafiol (Lewisburg, Pa.:

Bucknell University Press, 1983), 143.

60. Zweig, *Walt Whitman*, 128, also 133–142; Whitman quoted in Thomas, *Lunar Light of Whitman's Poetry*, 27. Thomas links Whitman's incorporating voice to his attempt to be a "mouthpiece," or "general partnership" of workers, independent yet not competitive but expansively collective. See, e.g., 27–30, 41–53.

61. Zweig, *Walt Whitman*, 138.

62. Lebeaux, *Thoreau's Seasons*, 62–110, compassionately and subtly details the strains in Thoreau's relationship with Emerson during Emerson's 1847 trip. Emerson himself, as Lebeaux suggests, may well have been masking a midlife crisis of his own (66–67). In *Young Man Thoreau*, 29–36, Lebeaux sketches Thoreau's father as "emasculated" yet with anger latent in his silences.

Chapter 4. Frederick Douglass's Self-Refashioning

1. *My Bondage and My Freedom*, ed. William L. Andrews (Urbana: University of Illinois Press, 1987; 1st pub. 1855), 151, hereafter cited in the text as *MB*.

2. *Narrative of the Life of Frederick Douglass, an American Slave* (New York: New American Library, 1968, 1st pub. 1845), 77, hereafter cited in the text as *N*. Among various discussions of the *Narrative*, Donald B. Gibson's "Reconciling Public and Private in Frederick Douglass's *Narrative*," *American Literature*, 57 (December 1985), 549–569, notes that Douglass minimizes his actual escape in part to make his fight with Covey the climax. In stressing Douglass's conflicting impulses, Gibson conflates the different editions, finding only "slight differences" (561).

3. The only comprehensive analysis of Douglass's revisions I have come across is Thomas De Pietro's "Vision and Revision in the Autobiographies of Frederick Douglass," *CLA Journal*, 25 (June 1983), 384–396. De Pietro argues that Douglass minimizes the aspects of "spiritual autobiography" in the *Narrative* to draw out sociological and political perspectives and to highlight his own quest for literacy as a pathway to rebellion.

4. Harriet Beecher Stowe, *Uncle Tom's Cabin, or, Life Among the Lowly* (New York: Harper & Row, 1965; 1st pub. 1852), 22.

5. In "Mothers, Husbands, and Uncle Tom," *Georgia Review* (Spring 1984), 131, Stephen Railton also notes how Stowe's narration holds firm the "linguistic line between genteel whites and lowly blacks," betraying "the anxiety as well as the allegiance she and her readers shared as a class." A reader for *Criticism*, where a version of this chapter was published (29 [Summer 1987], 341–370), suggests that *Uncle Tom's Cabin* provided Douglass with a narrative model for his genteel voice in *My Bondage and My Freedom*.

6. That perspective shaped my side of an interchange with Barbara Foley about her article "The Documentary Mode in Black Literature"; see "Forum," *PMLA*, 96 (January 1981), 105–106. Donald Gibson, "Reconciling Public and Private," argues that Douglass controls his aggressiveness throughout, in style as well as action; Douglass fights defensively, not to win (561, 563).

7. For a brief account of Covey (pronounced Coh-vee, with a long *o*) beyond Douglass's narrative, see Dickson J. Preston, *Young Frederick Douglass: The Maryland Years* (Baltimore: Johns Hopkins University Press, 1980), 118, 128–129. Covey, at that time twenty-eight years old and with a family, took no revenge on Douglass, Preston suspects, because Thomas Auld intervened and told Covey to be gentler. Perhaps ironically, within eighteen months after Douglass left, Covey had saved enough money for a 196-acre farm of his own. In the 1850 census he was listed as one of the district's wealthier farmers, with property worth twenty-three thousand dollars and five slaves. He died in 1875 with a very comfortable estate.

8. Henry Louis Gates, Jr., Preface to Harriet E. Wilson, *Our Nig; or, Sketches from the*

Life of a Free Black . . . (New York: Vintage, 1983; 1st pub. 1859), li–lii.

9. On sales figures, see Benjamin Quarles, Introduction to Douglass's *Narrative*, ed. Quarles (Cambridge: Harvard University Press, 1960), xiii–xiv.

10. Waldo E. Martin, Jr., *The Mind of Frederick Douglass* (Chapel Hill: University of North Carolina Press, 1984), 23, 27–29, 40–47. See also Peter F. Walker, *Moral Choices: Memory, Desire, and Imagination in Nineteenth-Century American Abolition* (Baton Rouge: Louisiana State University Press, 1978), 242–247, 258–260. Walker emphasizes Douglass's "hopeless secret desire to be white" (247) as well as the Garrisonians' racism. I'm indebted for this reference to Stephen Gould Axelrod. In *From Behind the Veil: A Study of Afro-American Narrative* (Urbana: University of Illinois Press, 1979), 17–26, Robert B. Stepto takes a more benign view of Garrison's and Wendell Phillips's prefatory materials. Though noting some tensions, he argues that they authorize Douglass's control of his narrative.

11. Preston's *Young Frederick Douglass* emphasizes the stability and relative protectiveness of Douglass's Eastern Shore slave background. He suggests that when Douglass was given back to Thomas Auld after Aaron Anthony's death, while the rest of his family went to a much more dreaded man and all the other twenty-eight slaves were kept with families, the division was done by Auld in Douglass's interest (90–91). Much later Douglass came to think that Auld sent him to Covey to try to do what was best for him (141). The 1855 edition tempers Douglass's criticism of Thomas Auld, adding that he was generous and humane and that Douglass had not been unhappy except during his months with Covey (172–173). Preston argues that readers then and now "want Frederick to have had a miserable childhood" and don't want him to admit he was a "favored slave" (173). Douglass finally visited the dying Auld, in an emotional reunion (185–186).

12. Martin, *Mind of Frederick Douglass*, 47. Andrews, Introduction to *My Bondage*, xxii, cites a Douglass letter to Senator Charles Sumner in 1852, saying his relationship to Garrison was "something like that of a child to a parent." Martin makes some parallels between the fight with Covey and the more protracted fight with Garrison as "psychological declaration[s] of independence," though, as he concludes, "the complicated problem of how to achieve black manly independence in the face of the racist paternalism of his white male colleagues, on the one hand, and his own psychological need to deal with his mysterious white patrimony, on the other, was never fully resolved" (47). Martin also notes Douglass's increasing equivocation about his father's white identity in the three editions (96–97). In *To Tell a Free Story: The First Century of Afro-American Autobiography, 1760–1865* (Urbana: University of Illinois Press, 1986), William L. Andrews argues that Garrison becomes the new climax in *My Bondage* (214–217, 233–239). Dickson Preston stresses Douglass's ambivalence about Aaron Anthony, who represented both brutality and lustful exploitation of slaves, yet also the self-made man Douglass so admired (*Young Frederick Douglass*, 23).

13. See Robert B. Stepto, "Storytelling in Early Afro-American Fiction: Frederick Douglass' *The Heroic Slave*," *Georgia Review*, 36 (Summer 1982), 355–368, on Douglass's break with Garrison after the trip to England as it becomes refracted in his novella.

14. Andrews, Introduction to *My Bondage*, sees Douglass's need for a home as central to his revisions, though he doesn't link "home" to whiteness and power. See also Andrews, *To Tell a Free Story*, 214–239, esp. 219–221 and 230–237. Andrews makes much more of Douglass's quest for black community than I do.

15. Martin, *Mind of Frederick Douglass*, 40–42; Walker, *Moral Choices*, 259–260. I am indebted here and in the following paragraphs to comments by Lee Clark Mitchell and Susan Kirkpatrick, the latter at a December 1986 MLA panel where a brief version of this chapter was given. See also Nathan Irvin Huggins, *Slave and Citizen: The Life of Frederick Douglass* (Boston: Little, Brown, 1980), 153–157, on Douglass's marriage and

his white women friends. Though illiterate, Anna prided herself on being a competent housewife. She "saw that he was met by parcels of fresh linen" at every stop on his travels (154). Huggins says Julia Griffiths stayed in the Douglass home for two years (156); Martin says 1848–1852. Huggins also asserts that Douglass "never left himself open to charges of infidelity" (156)

16. I am very grateful to Terry H. Pickett, who translated these unpublished materials, for sharing them with me. Pickett summarizes Ottilie Assing's life and friendship with Douglass in "Perspectives on a National Crisis: A German Correspondent Reports on America, 1853–1865." *Tamkang Journal of American Studies*, 4 (1988), 5–15. Assing left Douglass the interest on thirteen thousand dollars, the principal to go to the Society for the Prevention of Cruelty to Animals after his death (14). Another article by Pickett on Assing's friendship with Douglass is forthcoming in the *Georgia Historical Quarterly*. On Douglass's remarriage to Helen Pitts, see Huggins, *Slave and Citizen*, 157–159.

I am also indebted to Faith Berry for commentary on this chapter. As she informs me, Arna Bontemps declares that Douglass and his second wife bought a house once owned by Robert E. Lee (*Free At Last: The Life of Frederick Douglass* [New York: Dodd Mead, 1971], 271). Berry has found no confirmation of that, however, either at Cedar Hill, Douglass's home, or in other sources.

17. Walker, *Moral Choices*, 250–254. See also Martin, *Mind of Frederick Douglass*, 5, for a less provocative assessment of the picture. Walker is one of the few critics to emphasize Douglass's revisions. Martin stresses Douglass's need to affirm his shaky bond with his mother, e.g., 235–236.

18. Preston, *Young Frederick Douglass*, 9.

19. Ibid. On 129, for instance, Martin speaks of Douglass's "procapitalist bias" and "his bourgeois and assimilationist outlook." Douglass became a figurehead president of a black bank to encourage industry, thrift, and saving among freed Negroes; in 1874 the bank failed (103–104). Again and again he failed to see power in terms of social structure and groups, instead emphasizing power in individual terms as self-made manhood. Both Martin and Preston note that, as Martin puts it, "his bourgeois tastes found the rural, folk, and often unpolished quality of black expressive culture, like ecstatic religiosity, sorely wanting" (282). See also Preston, *Young Frederick Douglass*, 13–14, on his sense of superiority to the "Guinea niggers" from Africa. Martin cites Douglass's "blatant racialism" toward Africans and Mexicans (*Mind*, 217, also 209). Douglass's strong American Indian strain, from his grandmother, complicates this issue.

20. Martin, *Mind of Frederick Douglass*, 261–262; Douglass quoted 257, 261.

21. Douglass quoted ibid., 263. Valerie Smith, in *Self-Discovery and Authority in Afro-American Narrative* (Cambridge: Harvard University Press, 1987), 21–28, also emphasizes self-made manhood as an ideology that simultaneously gives his life meaning and traps him "in the very premises that contributed to his enslavement" (28).

22. See Walker, *Moral Choices*, 255–256; also Martin, *Mind of Frederick Douglass*, 15. Both Walker and Martin emphasize the hero's search for a lost patrimony. John Seelye notes that the Scots name means "the black one." See "The Clay Foot of the Climber: Richard M. Nixon in Perspective," in *Literary Romanticism in America*, ed. William L. Andrews (Baton Rouge: Louisiana State University Press, 1981), 130–131, and 125–134 on Douglass.

23. See Harriet A. Jacobs, *Incidents in the Life of a Slave Girl, Written by Herself*, ed. Jean Fagan Yellin (Cambridge: Harvard University Press, 1987; 1st pub. 1861). On Jacobs, see Andrews, *To Tell a Free Story*, 239–241, 247–263. I am indebted to Lee Clark Mitchell for suggesting this comparison to me.

Houston A. Baker, Jr., interprets the *Narrative* quite differently: that Douglass resolves his "lone existence plagued by anxiety" through adopting white, abolitionist, Christian language as his passport to freedom, without understanding how that language cut him off from himself. I think Douglass's alienation from himself is shaped much more by conventions of manhood than by public language. Also, Douglass uses Christianity more as a weapon than as a badge of identity. See Baker, *The Journey Back: Issues in Black Literature and Criticism* (Chicago: University of Chicago Press, 1980), 32–46. For a similar analysis, emphasizing the slave narrative as a genre responding to white expectations, see John Sekora, "The Dilemma of Frederick Douglass: The Slave Narrative as Literary Institution," *Essays in Literature*, 10 (Fall 1983), 219–226. I am indebted for this reference to Patricia Johnson.

24. Martin, *Mind of Frederick Douglass*, 81–91. Martin's discussion of Douglass's motives for allowing himself to be co-opted by the Republicans in the 1870s and 1880s is more complex.

25. Martin, *Mind of Frederick Douglass*, 73–74; see also 255, 130, 69.

26. Ibid., 209. On the "Secret Six," see Jeffrey Rossbach, *Ambivalent Conspirators: John Brown, the Secret Six, and a Theory of Slave Violence* (Philadelphia: University of Pennsylvania Press, 1982). Rossbach argues that the Secret Six, one of whom was Thomas Wentworth Higginson, hoped Brown's raid would stir blacks from laziness to more self-reliant habits of mind. I'm indebted for this reference to Bertram Wyatt-Brown.

27. Martin, *Mind of Frederick Douglass*, chap. 10 (253–278), connects Douglass's preoccupation with being a "Self-Made Man, Self-Conscious Hero" (the chapter's title) to Emerson; see esp. 255, 263–266.

28. Ibid., 140 (quotation), 147; Huggins, *Slave and Citizen*, 48–49.

29. Martin, *Mind of Frederick Douglass*, 150–156, also 5, where Martin suggests Douglass's feminism "might have represented in part his lifelong attempt to grapple with his stunted maternal tie." On feminists as a fund-raising constituency, see Stepto, "Storytelling," 356–357. Perhaps qualifying Douglass's feminism, the last version of his autobiography recounts his struggle with a racist private school, which refused to give his daughter "a refined and Christian education," despite his desire to have her "educated like the daughters of other men" (*Life and Times of Frederick Douglass* [New York: Collier Books, 1962; 1st pub. 1892] 268). In the 1860s, Douglass split with feminists, arguing that black male suffrage should take precedence over universal suffrage as a political priority. See Martin, 156–162; and Huggins, *Slave and Citizen*, 120–122.

30. Douglas quoted in Martin, *Mind of Frederick Douglass*, 11.

31. John Rock's March 5, 1858, speech is reprinted in *A Documentary History of the Negro People in the United States*, ed. Herbert Aptheker (Secaucus, N.J.: Citadel Press, 1951), 1:402–405, quotation 405.

Chapter 5. Two Genteel Women Look at Men

1. Dorothy Dinnerstein, *The Mermaid and the Minotaur: Sexual Arrangements and Human Malaise* (New York: Harper & Row, 1976); Nancy Chodorow, *The Reproduction of Mothering: Psychoanalysis and the Sociology of Gender* (Berkeley: University of California Press, 1978); also Carol Gilligan, *In a Different Voice: Psychological Theory and Women's Development* (Cambridge: Harvard University Press, 1982). On French feminism, see *New French Feminisms: An Anthology*, ed. Elaine Marks and Isabelle de Courtivron (Amherst: University of Massachusetts Press, 1980).

For a dismissive critique of recent feminist theories, see Nina Baym, "The Madwoman and Her Languages: Why I Don't Do Feminist Literary Theory," *Tulsa Studies in Women's Literature*, 3 (Spring/Fall 1984), 45–59. Baym finds in deconstructive feminism only a valorization of the weaker sex being desired by the masculine other, in "a language that is intensely private, politically ineffectual, designed to fail." Baym also accuses Freudian and Lacanian feminists of being "daddy's girl" masochists (50–51). While I agree with Baym's defense of pluralism and her call for research into how differences are culturally constituted, I disagree with her crisply adultomorphic view of the psyche.

2. Toril Moi, *Sexual/Textual Politics: Feminist Literary Theory* (London: Methuen, 1985), condemns the bourgeois humanism of American feminists and the radical anarchism of French feminists with equal Marxist fervor. K. K. Ruthven, in *Feminist Literary Studies: An Introduction* (Cambridge: Cambridge University Press, 1984), begins rather defensively as he fends off the charge of being phallocratic. Then he briskly and courteously surveys an enormous range of recent feminist criticism on the way to making a strong argument against separatism. For Mary Ryan's emphasis on how the new middle-class family worked together, through separate sex roles, not for upward mobility but for maintenance of the family's class status, see her *Cradle of the Middle Class: The Family in Oneida County, New York, 1790–1865* (Cambridge: Cambridge University Press, 1981), esp. 184, 242.

3. Twain, *Life on the Mississippi* (New York: New American Library, 1961; 1st pub. 1883), chap. 38, pp. 228, 231.

4. Ann Douglas, *The Feminization of American Culture* (New York: Knopf, 1977), 128. Douglas presents Hale as a conservative arbiter of taste who helped make women consumers. Ruth E. Finley, in *The Lady of Godey's: Sarah Josepha Hale* (Philadelphia: Lippincott, 1931), presents Hale as both a Victorian and a progressive reformer, 128–132, also 239: "Sarah Hale was not a suffragist, but she was the greatest feminist of her times." See 279–285 on the possible plagiarism of "Mary Had a Little Lamb," which Finley dismisses.

5. On the preeminence of *Godey's* and the taboo against mentioning the war, see Frank Luther Mott, *A History of American Magazines, 1741–1850,* (Cambridge: Harvard University Press, 1957; 1st pub. 1930), 580–594. Finley, *Lady of Godey's,* 176–179, ascribes that "signally obtuse mistake" to Louis Godey, whose policy permitting no religious or political discussion in the magazine was "almost a mania with him." By the 1850s, as Mott notes in his next volume, *Godey's* was overtaken by *Peterson's*; see *A History of American Magazines, 1850–1865* (Cambridge: Harvard University Press, 1938), 4, and 11 on Civil War circulation. Mott condescends to *Godey's* throughout, saying that all this magazine literature "did indeed need more virility in it." He blames women readers "for Longfellow and the others," and ultimately faults "the orthodox system of sentimental education for girls" (*Magazines, 1850–1865,* 48). A similar perspective shapes Fred Lewis Pattee, *The Feminine Fifties* (Port Washington, N.Y.: Kennikat Press, 1966; 1st pub. 1940).

6. Beste quoted in Nick Salvatore, *Eugene V. Debs: Citizen and Socialist* (Urbana: University of Illinois Press, 1982), 4–5. See also Lois W. Banner, *American Beauty* (New York: Knopf, 1983), which curiously slights *Godey's Lady's Book* in discussing antebellum women's fashions; and Karen Halttunen, *Confidence Men and Painted Women: A Study of Middle-Class Culture in America, 1830–1870* (New Haven: Yale University Press, 1982), 62–72, 81–91, 157–162, on *Godey's* and fashions. Halttunen emphasizes the uses of fashion by middle-class ladies to distinguish themselves from the vulgar (62–63) and discusses the calls for simplicity in *Godey's.* In the late 1840s, she notes, *Godey's* became less moralistic and more tolerant about ostentation, adopting a more lightly satiric tone (157–162).

7. Mott, *American Magazines, 1741–1850,* 590.

8. Mrs. S. J. Hale, "New-Year at Home," *Godey's Lady's Book,* 20 (January 1840), 3–4. Hale's opposition to public lecturing by women like Fanny Wright was of long standing. By 1836 Wright had become a symbol of the arch-deviant female, as Celia Morris Eckhardt says in her illuminating biography, *Fanny Wright: Rebel in America* (Cambridge: Harvard University Press, 1984), 244. On the other hand, Hale duplicitously advocates radical feminism and equality in her 1839 novel *The Lecturess: or Woman's Sphere,* "the earliest full-length treatment of a women's rights lecturer in literature," as David S. Reynolds notes in *Beneath the American Renaissance: The Subversive Imagination in the Age of Emerson and Melville* (New York: Knopf, 1988), 390. Hale's sympathetic heroine is a strong-willed champion of equality throughout her life, though suddenly recanting on her deathbed.

A fine, incisive account of Hale under her "mask of *mater familias*" is William R. Taylor, *Cavalier and Yankee: The Old South and American National Character* (Garden City, N.Y.: Doubleday, 1963), 92–119. Taylor sees her as a shrewd businesswoman (98) who left her child-rearing duties mostly to others, was a widow at age thirty-four, and lived most of her life in boardinghouses before dying at age ninety-one. Mott presents her as a high-church Episcopalian who dressed like a duchess (*Magazines, 1741–1850*, 583), while Taylor says she always wore black silk taffeta to signal her mourning. Taylor nicely pairs Hale with Daniel Webster: "They presided as master and mistress over the house of Whiggery" (119).

9. Nina Baym, *Novels, Readers, and Reviewers: Responses to Fiction in Antebellum America* (Ithaca: Cornell University Press, 1984), 210.

10. *Godey's Lady's Book*, 14 (May 1837), 210–211. Vols. 14–15 (1837) hereafter cited in the text.

11. Alicia Ostriker, *Stealing the Language: The Emergence of Women's Poetry in America* (Boston: Beacon Press, 1986), 40–41, on Dickinson; Bonnie G. Smith, *Ladies of the Leisure Class: The Bourgeoises of Northern France in the Nineteenth Century* (Princeton: Princeton University Press, 1981), 89. See also Alfred Habegger, *Gender, Fantasy, and Realism in American Literature* (New York: Columbia University Press, 1982), 3–37, especially chap. 5, on duplicity and bitterness about marriage in mid-century women's fiction.

12. T. S. Arthur, "Engaged at Sixteen," *Godey's Lady's Book*, 30 (January 1845), 3–5. I am indebted to Richard Smyth for alerting me to this story.

13. Here and elsewhere I'm indebted to John Moran for various discussions about *Godey's*.

14. Similarly, Fanny Wright observed that the "universally marked difference between men and women" reflected men's "fixed and steady occupation," giving "habitual exercise" to their energies. See Eckhardt, *Fanny Wright*, 99.

15. Melville, *Moby-Dick*, Norton Critical Edition, ed. Harrison Hayford and Hershel Parker (New York: Norton, 1967), 347; Ik Marvel [Donald G. Mitchell], *Reveries of a Bachelor, or A Book of the Heart* (New York: Scribner's, 1907; 1st pub. 1850), 74–75. In *Beneath the American Renaissance*, Reynolds links Mitchell's "purposefully disconnected style" to Dickinson's sense of the present's "momentousness" (34).

16. Rebecca Harding Davis, *Life in the Iron Mills or The Korl Woman*, ed. Tillie Olsen (Old Westbury, N.Y.: Feminist Press, 1972; 1st pub. 1861), 22. See also the bitter realism of the yeoman's wife at the end of Hawthorne's "Canterbury Pilgrims," describing how married love wears away into the man's gloomy roughness and the woman's peevish anger. *Nathaniel Hawthorne: Tales and Sketches ...*, ed. Roy Harvey Pearce (New York: Library of America, 1982), 164.

17. Anonymous, *The Young Man's Own Book ...* (Philadelphia: Key, Mielke and Biddle, 1832), 52, 117. Melville cites this book in *Typee*. See Neal L. Tolchin, *Mourning, Gender, and Creativity in the Art of Herman Melville* (New Haven: Yale University Press, 1988), 4, 44.

18. Also 105: "Women sometimes see at a glance what a man must go round through a train of argumentation to discover. Their *tact* is delicate, and therefore quicker in operation."

19. For a recent history of this law, see Norma Basch, *In the Eyes of the Law: Women, Marriage, and Property in Nineteenth-Century New York* (Ithaca: Cornell University Press, 1986).

20. Stowe, "Eliza: From My Aunt Mary's Bureau," *Godey's Lady's Book*, 20 (January 1840), 24.

21. Kirkland, *A New Home—Who'll Follow? Glimpses of Western Life*, by Mrs. Mary Clavers [pseud.], ed. William S. Osborne (New Haven: College & University Press, 1965; 1st pub. 1839), 37–38, hereafter cited in the text.

22. For useful overviews of Kirkland's literary career, see Annette Kolodny, *The Land before Her: Fantasy and Experience of the American Frontiers, 1630–1860* (Chapel Hill: University of North Carolina Press, 1984), 131–158, and William S. Osborne, *Caroline M. Kirkland* (New York: Twayne, 1972).

23. Osborne's Introduction places more emphasis than I do on Kirkland's penchant for making fun of herself as well as of romance illusions.

24. See Kolodny, *Land before Her*, 133–140, emphasizing the realism of women's isolation; also Habegger, *Gender, Fantasy, and Realism*, 38.

25. The first name comes at 92. On 71 she says mothers get used to children's noise much as "eels get accustomed to being skinned," though she then says how their play refreshes her.

26. Here I disagree in emphasis with Kolodny, who highlights Kirkland's sensitivity to landscape and gardening. Kolodny also discusses Kirkland as a mentor for prospective immigrants from the genteel middle class (*Land before Her*, 139–140, 147).

27. French feminist criticism might want to make a good deal more of the subversive energies in Kirkland's self-consciousness here than I do.

28. Kolodny, *Land before Her*, emphasizes the gender separation in such passages (140).

29. As John Seelye has suggested to me, there may be a strong dig here at the male equivalent of "Sorry, dear, I have a headache."

30. Nancy A. Hewitt, *Women's Activism and Social Change: Rochester, New York, 1822–1872* (Ithaca: Cornell University Press, 1984). The top, or "benevolent," women's group, Hewitt concludes, gave social standing and moral superiority to the affluent. It was hierarchic, deferential, and well organized. The next group, the "perfectionists," gave a sense of social and moral order for the upwardly mobile, mirroring the economic order pursued by their men. The third group, the "ultraists," was more radical and boldly activist, led by newly arrived agrarian Quakers. There were also groups of free black and working-class women (40, 228).

Hewitt challenges the separate-spheres argument, finding competition between women and sex-specific roles but not a battle between the sexes. Rather, it was "a struggle among various segments of the new urban middle classes for economic and political domination" (23).

31. I am borrowing the phrase from the title of Alfred Kazin, *An American Procession* (New York: Knopf, 1984).

32. I am taking issue here with a recent critical tendency to see little but interest-group politics in canon formation. In the first chapter of *Sensational Designs: The Cultural Work of American Fiction, 1790–1860* (New York: Oxford University Press, 1985), 3–39, Jane Tompkins comes very close to arguing for elite conspiracy as the source of Hawthorne's continuing reputation, while Nina Baym more arrestingly sees mainstream male criticism as foregrounding texts that allow critics to experience "beset manhood." See her "Melodramas of Beset Manhood: How Theories of American Fiction Exclude Women Authors," *American Quarterly*, 33 (1981), 123–139. For a fine recent book on American canon formation, arguing that every present creates its own past, see Richard H. Brodhead, *The School of Hawthorne* (New York: Oxford University Press, 1986).

33. William Kirkland, "British and American Monthlies," *Godey's Lady's Book*, 30 (1845), 271–275.

34. In 1833 when Lydia Maria Child first argued for immediate emancipation and the abrogation of laws prohibiting interracial marriage, so many subscribers cancelled subscriptions that her extremely popular children's magazine had to fold almost immediately. See Carolyn Karcher's Introduction to Child's *Hobomok and Other Writings on Indians*, ed. Karcher (New Brunswick: Rutgers University Press, 1986), xiii.

Chapter 6. Impassioned Women

1. See Nina Baym, "Melodramas of Beset Manhood: How Theories of American Fiction Exclude Women Authors," *American Quarterly*, 33 (1981), 123–139; and Jane Tompkins, *Sensational Designs: The Cultural Work of American Fiction, 1790–1860* (New York: Oxford University Press, 1985).

2. For a critique of feminist exclusivism, see K. K. Ruthven, *Feminist Literary Studies: An Introduction* (Cambridge: Cambridge University Press, 1984). A lively recent account of women's literary duplicity is Alicia Suskin Ostriker, *Stealing the Language: The Emergence of Women's Poetry in America* (Boston: Beacon Press, 1986).

3. Myra Jehlen, "Archimedes and the Paradox of Feminist Criticism," *Signs*, 6 (1981), 575–601. Toril Moi critiques this essay and others by American "bourgeois humanists" in *Sexual/Textual Politics: Feminist Literary Theory* (London: Methuen, 1985).

4. Joanne Dobson, "The Hidden Hand: Subversion of Cultural Ideology in Three Mid-Nineteenth-Century American Women's Novels," *American Quarterly*, 38 (Summer 1986), 223–242; Fanny Fern, *Ruth Hall and Other Writings*, ed. Joyce W. Warren (New Brunswick: Rutgers University Press, 1986). Quotation from Elizabeth Stoddard, in *The Morgesons and Other Writings, Published and Unpublished, by Elizabeth Stoddard*, ed. Lawrence Buell and Sandra A. Zagarell (Philadelphia: University of Pennsylvania Press, 1984), 131, hereafter cited in the text.

5. See Lydia Maria Child, *Hobomok and Other Writings on Indians*, ed. Carolyn L. Karcher (New Brunswick: Rutgers University Press, 1986).

6. Lawrence Buell, *New England Literary Culture: From Revolution through Renaissance* (Cambridge: Cambridge University Press, 1986), 356. On Cassandra's drive for autonomy, see also the Buell-Zagarell Introduction to *Morgesons*, xix.

7. Buell emphasizes the sea's function "as Lawrentian emblem of her passionate desire" (*New England Literary Culture*, 362). The object of Cassy's desire, however, remains vague. Is it voice, self, or a strong, gothic man? The Buell-Zagarell Introduction to *Morgesons* connects Stoddard to Dickinson, xii.

8. In *New England Literary Culture*, 355–358, Buell discusses the grandfather's discovery in relation to the provincial gothic genre.

9. Higginson's letter of August 16, 1870, *The Letters of Emily Dickinson*, ed. Thomas H. Johnson (Cambridge: Harvard University Press, 1958), 2:473.

10. A letter of Samuel S. Shaw to Henry Whitney Bellows, May 6, 1867, speaks of Elizabeth Melville's "belief in the insanity of her husband." Shaw and Bellows were concocting a plan "to make a sudden interference and carry her off, she protesting that she does not wish to go and that it is none of her doing." But Mrs. Melville was balking at the plan, because of her "imaginary and groundless apprehensions of the censure of the world upon her conduct," despite everyone's agreement "that her husband ill treated her so that she could not live with him." A subsequent letter of May 20 from Elizabeth Melville to Henry Whitney Bellows thanks him for his interest and "your long talk with me." "Whatever further trial may be before me," she says, she will "pray for submission and faith to *realize* the sustaining power of the Master's love." Walter Kring and Jonathan S. Carey, "Two Discoveries concerning Herman Melville," *Massachusetts Historical Society*, 87 (1975), 140–141, rpt. *The Endless, Winding Way in Melville: New Charts by Kring and Carey*, ed. Donald Yannella and Hershel Parker (Glassboro, N.J.: Melville Society, 1981) with strong rumors of wife-beating (19,22). Four months later, Melville's eighteen-year-old son Malcolm killed himself after Melville harshly disciplined him.

11. In *Private Woman, Public Stage: Literary Domesticity in Nineteenth-Century America* (New York: Oxford University Press, 1984), Mary Kelley explores the paradoxical, self-suppressing creativity of twelve genteel woman writers, each privileged by birth and

education for a public role yet constrained to reinforce the stereotype that woman's real place must be in the home. Two other books by sympathetic historians have titles summing up the dilemma. Carl Degler's survey of the centuries-long impasse between American women's self-fulfillment and their family role is aptly called *At Odds*, while Susan Conrad's fine study of intellectual American women such as Margaret Fuller carries the title *Perish the Thought*. Degler, *At Odds: Women and the Family in America from the Revolution to the Present* (Oxford: Oxford University Press, 1980); Conrad, *Perish the Thought: Intellectual Women in Romantic America, 1830–1860* (New York: Oxford University Press, 1976).

12. Edward Halsey Foster, *Susan and Anna Warner* (Boston: Twayne, [1978], 35; Kelley, *Private Woman, Public Stage*, 17–18.

13. Warner, *The Wide, Wide World* (New York: Feminist Press, 1987; 1st pub. 1850), 172, 189, 190, 194, hereafter cited in the text.

14. Tompkins, *Sensational Designs*, 167: "Mrs. Vawse is the most completely happy and fulfilled person in the novel because economically, socially, and emotionally she is the most independent."

15. Jane Tompkins suggests that Alice functions as the fairy godmother, while Aunt Fortune is the wicked stepmother (Ibid., 183).

16. Ellen's age is very hard to determine. On 295, after several months at Aunt Fortune's, John thinks she is twelve or thirteen, while Alice thinks she is ten or eleven and John half agrees. On 521, some three years later, after Ellen has been in Scotland for awhile, Lady Keith reports that Ellen is fourteen and a half years old. Tompkins, probably following Nina Baym, says Ellen is ten (*Sensational Designs*, 161). See Baym, *Woman's Fiction: A Guide to Novels by and about Women in America, 1820–1870* (Ithaca: Cornell University Press, 1978), 143. By the end (535) even Ellen is wondering "why every body calls me 'little;' I don't think I am very little."

17. Several critics note the pun on *misfortune*; only Margaret Klawunn, to my knowledge, picks up Warner's association of misfortune with Emerson. Klawunn's unpublished essay, for a graduate course at Rutgers University, cites Anna Warner's biography of her sister, *Susan Warner* (New York: Putnam, 1909), 252.

18. On 457–458, Mr. Van Brunt clearly bests Aunt Fortune's will, for Ellen's benefit. Arguably, however, she marries as much for business reasons as for love. Hawthorne, *The Scarlet Letter*, 2d ed., ed. Sculley Bradley et al. (New York: Norton, 1978; 1st pub. 1850), 181.

19. Hawthorne, *Scarlet Letter*, 185.

20. Ibid., 62. For Anna's comment that Susan wrote her book "in closest reliance upon God.... the book was written upon her knees," see Baym, *Woman's Fiction*, 142. In "Sparing the Rod: Discipline and Fiction in Antebellum America," *Representations*, 21 (Winter 1988), 67–96, Richard H. Brodhead links *Wide, Wide World* to *The Scarlet Letter* and other midcentury novels as narratives that help middle-class women internalize discipline through love. Brodhead sees Aunt Fortune as an example of old-style domestic economy and discipline, while Alice represents the new style of "moralizing lovingness" (80).

21. Most critics cite only the last part of this sentence. Helen Waite Papashvily, in *All the Happy Endings* (New York: Harpers, 1956), 1–14, was the first to argue that Warner's novel responded to the sensibilities of women who felt dominated against their will, though she concludes that the domestic novel kept women in their chains (209). Baym connects the sentimental tradition of tears to "rage and frustration" and powerlessness: "More than any of the other women, Susan Warner dealt with power and the lack of it" (*Woman's Fiction*, 144). In *Sensational Designs*, Tompkins echoes Baym's emphasis on powerlessness, paradoxically describing Ellen's self-conquest as a kind of autonomy that brings access to divine matriarchal power and female solidarity, or even a new Redeemer Nation based on moral women (151–165, 172). Tompkins's afterword to the Feminist Press edition more clearly depicts Ellen's powerlessness, and stresses the role of evan-

gelical Christianity in making women feel that they matter in the midst of patriarchal dominance and pervasive humiliations (584–608, esp. 599). Joanne Dobson ("The Hidden Hand," 227) sees a "subtext" of "strong, repressed anger at enforced feminine powerlessness"; her reading emphasizes narrative duplicity. Edward Halsey Foster, in *Susan and Anna Warner*, stresses what Tompkins calls the novel's "training narrative" side. For him, *Wide, Wide World* is not feminist; it presents a lesson in how to submit. Ann Douglas rather oddly stresses Ellen's "undeclared hostility to her culture's competitive forces" as the source of her allegedly unproductive helplessness; see *The Feminization of American Culture* (New York: Knopf, 1977), 63–64.

22. Just before that, the narrative speaks of Ellen's "most buoyant and elastic spirit": "it was not for one sorrow, however great, to utterly crush her. It would have taken years to do that."

23. Joanne Dobson makes John's horsebreaking central to her analysis of Ellen's suppressed fear and resentment. As Dobson rightly says, John is the prince in this fairy tale, yet a strangely abusive prince here: "He is merciless in his desire to dominate" ("Hidden Hand," 231–232). Warner, however, carefully steers Ellen toward understanding the rightness of John's actions and emphasizes that the horse is not being abused, in contrast to Saunders's abuse of Ellen's horse soon afterward. There John rescues Ellen, shows off his now docile Black Prince, and leaves her hungering for his kisses, which he returns to supply (397–403). Elizabeth Stoddard may have appropriated Charles Morgeson's horsebreaking from Warner and from Henrique in Stowe's *Uncle Tom's Cabin*. On John's censorship of novels, see 414, 477–478, 564.

24. Dobson, "Hidden Hand," 231. Alfred Habegger catches the chaste eroticism in Warner's depiction of male authority; see his discussion of Olive Schreiner's response to Warner's *Melbourne House* (1864), in *Gender, Fantasy, and Realism in American Literature* (New York: Columbia University Press, 1982), 13–14, also 18. Warner's "duplicity" purveyed erotic satisfaction in *Wide, Wide World*, even as Warner "outlawed the entire genre" of novels (14). Tompkins's Afterword associates John with "brutal sexuality," and highlights the book's sexualization of dominance—the "tears of orgasmic release" over "being psychically stripped" (599–600).

25. Tompkins, Afterword, 601. Tompkins emphasizes the contradiction between Ellen's spiritual submission and her capitalist drive for power and luxury.

26. Tompkins, *Sensational Designs*, 176. Tompkins's essay is itself duplicitous. At times she attributes a feminist onset of self-mastery and matriarchal power to the narrative, arguing for a paradoxical freedom through domestic roles. At other times, quite movingly at the end, she speaks of Ellen's apprenticeship as "an extinction of her personality" which leads to the joining of "punishment and sexual pleasure, humiliation and bliss" (179, 181–182). Gillian Avery, a well-known British author and authority on children's literature, gave a talk on various nineteenth-century children's books at the University of Florida, Autumn 1986. To see *The Wide, Wide, World* as a training narrative should qualify Habegger's differentiation of manhood from womanhood in *Gender, Fantasy, and Realism*, 41: "While a female is born to womanhood, manhood is never given. It must be fought for on the battlefield, or in some other competitive arena." Clearly Ellen has to fight just as hard to subdue herself into womanhood.

27. Sedgwick quoted in Kelley, *Private Woman, Public Stage*, 148.

28. Foster, *Susan and Anna Warner*, 46–47.

29. Stowe, *Uncle Tom's Cabin or, Life Among the Lowly* (New York: Harper & Row, 1965; 1st pub. 1852), 89, hereafter cited in the text.

30. For the Douglass quotation, see Waldo E. Martin, Jr., *The Mind of Frederick Douglass* (Chapel Hill: University of North Carolina Press, 1984), 198, from "Lesson of the Hour," April 16, 1888. Elizabeth Ammons sees the novel as an attack on conventional American manhood, defined by Stowe (in her *Key to Uncle Tom's Cabin*) as the drive "to be above

others in power, rank and station"; man "is *par excellence* an *oppressive animal.*" See Ammons's now-classic essay "Heroines in *Uncle Tom's Cabin,*" *American Literature,* 49 (May 1977), 66–79, reprinted in Ammons, *Critical Essays on Harriet Beecher Stowe* (Boston: G. K. Hall, 1980), 169, also 161 for a discussion of Legree as a "caricature" of "supermasculinity," which Stowe associates with the devil, Christ's antagonist."

Richard Yarborough observes that Stowe's "wholesale attack on male hegemony went largely unnoticed," because she keeps blacks and women "out of the white male sphere of direct political action," thus bounding her challenge "by the same assumptions that helped support the superstructure she strove to topple." Yarborough, "Strategies of Black Characterization in *Uncle Tom's Cabin* and the Early Afro-American Novel," in *New Essays on Uncle Tom's Cabin,* ed. Eric J. Sundquist (Cambridge: Cambridge University Press, 1986), 65–66. In "Sparing the Rod," Brodhead focuses on the problem of how to discipline Topsy and shows how the new disciplinary mode of mother love drives out the old mode of whipping and beating (84–88).

31. On the "Southern Hamlet" syndrome, see William R. Taylor, *Cavalier and Yankee: The Old South and American National Character* (Garden City, N.Y.: Anchor, 1963), 137–140.

32. Ammons, "Heroines in *Uncle Tom's Cabin.*" Philip Fisher argues that "Uncle" constitutes a familial, child's-eye view of Tom, mystifying the reality of his slavery; see chap. 2 of his *Hard Facts: Setting and Form in the American Novel* (New York: Oxford University Press, 1985), 119. However, Eric Sundquist notes that "Uncle" is "a conventional sign of kinship and familiarity in slave life" (Introduction to *New Essays,* 4).

33. Emerson, [July ?] 1847 journal, reprinted in *Selections from Ralph Waldo Emerson: An Organic Anthology,* ed. Stephen E. Whicher (Boston: Houghton Mifflin, 1957), 311.

34. Among the most important feminist studies of Stowe's novel are Ann Douglas, *Feminization of American Culture;* Ammons's essay; chap. 5 of Jane Tompkins, *Sensational Designs* (122–146, 1st pub. in *Glyph* 8 [1981]); and Gillian Brown, "Getting in the Kitchen with Dinah: Domestic Policies in *Uncle Tom's Cabin,*" *American Quarterly,* 36 (Fall 1984), 503–523. Edmund Wilson, *Patriotic Gore: Studies in the Literature of the American Civil War* (New York: Oxford University Press, 1962), 3–58, resurrected Stowe for modern critics, noting that by 1948 it was out of print (3).

35. On 228 Augustine says his father "could have divided Poland as easily as an orange, or trod on Ireland as quietly and systematically as any man living. At last my mother gave up, in despair. It never will be known, till the last account, what noble and sensitive natures like hers have felt, cast, utterly helpless, into what seems to them an abyss of injustice and cruelty, and which seems so to nobody about them."

36. Gillian Brown goes farthest in arguing that *Uncle Tom's Cabin* replaces the male marketplace with the female kitchen, or domestic economy. Agreeing with Jane Tompkins's assessment of the book as a feminist critique of American society, Brown adds that Stowe also sees conventional domestic ideology as patriarchal. Detaching the kitchen from the market, Stowe accomplishes "a utopian rehabilitation" of sentimental values ("Getting in the Kitchen," 507). To me the book seems more contradictory in its attack on the marketplace. The conservative aspect of Stowe's sentimental gender politics is highlighted by George B. Forgie, *Patricide in the House Divided: A Psychological Interpretation of Lincoln and His Age* (New York: Norton, 1979), 182–185.

37. Eric Sundquist more hesitantly advances a similar thesis about Stowe's implicit paternalist base; see his Introduction to *New Essays,* 32. Jean Fagan Yellin's essay concludes that whatever the radical thrust of Stowe's rhetoric, in practice she celebrates women who practice safely apolitical domestic feminism and racial colonization ("Doing It Herself: *Uncle Tom's Cabin* and Woman's Role in the Slavery Crisis," *New Essays,* 85–105. Alice Crozier usefully sets the novel in the tradition of New England providential history and denunciations of backsliding; see *The Novels of Harriet Beecher Stowe* (New York: Oxford University Press, 1969), 3–33, esp. 16.

38. I am indebted here to a graduate essay by Adeleke Adeeko at the University of Florida.

39. For reviewers' responses, see Nina Baym, *Novels, Readers, and Reviewers: Responses to Fiction in Antebellum America* (Ithaca: Cornell University Press, 1984), 219–223.

40. On urban vs. rural interests in the Northeast, see David M. Potter, *The Impending Crisis, 1848–1861*, ed. Don E. Fehrenbacher (New York: Harper Torchbook, 1976), 440–447, e.g., 443: "Lincoln received much less support in the urban North than he did in the rural North."

41. On the other hand, Mrs. Shelby and Chloe agree that women shouldn't work (257–258), and at St. Clare's plantation Tom takes over all the marketing and providing (204). Mrs. Shelby resembles Alice in *The Morgesons*, who takes over the management of Charles's business after her husband's death.

42. Sundquist, Introduction to *New Essays*, 19–20.

43. Claire Kahane, "Gothic Mirrors and Feminine Identity," *Centennial Review*, 24 (Winter 1980), 43-64, revised as "The Gothic Mirror" in *The (M)other Tongue: Essays in Feminist Psychoanalytic Interpretation*, ed. Shirley Nelson Garner, Claire Kahane, Madelon Sprengnether (Ithaca: Cornell University Press, 1985), 334–351.

44. See Crozier, *Novels of Harriet Beecher Stowe*, 29–33, for a fine summary.

45. Cassy's murder of her baby for its own good has been prefigured by the death of Prue's baby, starved by her white mistress (218). Cf. Gillian Brown, "Getting in the Kitchen," 521–522.

46. Sand's review is reprinted in Ammons's, *Critical Essays*, 3–4.

47. In "*Uncle Tom's Cabin* and Harriet Beecher Stowe: Beating Fantasies and Thoughts of Dying," *American Imago*, 40 (Summer 1983), 115–144, Alexander Grinstein applies conventional psychoanalytic perspectives to see sibling rivalry in Stowe's beating fantasies: father is beating the child I hate. At deeper levels, he argues, Stowe's beating fantasies express masochistic punishment and guilt for Oedipal wishes, especially for the death of her mother, and also her fear and guilt about seeming to be "a replacement child" for her dead sister Harriet, after whom she was named (135–143).

48. Richard von Krafft-Ebing, *Psychopathia Sexualis . . .*, trans. F. J. Rebman (Brooklyn: Physicians and Surgeons, 1938; 1st pub. 1886), 145: "That one man could possess, sell or whip another, caused me intense excitement; and in reading "Uncle Tom's Cabin" (which I read at about the beginning of puberty) I had erections." Case no. 57 insists that he was *"never spanked"* (149) and that he isn't at all effeminate (150). Krafft-Ebing coined the terms sadism and masochism. See Henri F. Ellenberger, *The Discovery of the Unconscious: The History and Evolution of Dynamic Psychiatry* (New York: Basic, 1970), 297–299.

49. Leslie Fiedler, *Love and Death in the American Novel*, rev. ed. (New York: Stein and Day, 1966), 264–269. St. Clare does twice call little Eva "Pussy" (186). Philip Fisher nicely counters the eroticization of death in such analyses when he observes, "to use death as the central image for suffering is to strengthen the passivity within sentimentality" (*Hard Facts*, 109).

50. See, for instance, Paul E. Johnson, *A Shopkeeper's Millennium: Society and Revivals in Rochester, New York, 1815–1837* (New York: Hill and Wang, 1978); Nancy F. Cott, *The Bonds of Womanhood: "Woman's Sphere" in New England, 1780–1835* (New Haven: Yale University Press, 1977), which emphasizes passionlessness as one way to enhance the status of woman's sphere; also Nancy A. Hewitt, *Women's Activism and Social Change: Rochester, New York, 1822–1872*, which differentiates among five quite separate women's groups in beliefs and behavior; and Barbara Leslie Epstein, *The Politics of Domesticity: Women, Evangelism, and Temperance in Nineteenth-Century America* (Middletown, Conn.: Wesleyan University Press, 1981), which stresses resentment.

51. On Tom as "the first fictional Christ figure in American literature," whose death helps to frame the Civil War as a "holy war," see Buell, *New England Literary Culture*,

189–190.

52. Thomas L. Haskell, "Capitalism and the Origins of the Humanitarian Sensibility," *American Historical Review*, 90, pt. 1 (April 1985), 339–361, pt. 2 (June 1985), 551–566, also rebuttals by David Brion Davis and John Ashworth with fifty-page reply by Haskell, "AHR Forum," *American Historical Review*, 92 (October 1987), 797–878.

53. In *Private Woman, Public Stage*, Mary Kelley observes, "Stowe did not eschew intimacy but Calvin's demands were so intense and unremitting that her own autonomy was continually threatened" (281). When his wife's novel became a runaway best seller, Calvin suddenly grew very fat. See Noel B. Gerson, *Harriet Beecher Stowe* (New York: Popular Library, 1976), 123–124. For Stowe's 1852 letter, see Jeanne Boydston, Mary Kelley, and Anne Margolis, *The Limits of Sisterhood: The Beecher Sisters on Women's Rights and Woman's Sphere* (Chapel Hill: University of North Carolina Press, 1988), 178–180.

Chapter 7.   Hard, Isolate, Ruthless, and Patrician

1. Michael Davitt Bell, *The Development of American Romance: The Sacrifice of Relation* (Chicago: University of Chicago Press, 1980), suggests that writers chose the label "romancer" to validate their sense of alienation and deviance (35) and that "romance in America was less a genre than a set of attitudes or problems" (148), partly intellectual and partly having to do with an emotional mixture of rage and need for attention. See also 29–36, on male writers' deviance and American literary culture. Edwin M. Eigner, in *The Metaphysical Novel in England and America: Dickens, Bulwer, Melville, and Hawthorne* (Berkeley: University of California Press, 1978), emphasizes the use of metaphysical allegory as a strategy of "hiding and hoodwinking," presuming a hostile audience yet also trying to engage readers in the creative process. See esp. chap. 2, 39–66.

2. Dana, *Two Years before the Mast: A Personal Narrative of Life at Sea*, introduction by May Lamberton Becker (Cleveland: World, 1946; 1st pub. 1840), 15, hereafter cited in the text. Dana's voyage occurred from 1834 to 1836. He graduated from Harvard in 1837 at the head of his class.

3. Robert Ferguson, *Law and Letters in American Culture* (Cambridge: Harvard University Press, 1984), 257–258.

4. See also 241: "We were determined to show the 'spouter' how things could be done in a smart ship with a good crew, though not more than half their number."

5. See also 90: "The Californians are an idle, thriftless people, and can make nothing for themselves."

6. Martin Green, *The Great American Adventure* (Boston: Beacon Press, 1984), 69–85, emphasizes the imperialistic aspects of Dana's narrative, 74–75 on "industry, frugality, and enterprise," also 83: "the WASP qualities of self-control, competence, and energy."

7. See also 277 ("a man must take a joke among sailors"), 370 ("An escape [from death] is always a joke on board ship.")

8. On Dana's relish for singing, see also 147, 180, 289–290. On 293–294, however, he finds an old salt's falsetto "ludicrous beyond measure."

9. Ferguson, *Law and Letters*, 263.

10. "They seem to be a doomed people . . . wasting away under a disease, which they would never have known but for their intercourse with Christianized Mexico and people from Christian America" (272).

11. Ferguson, in *Law and Letters*, discusses Dana's "depression" as he reenters Boston Harbor, connecting the depression to his father, 258–259. In the 1840's, as Brook Thomas notes, Dana assumed from the start that the commander of the *Somers* was innocent, "even though Mackenzie had hung three men to prevent what he thought, probably incorrectly, was the threat of mutiny." See Thomas, "The Legal Fictions of

Herman Melville and Lemuel Shaw," *Critical Inquiry*, 11 (September 1984), 43.

On Dana's reaction to the *Somers* incident, see also Robert L. Gale, *Richard Henry Dana, Jr.* (New York: Twayne, 1969), 63–64, also 65–72 on Dana's early career as a lawyer, sometimes defending sailors, more often defending companies. In 1848 he declared himself a Free Soiler, leading some Whig Bostonians to boycott him. Later, he courageously defended some fugitive slaves, even though he was severely beaten on the street by a hired boxer. See also *The Journal of Richard Henry Dana, Jr.*, ed. Robert F. Lucid (Cambridge: Harvard University Press, 1968), 1:xix–xxxii, on Dana's contradictory dualities within his conservative class position.

12. D. H. Lawrence, *Studies in Classic American Literature* (Garden City, N.Y.: Doubleday, 1951; 1st pub. 1923), 126, 128. Lawrence rhapsodizes about the flogging as "a natural form of human coition," a spontaneous "passional readjustment" natural to real men (129, 132).

13. Green, *Great American Adventure*, 82.

14. On the fragility of civilized identity in relation to *Typee*, see T. Walter Herbert, Jr., *Marquesan Encounters: Melville and the Meaning of Civilization* (Cambridge: Harvard University Press, 1980). A passage in Dana on a handsome sailor named Bill Jackson (100–101) anticipates *Redburn*.

15. Kim Townsend, "Francis Parkman and the Male Tradition," *American Quarterly*, 38 (Spring 1986), 103. Green, *Great American Adventure*, observes that "the two young Bostonians were determined not to grow up like their fathers" (70). His discussion of *The Oregon Trail* (101–115) concludes that Parkman transferred his Brahmin caste loyalty from the clergy to an "aristo-military caste" (105, 115). On American uses of violence to restore identity and, implicitly, manhood, see Richard S. Slotkin, *Regeneration through Violence: The Mythology of the American Frontier, 1680–1860* (Middletown, Conn.: Wesleyan University Press, 1973), a partially Jungian study; and Michael Paul Rogin, *Fathers and Children: Andrew Jackson and the Subjugation of the American Indian* (New York: Knopf, 1975), which draws on Melanie Klein's theories about infantile rage.

16. Parkman, *The Oregon Trail*, ed. David Levin (Harmondsworth, Eng.: Penguin, 1982; serialized 1847 in the *Knickerbocker Magazine*, 1st pub. 1849 as *The California and Oregon Trail*, 212, hereafter cited in the text.

17. Despite his scorn for the Indians' lack of restraint, he elsewhere (325) praises "the tranquillity of Indian self-control; a self-control which prevents the exhibition of emotion without restraining the emotion itself." Robert L. Gale, in *Francis Parkman* (New York: Twayne, 1973), connects Parkman's admiration of the will of Indian chiefs with his ambition to be chief of American historians (98).

18. On his memories of New England, see 135 on "savage life" vs. New England's "powerful and ennobling influences" which still reach him "unimpaired," 260 ("a vision rose before me of white kid gloves and silken mustaches"), 316 ("delicious associations of the gardens and peaceful homes of far-distant New England"—also 247), and 373 on Byron's "Childe Harold." Parkman's sense of Byron as unmanly is of a piece with Gale's more general comment, in *Francis Parkman* (99): "Parkman makes it painfully clear that he fancies himself more than a match for almost every specimen of manhood in the West."

19. See 252: "The Indians will soon be corrupted by the example of the whites, abased by whisky and overawed by military posts; so that within a few years the traveler may pass in tolerable security through their country. Its danger and its charm will have disappeared together."

20. On this passage, Martin Green, who links Parkman and Hemingway, comments in *Great American Adventure* (109), that Parkman wants to be a knight. See also Ernest Hemingway, *The Sun Also Rises* (New York: Scribner's, 1926), chap. 16.

21. Lawrence, *Studies in Classic American Literature*, 73 (on Cooper).

22. Gale, *Francis Parkman*, 112; finds these portraits delightful. In *Great American Adventure* (111–112), Green notes the polarity between the portraits of powerfully erotic young men and powerfully repellent old women, "shrill, abusive, and domineering."

23. Townsend, "Parkman and the Male Tradition," 98.

24. William H. Goetzmann, *Exploration and Empire: The Explorer and the Scientist in the Winning of the American West* (New York: Norton, 1966), 106–109. See also Henry Nash Smith's reassessment of the ideological aspects of his *Virgin Land*, "Symbol and Idea in *Virgin Land*," in *Ideology and Classic American Literature*, ed. Sacvan Bercovitch and Myra Jehlen (Cambridge: Cambridge University Press, 1986), 21–35.

25. Goetzmann, *Exploration and Empire*, 107. Goetzmann also distinguishes among the Spanish drive to conquer, the English drive to exploit, and the American drive to settle and make the land livable (108). Myra Jehlen, *American Incarnation: The Individual, the Nation, and the Continent* (Cambridge: Harvard University Press, 1986), emphasizes the land's function as a projective incarnation of liberal individualism, in contrast to Argentinian and Canadian responses of feeling intimidated by the land rather than presuming a destiny of exploitation. Goetzmann also notes the white man's expectation that Indians should adopt the Protestant work ethic and become civilized, self-reliant citizens (570–571).

26. Herman Melville, *Moby-Dick*, Norton Critical Edition, ed. Harrison Hayford and Hershel Parker (New York: Norton, 1967), 330.

Chapter 8. Devious Men

1. Harriet Beecher Stowe, *Uncle Tom's Cabin; or Life Among the Lowly* (New York: Harper & Row, 1965; 1st pub. 1852), 297. I am indebted to William Hunter for pointing out the strangeness of this passage.

2. Robyn R. Warhol has recently argued that women's narrations from this period are conventionally engaging, whereas men's narrations, including Hawthorne's, are conventionally distancing. See "Toward a Theory of the Engaging Narrator: Earnest Interventions in Gaskell, Stowe, and Eliot," *PMLA* (October 1986), 811–818, also her response in the March and May 1987 *PMLA* Forums. Also see Carroll Smith-Rosenberg's classic essay "The Female World of Love and Ritual," *Signs*, 1 (1975), 1–29.

3. Edgar Allan Poe, review of *Twice-Told Tales* (1842), excerpted in *Nathaniel Hawthorne's Tales*, ed. James McIntosh (New York: Norton, 1987), 331.

4. Harry Levin, *The Power of Blackness: Hawthorne, Poe, Melville* (New York: Vintage, 1958), 58.

5. See D. H. Lawrence, *Studies in Classic American Literature* (Garden City, N.Y.: Doubleday, 1951; 1st pub. 1923), esp. chaps. 8 and 9; Michael J. Colacurcio, *The Province of Piety: Moral History in Hawthorne's Early Tales* (Cambridge: Harvard University Press, 1984); and Philip Young, *Hawthorne's Secret: An Un-Told Tale* (Boston: David R. Godine, 1984). Young argues that Hawthorne's secret is incest, either as fantasy or fact, between himself and his sister Ebe, though Young's primary evidence is only an ancestral analogue.

6. Melville, "Hawthorne and His Mosses" (1850), reprinted in *Tales*, ed. McIntosh, 348.

7. *The Letters of Herman Melville*, ed. Merrell R. Davis and William H. Gilman (New Haven: Yale University Press, 1965), 125; Young, *Hawthorne's Secret*, 6.

8. James, *Hawthorne* (1879), excerpted in *Tales*, 352; Hawthorne, *The Scarlet Letter*, 2d ed., ed. Sculley Bradley et al. (New York: Norton, 1978), 113.

9. Hawthorne, *The House of the Seven Gables*, ed. Seymour L. Gross (New York: Norton, 1967; 1st pub. 1851), 2. Michael Davitt Bell, in *The Development of American Romance: The Sacrifice of Relation* (Chicago: University of Chicago Press, 1980), suggests that Hawthorne's choice of romance as a genre is really a choice of the deviant social identity of

"romancer" (xiii, 148, 30–36). A provocative essay by Walter Benn Michaels, "Romance and Real Estate," in *Raritan*, 2 (Winter 1983), 66–87, uses Hawthorne's preface to *The House of the Seven Gables* to argue that Hawthorne's sense of romance restores the property rights of impoverished aristocrats in the nonthreatening imaginative realm. A canny and subtle study of Hawthorne's teasing narrations is John Franzosa, "A Psychoanalysis of Hawthorne's Style," *Genre*, 14 (Fall 1981), 383–409. Franzosa links what he calls the "pseudo-intimacy" of Hawthorne's tone to Hawthorne's need to establish an elite group of readers and to conceal threats of aggression and abandonment.

10. Hawthorne, *Scarlet Letter*, 141. In *Rediscovering Hawthorne* (Princeton: Princeton University Press, 1977), Kenneth Dauber takes the hook in a nonaggressive way by arguing that Hawthorne opens an intimate intercourse with his readers. From a feminist rather than structuralist perspective Joyce W. Warren makes a similar argument, that Hawthorne tries to detach readers from masculine egotism and self-reliance to affirm sympathetic bonds with women and social attachments. See Warren, *The American Narcissus: Individualism and Women in Nineteenth-Century American Fiction* (New Brunswick, N.J.: Rutgers University Press, 1984), 208–225, 230. In "A Psychoanalysis of Hawthorne's Style," Franzosa says Hawthorne appeals not to intimacy but to indulgence (387). Dauber and Franzosa agree in seeing Hawthorne's rhetoric of sympathy as what Dauber calls "the chief bond of the elite community" (15).

11. "My Kinsman, Major Molineux" is usually dated 1832; McIntosh, in *Nathaniel Hawthorne's Tales*, 3, notes that it was published in 1831 but in a magazine dated 1832. The two most influential psychoanalytic interpretations are by Simon O. Lesser, *Fiction and the Unconscious* (New York: Vintage, 1962), 212–224, and Frederick C. Crews, *The Sins of the Fathers: Hawthorne's Psychological Themes* (New York: Oxford University Press, 1966), 61–62, 72–79. See also Peter Shaw, "Fathers, Sons, and the Ambiguities of Revolution in 'My Kinsman, Major Molineux,'" *New England Quarterly*, 44 (1976), 559–576, and his *American Patriots and the Rituals of Revolution* (Cambridge: Harvard University Press, 1981), 18–21, 190–191. On the historicist side, see Roy Harvey Pearce, "Robin Molineux on the Analyst's Couch: A Note on the Limits of Psychoanalytic Criticism," *Criticism*, 1 (1959), 83–90, reprinted in his *Historicism Once More* (Princeton: Princeton University Press, 1969); and especially Colacurcio, *Province of Piety*, 130–153.

12. Dauber, *Rediscovering Hawthorne*, 25–35; Carol Marie Bensick, *La Nouvelle Beatrice: Renaissance and Romance in "Rappaccini's Daughter"* (New Brunswick, N.J.: Rutgers University Press, 1985). See also Colacurcio's seventy-two-page analysis of "Minister's Black Veil," *Province of Piety*, 314–385.

13. Q. D. Leavis, "Hawthorne as Poet" (1951), excerpted in *Tales*, 367.

14. Hawthorne, "My Kinsman, Major Molineux," in *Tales*, 16–17, hereafter cited in the text.

15. Colacurcio, *Province of Piety*, 130–153, quotation 136.

16. Colacurcio, ibid., 142, suggests that the gentleman is the speaker of the Massachusetts House of Representatives, since his "hem-hem" could be clearing the throat for a speech, and since he reappears on the house balcony at the end. Thus Robin accosts the leader of his kinsman's opposition. Colacurcio sees this as a "pretty broad" joke; it seems to me that the narrator's emphasis on death drives out the humor.

17. Hawthorne's preface ostensibly locates the story in the 1730s. In *Province of Piety*, 149, Colacurcio calls the "Man in the Moon" reference "the single most improbable and astonishing formal detail in the entire story." For him it confirms the irrelevance of Robin's psychological story to the politics of the crowd's "congregated mirth." John McWilliams, Jr., in *Hawthorne, Melville, and the American Character: A Looking-Glass Business* (Cambridge: Cambridge University Press, 1984), 85–88, stresses the mob's violent demagoguery and Robin's passivity in responding to the "contagion."

18. Colacurcio, *Province of Piety*, 145.

19. *Tales*, 5n. McIntosh also points out Hawthorne's political pun on *party*, 11n.

20. Bensick, *La Nouvelle Beatrice*, 104–112; Crews, *Sins of the Fathers*, 134. Bensick curiously avoids the possibility of rape. She suggests that Beatrice has either inherited syphilis from her father or received it through inoculation (111). Crews notes that the narrative blames the father for the daughter's poisonous sexuality and that "Rappaccini has already committed a kind of incest by polluting Beatrice with his chemicals," but Crews restricts the idea of actual incest between father and daughter to the father's fantasy of Giovanni's marriage, which would be "vicariously incestuous." See also Gloria C. Erlich, *Family Themes and Hawthorne's Fiction: The Tenacious Web* (New Brunswick, N.J.: Rutgers University Press, 1984), 132, on "innuendoes of incest" between the sibling-like Giovanni and Beatrice.

21. In *Sins of the Fathers*, 125–130, Crews discusses the "hidden kinship" between Giovanni and Rappaccini. Robert Weisbuch, linking Giovanni to Aylmer in "The Birthmark," calls him "king of the voyeurs and prince of the narcissists," poisonous because of his "hybrid emotions" just as Rappaccini creates hybrid plants to compete with God. *Atlantic Double-Cross: American Literature and British Influence in the Age of Emerson* (Chicago: University of Chicago Press, 1986), 262–263. In "Beatrice Rappaccini: A Victim of Male Love and Horror," *American Literature*, 48 (May 1976), 152–164, Richard Brenzo links the three men through their competitive "enmity" and "irrational fears," scapegoated on Beatrice.

22. Bensick, *La Nouvelle Beatrice*, 105–108.

23. *Tales*, 209. John Franzosa, in "The Language of Inflation in 'Rappaccini's Daughter,'" *Texas Studies in Literature and Language*, 24 (Spring 1982), 1–22, notes that "the tale concludes with two rhetorical questions, neither of which allows for a definitive answer" (7).

24. Bensick, *La Nouvelle Beatrice*, 99–104.

25. Dauber, *Rediscovering Hawthorne*, 30–31.

26. Steven Mailloux, *Interpretive Conventions: The Reader in the Study of American Fiction* (Ithaca: Cornell University Press, 1982), 73–91; Nina Baym, *The Shape of Hawthorne's Career* (Ithaca: Cornell University Press, 1976), 105–112, excerpted in *Tales*, 427–430. In *La Nouvelle Beatrice*, Bensick argues that the narrator is intended as a parody of Concord transcendentalism, while in *American Romanticism and the Marketplace* (Chicago: University of Chicago Press, 1985), 62–70, Michael T. Gilmore argues that Rappaccini is a transcendental artist, Baglioni represents the ordinary pen-and-ink man writer, and Beatrice represents Hawthorne's writing, killed by the literary competition. Franzosa, in "Language of Inflation," associates the narrator with the language of economic inflation in the 1840s.

27. Lawrence, *Studies in Classic American Literature*, 93: "That blue-eyed darling Nathaniel knew disagreeable things in his inner soul. He was careful to send them out in disguise."

28. Erlich, *Family Themes*, 131–133, 42–45. Erlich criticizes Crews for applying Oedipal models to Hawthorne. See also her remarks on Hawthorne's ambivalent relation to masculinity, 8–9, 71–72, and 154–155. On fatherlessness and classic American writers, see Quentin Anderson, *The Imperial Self: An Essay in American Literary and Cultural History* (New York: Knopf, 1971), e.g., 15–16.

29. Erlich, *Family Themes*, xvii, 124–125.

30. Ibid., 68, 73, 118. It should be added that for part of Hawthorne's adolescence he lived away from Robert, in Maine.

31. James R. Mellow, *Nathaniel Hawthorne in His Times* (Boston: Houghton Mifflin, 1980), 610–611. Mellow's suggestion seems much more compelling to me than Philip Young's argument, in *Hawthorne's Secret*, for incest.

32. *The Scarlet Letter*, 140; *House of the Seven Gables*, 129, 123.

33. Erlich, *Family Themes*, 118–119.

34. Hawthorne, *The Blithedale Romance*, introduction by Arlin Turner (New York: Norton, 1958; 1st pub. 1852), 138, hereafter cited in the text.

35. See Louise DeSalvo, *Nathaniel Hawthorne* (London: Harvester Press, 1987), 97–118, esp. 110–113; John Harmon McElroy and Edward L. McDonald, "The Coverdale Romance," *Studies in the Novel*, 14 (Spring 1982), 1–16, esp. 8–9. Both accounts focus on the handkerchief and Coverdale's odd, instantaneous knowledge of where Zenobia is after he wakes from his dream. McElroy and McDonald, who argue that "Coverdale killed Zenobia in a burst of dammed-up sexual frustrations," note that Coverdale not only is the last to see her alive but knows exactly how deep the spot is now (twelve to fifteen feet). When he had passed it earlier that day he wondered how deep it was and whether anyone had drowned there (9). Beverly Hume also finds Coverdale guilty at least of murderous intent, in "Restructuring the Case against Hawthorne's Coverdale," *Nineteenth-Century Fiction*, 40 (March 1986), 387–399. Zenobia's rigidity strongly implies she was a victim of strangulation, like the woman whose recovery Hawthorne observed (392–394), though he thought she was a suicide.

36. See 74 ("Priscilla marked me out for the third place in her regards"), 92 ("I—though probably reckoned as a friend by all—was at best but a secondary or tertiary personage with either of them"), 116 ("My own part in these transactions was singularly subordinate. It resembled that of the Chorus in a classic play"), 141 ("How little did these two women care for me"), 158 ("Priscilla's heart... had room but for a very few dearest ones, among whom she never reckoned me").

37. Michael Davitt Bell, in *Development of American Romance*, 185–192, astutely discusses the acquisitiveness underlying Coverdale's false ideality. Bell emphasizes the connections between "Westervelt's spurious art" and Coverdale's "bogus Romanticism," which makes passion safe by reducing it to sentimentality and statues (186, 189). Coverdale's artistic evasions abet "Blithedale's sentimental language of social control" (191). In *Hawthorne, Melville, and the Novel* (Chicago: University of Chicago Press, 1976), Richard H. Brodhead focuses on Coverdale's self-deception, noting that prying curiosity displaces his erotic desire (101). What I take to be narcissism, both Brodhead and Joel Porte, in *The Romance in America: Studies in Cooper, Poe, Hawthorne, Melville, and James* (Middletown, Conn.: Wesleyan University Press, 1969), see as the narrative's diffuse sexual passion lurking under sentimental self-deception. Porte sees Coverdale as an artist afraid of his powers (130).

38. Coverdale has already retreated "moodily" from Priscilla, after she humiliates him (143). With Old Moodie, too, Coverdale presents physical features as fragments, oddly shifting Old Moodie's eye patch from the left to the right eye as the narration progresses (103, 189), as John McDonald has pointed out to me. Nina Baym, in *Shape of Hawthorne's Career*, discusses Coverdale as an artist of the genteel (202), though locating his background in middle-class cosmopolitan life (187). Richard Poirier, in *A World Elsewhere: The Place of Style in American Literature* (New York: Oxford University Press, 1966), 115–124, discusses Coverdale as a prefiguration of modernist sensibility, a rather masturbatory and self-regarding dandy who retreats from the romantic dream to an aestheticism that signals his superior sensibility. In *The Rhetoric of American Romance: Dialectic and Identity in Emerson, Dickinson, Poe, and Hawthorne* (Baltimore: Johns Hopkins University Press, 1985), Evan Carton cleverly re-entangles the "knot" of Hawthorne and Coverdale, stressing that the issue for Hawthorne is not whether Coverdale is unreliable but whether any narration can be reliable. Rather than set that evasiveness in social context, as I try to do, Carton more sympathetically sees it as fundamental to Hawthorne's exploration of imagination and actuality in the romance genre (228–252). Carton also links Coverdale with Moodie (282).

39. See also 51, for Coverdale's ironic awareness of his class consciousness.

40. *The Blithedale Romance*, Norton Critical Edition, ed. Seymour Gross and Rosalie Murphy (New York: Norton, 1978), 22n. Also see Brodhead, *Hawthorne, Melville, and the Novel*, 112. Almost every critic finds the last line appalling. Brodhead, for instance, says it undercuts the whole book: "If Coverdale's confession is true, then nothing else in the novel is" (115).

41. Edwin Haviland Miller, *Melville: A Biography* (New York: Braziller, 1975), 240–244. Miller conjectures that Melville reciprocally describes Hawthorne as Plinlimmon in *Pierre*. See also 118: "After Hollingsworth failed me, there was no longer the man alive with whom I could think of sharing all."

42. McElroy and McDonald, in "The Coverdale Romance," argue that Coverdale loves Zenobia and therefore that the secret analogy is, "Hollingsworth has just rejected Zenobia as she has rejected Coverdale" (4).

43. I am indebted to Samuel Kimball for several conversations about how Coverdale makes readers feel like Coverdale.

44. See James, *Hawthorne* (Ithaca: Cornell University Press, 1956; 1st pub. 1879), 105–109, esp. 108 on "the absence of satire." In *Sins of the Fathers*, Frederick Crews notes that *Blithedale* "remains the least admired of Hawthorne's longer narratives" (194), although its critical status seems to have risen considerably with Bell and other critics who read Coverdale ironically.

45. Brodhead, in *Hawthorne, Melville, and the Novel*, 92, points out that the narrative characteristically veils power battles in its conversations. In his more recent book, *The School of Hawthorne* (New York: Oxford University Press, 1986), 91–93, he also focuses on Blithedale as a "web of power" relations, and brilliantly discusses *The Bostonians* as James's revisionary reading of *Blithedale* to show "the inseparability of love, sexuality, and the will to power," elements that Hawthorne's narrative tries to polarize (148–157, quotation 153). In *Love and Death in the American Novel*, rev. ed. (New York: Stein and Day, 1966), 65, Leslie Fiedler calls *Blithedale* "an act of self-abnegation, public penance for being male." Later he observes that Zenobia must die because she "sinned in the flesh with men more masculine than he" (224).

An essay by Thomas F. Strychacz, "Coverdale and Women: Feverish Fantasies in *The Blithedale Romance*," *American Transcendental Quarterly*, 62 (1986), 29–46, develops the narrative's power dynamics and connects Coverdale's obsession with power to American patriarchal culture. Strychacz reverses my sense that a wish to be humiliated may go deeper in Coverdale than a will to power; he suggests that submission may be Coverdale's compensatory fantasy when dominance fails. John Carlos Rowe briefly discusses patriarchal power relations in *Blithedale*; see his *Through the Custom-House: Nineteenth-Century American Fiction and Modern Theory* (Baltimore: Johns Hopkins University Press, 1982), 67–68.

46. Lawrence, *Studies in Classic American Literature*, 118.

Chapter 9. Mrs. Hawthorne's Headache

1. Randall Stewart, *Nathaniel Hawthorne: A Biography* (New Haven: Yale University Press, 1948), 95, cites both the first quotation, which is from a letter to Horatio Bridge, February 4, 1850, rpt. in *Hawthorne: The Critical Heritage*, ed. J. Donald Crowley (New York: Barnes and Noble, 1970), 151, and the second quotation, which is from Hawthorne's *English Note-Books*, September 14, 1855.

2. D. H. Lawrence, *Studies in Classic American Literature* (Garden City, N.Y.: Doubleday, 1951), 13; see also his discussion of *The Scarlet Letter* as a "colossal satire" full of "inner diabolism" (92–110). At least two recent essays also question the narrator's reliability. David Van Leer, "Hester's Labyrinth: Transcendental Rhetoric in Puritan Boston," in *New Essays on "The Scarlet Letter*," ed. Michael J. Colacurcio (Cambridge:

Cambridge University Press, 1985), 57–101, declares that "the narrator is the novel's real hypocrite" (87), and indicts the narrator's pseudospiritual language. An essay more closely paralleling mine is Daniel Cottom, "Hawthorne versus Hester: The Ghostly Dialectic of Romance in *The Scarlet Letter*," *Texas Studies in Literature & Language*, 24 (Spring 1982), 47–67. Cottom argues that the narrator transcends nature with the evasiveness of romance while Hester is forced to accept a womanhood imprisoned in sexuality.

3. Anthony Trollope, "The Genius of *The Scarlet Letter*," in *The Scarlet Letter: An Annotated Text, Backgrounds, and Sources, Essays in Criticism*, 1st ed., ed. Sculley Bradley, Richmond Croom Beatty, and E. Hudson Long (New York: Norton, 1962), 242; see also "He is always laughing at something with his weird, mocking spirit" (244). The article in the Norton edition is a partial reprint of Trollope, "The Genius of Nathaniel Hawthorne," *North American Review* (September 1879), 203–222.

4. Trollope, "The Genius of *The Scarlet Letter*," 243; James, *Hawthorne*, introduction by Tony Tanner (London: Macmillan, 1967), 109–10. Taylor Stoehr, *Hawthorne's Mad Scientists: Pseudoscience and Social Science in Nineteenth-Century Life and Letters* (Hamden, Conn.: Archon, 1978), 116, stresses Chillingworth's function as "an evil chorus figure whose perspective has much in common with that of the reader and the author." An angry Salem Whig found nothing but Chillingworth in Hawthorne; see Benjamin Lease, "Salem vs. Hawthorne: An Early Review of *The Scarlet Letter*," *New England Quarterly*, 44 (1971), 110–17.

5. Anne W. Abbott, review of *The Scarlet Letter*, in *North American Review* (July 1850), rpt. in *Hawthorne: The Critical Heritage*, 166; E. P. Whipple, "Nathaniel Hawthorne," *Atlantic Monthly* (May 1860), rpt. in *Hawthorne: The Critical Heritage*, 344, 346. Whipple's 1850 review of *The Scarlet Letter* is also reprinted in *The Critical Heritage*, 160–62.

6. In arguing that close readings open out to questions of social history, I am opposing the antiformalist stance taken by Jane Tompkins in the first chapter of *Sensational Designs: The Cultural Work of American Fiction, 1790–1860* (New York: Oxford University Press, 1985), 3–39, arguing that critics have preserved Hawthorne's reputation at the expense of, say, Susan Warner's. I agree with Tompkins's larger contention that textual meanings are established by readers at any historical moment. But if I am right to say that *The Scarlet Letter* induces, replicates, and undermines the interpretive expectations of its contemporary readers, that posits a more ambivalent relation between text and community than the theory of interpretive community so far allows. Various writings by Tompkins, Stanley Fish, and Walter Benn Michaels have been developing the theory; Steven Mailloux usefully summarizes them and others in *Interpretive Conventions: The Reader in the Study of American Fiction* (Ithaca: Cornell University Press, 1982). Mailloux uses Hawthorne to orient the theory toward how texts constitute ethical judgments.

In emphasizing gender conventions, I am also resisting Michael J. Colacurcio's sympathetic critique of this chapter, which first appeared in *Nineteenth-Century Fiction*, 37 (March 1983), 552–575. In *New Essays on "The Scarlet Letter,"* Colacurcio urges a more deconstructive approach toward the text's meaning making. For him the text inexorably pushes meaning making toward Dimmesdale and presents Hester's sexuality as part of the metaphoric-theological generation of meanings (127, 134, also 19–20). While my chapter does remain open to the charge of romanticizing Hester or of polarizing the text's complexity as manhood vs. female subjectivity, Colacurcio's reading ultimately leaves one stranded in a complicated dead end, a nihilistic subversion of the narrator's evasive complicity with Dimmesdale's narcissism.

7. Hawthorne, *The Scarlet Letter: An Authoritative Text, Backgrounds and Sources, Criticism*, ed. Sculley Bradley, Richmond Croom Beatty, E. Hudson Long, Seymour Gross, 2d ed. (New York: Norton, 1978), 39, and 39–40 for subsequent quotations from the first chapter, hereafter cited in the text. For a similar close reading of the opening chapter, see Amy Schrager Lang, *Prophetic Woman: Anne Hutchinson and the Problem of Dissent in*

the Literature of New England (Berkeley: University of California Press, 1987), 164–165. Lang emphasizes the doubling latent in the oppositions.

8. Hyatt H. Waggoner, *Hawthorne: A Critical Study*, rev. ed. (Cambridge: Harvard University Press, 1963), 145; Nina Baym, *The Shape of Hawthorne's Career* (Ithaca: Cornell University Press, 1976), 124–35. Judith Fryer makes a more dubious argument for Hester's potential "androgyny" in *The Faces of Eve: Women in the Nineteenth Century American Novel* (New York: Oxford University Press, 1976), 74–84. See also Baym, "The Significance of Plot in Hawthorne's Romances," in *Ruined Eden of the Present: Hawthorne, Melville, and Poe: Critical Essays in Honor of Darrel Abel*, ed. G. R. Thompson and Virgil L. Lokke (West Lafayette, Ind.: Purdue University Press, 1981), 49–70.

9. See Edward Wagenknecht, *Nathaniel Hawthorne: Man and Writer* (New York: Oxford University Press, 1961), 17–18 and 150–53, for various remarks about Hawthorne's ambivalence concerning strong women.

10. Every Hawthorne commentator I've read has missed Hester's secret dream of reunion in hell. They assume she hopes for heavenly reconciliation. See, for example, Richard H. Brodhead, *Hawthorne, Melville, and the Novel* (Chicago: University of Chicago Press, 1976), 66; and Michael Davitt Bell, *The Development of American Romance: The Sacrifice of Relation* (Chicago: University of Chicago Press, 1980), 178.

11. I am indebted here and throughout this chapter to Richard Brodhead's incisive commentary on an earlier draft, as well as to helpful responses from Walter Herbert and *Nineteenth-Century Fiction*'s two readers. On Anne Hutchinson and *The Scarlet Letter*, see Lang, *Prophetic Woman*, 161–192. Lang's complex reading presents Hester as proud and self-reliant, not loving.

12. Nancy Chodorow, *The Reproduction of Mothering: Psychoanalysis and the Sociology of Gender* (Berkeley: University of California Press, 1978).

13. This view of first name as implying intimacy and last name as social code could reflect the narrator's patronizing. Also, as with Robin Molineux, Hester's relative freedom from her last name suggests her dangerous susceptibility to passion, at least in the narrator's eyes.

14. Brodhead, *Hawthorne, Melville, and the Novel*, 56–57, emphasizes Pearl's oscillation between incompatible modes, especially in this scene. Most critics simply see Pearl as Hester's double. For a fascinating essay focusing on Hawthorne's ambivalent gender expectations as a parent, see T. Walter Herbert, Jr., "Nathaniel Hawthorne, Una Hawthorne, and *The Scarlet Letter*: Interactive Selfhoods and the Cultural Construction of Gender," *PMLA*, 103 (May 1988), 285–297. Herbert sees Una's later nervous breakdown as a counter-text to Pearl's transformation from embattled brat to True American Womanhood, though that transformation becomes only one among "a continuous scrimmage of meanings" (288) emerging from unresolved gender conflicts in Hawthorne's life as well as in his writing.

15. My analysis of this scene opposes the more narcissistic readings offered by John Irwin, *American Hieroglyphics: The Symbol of the Egyptian Hieroglyphics in the American Renaissance* (New Haven: Yale University Press, 1980), 250–251, which stresses the interplay of mirrors with absence; and by Sharon Cameron, *The Corporeal Self: Allegories of the Body in Melville and Hawthorne* (Baltimore: Johns Hopkins University Press, 1981), 84, which stresses Pearl's connection to the letter as part of Hester's body. Both readings illuminate narrative doublings and problems of identity but avoid the interpersonal issues that generate narcissistic fears. Cameron in particular reduces feelings of anger to acts of violence.

16. This reading differs from Christian readings that see Dimmesdale's "tongues of flame" eloquence as the romance's central truth; e.g., see Roy Male, "Hawthorne's Literal Figures," in *Ruined Eden of the Present*, 90. My reading also differs from those that see Dimmesdale's guilt in primarily sexual terms; see Joel Porte, *The Romance in America:*

Studies in Cooper, Poe, Hawthorne, Melville, and James (Middletown, Conn.: Wesleyan University Press, 1969), 98–114. In several places, most recently in " 'The Woman's Own Choice': Sex, Metaphor, and the Puritan 'Sources' of *The Scarlet Letter*," in *New Essays on "The Scarlet Letter"*, Michael J. Colacurcio suggests that Dimmesdale's remorse for adultery is really his fear of idolatry, of putting Hester before God (118).

17. Baym, "The Significance of Plot," makes a strong argument for Hester's consistent social power. Baym also stresses Dimmesdale's moral inadequacy, though the sexism she attributes to Darrel Abel should be lodged with the narrator. I think Baym overstates Hester's consistency and underplays the narrator's ambivalence. The narrator's Catholic associations for Hester—the "sainted" Anne Hutchinson (Hawthorne omits the e from her first name), the "madonna" that a "Papist" would have seen, and here a "Sister of Mercy" whose letter "had the effect of the cross on a nun's bosom" (118)—may be meant to evoke suspiciousness as well as approval, given the anti-Catholic feelings running so high in the 1850s.

18. The narrator twice implies that Chillingworth had been detained against his will by Indians for much of that time. Chillingworth is called "Master Prynne" by a townsman in chapter 3. His "Peace, Hester, peace!" concluding chapter 14 (126) parallels Dimmesdale's later "Hush!"

19. See Baym, "The Significance of Plot," in *Ruined Eden of the Present*; and Michael J. Colacurcio, "Footsteps of Anne Hutchinson: The Context of *The Scarlet Letter*," *ELH*, 39 (1972), 459–94, an essay that rightly connects Hester to Anne Hutchinson and Dimmesdale to John Cotton but wrongly reduces Hester's radical perceptions to her sexuality. Colacurcio concludes that both the teller and the tale force Hester to abandon conclusions to which we are sympathetic. Lang, in *Prophetic Woman*, also finds that Hester's dangerous multiplicity is conventionalized or put in its woman's place, but wrongly says Hester repents. Lang also accepts the narrator at face value, intriguingly seeing his voice as an embroiderer-double of Hester, but she reduces Hester to the narrator's fear of unchecked individualism.

20. Morton Cronin, "Hawthorne on Romantic Love and the Status of Women," *PMLA*, 69 (1954), 98. See also Frederic I. Carpenter's fine essay "Scarlet A Minus," *College English*, 5 (1944), 173–80; rpt. in both Norton Critical Editions of *The Scarlet Letter*.

21. Recent criticism has begun to explore these oscillations. See esp. Brodhead, *Hawthorne, Melville, and the Novel*; Kenneth Dauber, *Rediscovering Hawthorne* (Princeton: Princeton University Press, 1977), though Dauber is taken in by the narrator's claims for intimacy; and Edgar A. Dryden, *Nathaniel Hawthorne: The Poetics of Enchantment* (Ithaca: Cornell University Press, 1977), which argues for Hawthorne's alternation between postures as his way of managing "a menacing otherness at his own center" (21).

22. See Leslie A. Fiedler, *Love and Death in the American Novel*, rev. ed. (New York: Stein and Day, 1966), 437; and Baym, *The Shape of Hawthorne's Career*, who differs from my view in saying that at the end "the two shattered personalities become whole again and the symbolic characters disappear" (130).

23. Irwin, *American Hieroglyphics*, 239–284; Frederick C. Crews, *The Sins of the Fathers: Hawthorne's Psychological Themes* (New York: Oxford University Press, 1966), 136–153. Irwin attributes Dimmesdale's guilt to the opposition between his "true" self and his false public role and presents Hester as the double for a Dimmesdale-like narrator. Crews's more ambivalent reading mocks Hester for "prating" of freedom, yet equally condemns the minister's anxious egotism. For Crews, Dimmesdale finally achieves "heroic independence" of Hester by sublimating his libido in oratory; Hester "lacks the detachment to appreciate Dimmesdale's final act of courage." Yet that act is simultaneously an "egocentric confession" and a "suicide" to relax compulsive guilt by expelling libido (143–152). Baym, *The Shape of Hawthorne's Career*, 138–139, briefly suggests a Freudian perspective, that Pearl might be Hester's id and Chillingworth Dimmesdale's superego.

24. In *Rediscovering Hawthorne* Dauber astutely discusses the shift toward Dimmesdale as allegory's socialization of the forest's romance world. Brodhead, *Hawthorne, Melville, and the Novel,* associates interpretive openness with Hester's symbolic mode and says that Chillingworth embodies tendencies toward allegorical rigidity and the punitive realism of a hierarchic male society. Bell, *The Development of American Romance,* 176–177, similarly argues that Hester's rebellion is "the central 'story'" but that she, as well as society, represses herself to become "a victim of allegory." Both Poe and Henry James vehemently opposed Hawthorne's allegorizing as artistically destructive, a perspective sometimes adopted by Hawthorne himself. In *The School of Hawthorne* (New York: Oxford University Press, 1986), 184, Brodhead suggests that symbolic allegory is Hawthorne's way of both dramatizing and critiquing the "daimonization" of a self by showing how obsessions reduce a self's wholeness to "the expressive flatness of emblematic signs."

25. Abbott, review of *The Scarlet Letter,* in *Hawthorne: The Critical Heritage,* 165. Bell, *The Development of American Romance,* 178, suggests that even God "becomes a kind of allegorical double" for Dimmesdale's "guilty self-justification." Leslie Fiedler, *Love and Death in the American Novel,* 235, describes this passage as "an equivocation which undercuts, at the last moment, the whole suggested meaning of his book."

26. See Hélène Cixous, "sorties," in *New French Feminisms: An Anthology,* ed. Elaine Marks and Isabelle de Courtivron (Amherst: University of Massachusetts Press, 1980), 91–92, on the reduction of the woman to the maternal implied in the ascension of man to the father. In *Prophetic Woman,* 186–187, Lang notes that Dimmesdale incorporates Hester into his redemption much as Emerson incorporates womanhood into his version of transcendence.

27. As John Franzosa has established for "The Custom-House," anger and dependence are issues more basic than guilt and sexuality. See "'The Custom-House,' *The Scarlet Letter,* and Hawthorne's Separation from Salem," *ESQ,* 24 (1978), 57–71. Franzosa argues that a guilty identity balances impulses toward hostile intrusion and isolated self-possession and allows inauthetic identity with the narrator's community. Baym defends Hawthorne's mother from Hawthorne in "Nathaniel Hawthorne and His Mother: A Biographical Speculation," *American Literature,* 54 (1982), 1–27. While suggesting that Hawthorne's various presentations of his mother mask her "oppressive" presence in his psyche, Baym sees *The Scarlet Letter* as a creative reversal that temporarily frees Hawthorne from dependency on maternal power. On Hawthorne's relation to Robert Manning, see Gloria C. Erlich, *Family Themes and Hawthorne's Fiction: The Tenacious Web* (New Brunswick, N.J.: Rutgers University Press, 1984).

28. The phrase is Whipple's (*Hawthorne: The Critical Heritage,* 161–62). Henry F. Chorley, in a review in the *Athenaeum,* June 15, 1850, praised *The Scarlet Letter* for being "so clear of fever and of prurient excitement" because "the misery of the woman" is always present (rpt. in *Hawthorne: The Critical Heritage,* see 163); E. A. Duyckinck, in a review in *Literary World,* March 30, 1850, was happy to see a "writer who has lived so much among the new school" handle "this delicate subject without an infusion of George Sand" (rpt. in *Hawthorne: The Critical Heritage,* see 156–57). On the other hand, both Abbott's review and the review by Orestes Brownson in *Brownson's Quarterly Review* (October 1850), condemn the romance because Hester is not sufficiently repentant, as does the infamous review by Arthur Cleveland Coxe in the *Church Review* (January 1851) (rpt. in *Hawthorne: The Critical Heritage;* see 165–166, 177–178, and 183).

Chapter 10. Ahab's Queenly Personality

1. Robert Zoellner, *The Salt-Sea Mastodon: A Reading of "Moby-Dick"* (Berkeley: University of California Press, 1973), ix. Despite current critical practice, I am deleting the hyphen from *Moby Dick* except when the title is cited with the hyphen. The only reason

for including it seems to be its presence in the title of the American edition, since the whale's name always appears without the hyphen. Harrison Hayford and Hershel Parker, the editors of the Norton Critical Edition, treat the issue as an unresolved question and acknowledge that their policy "has been conservative" ([New York: Norton, 1967], 477). Melville himself cites the title without a hyphen in his letter to Sophia Hawthorne (ibid., 568). Given Melville's notorious sloppiness about punctuation, the hyphen seems to me to be a canonized mistake.

2. The most influential psychoanalytic study of Melville is Edwin Haviland Miller's *Melville* (New York: George Braziller, 1975), 172–219 on *Moby Dick*. Martin Bickman's "Melville and the Mind," in *A Companion to Melville Studies*, ed. John Bryant (Westport, Conn.: Greenwood Press, 1986), 515–541, is an admirably detailed and judicious review of psychological scholarship. Recent political studies include Joyce Sparer Adler, *War in Melville's Imagination* (New York: New York University Press, 1981), 55–78 on *Moby Dick*; James Duban, *Melville's Major Fiction: Politics, Theology, and Imagination* (Dekalb: Northern Illinois University Press, 1983), 82–148 on Ishmael's complicity with Ahab's racist expansionism; and Michael Paul Rogin, *Subversive Genealogy: The Politics and Art of Herman Melville* (New York: Knopf, 1983), mixing psychological insights with Melville's uses of his family's history.

In *American Romanticism and the Marketplace* (Chicago: University of Chicago Press, 1985), Michael T. Gilmore sees *Moby Dick* as an allegory of alienated labor in a commodifying economy, with Ishmael as artisan and Ahab, more problematically, as factory worker, 113–131, esp. 115–121. Robert Shulman, *Social Criticism and Nineteenth-Century American Fictions* (Columbia: University of Missouri Press, 1987), 197–210, similarly presents Ishmael as a manly, democratic artisan; Ahab represents the authoritarian, alienated personality type. The most exuberant critique of Ahab as modern authoritarian personality is in *Mariners, Renegades and Castaways: The Story of Herman Melville and the World We Live In* (London: Allison & Busby, 1985; 1st pub. 1953), where C. L. R. James argues that Ahab represents the essence of the modern totalitarian personality, which thrives because of liberal intellectuals like Starbuck and Ishmael. James mocks psychoanalysis, which (he says) has helped to make intellectuals effete, incestuous, and homosexual (e.g., 97–98, 109–110).

3. See especially Zoellner, *Salt-Sea Mastodon*; and Adler, *War in Melville's Imagination*. The seminal essay shifting attention from Ahab to Ishmael is Walter Bezanson, "*Moby-Dick*: Work of Art," in "*Moby-Dick*": *Centennial Essays*, ed. Tyrus Hillway and Luther S. Mansfield (Dallas: Southern Methodist University Press, 1953), 30–58. Donald E. Pease sets the Ishmael = freedom, Ahab = totalitarianism interpretation in a Cold War context; see "Melville and Cultural Persuasion," in *Ideology and Classic American Literature*, ed. Sacvan Bercovitch and Myra Jehlen (Cambridge: Cambridge University Press, 1986), 384–417.

4. See, for instance, Richard Brodhead, *Hawthorne, Melville, and the Novel* (Chicago: University of Chicago Press, 1976), 134–162, which explicates Ishmael and Ahab as contradictory literary genres, or Edgar A. Dryden, *Melville's Thematics of Form: The Great Art of Telling the Truth* (Baltimore: Johns Hopkins University Press, 1968), 83–113, which presents Ishmael as a storyteller who describes the "truth": all forms are fictions, he and Ahab are actors, and meaning itself is constructed by "a mind which has turned away from the chaos and confusion of the world toward a contemplation of its own activity" (84)—a deconstructionist on the masthead. Edwin Eigner gains a Mapple's-eye-view stability by presenting both Ahab and Ishmael as blasphemous questers after mastery, with Ishmael saved from himself at last. See Eigner, *The Metaphysical Novel in England and America: Dickens, Bulwer, Melville, and Hawthorne* (Berkeley: University of California Press, 1978), 81–82, 96, 111–113, 215–216, 223–225.

5. See Michael Davitt Bell, *The Development of American Romance: The Sacrifice of Relation*

(Chicago: University of Chicago Press, 1980), 217–233. Joyce Warren, *The American Narcissus: Individualism and Women in Nineteenth-Century American Fiction* (New Brunswick: Rutgers University Press, 1984), assesses *Moby Dick's* narcissism with a strong, if simple, feminist critique, emphasizing Melville's biography.

6. Conrad's letter of January 15, 1907, to Humphrey Milford, who had asked him to write a preface, is reprinted in Frank MacShane, "Conrad on Melville," *American Literature*, 29 (January 1958), 463–464. Bell notes his bafflement in *Development of American Romance*, 224, 233. Neal L. Tolchin, *Mourning, Gender, and Creativity in the Art of Herman Melville* (New Haven: Yale University Press, 1988), 117–137, argues that in *Moby Dick* Melville tries to exorcise his mother's rage and grief through Ahab, but Victorian mourning conventions block the expression of feeling. My discussion of insincerity and narcissism is also indebted to Suzanne Stein's 1986 Rutgers University dissertation, "The Pusher and the Sufferer: An Unsentimental Reading of *Moby-Dick*." Stein explores the narcissism in Ahab's pose of tragic hero and in Ishmael's need to see Ahab that way. In *Studies in Classic American Literature* (Garden City, N.Y.: Doubleday, 1951), D. H. Lawrence notes of *Moby Dick*, "As a soul history, it makes one angry" (160, also 157–158).

7. Melville, letter to Sarah Huyler Morewood, September 12, 1851, reprinted in the Norton Critical Edition of *Moby-Dick; or, The Whale*, ed. Harrison Hayford and Hershel Parker (New York: Norton, 1967; 1st pub. 1851), 564 (all citations are from this edition; they will be given in the text). See his letter to Sophia Hawthorne (January 8, 1852), reprinted 568: "It really amazed me that you should find any satisfaction in that book. It is true that some *men* have said they were pleased with it, but you are the only *woman*—for as a general thing, women have small taste for the sea." See also Nina Baym, "Melodramas of Beset Manhood: How Theories of American Fiction Exclude Women Authors," *American Quarterly*, 33 (Summer 1981), 123–139. Baym applies her phrase primarily to male critics of classic American literature, but texts such as *Moby Dick* abet that male tradition. Richard Brodhead calls it "so outrageously masculine that we scarcely allow ourselves to do justice to the full scope of its masculinism," especially its "quest for absolute potency." See his Introduction to *New Essays on Moby-Dick*, ed. Brodhead (Cambridge: Cambridge University Press, 1986), 9–10.

8. For a discussion of Melville's review of Parkman, see Lee Clark Mitchell, *Witnesses to a Vanishing America: the Nineteenth-Century Response* (Princeton: Princeton University Press, 1981), chap. 7. Mitchell argues that Queequeg and Ahab each "educates Ishmael in alternative responses to experience" (206), with Queequeg challenging Ahab's absolutism. Robert K. Martin argues that homosexual bonding, particularly in the Queequeg-Ishmael friendship, challenges both Ahab's patriarchal aggression and the American ideal of heterosexual manhood based on conquest and ownership. See his *Hero, Captain, and Stranger: Male Friendship, Social Critique, and Literary Form in the Sea Novels of Herman Melville* (Chapel Hill: University of North Carolina Press, 1986), 67–94. Martin also highlights the masturbatory aspects of Ishmael's play with language, arguing that by combining democratic fraternity with masturbation Melville tries "to undermine the cult of earnest productivity" (16, also 63 on mutual masturbation vs. penetration).

9. For a more psychoanalytic gloss on this passage and on Queequeg, see my essay on *Moby Dick* in *Psychoanalysis and Literary Process*, ed. Frederick Crews (Cambridge, Mass.: Winthrop, 1970), 78–85.

10. Donald G. Mitchell's book (pub. under the pseudonym of Ik Marvel) is a meditation on male needs for intimacy. Without a good woman, he muses, you wake "with a shudder into the cold resolves of your lonely and manly life" (*Reveries of a Bachelor* [New York: Scribner's Sons, 1907; 1st pub. 1850], 120). A boy without love, he says later (167), "will find pride, self-indulgence, and an iron purpose coming in to furnish other supply for the soul that is in him." To a man hurt by love, "Business, and pursuits of ambition or of interest, pass on like dull, grating machinery" (270). In "Call Me Ishmael, or How to

Make Double-Talk Speak," *New Essays on Moby-Dick*, 73–108, Carolyn Porter argues that Ishmael's "miraculous talent for destabilizing our perspective without provoking our hostility" depends on his ability to speak both as alien and as authority, sponging and plundering from his culture (94, 99).

11. On the phantom as worried stepmother, see Louise Dutney's appendix to my essay, "Class Conflicts in Teaching *Moby-Dick*," *Approaches to Teaching Melville's "Moby-Dick*," ed. Martin Bickman (New York: MLA, 1985), 91, 94–95. Or the phantom might be "the consoling spirit of his dead mother," John Seelye suggests in *Melville: The Ironic Diagram* (Evanston, Ill.: Northwestern University Press, 1970), 61.

12. I'm indebted for this formulation to a University of Florida student, Knan Lee, and also to Suzanne Stein's dissertation.

13. Melville, *White-Jacket or The World in a Man-of-War* (New York: Library of America, 1983), chaps. 33–35, quotations 496, 501, hereafter cited in the text.

14. Rogin, *Subversive Genealogy*, 90–97; Richard H. Brodhead, "Sparing the Rod: Discipline and Fiction in Antebellum America," *Representations*, 21 (Winter 1988), 67–96.

15. I'm indebted to John Seelye for reminding me of *White-Jacket's* relevance here.

16. Lawrence, *Studies in Classic American Literature*, 173.

17. Rogin, *Subversive Genealogy*, 118. On monomania, see Henry Nash Smith, *Democracy and the Novel: Popular Resistance to Classic American Writers* (New York: Oxford University Press, 1978), 35–42. Smith is uncommonly candid about his inability to make sense of the narration (37, 44–48, 53–54). An earlier essay by Smith, "The Image of Society in *Moby-Dick*," *Centennial Essays*, 59–75, also raises the issue of narrative incoherence, while explicating Ishmael's "philosophical anarchy" (66) as a response to competitive capitalism. See Rogin, *Subversive Genealogy*, 120–121: "Ahab carries to its extreme the egotistic, bourgeois desire for power, to be alone in the world and to possess it.... He reveals the rebellion and the desire for domination entangled in the wish to be free."

18. In *American Romanticism and the Marketplace*, Michael Gilmore usefully summarizes key economic changes from 1815 (2–5) and emphasizes the increasing class segregation. See also my discussion and notes in Chapter 3.

19. See James, *Mariners, Renegades and Castaways*, 72.

20. Zoellner, *Salt-Sea Mastodon*, 91–117.

21. Martin Leonard Pops, in *The Melville Archetype* (n.p.: Kent State University Press, 1970), 65–87, explains the whale's "dichotomous nature" in more Jungian terms, as a double realm of God and sexual energy. If Ahab strives to penetrate the male wall and reach the female principle, his quest is also a "heroic attempt to emancipate himself from the Mother through 'regenerative' incest" (85).

22. In *Herman Melville* (London: Methuen, 1950), 172, Newton Arvin says of this passage, "Ahab's 'ivory' leg is an equivocal symbol both of his own impotence and of the independent male principle directed cripplingly against him." Arvin's study remains a powerfully ambivalent account of manhood in *Moby Dick*. He speaks of the "butchery and carnage" at the heart of *Moby Dick* (160), while he admires Melville's ability to lift that destructiveness to an imaginative level. Arvin also sees the unconscious center of the book as suicide and murder, counterbalanced by Melville's commitment to love and friendship (170–171). In *Melville and Male Identity* (Rutherford, N.J.: Fairleigh Dickinson University Press, 1980), Charles Haberstroh, Jr., says Ahab and Ishmael are twinned in alienation and hungering for dominance (100). Haberstroh agrees with Edwin Miller, who asserts in *Melville* that Ahab and Ishmael "are frightened boy-men" (218).

23. Harold Beaver, an exception, extensively annotates "The Candles" with gnostic references. For him, Ahab "is now wholly at the command of the 'fallen Mother,' " as Sophia and Kali defy the Demiurge. See *Moby-Dick*, ed. Beaver (New York: Penguin, 1972), 927–930. In *Melville's Later Novels* (Athens: University of Georgia Press, 1986), 91–124, William B. Dillingham also reads Ahab as a gnostic heretic. In *Melville's Quarrel*

with God (Princeton: Princeton University Press, 1952), 229–232, Lawrance Thompson sees "The Candles" as the book's blasphemous climax. Leon Howard more prosaically links Ahab's fire imagery to Carlyle; see Howard, *The Unfolding of Moby-Dick*, ed. James Barbour and Thomas Quirk (Glassboro, N.J.: Melville Society, 1987), 42. Robert Milder links Ahab to Goethe, and stresses the literariness of his demonism; see *"Nemo Contra Deum . . .: Melville and Goethe's 'Demonic,' "* in *Ruined Eden of the Present: Hawthorne, Melville, and Poe, Critical Essays in Honor of Darrel Abel*, ed. G.R. Thompson and Virgil L. Lokke (West Lafayette, Ind.: Purdue University Press, 1981), 205–244. Among other things, for instance, "The Candles" is an implied pun on the word surfacing two chapters later, "lucifers."

24. Richard Sewall, *The Life of Emily Dickinson*, (New York: Farrar, Straus & Giroux, 1974), 2:515.

25. Warner Berthoff, *The Example of Melville* (Princeton: Princeton University Press, 1962), 42–46. (As Edwin Miller observes of Ishmael's ostensibly strong, sure masculine voice, he is trying to cut the legs off both people and ideas; *Melville*, 218.) Hershel Parker's 1963 dissertation originally had a chapter demonstrating how Melville started to identify with defiant Satanic sufferers as he finished *Moby Dick*. But "the substitute director said that if I was right, Melville was crazy, so the chapter was junked." *Nineteenth-Century Fiction*, 39 (December 1984), 361.

26. Amariah Brigham, *An Inquiry concerning the Diseases and Functions of the Brain, the Spinal Cord, and the Nerves* (New York: Arno Press, 1973; 1st pub. New York, 1840), 240, 247. Brigham observes that one can sometimes cure women of hysteria either by forcing them to exercise or by burning their feet with a hot poker, to make them afraid of having a fit again (248–249).

27. Carroll Smith-Rosenberg, "The Hysterical Woman: Sex Roles and Role Conflict in 19th Century America," *Social Research*, 39 (1972), 651–678, reprinted in *Disorderly Conduct: Visions of Gender in Victorian America* (New York: Oxford University Press, 1986), 197–216; Jean Strouse, *Alice James: A Biography* (Boston: Houghton Mifflin, 1980); Juliet Mitchell, *Women: The Longest Revolution: Essays on Feminism, Literature and Psychoanalysis* (London: Virago Press, 1984), 307. Also see Carol Gilligan, "The Conquistador and the Dark Continent: Reflections on the Psychology of Love," *Daedalus*, 113 (Summer 1984), 75–95, for a critique of the depersonalization of women in the post-Freudian terminology of object relations, implicit in Freud's studies of female hysteria. See also T. Walter Herbert, Jr., "Nathaniel Hawthorne, Una Hawthorne, and *The Scarlet Letter*: Interactive Selfhoods and the Cultural Construction of Gender," *PMLA*, 103 (May 1988), 285–297, for a fine analysis of how Hawthorne's gender ambivalences helped to induce hysteria in his daughter.

28. Emerson, *Emerson in His Journals*, ed. Joel Porte (Cambridge: Harvard University Press, 1982), 414, entry ca. 1851. In *Women: The Longest Revolution*, 290, Mitchell speaks of the hysteric's voice as the woman's masculine language talking about feminine experience, unable to be disruptive except within patriarchal law.

29. I'm indebted for this point to Marilee Lindeman, who also suggested an idea I've appropriated in the next paragraph, that Ahab calls God a bastard. In *Prophetic Woman: Anne Hutchinson and the Literature of New England* (Berkeley: University of California Press, 1987), Amy Schrager Lang suggests that various nineteenth-century male writers similarly absorb stereotypical female energies into their self-images.

30. Roland Barthes, *The Pleasure of the Text*, trans. Richard Miller (New York: Hill & Wang, 1975), 53. In *Hero, Captain, and Stranger*, Robert Martin draws too simple a polarity between patriarchal, aggressive, and phallic Ahab and Ishmael's delight in homosexual chumship. Ahab also flaunts an abstracted homoerotic desire here. A fine essay by Samuel Kimball, "Uncanny Narration in *Moby-Dick*," *American Literature*, 59 (December 1987), 528–547, connects Ishmael's narration to suppressed matricide and still more pervasive

fears of infanticide.

31. Arvin, *Herman Melville*, 30; Tolchin, *Mourning, Gender, and Creativity*, 128–134, on "The Candles." Tolchin explains Ahab's rhetorical inauthenticity as a parody of Victorian grieving, and links the scene to parlor theatricals, though Ahab's grief outstrips the genres. Tolchin also links the "queenly personality" to Melville's mother, who blocked his mourning with her own.

32. Eve Kosofsky Sedgwick, *Between Men: English Literature and Male Homosocial Desire* (New York: Columbia University Press, 1985), 102 (on James Hogg's *Confessions of a Justified Sinner*), also chaps. 5 and 6 on paranoid gothic, esp. 90–92, 114–117; Vivian R. Pollak, *Dickinson: The Anxiety of Gender* (Ithaca: Cornell University Press, 1984), 133, 150–156 on self-loathing as a transformation and suppression of homosexual desires. Jeffrey Steele briefly suggests a Lacanian perspective on Ahab, that he is voicing messages from the other within the self; see *The Representation of the Self in the American Renaissance* (Chapel Hill: University of North Carolina Press, 1987), 176–177. Steele's book has its own Melvillean doubleness, moving toward Jungian perspectives on androgyny, especially in Whitman and Margaret Fuller, while emphasizing the exposure of uncanny otherness in Poe, Hawthorne, and Melville. For a Lacanian analysis of father-son issues in various Melville novels, see Regis Durand, "The Captive King: The Absent Father in Melville's Text," in *The Fictional Father: Lacanian Readings of the Text*, ed. Robert Con Davis (Amherst: University of Massachusetts Press, 1981), 48–72.

33. Shakespeare, *King Lear*, ed. Kenneth Muir (London: Methuen, 1972), 80 (II.iv.54–55).

34. Rogin, *Subversive Genealogy*, 93–94.

35. Sigmund Freud, "Analysis Terminable and Interminable," in *Therapy & Technique*, ed. Philip Rieff (New York: Crowell Collier, 1963), 270.

36. Zoellner, *Salt-Sea Mastodon*; Adler, *War in Melville's Imagination*. Two useful recent anthologies of feminist criticism are *New French Feminisms*, ed. Elaine Marks and Isabelle de Courtivron (Amherst: University of Massachusetts Press, 1980); and *The (M)other Tongue: Essays in Feminist Psychoanalytic Interpretation*, ed. Shirley Nelson Garner, Claire Kahane, Madelon Sprengnether (Ithaca: Cornell University Press, 1985). In *Hero, Captain, and Stranger*, Robert Martin similarly argues that Ishmael's survival restores "the feminine and maternal" beyond "the imposition of exclusive white male power" (70). James McIntosh makes a more complicated argument for Ishmael's "passive, shifty, elusive" fluidity of consciousness as that of a "visionary survivor"; see "The Mariner's Multiple Quest," in *New Essays on Moby-Dick*, 49–50. Joseph Allen Boone argues that Ishmael softens Ahab's rigid masculine self-hatred by accepting "the 'maternal' or 'feminine' within himself," though not securely. See *Tradition/Counter/Tradition: Love and the Form of Fiction* (Chicago: University of Chicago Press, 1987), 241–252, quotation 247.

37. Baym, *Woman's Fiction: A Guide to Novels by and about Women in America, 1820–1870* (Ithaca: Cornell University Press, 1978), 145.

38. The most detailed and reliable account of Melville's childhood is still William H. Gilman, *Melville's Early Life and "Redburn"* (New York: New York University Press, 1951), 5–82, though Gilman interprets the family dynamics much more benignly than I do. Gilman stresses Allan Melvill's "profound veneration for his ancestors and an all-possessing love for his wife and children" (12), along with "his petty vanities and servility to the *haut monde*" (13). Gilman presents Maria as "essentially a simple, domestic, and somewhat provincial woman" (18) whom Melville unfairly maligns in *Pierre*, yet a mother whose "severe" discipline belied her periodic depressions (20). In a letter Allan calls young Herman "very backward in speech & somewhat slow in comprehension, but... of a docile and amiable disposition" (28), as opposed to Gansevoort, "who, according to his doting father, was 'considered rather more than an ordinary genius' " (30). Gilman concludes, "Herman always seems to have been 'a good boy,' " as Allan called him (39).

Miller's discussion of Allan and Maria, in *Herman Melville*, 53–89, stresses Allan's shallow dandyism, his use of the rod (66–67, countered by Gilman, 21), and Maria's depressions (75). He cites the incident of the bedside stool sitting as a family legend (77), and also notes Melville's laconic remark to a niece that his mother "hated him" (88). Haberstroh's *Melville and Male Identity* emphasizes Melville's idealization of his father as a cosmopolitan gentleman (13–19) and the lost, outraged boy submerged in Melville's fake persona of the responsible man (22–28, 75). Haberstroh sees *Pierre* as an attempt to murder the orphan self that Melville hated at the center of his own psyche (22, 104). In *Subversive Genealogy*, Rogin recurrently analyzes clothing imagery in Melville's work in relation to Allan's profession as clothing importer (e.g., 140–141) and suggests that Ishmael wants a patriarchal beating to get free of maternal power (188–189).

39. Tolchin, *Mourning, Gender, and Creativity*, passim, also 137 on experiencing grief as choking; *Redburn: His First Voyage*, end of chap. 7. In "Allan Melvill's Death: A Misdiagnosis," *Melville Society Extracts*, 67 (September 1986), 9–11, Susan Weiner and William J. Weiner argue that critics are wrong to romanticize Allan's death as madness. His delirium arose from biological rather than psychiatric causes, they say, and Melville himself interpreted his father's delirium as due to a fever. The characterization of Ahab makes their case more tenuous.

40. Tolchin, *Mourning, Gender, and Creativity*, 18–19 on Allan's "probable premarital sexual liaison" and 140 on its relevance to *Pierre*. Tolchin speculates that Herman knew about it, while his mother didn't. But Henry A. Murray, Harvey Myerson, Eugene Taylor, in "Allan Melvill's By-Blow," *Melville Society Extracts*, 61 (February 1985), 1–6, say the two ladies visited the Melvill house, and "were sent away by Mrs. Melvill" (2). See also T. Walter Herbert, Jr., *"Moby-Dick and Calvinism: A World Dismantled* (New Brunswick, N.J.: Rutgers University Press, 1977), 26–68, on Allan's death and Maria's use of Calvinism to see Allan as a "Child of the Devil" (57–68). I'm indebted here to conversations with Walter Herbert and Neal Tolchin about Maria's rage and to Suzanne Stein's ideas about narcissistic trauma.

41. Harry Stack Sullivan, *The Interpersonal Theory of Psychiatry*, ed. Helen Swick Perry, Mary Ladd Gawel (New York: Norton, 1953), 214–215, and more generally his discussion of rage behavior as the substitution of a "bad-me" in place of "the generic need for tenderness" (201–216). See also Alice Miller, *Prisoners of Childhood: The Drama of the Gifted Child and the Search for the True Self*, trans. Ruth Ward (New York: Basic, 1981), for an eloquent psychoanalytic account of how a mother's narcissistic resentments can bring about depression, grandiosity, and narcissistic disturbance in the gifted child. Miller's two later books focus on child abuse, too simply I think. Her psychoanalytic views would reinforce Edwin Haviland Miller's emphasis on Allan Melvill's use of the rod.

From a more Freudian perspective, Otto F. Kernberg writes of what underlies narcissistic exploitation of others: "a hungry, enraged, empty self, full of impotent anger . . . and fearful of a world which seems as hateful and revengeful as the patient himself." He links the narcissistic personality to cold, hostile mothering. See his *Borderline Conditions and Pathological Narcissism* (New York: Jason Aronson, 1975), 233–235.

42. Charles Olson, "Letter for Melville 1951," in *A Controversy of Poets*, ed. Paris Leary and Robert Kelly (Garden City, N.Y.: Doubleday, 1965), 304–311, cited by Bickman, "Melville and the Mind," 520.

43. Julia Kristeva, *Powers of Horror: An Essay on Abjection*, trans. Leon S. Roudiez (New York: Columbia University Press, 1982). Kristeva's book offers a richly suggestive frame for interpreting the interplay of passivity and narcissism in *Moby Dick*: "the abject" (Ahab) tries to cleanse himself of maternal loathing by joining with the hostile father, while "the deject" (Ishmael) constantly "*strays* instead of getting his bearings" (6–9). Such an "I" seeks a fetish as a "life preserver" to stand in the place of abyss and horror: the whale for Ahab, and language itself, "our ultimate and inseparable fetish" (37) for Ishmael.

Like Ishmael, Kristeva cannot make up her mind whether mother's loss or mother's loathing is the abyss. Analytically, for most of the book, especially in her discussion of Céline, Kristeva presumes deprivation as the first abyss. It seems to me, however, that her more original focus on maternal loathing is where her own highly charged, if abstracted feelings emerge (e.g., 6, 64, 77–78, 157–159). Ultimately Kristeva defines the experience of self as the abjection of the loathing/absent mother to father's otherness and power. Even feminism for her is "the last of the power-seeking ideologies" (208). Her Lacanian alternative is a state of nonself, also prefigured in abjection.

44. Herbert, *"Moby-Dick" and Calvinism,* 141.

Index

Library of Congress Cataloging-in-Publication Data
Leverenz, David.
    Manhood and the American renaissance.
    Bibliography: p.
    Includes index.
    1. American literature—19th century—History and criticism. 2. Masculinity (Psychology) in literature.
3. Sex role in literature. 4. Men in literature.
I. Title.
PS217.M37L48 1989   810'.9'353   88-47914
ISBN 0-8014-2281-7 (alk. paper)